Between Borders

Between Borders

The Great Jewish Migration from Eastern Europe

TOBIAS BRINKMANN

OXFORD
UNIVERSITY PRESS

Oxford University Press is a department of the University of Oxford. It furthers
the University's objective of excellence in research, scholarship, and education
by publishing worldwide. Oxford is a registered trade mark of Oxford University
Press in the UK and certain other countries.

Published in the United States of America by Oxford University Press
198 Madison Avenue, New York, NY 10016, United States of America.

© Oxford University Press 2024

All rights reserved. No part of this publication may be reproduced, stored in
a retrieval system, or transmitted, in any form or by any means, without the
prior permission in writing of Oxford University Press, or as expressly permitted
by law, by license, or under terms agreed with the appropriate reproduction
rights organization. Inquiries concerning reproduction outside the scope of the
above should be sent to the Rights Department, Oxford University Press, at the
address above.

You must not circulate this work in any other form
and you must impose this same condition on any acquirer.

Library of Congress Cataloging-in-Publication Data
Names: Brinkmann, Tobias, author.
Title: Between borders : the great Jewish migration from Eastern Europe /
Tobias Brinkmann.
Other titles: Great Jewish migration from Eastern Europe
Description: New York, NY : Oxford University Press, [2024] |
Includes bibliographical references and index.
Identifiers: LCCN 2024015162 (print) | LCCN 2024015163 (ebook) |
ISBN 9780197655658 (hardback) | ISBN 9780197655672 (epub)
Subjects: LCSH: Jews, East European—Migrations—History—19th century. |
Jews, East European—Migrations—History—20th century. |
Europe, Eastern—Emigration and immigration—History—19th century. |
Europe, Eastern—Emigration and immigration—History—20th century.
Classification: LCC DS135.E83 B64 2024 (print) | LCC DS135.E83 (ebook) |
DDC 304.8089/92409034—dc23/eng/20240403
LC record available at https://lccn.loc.gov/2024015162
LC ebook record available at https://lccn.loc.gov/2024015163

DOI: 10.1093/oso/9780197655658.001.0001

Printed by Sheridan Books, Inc., United States of America

Contents

Acknowledgments vii
Abbreviations ix

Introduction 1

1. Early Jewish Migration from Lithuania 12
2. The 1881–1882 Pogroms and the Brody Crisis 31
3. Jewish Mobilities and the Business of Migration 51
4. Migrant Journeys 75
5. Protective Umbrella: The Transnational Jewish Support Network 101
6. The First World War and Its Aftermath: Displacement and Permanent Transit 128
7. The Interwar Years: Alternative Destinations and Dead Ends 162
8. A Not So Typical Journey 189
9. Jewish Migrations or Wandering Jews? 206
10. Migrants Become Immigrants 234

Conclusion: Migrants *and* Refugees 244

Notes 253
Selected Bibliography 295
Index 309

Acknowledgments

I dedicate this study to Malvin and Lea Bank, who endowed a position for a historian researching Jewish migration at Penn State's Jewish studies program. The endowment allowed me to conduct research at archives in Israel, North America, and Europe. The College of Liberal Arts, the History Department, the Arts and Humanities Institute, and the Jewish Studies Program at Penn State generously assisted my research by providing additional support and teaching leaves. I also received support from the History Department and the Parkes Institute for the Study of Jewish/Non-Jewish Relations at the University of Southampton, where I taught from 2004 to 2008. The Minda de Gunzburg Center for European Studies at Harvard University and its staff assisted me during my stay as John F. Kennedy Memorial Fellow in 2007–2008. The Rabbi Harold D. Hahn Memorial Fellowship at the American Jewish Archives in Cincinnati enabled me to research the extensive World Jewish Congress collection in 2007–2008.

Several scholars and institutions made it possible for me to present my research. I want to extend special thanks to the German Historical Institute in Washington, D.C., whose director, Simone Lässig, invited me to several conferences about migration and Jewish history. I also want to thank Steven Weitzman and Elisheva Baumgarten for inviting me to a summer school for graduate students at the Hebrew University in Jerusalem in 2015 that focused on Jewish migrations. During the summer of 2018 I taught at the University of Nanjing as part of a grant by the Henry Luce Foundation. I want to thank Professors Lihong Song and Xu Xin and their students and colleagues in Nanjing for their hospitality and for valuable feedback. And I am grateful to the staff at the Kaplan Centre for Jewish Studies and Research at the University of Cape Town for welcoming me and other scholars over the years, especially to Adam Mendelsohn, who provided helpful feedback to an early draft of the manuscript.

I am particularly indebted to Derek J. Penslar and Christhard Hoffmann, who wrote many references over the years and read early versions of the manuscript. During visits to Berlin I discussed the project with Reinhard Rürup before he passed away in 2018. I also want to thank Tony Kushner, Eli

Lederhendler, Leslie Page Moch, Jonathan Sarna, and Dorothee Schneider for writing references for me. John Klier gave me invaluable advice on how to transition to the British academic system and shared some of his findings about the 1881–1882 pogroms. I always enjoyed meeting with Richard S. Levy when I passed through Chicago. I greatly miss both.

The anonymous reviewers and the faculty delegates of Oxford University Press made useful suggestions for revisions. I could not have written this book without the students I have been teaching at the University of Southampton and at Penn State. They raised crucial questions that helped me to shape this project. I received feedback and support from more people than I can name here. I am particularly grateful to Eliyana Adler, Mary Al-Sayed, Yaakov Ariel, Israel Bartal, Dean Bell, Inka Bertz, Anna Cichopek-Gajraj, Jonathan Dekel-Chen, Hasia Diner, Verena Dohrn, Josef Ehmer, Gennady Estraikh, Hannah Ewence, Torsten Feys, Lloyd Gartner, Lori Ginzberg, Daniela Gleizer, Arthur Goldhammer, Jaclyn Granick, Abigail Green, Daniel Greene, Jeffrey Gurock, Anna Holian, Dietlind Hüchtker, Christoph Jahr, Drew Keeling, Rebecca Kobrin, Markus Krah, Nathan Kurtz, Boerries Kuzmany, Fred Lazin, Ruth Leiserowitz, Rainer Liedtke, Olaf Matthes, Guy Miron, Matthias Middell, Jan Musekamp, Marion Neiss, Frank Nesemann, Jochen Oltmer, Francesca Piana, Dorota Praszalowicz, Markian Prokopovych, David Rechter, Davide Rodogno, Marsha Rozenblit, Joshua Shanes, Lisa Silverman, Yael Siman, Annemarie Steidl, Swen Steinberg, Adam Sutcliffe, Gregor Thum, Mark Tolts, Heléna Tóth, Hollace Weiner, William Weitzer, Marcin Wodzinski, Steven Zipperstein, and Aristide Zolberg. Joachim Schloer generously shared a number of sources with me, and I am particularly grateful that he (re-)published the little-known works by Sammy Gronemann.

Several archivists and librarians assisted me during the research phase. At the Hamburg State Archive Nina Schwenke kindly permitted me to reproduce some of the photographs of Jewish migrants taken by Johann Hamann in Hamburg in 1907. Dana Hermann and Gary Zola at the American Jewish Archives in Cincinnati and Frank Mecklenburg at the Leo Baeck Institute in New York also provided important assistance.

At Oxford University Press Nancy Toff, often made time for me in her busy schedule and gave invaluable advice. Chelsea Hogue provided much support during the production. Several close friends assisted me during my own journeys. I want to mention in particular Carsten and Elzbieta Hartkopf in Frankfurt, Sabine Hillebrecht in Berlin, Dan and Michaela Levene as well as Frances Clarke in Southampton, George and Virginia Dick in Chicago, and, last but not least, my partner, Michele Barosh, and her son, Jonah Barosh.

Abbreviations

AJA	American Jewish Archives, Cincinnati
AJC	American Jewish Committee
AZ	*Allgemeine Zeitung des Judenthums*
CAHJP	Central Archive for the History of the Jewish People, Jerusalem
CNR	Canadian Northern Railway
CPR	Canadian Pacific Railway
CZA	Central Zionist Archive, Jerusalem
D.C.KfRJ	Deutsches Central-Komitee für die Russischen Juden
DIGB	Deutsch Israelitischer Gemeindebund
DP	displaced person
FO	Foreign Office (British government)
GeSta	Geheimes Staatsarchiv (Prussian Privy State Archive), Berlin
GPO	Government Printing Office
HAPAG	Hamburg-America Line (steamship line)
HIAS	Hebrew Sheltering and Immigrant Aid Society
HICEM	HIAS-JCA-Emigdirect
IJA	Institute for Jewish Affairs
ILO	International Labor Organization
IMM	International Mercantile Marine Company
IRO	International Refugee Organization
JCA	Jewish Colonization Association
JDC	American Jewish Joint Distribution Committee
LBI	Leo Baeck Institute, New York
LNA	League of Nations Archive
NCJW	National Council of Jewish Women
NDL	North German Lloyd (steamship line)
NLIL	National Liberal Immigration League
OeStA/AVA	Austrian State Archive/General Administrative Archive, Vienna
OSS	Office for Strategic Services
UNRRA	United Nations Relief and Rehabilitation Administration
WJC	World Jewish Congress
YIVO	Yidisher Visnshaftlekher Institut (Jewish Scholarly Institute)

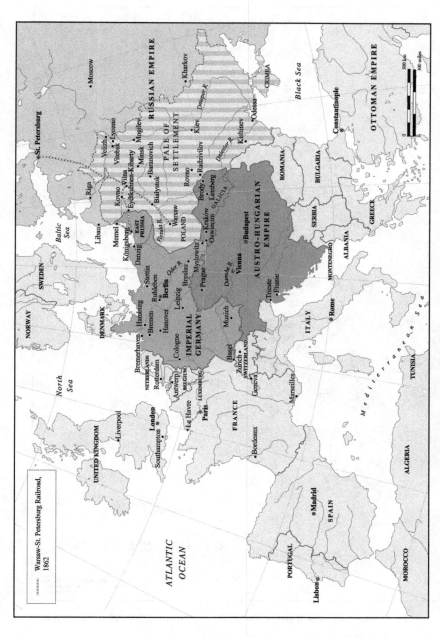

Map of Europe in July 1914 with the railroad line from Warsaw to St. Petersburg and the branch line from Vilna to Königsberg. *Created by Tobias Brinkmann and Isabelle Lewis.*

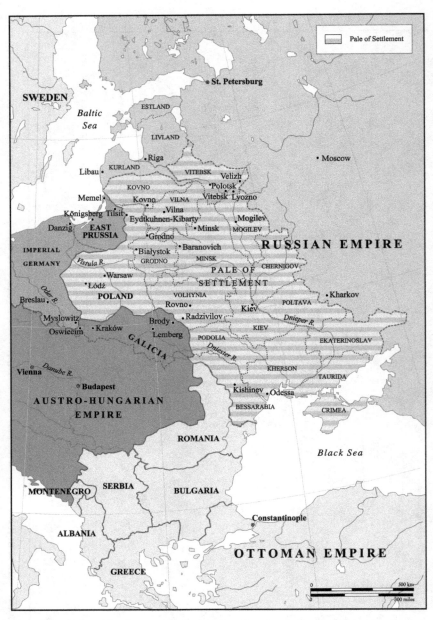

Map of the Pale of Settlement in the Russian Empire and adjacent territories in July 1914. *Created by Tobias Brinkmann and Isabelle Lewis.*

Introduction

Migration is a defining aspect of the Jewish experience. Since biblical times Jewish migrations have been widely associated with flight from persecution. Long before the Holocaust, accounts of Jewish history highlighted antisemitism and expulsions as overarching causes for Jewish population movements. In the 1904 *Jewish Encyclopedia* Joseph Jacobs characterized Jewish history as a constant chain of "forced" movements "from country to country." Since the 1980s specialist scholars have shifted to more differentiated interpretations of Jewish migrations. Yet the lachrymose view of Jewish migrations persists in popular publications, textbooks, and even scholarly studies, especially surveys of global migration and refugee issues. In an informative 1996 book about global migrations, Thomas Sowell begins the chapter on the Jews with this sentence: "The tragic history of the Jews as a people wandering the world through centuries of persecution has been . . . remarkable for their achievements." In the chapter Sowell plays down the agency of Jews as migrants.[1]

Howard Sachar, whose books about modern Jewish history have been widely assigned at American colleges and universities until recently, took a more nuanced view, acknowledging the impact of economic factors. Yet even in the revised 1990 edition of a survey that was first published in 1958 he continued to describe Jewish migration from Eastern Europe after 1880 as "flight." The author of a recently published history of refugees in Europe after 1492 asserts that the Jewish "emigration" from the Russian Empire before 1914 "can be viewed in large part as a flight from religious and ethno-national persecution." The respective subchapter is titled "Flight from Pogroms." Even a superficial search for the phrase "fled the pogroms" in contemporary newspapers and magazines yields dozens of results about Jews leaving the Russian Empire before 1914.[2]

The view of forced migration as a supposed Jewish habitus can be traced to the Christian stereotype of the "Wandering Jew." According to a legend that first emerged in thirteenth-century Europe, the Jewish figure that is sometimes called Ahasverus was condemned to wander until the second coming of Christ because he struck or cursed Jesus on the way to the crucifixion. Like Ahasverus, "the" Jews remain permanent outsiders without a home. Wherever they settle, they cannot stay. The "Wandering Jew" became a staple of literary discussion during the nineteenth century. The ten-volume novel *Le Juif Errant* (1844) by French writer Eugène Sue found enormous appeal and was translated into English. In the early twentieth century, the view of the Jews as a "wandering people" became influential among Zionist authors. To reinforce the case for "normalization," or permanent settlement in a Jewish homeland, they depicted Jewish life in the Diaspora as a period of suffering characterized by oppression and frequent expulsions. This view was suggestive because the rise of Zionism coincided with strong Jewish migration from the Russian Empire and Romania, where Jews faced manifold restrictions and growing violent persecution. Zionist leaders and authors frequently referenced the Exodus. The charismatic founder of the Zionist World Organization, Theodor Herzl, styled himself as a modern Moses.[3]

After 1890 the number of Jewish migrants moving to the United States and more far-flung destinations such as South Africa grew dramatically. In 1904, the year Jacobs's *Jewish Encyclopedia* article was published, more than 100,000 Jews moved to the United States, primarily from the Russian and Austro-Hungarian empires. They made up more than 13 percent of U.S. immigrants. In the previous year, a notorious pogrom in Kishinev had shocked the world. Between 1903 and 1906 hundreds of anti-Jewish attacks claimed Jewish lives across the Russian Pale of Settlement, the western provinces of the Russian Empire where Jews were allowed to live. The Russian authorities appeared unable or unwilling to stem the violence. It is understandable that most observers considered the pogroms the overarching cause for the strong migration.

A closer reading of pre-1914 reports about Jewish migrations, however, betrays surprisingly differentiated interpretations. Several Jewish social scientists, journalists, and aid organizations in continental Europe published accounts about the causes of the Jewish "mass migration." Based on the analysis of available data these authors judged economic and demographic factors as decisive. After all, the Jewish mass migration between 1870 and 1914 was part of an unprecedented upheaval. Millions of people around the globe were on the move as expanding transportation networks connected little-developed rural regions to globalizing markets for labor, services, and goods.

Between 1841 and 1891, when most European countries experienced strong growth, Ireland's population decreased from more than 8 million to less than 5 million, due largely to strong migration to the United States, Britain, and other destinations. Norway's demographic development also stands out. The almost 200,000 Norwegians who moved to the United States during the 1880s represented close to 10 percent of the country's population, and migration from Norway to the United States remained strong until 1914. Norway's demographic growth slowed down significantly in this period. After 1900, the number of Italian migrants registered at U.S. ports frequently exceeded by far that of Jews from Eastern Europe. Between 1880 and 1914 more than 4 million Italians moved to the United States, primarily from the country's little-developed Mezzogiorno. Like Jewish and many Irish immigrants, Italian immigrants clustered in a few cities, especially New York. The rates for Italian nationals who returned to their home villages and towns exceeded 60 percent in some years after 1900. Jewish remigration rates were much lower but not negligible.[4]

Indeed, in his entry on migration in the *Jewish Encyclopedia* Jacobs conceded that "in recent times a new kind of migration has taken place, due partly to economic causes and partly to persecution." St. Petersburg journalist L. Wygodski, the author of the subsequent section on migration from Russia, stressed that the pogroms were merely the "stimulus." The "true cause" of the mass migration was the miserable economic situation of the Jewish population. He identified networks as crucial drivers of the migration and traced fluctuations in the number of migrants to business cycles of the U.S. economy. In recent years several studies have backed up his remarkably far-sighted assessment. Even in the aftermath of the First World War, when Russian, Ukrainian, and Polish nationalists massacred tens of thousands of Jews, displacing many more, Jewish scholars discussing Jewish migration remained committed to critical and differentiated approaches, rejecting simplistic explanations. The "lachrymose" view of Jewish migrations became dominant in the scholarly literature only during and shortly after the Holocaust.[5]

The migrations of millions of people of different cultural backgrounds across long distances were closely intertwined with concerted efforts to better comprehend this seemingly unprecedented phenomenon. Much of the early literature concentrated on the respective national and local spheres. Few authors who wrote about migration before the 1920s were affiliated with universities; instead the publications ranged from journalistic accounts and studies written by independent scholars, urban reformers, and members of migrant aid associations to biased texts whose authors identified migration as a "racial" threat and a grave risk to public health. In several European countries, nationalists, politicians, and military leaders expressed concern about the impact of mass *emigration*, especially since most departing migrants were young men, women, and children. In the United States, Britain, and other destination countries social scientists, public health officials, and urban reformers began to take a closer look at actual *immigrants*. An early example is a scientific study anthropologist Franz Boas conducted in New York around 1910. Using the measurements of the head shapes of more than ten thousand immigrants from different parts of Europe and their American-born children, the study traced significant differences between parents and children to environmental factors, rejecting widespread views that supposed racial differences were biologically determined. Boas's research was funded by the U.S. Congress, as part of a concerted effort to learn more about immigrants and immigration.[6]

Early on, serious scholarship about Jewish migration stood out because it transcended national debates about the benefits and supposed threats associated with mass migration. Around 1900 it became clear that the dramatic increase in Jewish migration from Eastern Europe marked a decisive shift. Even committed Zionists conceded that a homeland to accommodate millions of Jews from Eastern Europe could not be established in the short term. At the same time Jewish aid associations, which had supported migrants along the main transit routes and in the receiving countries for decades, began to move from situational crisis management to a more sustained approach that depended on coordination across borders but also on the collection and analysis of data. Jewish (and other) aid workers lobbied with government officials on both sides of the Atlantic and nonstate actors, such as steamship line companies. Jewish community leaders made concerted efforts to refute falsehoods spread by antisemitic agitators and spoke up against migration restrictions in different countries. Before 1914, the soft power of Jewish aid associations was not negligible, as this study will show.

The First World War constituted a turning point. A massive refugee crisis and a shift to restrictive migration policies in the United States and other destination countries after 1918 greatly exacerbated the situation of "unwanted" Jewish (and other) minorities in Eastern Europe. A large number of Jews who had been displaced during and after the war, many of whom had become stateless, were stranded in a situation that can best be described as "permanent transit," unable to return to their homes and unable to join relatives and acquaintances in the United States and a few other preferred destinations. Jewish migration to Mandate Palestine increased during the 1920s, but the remigration rates were high. The Great Depression, the rise of openly antisemitic regimes in Germany, Poland, and Romania whose leaders promoted violent persecution, and the forced expulsion of Jewish populations corresponded with increasingly desperate efforts by Jewish representatives and aid workers to find safe havens. Already in the 1920s Jewish aid organizations began compiling lengthy reports about destinations for Jewish "resettlement" in East Africa, Latin America, and the Caribbean. During the 1930s and 1940s the affliction of "unwanted" Jews who were sometimes literally stranded in the no man's land between borders gave rise to influential studies and concepts that shaped the emerging field of migration and refugee studies.[7]

Why did the view of Jewish migration from Russia as the latest chapter of continuous Jewish flight cast a long shadow over the scholarship for decades after the Holocaust? And why does the pre-1914 flight narrative continue to linger in the general historiography and popular memory? The answer to these questions leads to a striking research gap that is the subject of this book. On a first glance, few fields in modern Jewish history appear better studied than Jewish migrations. Yet works published after the 1940s deal almost exclusively with a single aspect: Jewish *immigration* and its repercussions.[8] After the founding of the State of Israel in 1948, the problem of permanently displaced Jews and the debate about a wider range of causes and the general implications faded into the background. Instead, Jewish immigration emerged as a redemptive success story of Jews who had "escaped" from Europe and countries of the Middle East and Maghreb to the "promised lands" of the United States and Mandate Palestine/Israel, where they reinvented Jewish *Gemeinschaft*.

The rising interest in ethnicity during the 1960s also explains why many American scholars began to research specific ethnic groups (often their own), as if different ethnic groups existed in complete isolation from each other before, during, and after the journey across the Atlantic. Indeed, not all Jews or Italians migrated because they were Jews or Italians (or Jewish Italians in a few cases) but because they were looking for a better life for themselves and their families. Yet it is also true that most members of specific ethnoreligious groups frequently shared certain economic profiles. Before 1800 European Jews were forced into proto-capitalist niches on the margins of feudal societies, while many Christians were tied to the land or to specific occupations. Scholars have debated the long-term impact of economic profiles and specific proficiencies, especially as migrants were hired for industrial jobs that demanded completely new skills. Migrants may have arrived with different cultural and linguistic backgrounds, but they became part of the industrial working class in northern U.S. cities after the American Civil War.[9]

The growing appeal of the ethnicity concept and the focus on immigration among American Jewish authors during the ethnic revival of the 1960s and 1970s were also attempts to come to terms with the irrevocable destruction of Jewish life in Eastern Europe during the Holocaust. In the award-winning epic *World of Our Fathers* (1976), one of the most widely read accounts of Jewish immigrants in the United States, author Irving Howe portrayed Jews on the move as refugees driven from their homes. The Jewish migration from Eastern Europe between 1881 and 1914, as he put it emphatically, was "comparable in modern Jewish history only to the flight from the Spanish Inquisition." Desperate attempts by Soviet Jewish refuseniks to emigrate during the 1970s only reinforced the bleak view of Jewish migration from Russia before 1914.[10]

Historians in Israel crafted their own distinctive narrative by depicting Jewish immigration to Palestine as a succession of distinctive *aliyot*. The Hebrew term *aliyah* refers to the return of exiled Jews to the ancient land of Israel and describes the act of moving up. According to this narrative, Jews moving to Palestine before 1914 were few in number but committed Zionists who built flourishing agricultural colonies. Jews who migrated elsewhere, a far larger number, are consigned to the background if they are mentioned at all. In recent years this view has been revised. Before the 1930s most Jewish Palestine migrants looked for better economic opportunities, and many settled in towns and cities rather than agricultural regions.[11] Authors covering Jewish immigration usually have devoted only fleeting attention to the causes. Most do not discuss the journeys of Jewish (and other) migrants. Little is known about Jews and others who returned to their home countries, were prevented from entering destination countries, or were permanently displaced after 1914.[12] Scholars discussing Jewish immigration tend to ignore non-Jewish migrants. In a similar vein, most studies about German or Polish migrants moving to the United States during the nineteenth century exclude Jewish migrants. As a result, surprisingly little is known about ties between migrants of different ethnic and religious backgrounds originating in the same places in Central and Eastern Europe.[13] Much of the scholarship deals with Jewish migration from just one point of origin, the "cursed" Russian lands, to the two main destinations, the United States and (Mandate) Palestine/Israel. The global dimension of Jewish migration from Eastern Europe after 1860 has not been sufficiently explored.[14]

The rise of Holocaust studies after the 1970s has illustrated the shortcomings of looking just at those who managed to immigrate. Desperate attempts by German and Austrian Jews to escape Nazi persecution by fleeing to Shanghai, North Africa, Latin America, and the Caribbean during the 1930s and early 1940s are well documented. Hundreds of personal testimonies and memoirs trace the experiences of Jewish refugees from Central Europe. Many German and Austrian Jews were still waiting for immigrant visas when German troops occupied countries they had considered safe, such as the Netherlands and France. In marked contrast, relatively few Eastern European Jews managed to escape. They faced closed gates wherever they turned. In the wake of the notorious Kristallnacht pogrom in November 1938 the Roosevelt administration belatedly relaxed the immigration policy for German and Austrian Jews, but the rigid quotas excluding Jews (and others) born in Eastern Europe remained in place. Few survived regardless, whether they were deported from or murdered in Western, Central, or Eastern Europe. Apart from a few memoirs, diaries, and desperate letters, few documents remain that shed light on their journeys. Indeed, some of the most important sources are the memoirs of Holocaust survivors.

In recent years scholars have made a concerted effort to analyze long-ignored Yiddish sources such as interviews conducted in the immediate aftermath of the Holocaust, accounts by Polish Jews who fled to the Soviet Union, and Yizkor books that document the history and memory of hundreds of destroyed Jewish communities across Eastern Europe.[15] Very few scholars have researched the system of deportations to ghettos and extermination camps by rail based on the testimony of survivors and other sources. Apart from a short essay by pioneering Holocaust historian Raul Hilberg, the role of various, largely state-owned European railroads in the history of the Holocaust remains understudied.[16]

Why devote a book-length study to seemingly mundane journeys of Jewish and other migrants and refugees? Researching transit journeys of Jews from Eastern Europe between the 1860s and the aftermath of the Holocaust transcends another powerful narrative that continues to shape much of the scholarship in modern Jewish history and refugees. Ironically, historical migration studies and modern Jewish history, two fields with an obvious predilection toward transnational perspectives, remain beholden to the nation-state paradigm. The same states that emancipated their Jewish populations after the late eighteenth century defined and categorized those crossing their borders. The terms "immigrant" and "emigrant" were coined by bureaucrats to distinguish between different types of cross-border movement. States have been regulating migration (and Jewish life) differently over time. Diverging statistical and legal systems and linguistic distinctions make comparisons challenging. Therefore, few authors who cover the history of immigrants venture beyond national borders. Important exceptions are recent publications about the migrations of small groups of Sephardi Jews whose authors have retraced the global journeys between the Levant, Latin America, and Africa. This study looks beyond the traditional centers of Jewish life, at the spaces in between—in a period when new centers in America and Palestine/Israel were emerging and the dominant center of Jewish life in Eastern Europe faced an uncertain future.[17]

Terms such as "illegal" and "undocumented" migrants are often used uncritically even though states have been defining "illegal" migration differently over time. A migrant can be considered a deserving political refugee on one side of a border but treated as an unwanted economic migrant on the other. Following regime changes welcome refugees can be recategorized as unwanted economic migrants. In a study of twentieth-century migration to the United States, historian Mae Ngai emphasizes a seemingly obvious point: the illegal (im)migrant is a legal construct. The term "migrant" itself has to be used carefully. After the First World War nation-states such as Romania began to label Jews and members of other unwanted minority populations as "migrants" to justify their exclusion, expulsion, or "resettlement," the term the Nazi regime would use as a cipher for systematic mass killings during World War II.[18]

The mutual influences between changing migration policies enacted by different states remain little understood. Migration historian Adam McKeown has pointed to links between Chinese exclusion policies in the United States, Canada, South Africa, Australia, and other destination countries between the late nineteenth century and the 1940s. This study raises a similar argument relating to Jewish migrants from Eastern Europe. Before 1914 the overwhelming majority moved to the United States, and smaller groups settled in Western Europe and more far-flung destinations in Latin America, South Africa, and Palestine. Already in the early 1880s American Jewish observers grasped that Chinese exclusion could serve as a blueprint for excluding other "races" that were considered "undesirable." The American lawmakers who drafted restrictive immigration bills in 1921 and 1924 specifically sought to exclude unwanted "races," not least Jews from Eastern Europe. After 1918 several other major destination countries, such as Britain, Canada, and Argentina, also began to exclude Jewish migrants.

Ellis Island makes repeated appearances in this book, not as a celebrated gateway but in its lesser-known role as an offshore transit and deportation facility, especially after the mid-1920s. Many "unwanted" migrants never even reached Ellis Island. Aristide Zolberg was one of the first scholars who pointed to the far-reaching repercussions of America's immigration restrictions after 1921 for the migration policies of other states. State officials in Central Europe and the transatlantic steamship lines coordinated their treatment of transmigrants from the Russian and Austro-Hungarian empires already during the 1880s to ensure they adhered to U.S. immigration regulations, a practice Zolberg described as American "remote control."[19]

The focus of most migration scholars on the modern state and the legal categorizations state officials applied to people on the move has obscured the influence of humanitarian organizations and private businesses facilitating journeys across borders, before and after 1914. Retracing the journeys of Jewish migrants from Eastern Europe across borders (and national historiographies) after 1860 sheds light not just on individual agency but also on nonstate actors operating between and beyond borders: Jewish and other migrant aid associations, railroad companies, steamship lines, travel agents, and smugglers. Authors of richly illustrated coffee-table books about the great ocean liners rarely discuss the backgrounds of crew members and the experiences of passengers traveling in steerage, several decks below the luxurious first-class quarters. The history of several Jewish aid associations is well researched, albeit almost exclusively in their respective national setting. It is hardly known that after 1870 most members of the Paris-based Alliance Israélite Universelle lived in Imperial Germany. Apart from a pioneering study about its state-of-the-art school network in the Ottoman Empire little has been written about the assistance Alliance members provided in different parts of Europe and the Levant to local Jews and Jewish migrants before and after 1914.[20]

More than a few Jewish entrepreneurs played prominent roles in the mobility business during the nineteenth century, on both sides of the Atlantic. Some scholars covering the dramatically increasing migration from the

Russian Empire after 1870 recognize the impact of an improving transportation network but provide only limited information about its builders. In 1862 a group of investors led by Emile and Isaac Pereire, two Sephardi brothers from Paris, completed the Warsaw–St. Petersburg railroad that connected northern Russia, Lithuania, and Poland with Central Europe—and thus provided access to North Sea ports with regular transatlantic service. Most migrants from the Russian Empire traveled on steamers of the Hamburg-America Line (HAPAG) and its affiliated carriers. Albert Ballin, HAPAG's chief executive after 1900, was one of the most influential Jewish mobility entrepreneurs of his time.[21]

The main protagonists of this book are migrants, facilitators, and mostly Jewish authors who wrote about Jewish and general migration after 1860. Facilitators comprise smugglers on the border, ticket agents, railroad investors, employees and executives of steamship lines—service providers whose businesses depended on relatively permeable borders. Representatives of Jewish aid associations were facilitators of a different kind. They did not charge migrants but extended support, gave advice, and lobbied on their behalf. State officials, legislators, and observers, including journalists and writers, populate the supporting cast. After 1914, when states began restricting migration and hundreds of thousands of Jews had lost their homes, different protagonists moved to center stage, Jewish representatives who pondered solutions for permanently displaced people and Jewish scholars who laid the conceptual foundations for migration and refugee studies.

Most of the men and a few women who wrote about Jewish migration during the twentieth century were themselves Jewish migrants. They were born between the 1870s and 1890s and followed similar paths that took them from the Russian Empire via interwar Berlin and Paris to New York in the early 1940s. Several were close collaborators. Only a handful managed to obtain university positions, sometimes late in life. They earned income as journalists, aid workers, translators, and even language teachers, or worked for small Jewish research institutes.

The sources for this study range from personal letters, memoirs, and business files to reports of Jewish aid associations and Jewish communities, the personal papers of scholars, rabbis, and Jewish representatives, government records, court files, newspapers, and photographs, as well as scholarly and literary publications. The dispersion of the sources in archives across Europe, North America, Israel, and beyond is part of the challenge of writing a book that retraces the journeys of migrants through different countries and territories over almost a century. The limited use of Yiddish- and Russian-language sources is a conscious choice. Instead of analyzing debates about Jewish migration in Yiddish publications around the globe (a fascinating subject in its own right), this study seeks to examine encounters and exchanges between Jews from Eastern Europe and others: the representatives of Jewish communities in transit and destination countries such as Germany, Britain, and the United States, state officials and legislators, a wide range of nonstate actors, as well as the broader and scholarly public spheres. Early on Yiddish-speaking migrants acted as brokers who specifically targeted Jewish and general audiences who did not read Yiddish. They were journalists, aid workers, writers, and scholars. Frequently this betrayed attempts to normalize the view of Jewish migrants and migrations and dismiss widespread stereotypical perceptions of Jewish migrants.

A particularly important language in these exchanges was German. Germany and the Austro-Hungarian Empire were major points of passage for Jewish migrants from the Russian Empire. Many young Jews (and non-Jews) from Eastern Europe attended universities in Germany, Austria, and Switzerland before the 1930s, often publishing dissertations and other works in German. For decades German was the official language of the World Zionist Organization. German remained a major Jewish lingua franca even after 1933, not least in the sphere of secular and religious Jewish organizations. For instance, during the second half of the 1930s the World Jewish Congress (WJC) conducted its meetings in Geneva in German. The minutes were translated into English for the staff at the WJC's New York office.[22] Russian-language sources are of limited importance for a study dealing not with Russian policies toward Jewish "emigration" but with the journeys of migrants who overwhelmingly left the Russian Empire days after they had departed from their hometowns.[23]

1
Early Jewish Migration from Lithuania

In November 1865, Isaak Rülf was heading to Memel (Klaipeda), a remote port on the Baltic in the far northeastern corner of Prussia. After serving a small community (*Gemeinde*) in Mecklenburg as assistant rabbi for several years, Rülf was looking for a new challenge. Memel's Jewish community was young and needed leadership. In the 1850s small groups of Polish and Lithuanian Jews had moved to the port and organized their own private synagogues. In 1862 the Prussian government, which closely supervised religious life, organized a Jewish community. But different Jewish factions continued to pray separately. The new rabbi was expected to bridge the divisions. Rülf was in his mid-thirties and had recently defended his doctoral dissertation. He was clearly tempted by the chance to lead a new *Gemeinde*.

Few places in Prussia were more isolated than the windswept borderland of East Prussia, a sparsely settled region known for its harsh winters. It is not known how Rülf traveled to Memel. Taking the boat from Stettin (Szczecin) across the Baltic Sea was not an enticing option during the stormy fall months. He probably headed to East Prussia on a newly completed rail line. The journey through little-developed eastern provinces to the East Prussian capital Königsberg (Kaliningrad) was a voyage back in time. Shortly before Rülf's arrival a branch line had been extended from Königsberg to Tilsit (Sovetsk), on the shores of the Neman River, known in German as the Memel River. Memel itself would be connected to Prussia's rail network only in the mid-1870s. From Tilsit travelers bound for Memel had to continue the rest of the journey by carriage or boat.[1]

Just after Rülf's arrival, Lithuanian Jews fleeing starvation and disease sought support from the small Jewish communities in Memel and other towns in East Prussia. Earlier than many others Rülf grasped that strong Jewish migration from Lithuania would last for years, if not decades. The 1868–1869 migration crisis serves as a lens to look beyond the (stereotypical) perceptions of "Litvaks" by established Jews in Central and Western Europe at the actual migrants. Apart from Rülf, who would emerge as an important advocate for Jewish migrants, the main protagonists of this chapter are a group of prominent French and Prussian Jews who organized an aid effort for Lithuanian Jewish migrants in 1869 and a Jewish teenager who left his Lithuanian village in the mid-1870s.

A decade before Rülf moved to Memel the local Jewish population began to increase following an unexpected economic boom. The British and French blockade of Russia's Black Sea ports during the Crimean War (1853–1856) put the spotlight on Memel and Königsberg. Prussia was not involved in the conflict. Almost overnight East Prussia emerged as a major gateway for Russian grain and timber exports. After the war both ports retained some of the lucrative Russian business. Even Tilsit's small river port benefited from the growing trade after the town was connected to Prussia's rail network. In the late 1850s the Prussian government funded the construction of a rail line from Königsberg to the Russian border and lobbied in St. Petersburg for a link on the Russian side.

Prussian officials were keen to boost the economic development of the remote province, which lagged far behind the industrial growth regions on the Ruhr and in Upper Silesia. Already during the first half of the nineteenth century Jewish peddlers and artisans had flocked to Memel from surrounding Lithuanian towns during the summer. The expanding Russian timber trade created hundreds of new jobs and economic niches attracting migrants. Jewish brokers began managing the transportation and processing of timber. Large tree rafts were floated from central Lithuania to Memel, where the timber was processed and shipped across the Baltic Sea. Memel's population increased from ten thousand in 1850 to almost twenty thousand in 1870. The Jewish population grew from a few families to almost nine hundred residents by 1867.[2]

The Russian border surrounded Memel's outskirts and was only superficially demarcated in some areas. Local smugglers used hidden paths or bribed Russian guards. The more relaxed Russian border regime after the Crimean War and the expanding trade along the border led to growing Jewish settlement across East Prussia. In the backward eastern borderland Prussian officials tolerated foreign migrants before 1880, not least for economic reasons. Citizenship was a different matter. The government was reluctant to naturalize foreigners and their descendants, even if they had lived in Prussia for decades and owned businesses. As a result of the eighteenth-century partitions of Poland, Prussia had gained a large number of Polish speakers and a not insignificant Jewish population, especially in the province of Posen, where German speakers were a minority. Most inhabitants of East Prussia spoke German dialects, but in rural parts of the province many preferred Masurian, a Polish dialect, and northern counties were home to Lithuanian speakers. During the first half of the nineteenth century many Polish speakers in Prussia's eastern provinces resisted a repressive Germanization policy. Therefore, the Berlin government was concerned about potential unrest and uncontrolled migration across the eastern border.[3]

Their large foreign membership distinguished the Jewish communities in Memel and several smaller East Prussian towns from those in other parts of Prussia at the time. East Prussia's only major city, Königsberg, had a sizable, albeit highly fluctuating number of foreign Jews among its residents. According to several estimates, in 1880 about 40 percent of Königsberg's 5,324 Jews had been born in the Russian Empire. Many were involved in the grain trade. The actual number of Lithuanian Jews in Königsberg may have been far higher because the Jewish community did not formally register Jewish sojourners and seasonal business travelers.

The little-known Lithuanian Jewish migration to towns and cities in East Prussia betrays the surprising openness of the economy in the East Prussian borderland before 1880. Most migrants were self-employed. They created jobs, notably in the timber and grain business, and promoted cross-border trade. Local officials explicitly welcomed Jewish migrants because they provided a much-needed boost to stagnant economies. Repeatedly, Memel's city council backed citizenship applications by successful Jewish business owners. As late as 1884 the city council managed to override the objections of the provincial government against the citizenship application of a timber entrepreneur, who on some days employed up to eighty men in his sawmill. The Königsberg authorities also supported citizenship applications by Jewish grain brokers during the 1870s.[4]

The reluctance of governments to naturalize foreign migrants partly explains why the German states did not become a major destination for Jews from the Russian Empire, even before Prussia shifted to a harsh anti-immigration policy in the 1880s. Outside of East Prussia only the Jewish community in Saxony's commercial center, Leipzig, had a majority of foreign members. During the eighteenth century Leipzig had emerged as a hub for the European fur trade. Jewish merchants from the East Galician border town Brody played a leading role in the lucrative trade. As more Polish Jews obtained the right to settle in Leipzig after 1815 the fur business expanded. By 1900 a majority of Leipzig's six thousand Jews were foreigners. Even the children born in Saxony to foreign parents rarely were able to obtain Saxon citizenship. The Saxon government handled citizenship applications even more rigidly than its Prussian counterpart. The Leipzig Jewish community stands out because it deprived foreign Jews of the right to vote in *Jewish community* elections until 1918.[5] In Memel foreign Jews had the right to vote, but before the arrival of Rülf in 1865 interactions between Litvaks, a smaller group from formerly Polish territories in Prussia and Russia, and the few German-speaking Jews were limited. The leading intellectual figure of Memel's Litvak community was rabbi Israel Salanter, a respected Orthodox rabbi who had settled in Memel around 1860. Just when Rülf developed a growing interest in Jewish life in Lithuania, Salanter looked west. He traveled repeatedly to Berlin and even Paris, and around 1870 he settled in Königsberg.[6]

Rülf's first months in Memel were challenging. Most Litvaks shunned him. This began to change when, months after his arrival, Rülf successfully saved Jankel Widutzky, a runaway Jewish teenager, from conversion to Protestantism. He forced a reluctant English missionary to return the boy to his parents in Vilna. The matter briefly caught the attention of the German Jewish public still unsettled by the notorious Mortara affair. In 1858, a Catholic nanny in Bologna, which then belonged to the Papal States, claimed to have secretly baptized the Jewish boy Edgardo Mortara. The papal authorities seized the child and Pope Pius IX adopted him, refusing to return him to his parents. The Mortara affair illustrated the need for a stronger Jewish voice, triggering the founding of the Alliance Israélite Universelle in 1860. The emergence of nongovernmental humanitarian organizations like the Alliance reflects a growing sense of shared responsibility among recently emancipated Jews in Western and Central Europe for Jews in the Ottoman Empire and Eastern Europe. Supporting Jews in need did not conflict with new national loyalties. As Western Jews became respected members of the urban bourgeoisie and committed citizens of rising nation-states, most Jews in the Russian and Ottoman empires lived in great poverty, were deprived of basic rights, and had limited economic prospects. The Alliance combined a patronizing mission to "civilize" and educate these Jews with sincere attempts to lobby for Jewish rights, provide material support, and publicize anti-Jewish discrimination and violence. The Alliance resembled other transnational humanitarian organizations that were established in the same period, especially the International Committee of the Red Cross (1863).[7]

After Rülf contacted the Alliance, its members encouraged him to publish a small pamphlet about the Widutzky affair. To Rülf's disappointment the text did not enhance his reputation beyond Memel. His courageous stand against public attacks by the English missionary, however, earned him respect among Litvaks in Memel.[8] In the following decades Rülf did much to make the Jewish community a visible and respected part of the city's society. To improve his modest salary the rabbi assumed the editorship of the local newspaper, the *Memeler Dampfboot* (Memel Steamboat) in 1872. Unlike comparable papers in rural Prussia the *Dampfboot* condemned the rising antisemitic movement in Germany. Rülf also provided religious instruction for Jewish children who attended Memel's public school. Parents from nearby towns in Lithuania soon began sending their children to Memel. One of Rülf's students was the later Zionist leader David Wolffson.[9]

Soon after his arrival in Memel Rülf realized that Memel's proximity to the border put him in a unique position to inform the Jewish public in Central and Western Europe about Jewish life in the Russian Empire. The first extensive reports he wrote in 1868 and 1869 about Memel and Lithuania reflect the economic divide between rural towns with tiny Jewish communities in East Prussia and Lithuanian towns overwhelmingly settled by destitute Jews. In the late 1860s the gulf between Prussia and the Lithuanian provinces was widening. Prussia's economic transformation and its rise to a major European power had repercussions even in its little-developed eastern hinterland. Rülf's early depictions of Lithuanian Jews reflect widespread stereotypes about *Ostjuden* (eastern Jews) among educated Jews in the German states and Western Europe. In an 1868 article for the *Allgemeine Zeitung des Judenthums*, the main German-language Jewish weekly, the rabbi characterized the few "German Jews" in Memel as hard-working, successful, and benevolent. Most members of his *Gemeinde*, however, were "Russian and Polish Jews," primarily small traders and artisans, especially tailors. Quite a few shunned "productive" occupations to study in the Beth Hamidrasch. Their families lived in great poverty. In passing Rülf mentioned that Jews on the other side of the border were struggling even more. "The misery, the need, the coarseness, the dirt, and the dishonesty of these people are beyond description." It would hardly be possible to alleviate Jewish suffering because, in Memel "we are surrounded by hordes of starving people." Rülf also emphasized that sending money and supplies was not a viable solution. In his view the massive problem required a sustained approach. Men and women would have to be trained to become self-sustaining farmers and artisans, and they would have to be resettled to more prosperous regions in the interior of the Russian Empire.[10]

In late May 1869 Rülf took his first trip across the border to Kovno (Kaunas), which he described as an almost "purely Jewish town." Like other travelers Rülf was shocked by the extent of misery there. He encountered groups of children, "naked, wretched, demoralized, not resembling humans." It is important not to lose sight of the fact that most Christians in the region were also poor. Yet Rülf felt that Jews lacked any protection. He met Kovno's Russian governor, who shared his view that the only way to resolve Jewish suffering was resettlement. The visit sparked a profound change in Rülf's perception of *Ostjuden*—and of his own Jewish identity. "Deep sentiment gripped my heart, I saw myself transplanted to Erez-Israel, the dear ancient home of the fathers. Can I deny it? My heart is with my people, is attached to land where the fathers lived."[11]

The sudden realization that he was closely related to the downtrodden Jews in Kovno marks a departure from Rülf's initial unfavorable descriptions. He accepted an invitation to preach a sermon at a Kovno synagogue. Rülf decided to talk about Jewish emancipation: "This is not our struggle. This is the struggle of the world. By pursuing our interest, we are furthering the welfare of humankind." This sentiment echoes a basic principle of Reform Judaism: the obligation of Jews to spread universal ethical truths. In the following section Rülf specifically referred to "human and brother rights of all people in the world." As Russian subjects living in the Pale of Settlement, the members of his audience lacked basic rights. In 1861, the new reform-minded tsar Alexander II had liberated Russian serfs. The implementation was haphazard and exacerbated social tensions. Yet during the 1860s the government provided privileges to small groups of Jewish university graduates, professionals, artisans, and army veterans, fueling hopes for further improvements. In neighboring Prussia, Jewish emancipation was nearing completion. For Rülf, securing full citizenship for Jews was part and parcel of a broader emancipation project that was not limited to specific groups.

The rabbi did not hide his relief when he returned to Prussia. "Praised be my Prussia, praised be its people, praised be your officials, praised be your government, that is truly the expression with which I want to conclude my journey to Russia." This was not so much a patriotic statement as a thinly veiled denunciation of the tsarist government. Prussian Jews stood on the threshold of full emancipation, while the tsar did little to alleviate the miserable condition of his Jewish subjects.[12]

The 1869 Lithuanian Migration Crisis

Rülf's visit to Kovno was part of a fact-finding mission. Jewish communities in Prussia's eastern provinces had long assisted destitute Jews coming across the border. The overwhelming majority of the early Jewish migrants hailed from central Lithuania. Before the late 1860s their numbers were limited because East Prussia, a thinly settled province, offered few job prospects outside of the agricultural sector. This state of affairs changed in the fall of 1868, when larger groups of desperate Jews came across the border seeking help.

In the mid-1860s bad weather led to a series of disappointing harvests in East Prussia and the Memel region. The situation worsened considerably when it rained throughout the summer of 1868.[13] In a region overly dependent on subsistence farming the repeated loss of the harvest was disastrous. In early 1868 Rülf forwarded a call for support by a committee of Memel's civic leaders to the *Allgemeine Zeitung*. Memel's established citizens had taken steps to support the neediest but sought funds from other parts of Prussia. The call did not mention Jews and was signed by Rülf and two Protestant businessmen. Persistent rain during the summer months of 1868 affected the Kowno and Suwalki provinces on the Russian side of the border, leading to extensive flooding. Most members of the rural population owned small gardens and some livestock, but bad harvests and limited food supplies led to an increase of typhus and cholera cases. Jews were hit harder. Demand for clothes, tools, and other goods made and sold by Jewish artisans and traders decreased or simply vanished. Food stocks were quickly exhausted. Small children and older women and men were particularly vulnerable because they depended on others. As a result, a growing number of Jews walked across the border in the fall months of 1868 pleading for help.

The available sources do not mention large groups of non-Jews seeking support. Jews knew they could expect some support from fellow Litvaks on the other side of the border. In December 1868 Rülf informed Jewish communities in the German states about the looming crisis. In January 1869, the *Allgemeine Zeitung* published his first harrowing account. Rülf specifically mentioned the death of Jewish children in the town of Telz (Telsiai), which would later become known for its yeshiva. In other towns, dozens of Jews had contracted or had already died from typhus. In the following months local committees formed across the German states to raise funds.[14]

Before the 1860s the number of poor migrants seeking support from Jewish communities was limited. Jews from the Russian and Austro-Hungarian empires moved, often seasonally, within the borderland region but rarely beyond it. Those who lived far from the border lacked means and information to travel, not to mention access to a reliable transportation infrastructure. In Central Europe Jewish poverty was declining dramatically. Between 1820 and 1850 most Jews in the German states made the move from the margins of rural economies to the urban bourgeoisie, often in a single generation. This unprecedented social mobility was closely associated with migration. Most Jews moved to nearby cities such as Frankfurt, Cologne, and above all Berlin. More than 100,000 rural Jews joined the large migration from the German states to North America between the 1820s and 1880s. Here too most prospered. Available sources from Europe and the United States do not hint at larger groups of Jewish migrants who required assistance. Jewish communities in port cities, notably New York and London, encountered poor migrants on a more frequent basis after 1820, but before 1880 the provision of assistance for migrants was largely handled on the local level.[15]

In 1868–1869, for the first time in living memory, the small Jewish communities in East Prussia could not cope with the rising number of destitute Jews. None of the Jewish observers in the vicinity of the border contested that these Jews were fleeing great misery. The crisis occurred at a particularly inconvenient moment for Prussian Jews. Right-wing Prussian politicians had long warned that "masses" of Russian Jews and Poles would "stream" across the poorly guarded eastern border. On June 15, 1847, during a debate over a Jewish emancipation bill in the recently convened Prussian Landtag (assembly), a young landowner rose to speak against full Jewish emancipation. Jews, he stressed, could and should not become civil servants of a Christian state such as Prussia. In larger cities, such as Berlin, they tended to be "respectable," but in rural parts of Prussia Jews were systematically exploiting poor farmers. Even worse, should the legal and social condition of "Polish" Jews in the Prussian province of Posen improve as envisaged by the emancipation bill, "millions of Russian Jews who are not feeling at home [in Russia] might be lured" across the border.

The emancipation bill passed but excluded Jews from certain positions in the civil service and legal system. Jews in the largely Polish-speaking province of Posen remained disadvantaged. After 1847 the archconservative opponent of Jewish emancipation would embark on a remarkable political career. After spending several years as Prussia's ambassador in Paris and St. Petersburg, Otto von Bismarck was appointed Prussian prime minister in 1862. Enjoying much support from fellow aristocratic landowners, Bismarck quickly gained the trust of the new Prussian king Wilhelm I and emerged as a powerful driving force behind Prussia's rise to a major European power.[16]

On July 3, 1869, just when the Lithuanian migration crisis gripped the Jewish public, Prussia fully emancipated all permanent Jewish residents within its borders. The emancipation edict did not apply to recently arrived migrants from other states or their Prussian-born children. In April 1869, a few months before full emancipation was formally enacted, the Jewish community in Berlin sponsored a concert in its recently dedicated imposing New Synagogue to raise funds for suffering Jews in the Lithuanian provinces. The king and leading Prussian aristocrats attended the service. Prime Minister Bismarck stayed away. To express his respect for the Jewish tradition the monarch did not remove his hat during the concert. While the king's visit constituted a great honor, the *Allgemeine Zeitung* reminded readers that the *Kreuzzeitung*, Prussia's main conservative paper, continued to promote anti-Jewish hatred in its editorials.

Lingering hostility in the upper echelons of the Prussian state to migration from the Russian Empire and widely held anti-Jewish stereotypes precluded the possibility of allowing even a handful of Jewish refugees from Lithuania to remain in Prussia for more than a few weeks. Jewish community leaders knew they had to solve the crisis on their own, and as quickly as possible. Apart from keeping the Prussian government on the sidelines, Jewish communities faced a Jewish public that was at best indifferent toward Jewish misery in Eastern Europe. As full emancipation appeared within grasp during the mid-1860s Jews in the German states had distanced themselves from their eastern coreligionists. Negative images of *Ostjuden* were widespread. Even open-minded commentators and observers like Rülf deplored the primitive state of Jewish life in Russia and expressed the need for a thorough education and modernization program. A crucial term in this discussion was "productivization" (*Produktivierung*): Jews in Russia would prosper only if they would earn income as productive artisans and farmers, rather than studying the Talmud.[17]

The most immediate challenge facing Jewish community leaders in Prussia's eastern borderland was the need for an overarching Jewish institution that could coordinate support, raise funds, and distribute aid where it was needed. Just as the crisis reached a critical phase in July 1869, Jewish delegates congregated in Leipzig to establish the Deutsch Israelitischer Gemeindebund (DIGB), a federation of Jewish communities from the German states and parts of the Austro-Hungarian Empire. The delegates expressed their support and elected a committee to deal with the aid effort and raise funds. But without a central office and staff the new organization could not manage the crisis.[18] During the spring months the *Allgemeine Zeitung* coordinated the relief effort. In May 1869, the paper began devoting a lengthy section in almost every issue to the crisis in "West Russia." It published letters from rabbis representing affected communities and lay leaders involved in fundraising efforts. The paper's editor, Reform rabbi Ludwig Philippson, moderated the discussion. Without overarching institutions, the editor of the widely read weekly was in a unique position to speak on behalf of Jews in Central Europe. Like his counterparts in other countries, for instance American rabbi Isaac Mayer Wise, who also edited a national Jewish weekly, Philippson played an outsized role in shaping Jewish public opinion.

Rülf regularly dispatched reports to the *Allgemeine Zeitung*. After his return from Kovno in early June 1869 he demanded an immediate mass resettlement of Jews from Lithuania to Russia's southern provinces, where the economic conditions for settlement were more promising than in the overpopulated Lithuanian towns. A commentator familiar with the restrictive Russian policies toward Jewish subjects expressed doubt about the proposal because Jews and foreigners could not legally acquire land. He also wondered what employment Jewish artisans and peddlers would find. Other commentators demanded the Russian government adopt the successful Prussian gradual emancipation policy. On the eve of full emancipation Prussian Jews did not huddle "close together" in Jewish neighborhoods (like their Russian coreligionists); Jewish *Gemeinden* were financially stable; and Jews had become respected and "intelligent" members of Prussia's bourgeoisie.[19]

Rabbi Abraham Treuenfels from Stettin bluntly suggested a different plan: "Emigration, organized emigration on a grand scale." Palestine and the Russian interior were not viable options, unlike America with its rapidly growing economy. If tens of thousands of poor Irish could move to the United States, fifty thousand Jews from western Russia should be able to do the same. In hindsight, this assessment appears prophetic. Treuenfels was hardly the first German Jew who presented America as a solution. In 1846 none other than Philippson had suggested Russian Jews should move to Texas to escape government oppression. Treuenfels's disparaging comments about Russian Jews betray a lack of compassion and knowledge. Hundreds were "begging all over Germany," he wrote; his city had become a "gateway for hordes" of Russian Jews. Some continued their journey to Denmark and Sweden; others headed west, relying on the support of local Jewish communities, supposedly to earn money for a passage to America. The rabbi accused the *Gemeinde* in Königsberg of exporting the migration crisis to Stettin and other cities further west.[20]

Instead of moving poor Jews from one community to the next, Treuenfels suggested, it was necessary to act "reasonably, with a plan in mind, and collectively." Sending large groups of poor Lithuanian Jews to America would remove unwelcome Jews from Prussia. The infrastructure for such a project, Treuenfels pointed out, was already in place. Agricultural laborers from East Prussia, Pomerania, and Mecklenburg heading to the United States usually traveled by train to the ports of Hamburg and Bremen. He expected American Jews to accommodate the arrivals: "What these people [the Jews from Russia] should do over there? We say frankly, we have taken them across [the ocean], now American Jews may take care of them." Treuenfels expressed dismay over the lack of cooperation between Jewish communities. Since the migration threatened the status of all Prussian Jews it was necessary to cooperate and act decisively. Tellingly, the contributors whose letters the *Allgemeine Zeitung* printed all agreed that the Lithuanian Jews should be sent to a distant place.[21]

In his role as editor of the main Jewish weekly in Central Europe Philippson could collect, channel, and publish information, not least calls for donations, but he could not supervise the distribution of aid to affected communities and migrants. During the summer of 1869 he approached the Alliance. Its president, Adolphe Cremieux, suggested a meeting in Berlin.[22] For the Alliance the crisis came at an opportune moment. A growing number of Jews in the German states were becoming members and organizing local Alliance chapters. One of the first was the rabbi of the Jewish community in Königsberg, Isaac Bamberger. The DIGB meeting may also have influenced Cremieux's decision. Before a rival organization could emerge, it was in the interest of the Alliance to involve its German members in the aid effort. This development marks an important moment: an overarching Jewish organization that was not tied to a single donor or a specific community stepped in to manage a crisis involving Jewish migrants in a distant foreign territory.

On October 11, 1869, more than forty men convened in Berlin: Rülf, Bamberger, representatives of larger Jewish communities in the German states, and the Alliance leadership. Philippson was unable to attend. Cremieux missed the main meeting but arrived in time for several informal follow-up discussions. The key figure was Albert Cohn, the de facto executive director of the Alliance. For almost three decades he had supervised the philanthropic projects of the Paris branch of the Rothschild family. He could draw on a network of contacts across Europe and the Ottoman Empire. Rülf and two representatives from other East Prussian communities spoke first, informing the attendees about the "horrible conditions" affecting Jews in Lithuania. They blamed discriminatory state policies but also unenlightened rabbis who were either "extremely" orthodox or subservient to the government. Their description of Russian Jews betrays deep-seated stereotypes echoing earlier descriptions: "This population is unable to perform almost any productive work. That is the sad picture of the conditions, not just among the Jews in West Russia [Lithuania] but among all Russian Jews." No Jewish delegate from the Russian Empire had been invited to refute these claims. The participants elected a small committee, which continued to deliberate for several days. Cohn announced a donation of 300,000 francs by the Paris Rothschilds to assist Jewish emigration from Russia. Alliance chapters in France and the German states had already raised 70,000 francs.[23]

Bamberger was appointed head of a "main border committee" in Königsberg. Apart from coordinating its activities with the Alliance main office in Paris, the committee was tasked with supporting the neediest, funding efforts to improve the (secular) education of young Jews of both sexes, and training Jews to become farmers and artisans. The children of Jewish migrants from Russia were to receive a thorough education and job training. The Alliance vowed to "organize" the emigration and consult with the Russian government. Only younger men and their families who were "able and willing to work" would be considered for emigration to the United States. For that purpose, the Alliance announced it would reach out to American Jews to make sure that the new arrivals were cared for. The resettlement of Jews to the Russian interior was not mentioned.

The committee initially concentrated on job training schemes and education. Boys from the Kovno region were trained as artisans or sent to local schools in East Prussia. A few younger men attended rabbinical seminaries in Berlin and Breslau (Wrocław), almost certainly with the expectation that they would return to the Pale and help modernize traditional communities. To mitigate concerns by American Jews, the Alliance brokered a deal with the newly founded Hebrew Emigration Aid Society in New York. Only carefully selected industrious Jews would be sent to America. The 1870–1871 Franco-Prussian War delayed he resettlement effort. But by early 1872 more than five hundred Lithuanian Jews had made the journey. A significantly larger group of migrants was sent home. Philippson was pessimistic about the prospects for Jewish life in the Russian Empire. After admonishing his readers for making insufficient donations, he compared the Lithuanian migrants with Sephardi Jews who had been expelled from Spain and found asylum in Amsterdam. Lithuanian Jews were the "Marranos of the 19th Century." Philippson distinguished between "two types" of these new "Marranos." "Landläufige Gestalten" (the usual suspects), was code for vagrants and beggars. In contrast, he wrote, honest and hard-working merchants and artisans who reluctantly asked for support were deserving.[24]

The 1869 crisis showed that the Alliance had emerged as the helping hand of the Jewish Diaspora. Unlike Philippson's weekly paper, a professional organization with access to funds could assist local Jewish communities with crisis management. Neither Prussian nor American Jews, not to mention Jews in the Russian Empire, had been able to establish organizations that could coordinate a similar aid operation. As more Jews rose into the middle class across Europe and North America and subscribed to Jewish weeklies, the Alliance and its sister associations could reach out to more donors and act quickly by drawing attention to the crisis, publishing fundraising calls, and providing targeted assistance where it was needed.

German Jewish leaders, including Philippson, continued to embrace the Alliance and its mission, even after the divisive Franco-Prussian War. In 1872 German and French Jewish leaders met in Brussels to discuss the precarious situation of Jewish communities in the Romanian principalities. Philippson's paper emphasized the spirit of "solidarity" and the "harmonious" character of the discussions, at a time when German and French officials were barely on speaking terms. The war did not slow down the expansion of Alliance chapters across Germany. By 1880, most members of the Alliance lived in Imperial Germany, even though the leadership was composed of a small group of Paris Jews. Jews in Germany and the United States struggled to establish similar organizations for decades, largely because Jewish communities in both countries were more dispersed and experienced strong growth during the second half of the nineteenth century.[25]

Networking across borders within and even beyond Europe to solve a specifically Jewish crisis was still a new experience, as was a public and controversial discussion about possible solutions. The ambivalent perception of the migrants as victims of a Russian state unwilling to do much for its subjects but also as unproductive and prone to begging would shape the organized assistance of Jewish migrants from Eastern Europe into the twentieth century.

To counter widespread anti-Jewish stereotypes Jewish aid associations such as the Alliance and later the Jewish Colonization Association turned to a specific policy that had roots in the emancipation debate in the German states. Jewish community leaders promoted transforming poor and economically marginalized Jews into productive and hard-working model citizens. Even though the prospects for Jewish farmers and artisans appeared increasingly gloomy in industrializing economies after the middle of the nineteenth century, Jewish aid organizations developed a wide range of training schemes for poor Jews well beyond 1914.[26] During the 1880s Jewish advocates of that policy were taken more seriously. The U.S. 1882 Immigration Act explicitly excluded "any person unable to take care of himself or herself without becoming a public charge." After the 1890s Zionism provided another boost to the productivization policy.[27]

A Litvak Moves to America

The 1868–1869 migration crisis marks a turning point because for the first time Jewish representatives from different parts of Europe came together to debate the implications of rising Jewish migration from the Russian Empire and coordinate support across borders. No Jews in the Russian Empire participated in the discussions or were invited to the Berlin conference. Although the crisis marks the beginnings of a transnational support network, its impact on the actual migration was limited. Only a few Litvaks were dispatched to Western Europe and the United States. The extensive coverage of the 1868–1869 crisis in the Jewish press obscures a barely noticed but steadily growing migration of Jews from the northern Pale through Central Europe to Britain and the United States. These migrants overwhelmingly traveled on their own. Few asked Jewish communities along the transit routes for assistance. In an 1874 letter to the Anglo-Jewish Association, Cremieux noted the growing emigration of "young and industrious men" from Lithuania. Networks were a crucial catalyst. Early migrants sent back information about the economic conditions and sometimes money for their relatives' passage.[28]

Already in 1864, the United Hebrew Relief Association of Chicago noted the presence of *Ostjuden* in the city. Its board members were prospering Jewish immigrant entrepreneurs from Bavaria and the Palatinate. The use of the German term in an otherwise English text hints at a stereotypical view of supposedly unproductive men who neglected their families by studying the Talmud and relying on donations from other Jews. Yet few Jewish immigrants from Lithuania actually asked established Chicago Jews for support. Apart from disparaging comments in local Jewish sources, the movement of young Lithuanian Jewish men and women was little noticed and not newsworthy. The migrants built their own aid networks, often *Landsmanshaft* congregations. In 1870 migrants from the town of Mariampol (Marijampole) organized a small benevolent society, which became the nucleus of Chicago's Orthodox congregation Ohave Sholom Mariampol.

Hardly any research has been conducted on the journeys and travel routes of average migrants. Their recollections were shared orally and became part of family histories. Apart from a few mementos, such as birth certificates, photographs of ancestors, random letters, and steamship tickets, few sources remain. One of the migrants who recorded his migration experience was a respected Chicago businessman and Zionist who published a detailed memoir of his "first eighty years" in 1939.[29] Bernard Horwich was born in 1861 in Poniemon (Panemune), a tiny village located on the banks of the Neman River on the outskirts of Kovno. He and his brothers grew up in a strictly Orthodox household. Their father had moved to Poniemon as a young man to study the Talmud. After marrying a local woman, he joined other Jews in the timber trade. He leased forest tracts from landowners and the government, hiring local workers to cut down trees. The timber was sold locally or shipped down the river in large rafts to Memel. His income fluctuated and barely sustained the growing family. Horwich had five brothers. One attended a yeshiva in Vilna; another trained as an artisan in Odessa. Jews from the village were already moving to America when Horwich was a boy. He recalls reading letters from America to their illiterate parents.

After his bar mitzvah Horwich joined his father on business trips and earned some money. He realized he had to figure out what to do with his life. He could stay put, marry, and establish himself in the timber business, like his father. Unlike his brother at the yeshiva Horwich did not want to become a rabbi or Talmudic scholar. Knowledge about Jews who had already left and the constraints of the religious tradition persuaded him to leave. One Saturday Horwich's father saw him riding in a carriage with a peasant. He was deeply hurt by his son's flagrant violation of the sabbath. After agonizing for several days Horwich made up his mind. The fourteen-year-old declared that he would not remain in Poniemon. As he put it, "I felt I was independent.... Father consented to my going, and a few weeks later I headed to Königsberg, finally realizing my dreams."[30]

For many Jews in Lithuania Königsberg appeared to be the gateway to a better future. Horwich does not specifically discuss the precarious economic situation in the Lithuanian provinces but hints at limited prospects for young Jewish men and women. For many migrants the East Prussian capital served as a first stopover. Unlike Russian ports on the Baltic Königsberg's port, Pillau, was usually ice-free during the winter months. The completion of the cross-border railroad to Kovno, Vilna, and St. Petersburg in 1862 and of another line to Brest-Litovsk in 1873 fortified Königsberg's position as a hub for the lucrative Russian grain trade. For several years after 1880 the city was Imperial Germany's leading port for grain shipments, benefiting from another blockade of Russia's Black Sea ports during the Russian war with the Ottoman Empire in 1877–1878.[31]

Like almost all Jewish migrants leaving the Russian Empire, Horwich traveled by train. His mother insisted that her husband accompany her son on the short train journey to the border at Kibarty. Horwich recalls that a bribe by his father let him leave Russia without a passport: "Six roubles in cash to the right party fully took care of the law."[32] In 1875 no passport was required to enter Prussia, and Horwich does not mention controls in Eydtkuhnen, on the Prussian side of the border. In Königsberg, Horwich boarded with an acquaintance of his father. His plan to establish himself as a grain broker fell apart before he even arrived in the city. Naively, the teenager entrusted most of his savings to a swindler who preyed on young Jewish migrants on the train. Too proud to return home, Horwich clerked in a small store, earning a sufficient income but not enough to launch his own business. With a partner, he moved to the East Prussian border town of Tilsit, where he ran a modestly successful store for agricultural goods.

Before the mid-1880s the Prussian government tolerated Jewish and other Russian sojourners, as long as they were employed and did not create trouble or become destitute. Shortly after his arrival in Königsberg Horwich even went to the police to file a complaint about the swindler on the train. In early 1880 he decided to move on. He was nineteen years old, still single, and possessed reliable information about opportunities in America. He also worried about his legal status after he heard the Prussian state considered restricting foreign labor migration. A cousin who had settled in New York several years earlier sent him a prepaid ticket. In Hamburg he boarded a steamer for Liverpool and New York. Soon after his arrival he relocated to Chicago, a rapidly growing city, that appeared more promising than New York. He began peddling stationery in Chicago's streets and later set up a scrap business.[33]

Up to this point his story follows a fairly typical pattern. Horwich was a young man with little money from a small village looking for independence and a better life. Unlike most Christians from Lithuania, he could read and write, a crucial skill. Instead of moving straight from his hometown to America he sojourned in East Prussia for several years. And like other migrants he sent some of his earnings to his family. Horwich did not exactly know what to expect in Königsberg, and later in New York and Chicago, but he obtained information about the destinations and relied on relatives and acquaintances. Horwich rose relatively quickly from a street peddler to a modestly wealthy business owner. He noticed a potentially lucrative niche collecting used bottles and selling them to breweries. He employed helpers and expanded the small business. An attempt by the breweries to take control of the bottle redistribution briefly appeared to threaten his enterprise. He diversified, investing in other ventures in the scrap sector. At least two of his brothers also left their home village at a young age, one moving to Vilna and one to Odessa. By the early 1890s all of Horwich's five brothers had settled in Chicago.

The migration of siblings shows the importance of kinship and networks in the migration process. In 1893, the Horwich brothers hosted their father on the occasion of the Columbian World Exposition. During the 1890s Horwich became an early leader of Chicago's emerging Zionist movement. Unlike most fellow migrants from Lithuania, he joined a Reform congregation and socialized with members of the Jewish business establishment, albeit without cutting his ties to more recent immigrants. His surprisingly candid memoir leaves no doubt that his migration was driven by a quest for better economic prospects. He missed his parents and faced more than a few challenges along the way, but he did not regret his decision to leave.[34]

Most authors devote only fleeting attention to Lithuania as a region of origin before 1881.[35] Even a cursory glance at Jewish communities in different parts of the world demonstrates the importance of the two districts Kovno and Vilna and the adjacent Polish districts of Suwalki and Lomza as regions of origin in the decades before 1900. When Horwich reached Chicago in 1880 he joined a growing community of Lithuanian Jews. Poniemon was a tiny village, but Horwich was not the first Poniemon Jew who settled in Chicago. At least one member of a Poniemon family, later known by the name Bregstone, had reached Chicago in 1878. Other Bregstones settled in New York and Scranton, Pennsylvania, during the 1870s. Of the almost three thousand Jews in Sweden in 1880 about 40 percent had been born in the Russian Empire before 1865, overwhelmingly in the small Suwalki district—an example of chain migration. Most left Sweden for the United States within a few months or years of each other. A large migration network from the vicinity of Kovno completely transformed the small Jewish community in South Africa between the late 1880s and the 1910s.

Litvaks also represented a prominent group in the vibrant Jewish immigrant neighborhoods in London's East End, Boston's North End, and Manhattan's Lower East Side during the 1870s, and in many smaller cities, for instance, in the Irish capital, Dublin. It is likely that most belonged to migration networks from specific places in the Kovno, Vilna, or Suwalki districts. Studies about Jewish migrants in London hint at a high level of transmigration before 1914. After sojourns in Königsberg, Berlin, Sweden, or Odessa, Litvaks moved to London or northern cities such as Leeds for a few weeks or months to earn some money before continuing their journey to New York and beyond. Others traveled by train from London to Southampton, where they embarked on Union Castle Line steamers for Cape Town and from there by train to Johannesburg.[36]

Bernard Horwich belonged to the millions of young men and women who left rural parts of Europe for nearby and distant cities. The act of migration freed young men like Horwich from religious and social constraints. Moving to a distant destination was usually not a rejection of tradition and family, nor was it a one-way street. Migrants relied on relatives and friends who had already moved across the Atlantic. Tickets bought in the United States and sent to relatives and friends back home became increasingly common after 1870. Even when he earned a relatively limited income in Königsberg and Tilsit, Horwich sent money to his family in Poniemon. As the economic conditions in smaller towns in the Russian Empire, not least in Lithuania, deteriorated further after 1880, Jewish families depended on remittances from migrants. Horwich's extended journey and that of his brothers indicates that migrations to nearby cities overlapped with migrations across Russia's western border and across the Atlantic. The available sources indicate that Jews left the northern part of the Russian Empire earlier and in larger numbers than members of other groups, such as Lithuanians, Poles, and German speakers. The limited data also point to the migration of families because a disproportionate share of Jewish women, children, and older men and women relocated to the United States. The gender ratio among Jewish migrants was almost balanced. And remigration rates for Jews were lower than for non-Jewish Eastern Europeans but not negligible. These differences can be traced to the distinctive economic profile of Jews and to the lack of economic prospects in small rural towns in the northern Pale.[37]

The 1869 migration crisis was the result of widespread poverty and lack of economic opportunities in the northern part of the Russian Pale. Before 1869 established Jews in Western Europe considered anti-Jewish discrimination and violence but also calamities like disease outbreaks affecting Jewish communities in the diaspora as the main challenges requiring a coordinated Jewish response. The Lithuanian crisis added migration to the agenda. For the first time Jews in Central and Western Europe debated the implications of a prolonged Jewish migration from the Russian Empire. Migration was not a distant problem but affected the public reputation of Jewish communities in the transit and destination countries. The migration of poor Jews required concerted action across borders—by Jewish leaders who were recently emancipated citizens of different states which sometimes were involved in military conflicts or had strained relations. The response to the 1869 crisis laid the groundwork for a loosely linked transnational Jewish support network, with the Alliance as a key actor. The story of Bernard Horwich illustrates that a wide gulf separated distorted perceptions of *Ostjuden* from actual migrants who often planned their journeys carefully and were not vagrants or beggars. Horwich was one of thousands of young Litvaks who moved to the United States before 1880. His experience shows the impact of agency and of networks comprising families and acquaintances from small towns in Lithuania.

The public discussion about the Lithuanian crisis hints at three larger issues connected with Jewish migration before 1880: the question of rights for Jews in the Russian Empire, the legal status of migrants in transit, and the resettlement of Russian Jews to a more suitable territory. Several commentators in the German states recognized that, just as they themselves were being emancipated, Lithuanian Jews were unwanted and unprotected subjects whose fate did not much concern the St. Petersburg government. In this context, Rülf's emphatic 1869 sermon is noteworthy. The effort to emancipate Jews in and beyond Europe was part of a broader struggle for universal rights. Another point deserves more attention. Already in the late 1860s Rülf and other rabbis as well as the Russian governor of Kovno discussed the mass resettlement of Lithuanian Jews as one solution to address Jewish poverty.[38]

2
The 1881–1882 Pogroms and the Brody Crisis

In early 1882 the Russian police in Velizh, a small provincial town in the northern Pale of Settlement, searched the living quarters of a young teacher and hauled him to the station for an interrogation. Following the assassination of Tsar Alexander II by a group of young terrorists the previous year, the authorities resorted to mass arrests and expanded the search for potential anarchists.

The teacher had every reason to be worried. Three years earlier, as a student at the Vilna teacher seminar, he had joined a secret anarchist cell. He knew the police were investigating the group. In a coded letter his mother had informed him that one of his friends had already been detained. It is easy to understand why he and other students sympathized with the anarchist cause. Already as a small child he had been confronted with Russian state brutality. The harrowing image of bodies covered in white shrouds, hanging on gallows on a field outside of Vilna—Poles executed after the failed 1863 uprising—burned itself into the memory of the three-year-old boy. He spent his early childhood in a tight-knit Jewish world shaped by religiosity and widespread poverty. When he was six years old, the family moved to nearby Vilna. As a teenager he attended a yeshiva but developed an interest in Russian literature. Like the young Bernard Horwich, he began to distance himself from the religious tradition. His decision to attend the teacher seminar led to a break with his observant father.[1]

The interrogation revealed that a friend of the teacher in Vilna had fallen into the clutches of the investigation. To his surprise the police did not detain the teacher but told him not to leave town. Certain he would be arrested, he raised some money from local acquaintances and took off. Moving carefully to avoid police patrols, he made his way by boat and carriage to Mogilev, a journey that took several days. Here, he spent three weeks to obtain forged papers and consider his options. Where to go? Staying in Russia probably meant Siberian exile. One man tried to persuade him to go to

Between Borders. Tobias Brinkmann, Oxford University Press. © Oxford University Press 2024.
DOI: 10.1093/oso/9780197655658.003.0003

Palestine. America seemed more promising for building Socialist colonies than Switzerland or Paris, preferred destinations for Russian dissidents. Still undecided, he traveled south by boat on the Dnieper River. Twice he barely eluded the police. In Kiev a trustworthy person bought him a train ticket; doing so himself with forged papers would have been too risky. He boarded the train, bound for the Austrian border.

The pogroms in the southern provinces—far from where he lived—and increasing Jewish migration feature in his account, but not prominently. The Jews he met on the train were not fleeing pogroms. Like the young teacher, most were educated young men with leftist leanings. Several belonged to Am Olam (Eternal People), a society that had formed in Odessa in the previous year to establish Socialist colonies in the United States. The group on the train hailed from the southern town of Balta in Podolia, the scene of a major pogrom on April 29, 1882, weeks after the young men on the train had left the town.

In Zdolbunova outside of Rowno (Rivne) the migrants transferred to the branch line toward Lemberg (Lviv). The teacher hesitated to buy a ticket for the last portion of the journey, fearing he would have to show his forged passport. His concerns were unfounded; the train conductor accepted a bribe. Several smugglers openly walked up and down the aisles calling for customers. The teacher chose a red-bearded Jewish man. From the train station in Dubno the smuggler and his Christian helpers took the group on a horse-drawn carriage to a small hut outside of the border town Radzivilov, where they waited until the evening. After demanding and receiving more money, the smugglers led the migrants toward the border. In the darkness they lost any sense of direction or time. Reasoning it was better to be caught by Russian border guards without papers, the teacher tossed the forged passport. He did not need papers to enter the Austrian Empire.[2]

The next morning the exhausted migrants walked into the Galician border town of Brody. The teacher was too tired to fully grasp the strange scenery. Thousands of Jews were camping out in makeshift tents all over town. Following a wave of pogroms in provinces near the Black Sea, large groups were flocking to Brody, most with unrealistic expectations that they would be taken to America free of charge. Even though he does not mention it in his memoir, these rumors may have influenced the teacher himself to head to Brody. According to Leo Goldenstein, a member of the local Jewish aid committee, several local businessmen were a major source of the rumor campaign, hoping to derive income from the aid operation. In response, the committee contacted Jewish papers and rabbis in Russia to discourage Jews from coming to Brody, with limited success.

The teacher hardly mentions the migration crisis in his account. He wrote a letter to his mother, got a haircut, bought new clothes, and socialized with locals. He was struck by the dilapidated state of the town and the abject poverty of the local Jews. Some tried to persuade young migrants to marry their daughters and take them to America. The wife of the red-bearded smuggler even offered her teenage cousin for sex. After several days the teacher decided to join the Am Olam group from Balta on their journey to America. Did he pay for his passage or accept support from an aid committee in Brody? He avoided discussing this matter but pointed out that relying on the aid committee was certainly an attractive option, even for migrants with sufficient funds. With a larger group he traveled via Lemberg, Breslau, Berlin, Hamburg, and Liverpool to Philadelphia, only a few weeks before Jewish aid associations stopped funding the journeys of larger groups of Jewish migrants stranded in Brody.[3]

The teacher recalled his passage through Brody more than forty years later, in the early 1920s, when he could look back on a truly remarkable career. At that time Abraham Cahan was one of the most successful and illustrious Jewish immigrants of his generation. Instead of joining an agricultural colony he found a job as a tobacco worker on New York's Lower East Side and began submitting articles to Yiddish newspapers. In 1897 Cahan and several fellow journalists founded the *Forverts* (Forward) as a less dogmatic alternative to the Socialist *Arbeiter Zeitung*, which he had coedited in the early 1890s. The daily's name was inspired by Germany's revered Social Democratic *Vorwärts* paper. Cahan had a canny sense of his readers' interests and needs. He believed a successful paper had to offer more than just news and political commentary. The *Forverts* was designed as an indispensable companion, advising readers on how to cope with their daily struggles. Readers could draw on a range of services, such as English classes, vaccinations, and summer camps. Staff members even intervened on behalf of relatives detained at Ellis Island.

Cahan worked hard to channel readers' emotions and views and give them a voice. In 1906 he launched an advice column, "Bintel Briefe" (Bundle of Letters), which epitomized the paper's role as a broker between the old world and the new. He encouraged his anonymous letter writers to open up. He did not shy away from touching on his readers' intimate lives because he felt only his paper provided a forum for discussing taboo subjects such as sex. After difficult beginnings—Cahan walked away from the paper for several years before returning as editor with absolute control—the *Forverts* became an institution with a daily circulation that exceeded 100,000 by 1910 and 275,000 in the late 1920s. In 1912 the *Forverts* moved into its own skyscraper, which towered over the Lower East Side, home to hundreds of thousands of Jewish immigrants. Today the building houses luxury condos, but the portraits of four Socialist leaders on the building's portal have been preserved: Karl Marx; Friedrich Engels; Ferdinand Lasalle, the Jewish cofounder of the German Social Democratic Party; and the party's leader in 1912, August Bebel. Cahan's moderate Socialist views, his pragmatism, and his lack of enthusiasm for Zionism made him the target of frequent polemic attacks. Like other leading figures on the Lower East Side, Cahan was known for his vanity. He remained unfazed. His memoir, *Bleter fun mein Lebn* (Leaves of My Life), covered five thick volumes. The description of his life's remarkable journey, portraying the author as plucky hero, not so implicitly evokes Homer's *Odyssey*.[4]

His short sojourn in Brody marked a decisive moment in Cahan's life. For three weeks he found himself between two worlds. He and the other young Jews had left Russia behind, but America was still distant and an imagined rather than a real place. In Brody Cahan made up his mind to go to America. He did not personally witness pogroms and did not describe encounters with pogrom victims during his journey. Yet he did point out that the 1881–1882 pogroms turned the Jewish migration from a trickle to a mass movement. This statement reflects his viewpoint in the mid-1920s, after more than 2 million Jews had moved to America. His prediction that future historians would interpret the Brody crisis as a turning point in modern Jewish history turned out to be far-sighted, even from the vantage point of the 1920s.

The view of the pogroms as the overarching cause for the Jewish migration from the Russian Empire (and adjacent territories) continues to linger. A search for the phrase "fled the pogroms" in contemporary newspapers and magazines yields dozens of results. According to a recent article about Lithuanian immigrants in Chicago in the *Economist*, "at the turn of the twentieth century thousands of Litvaks (Lithuanian Jews) fled the pogroms under Russian rule, while mostly blue-collar [Christian Lithuanian] workers came for jobs in the stockyards." This statement is misleading. Pogroms did occur in the northern Pale before 1914, but they were rare compared to the more frequent violence in the southern provinces and certainly were not the single cause behind the mass migration of Lithuanian Jews to Chicago and other American cities around

1900. Chicago was an early destination for Jewish migrants seeking better economic opportunities. Jewish men and women who settled in Chicago after 1870 often found employment in the garment sector.[5]

Although scholars writing about Jewish life in the Russian Empire have largely dismissed the pogrom thesis in recent decades, the view that the pogroms were the major cause driving Jewish migration remains influential in studies about general migration history. A synthesis about twentieth-century global migration traces Jewish migration from the Russian Empire between 1903 and 1905 exclusively to pogroms. In a recently published study about U.S. immigration policy the author writes, "The first large group of Jews fleeing Russia landed in New York [in 1881] and so began the 'new immigration' wave from southern and eastern Europe that would last for four decades." Dozens of similar examples could be cited.[6]

It is important to stress that anti-Jewish violence and restrictive policies by the tsarist government made a lasting and deep impact on the Jewish population in the Russian Empire. The *perception* that the authorities instigated the pogroms or at least did not attempt to prevent the violence was widespread. More important, especially younger Jews had little hope of improvement and all Jews lived in growing fear, especially after the notorious and widely reported 1903 Kishinev pogrom. Economic pressure exacerbated the situation of many families who had to provide for children and elderly family members. Yet a sharp distinction between economic migrants and refugees fleeing persecution does not accurately describe the experience of Jews who left Eastern Europe before 1914.

Early authors writing about Jewish migration were quite aware of the complex motives influencing the decisions of Jews seeking to leave the Russian Pale. During the middle decades of the twentieth century older interpretations were sidelined by a suggestive but one-sided narrative that traced Jewish migration from Eastern Europe before 1914 almost exclusively to persecution. When and where did the view of the pogroms as overarching cause of the Jewish migration from Eastern Europe originate? And who were the Jews Cahan encountered in Brody, if they were not pogrom refugees?

Assessing the Causes of Jewish Migrations

The first decade of the twentieth century marked a decisive phase in the history of the Jewish mass migration from Eastern Europe. The shocking 1903

Kishinev pogrom attracted worldwide attention. Following the Russian defeat in the war against Japan in early 1905 anti-Jewish violence surged and spread to the northern Pale of Settlement, where most migrants originated. A new wave of pogroms in the southern provinces between 1903 and 1906 coincided with a dramatic increase of Jewish migration. In 1905, following a prolonged public debate, the British Parliament passed the Aliens Act, a restrictive immigration bill that implicitly targeted Jewish immigrants from Eastern Europe. The Prussian government tolerated transmigrants but took a harsh line against unwanted migrants who tried to settle in Berlin and other cities. Between 1904 and 1906 the Prussian authorities deported hundreds of "illegal" Russian Jewish migrants from Berlin. Even more concerning was the likelihood of the passage of more through immigration restrictions in the United States.[7]

In 1907 the U.S. Congress appointed a committee to investigate immigration. Most members of the so-called Dillingham Commission considered immigration a "problem." The prospect of growing violence against Jews in the Russian Empire and Romania and the increasing likelihood of migration restrictions in the main destination countries was a matter of serious concern for Jewish community representatives in the United States and Europe. If the United States switched to a more restrictive immigration policy, where would Jews facing violence and discrimination be able to go? Would other countries follow the British example? Jewish leaders in the United States and Europe understood the potential repercussions of a more restrictive American immigration policy. Should the United States close its doors, agonized the Hilfsverein, the leading German Jewish aid association in 1911, "a catastrophe would ensue, so terrible, that it will overshadow the persecutions and pogroms."[8]

Leaders of Jewish communities in Europe and the United States lobbied against restrictions by highlighting Jewish suffering in Russia and Romania. This was a sensible strategy because the violence was real. It appeared that the Russian government did little to prevent violent attacks against Jewish civilians and address the precarious economic situation of Jewish and other subjects. The situation was even worse in Romania, one of the poorest countries in Europe. To mitigate the impact of increasing unrest among Christian peasants, the government openly condoned violent attacks against Jews. Reports by Jewish aid associations and Jewish newspapers frequently depicted Jewish migrants as "refugees" fleeing violent persecution. For the general press and the Jewish public in different countries the link between rising violence and strong Jewish migration appeared suggestive. Yet a closer look at contemporary texts about actual migrants betrays surprisingly differentiated assessments. In a 1905 essay the executive director of the Hilfsverein, Bernhard Kahn, deplored widespread anti-Jewish violence in Russia and expressed concern about potential American immigration restrictions. However, Kahn stressed that the main causes driving the migration were economic.[9]

Jewish migration emerged as a prominent topic requiring serious and thorough analysis around 1900, when record numbers of Jews (and non-Jews) were leaving Eastern Europe. In 1904 the number of Jews entering the United States crossed the 100,000 annual threshold for the first time. These Jews constituted about 10 percent of the annual net immigration, a huge number for members of a relatively small group. It is estimated that not more than 250,000 Jews had lived in the United States around 1880. Rapidly expanding communities such as in Buenos Aires and Johannesburg were composed almost entirely of new arrivals. In Britain and the United States calls for limiting mass immigration gained political support. Antisemites linked Jewish immigrants from Eastern Europe with capitalist exploitation and, sometimes in the same vein, with left-wing political radicalism. At this critical juncture Jewish aid associations and communities in different parts of the world began to collect and publish extensive data about the causes of the migration and the actual migrants. This information was used to refute stereotypical perceptions of Jewish migrants and to lobby effectively against looming migration restrictions.[10]

The concise entry for "Migration" in the eighth volume of the *Jewish Encyclopedia* (1904) reflects the lack of information. St. Petersburg journalist L. Wygodski, who contributed the short section about Russia, carefully distinguished between economic factors and persecution, emphasizing that "the true cause [behind the strong migration] was undoubtedly the very unfortunate economic condition of the Jewish population in Russia. . . . [T]he riots merely supplied the stimulus." Wygodski likely wrote this passage before the 1903 Kishinev pogrom. His article reflects how he struggled to grasp the unfolding mass movement, which clearly represented a momentous shift.[11] The authors of early texts about the migration often hailed from the Russian Empire, had some university training, and moved in Zionist or Bundist circles. Their work straddled several disciplines, notably demography, economics, statistics, and law. They explicitly rejected political propaganda and stereotypical images of the Wandering Jew, emphasizing the need for critical scholarship.

The first in-depth scholarly study about Jewish mass migration from Eastern Europe is the 1913 dissertation by statistician and demographer Liebmann Hersch. Hersch grew up in modest circumstances as the son of a journalist in a small town in northern Lithuania. Migration shaped his upbringing. When he was a child, his father joined a growing number of Jews from the vicinity of Shavli (Siauliai) who settled in South Africa in the early 1890s, leaving his family in Lithuania. After the death of his mother a local teacher adopted Hersch and his five siblings. Eventually the father returned. After remarrying he moved the family to Warsaw. Hersch enrolled at Warsaw University to study mathematics. His activities as a member of the leftist Bund aroused the suspicion of the tsarist police. He left for the University of Geneva, where he studied demography. Even before he completed his doctoral dissertation on Jewish migration Hersch began teaching demography and statistics in his department. He belonged to a handful of Jewish scholars publishing works on Jewish social science and history who obtained permanent positions at well-regarded research universities during the interwar period. In 1927 the University of Geneva promoted him to a full professorship.[12]

In his 1913 dissertation, "Le juif errant d'aujord hui" (The Contemporary Jewish Migrant), Hersch carefully weighed several explanations. He did not judge Jewish migration as a distinctive development and drew comparisons to other groups. Economic factors were decisive but could not be studied in isolation. Although the title hints at the image of the Wandering Jew, Hersch explicitly rejected this stereotype as misleading. Based on extensive statistical material he carefully analyzed differences between the internal and overseas migrations of Jews and others from the Austro-Hungarian and Russian empires. He accurately traced a decline of the Jewish and general transatlantic migration in 1907–1908 to a recession in the United States. The legal discrimination and settlement restrictions imposed on Jews in the Russian Empire, he argued, caused growing economic hardship. Therefore, Russian Jews were more likely to look for better opportunities elsewhere than their coreligionists from the Austrian province of Galicia who did not face formal restrictions. Hersch examined published statistics critically. He questioned the reliability of the data provided by the *Jewish Encyclopedia*.[13]

In the same year that Hersch completed his dissertation another young migrant from the Russian Empire, Wladimir Wolf Kaplun-Kogan, published the study *Die Wanderbewegungen der Juden* (The Migrations of the Jews), which was almost certainly a dissertation he completed at the University of Cologne in economics. Relatively little is known about Kaplun-Kogan. He was probably born in Crimea. During the 1920s he was affiliated with a research institute at the University of Breslau. After 1933 he lived in Stockholm, where he died in 1948. Kaplun-Kogan took a more expansive view than Hersch, tracing Jewish migrations from the biblical period to the present. He dismissed the interpretations of nineteenth-century Jewish historians such as Heinrich Graetz who stressed the impact of persecution. The available data did not support the claim that the pogroms had caused the Jewish mass migration after 1880: "It was not legal restrictions and pogroms that caused Jewish emigration [from Russia] but rather—primarily—the country's economic development."[14]

The decline of the feudal system and the rise of capitalist production in the Russian Empire had displaced Jews and peasants. Jews were hit harder by the economic transformation because they lost their roles as middlemen and artisans, forcing them to look for new opportunities. Moving to territories east of the Volga and the Ural Mountains was an option for Russian peasants looking to farm their own land, but not for Jews who lacked the necessary skills and were restricted to the Pale of Settlement. In cities in Russian Poland, Jews from the Pale had to compete with non-Jews for housing and industrial jobs, making migration to Britain and the United States more feasible. Kaplun-Kogan observed, correctly, that Jewish migration from the Russian Empire was not a post-1881 phenomenon but had already increased in the early 1870s.

Kaplun-Kogan's short introduction, titled "The Jewish Question as a Problem of Migration," contradicts his sound analysis and betrays Zionist influences. Kaplun-Kogan depicts the Jews as a "people on the move" and as "a foreign element in the organism of host peoples." This view was popular with other Zionist authors and was influenced by the Christian stereotype of the Wandering Jew. In 1919 he published a revised study about Jewish migration after 1880. By then his view of Zionism had shifted. He relegated Theodor Herzl to the "epoch of utopianism and dilettantism" and did not revisit the discussion about the Jews as a "wandering people." Instead, he proposed a model to explain Jewish migrations that was influenced by Hersch's discussion of economic and political causes. To analyze the migration, he wrote, scholars should distinguish temporary "political-legal" factors such as the restrictions Jews had faced in the Russian Empire from "long-term" economic factors. He identified three distinct cases. In Romania only "political-legal" factors applied because restrictions prevented Romanian Jews from pursuing economic opportunities in a backward agricultural setting. Russia constituted a combination of "political-legal" and economic factors, whereas Jewish migration from the Austrian province of Galicia was almost exclusively related to economic factors.[15]

Among the Zionist texts about migration a 1905 essay by an obscure Russian author stands out. Zwi Avraami (almost certainly a pseudonym) traced Jewish emigration to "pressures" that resulted from discrepancies in economic development. Avraami was the first author who noted the reversal of a pattern that he regarded as characteristic for Jewish migrations in Europe after the late medieval period. Traditionally Jews had moved to economically less developed areas—from Spain to the Ottoman Empire in the 1500s and from Central Europe to the Polish Empire in the 1400s and 1500s. The rise of a capitalist mode of production reversed this pattern: a growing number of Jews were leaving economically backward regions in Eastern Europe for industrial societies such as the United States and England during the 1880s. Unlike other Zionist authors, Avraami did not touch on expulsion or persecution, and he avoided the image of the Jews as "wandering people." Rather he considered individual agency to be decisive.[16]

Beyond publications by a few Jewish scholars and aid officials, Jewish migration attracted little scholarly interest before 1914. An exception is the multivolume report of the Dillingham Commission. Most members of the commission favored restrictions and prepared the ground for the closed-door U.S. immigration policy that went into effect after 1917. The extensive report, forty volumes in total, betrays the influence of social science and economics. The commission collected extensive statistical material and even toured ports in Europe. The reports contain firsthand accounts by U.S. immigration inspectors and consular officials about the main travel routes and the social and economic conditions in different parts of Europe. The commission funded several studies. One of the most influential was the detailed analysis of the physiology of immigrants conducted by anthropologist Franz Boas.

The final report identified "economic conditions" as the overarching cause for European migration to the United States. The data that U.S. immigration officials began gathering after 1891 revealed that about a third of the migrants returned to Europe after working in the United States for periods ranging from several months to several years. This finding challenged widely held perceptions about migration as unidirectional. For the lengthy and detailed section about the migration of "Hebrews" from the Russian Empire the Dillingham Commission relied on a memorandum provided by the Baron de Hirsch Fund, which later became known as the Jewish Colonization

Association (JCA). During the first decade of the twentieth century this Paris-based organization maintained dozens of offices in the western part of the Russian Empire to advise potential colonists. The office staff collected data and other information about migrants who were considering moving to the Americas. Based on a wealth of statistical material JCA officials came to a similar conclusion as Hersch and other Jewish scholars: the impact of violent persecution was limited, but settlement and occupation restrictions exacerbated the dire economic situation of the Jewish population in Russia.[17]

The authors of early scholarly studies linked Jewish migration before 1914 with economic factors. The view of the 1881–1882 pogroms as the single overarching cause driving Jewish "flight" from Russia—and implicitly from Eastern Europe and beyond before 1914—did not gain traction until the 1940s. Unlike earlier authors who were social scientists and journalists, several of the post-1940 authors were historians who had made their own precarious migrations from Europe to the United States in the wake of the Holocaust.

In 1942, on the eve of the Holocaust, Zosa Szajkowski published the first extensive article about the beginnings of the Jewish "mass migration" in 1881–1882. He had just reached New York after a dramatic flight from France that took him through North Africa. He had lost contact with his family in German-occupied Poland. Szajkowski probably drew on research he had conducted on the eve of the German occupation of Paris as part of his work as a research student with historian Elias Tcherikover at Yidisher Visnshaftlekher Institut (YIVO), a Jewish scholarly institute. Relying almost exclusively on the French Jewish weekly *Archives Israélite* and other French sources, he characterized Brody as a "temporary asylum for the refugees from the historic wave of pogroms unleashed by the Tsarist regime." Since he referenced Cahan's memoir, Szajkowski must have been aware that he was fulfilling the vision of the famous journalist, who still edited the *Forverts* in the 1940s.[18]

In his influential 1948 survey of Jewish migration history, *To Dwell in Safety*, historian Mark Wischnitzer described the year 1881–1882 as "the decisive year in the history of modern [Jewish] migration." The migration crisis marked the "foundation[s] for the greatest population shift of the Jews in their entire history." Wischnitzer was certainly not the first Jewish historian who emphasized the significance of that year, but he helped to popularize the view that the 1881–1882 pogroms caused large-scale Jewish migration. The pogroms, he argued, were "incited and directed by Russian government officials." As violent attacks against Jewish civilians spread from Elisavetgrad in central Ukraine to neighboring towns, "the persecuted Jewish inhabitants fled in panic toward Russia's western border." Renewed outbursts in March 1882 supposedly caused another Jewish refugee wave. According to Wischnitzer, thousands of desperate Jewish "refugees" converged in the Austrian border town Brody in the summer of 1881 and again in 1882. After a concerted effort, Jewish aid organizations evacuated the "refugees" to destinations in other countries. Contemporary newspapers and the reports of Jewish aid associations appeared to back this view.[19]

Wischnitzer's own biography raises questions about this account. He was born in 1882 in Rowno (Rivne) in Volhynia, a town that was not affected by the 1881–1882 pogroms. Although his parents belonged to the Jewish petite bourgeoisie, Wischnitzer must have been familiar with the dire economic situation of the rural population. During the 1890s he attended Brody's respected *Gymnasium* (high school), barely a decade after the dramatic events of 1881–1882. Wischnitzer's sojourn in the Galician border town coincided with a strong increase in Jewish transit migration. Yet in his otherwise detailed survey of Jewish migration history he paid little attention to economic factors. He did not mention that a disproportionate number of Jewish migrants originated in Lithuania, where no pogroms occurred in 1881–1882.

Wischnitzer almost completely ignored Jewish migration from Galicia, even though he had published work on the economic history of Brody Jews. The Austrian province was notorious for abject poverty. The 1890s witnessed growing migration of Jews and non-Jews to Vienna and North America. Between 1880 and 1914 well over 300,000 Jews left Galicia, primarily for the United States. Taking natural growth into account, these migrants represented over 25 percent of Galicia's Jewish population. Unlike their coreligionists in the Russian Empire and Romania, Jews in Galicia had been fully emancipated in 1867. Anti-Jewish violence in Galicia was rare before the First World War. A notable exception was a wave of pogroms that spread through western and central Galicia in 1898. The violence caused Jewish migration, albeit primarily on the regional level, from small rural towns and villages to nearby cities within the province. The Austrian authorities prosecuted over thirty-eight hundred alleged perpetrators. Twenty-three hundred were sentenced to prison terms. Most were male Polish-speaking peasants and laborers. A few perpetrators moved to America to avoid prosecution.[20]

Why did Wischnitzer and Szajkowski take a one-sided view of Jewish migration in the early 1880s, even though they clearly knew that other factors had driven Jewish migration, not least from Galicia? And why would their interpretations influence the perception of Jewish migration from Eastern Europe for decades? Like other authors writing about Jewish migration after 1940 Wischnitzer and Szajkowski had escaped Nazi persecution and lost close family members in the Holocaust. Before the establishment of the State of Israel in 1948, the situation for Jewish Holocaust survivors and Jews who had escaped to distant destinations such as Shanghai appeared hopeless. Most were stateless and depended on support from Jewish aid organizations. This partly explains why Szajkowski, Wischnitzer, and other Jewish authors put much emphasis on the longue durée of persecution as the overarching cause for Jewish migration. The view of Jewish migration as a series of forced movements throughout the history of the Jewish Diaspora also resonated with the founding myth of the State of Israel. Until the 1990s leading Israeli historians like David Vital echoed the assessment of Zionist scholars before 1948, that during the long period of *Galut* (exile) the Jews were permanent outsiders and often forced to move.[21]

The 1881–1882 Brody Crisis Revisited

Contemporary newspapers, reports by Jewish aid associations, and several studies published by Börries Kuzmany and John Klier in the past decade allow for a closer look at the background of the pogroms in the southern provinces in 1881–1882 and the Brody crisis. In the eighteenth century Brody emerged as a trading hub thanks to its location on the western border of the Russian Empire. During this period Jewish life in the town flourished. By the 1880s, as Cahan observed, Brody and its Jewish community had fallen on hard times. Two places in Brody were associated with mobility and offered a ticket to a better future: the small train station and the German-language *Gymnasium* that Wischnitzer attended in the 1890s. Curiously, no author touches on a seemingly mundane point: that Cahan was by no means the only migrant who traveled to Brody by train. The railroad line from Lemberg reached Brody in 1870, and the connecting Russian line from Rowno to the border was completed in 1873. Brody's economy did not derive substantial benefits from the railroad, however. Goods that had once been bought and sold in Brody's stores and streets now bypassed the town. Local businesses and smugglers derived modest income from the rising number of migrants who had to interrupt the train journey to avoid Russian border guards. Since few Russian subjects carried the required passport to leave the Russian Empire legally, most took the train to Dubno or Radzivilov, hired a smuggler, and walked across the border to Brody's train station. Some migrants also traveled in the other direction. Without the Russian passport they too relied on smugglers.[22]

The expanding railroad network was a much more decisive factor than the pogroms in explaining the scale of the crisis in Brody in 1881–1882. When the first large groups of Russian Jews reached Brody in the spring of 1881, local Jews appealed to the main Austrian Jewish aid association, the Israelitische Allianz. Initially, the Austrian authorities and the public expressed much sympathy. To Western journalists it appeared obvious that the Jews congregating in Brody were pogrom refugees hailing from towns in central and southern Ukraine affected by anti-Jewish violence. The Israelitische Allianz was unprepared, forcing its mother organization, the Alliance Israélite Universelle, to step in. In August 1881 the Alliance dispatched Charles Netter, one of its most capable crisis managers, to Brody. Before the winter set in, most migrants had left for the United States and other destinations. Many had received support from the Alliance.

Following renewed anti-Jewish outbursts in the southern provinces in April 1882, far more Jews congregated in Brody than in 1881. In May 1882, the Russian government severely restricted Jewish settlement and business activities in the Pale. And throughout the year the Kiev authorities expelled hundreds of Jews without settlement permits from the city. To outside observers it seemed obvious that the pogroms, the notorious May Laws, which severely restricted Jewish settlement and business activities in the Pale, and the Kiev expulsions were part of a grand Russian scheme to push out oppressed and impoverished Jews. Historian John Klier, the author of an in-depth study about the 1881–1882 pogroms, has dismissed this view. The St. Petersburg government, he shows, did not instigate the pogroms but rather attempted to stem the violence, killing dozens of pogrom perpetrators. The Kiev expulsions were not connected with the May Laws or the pogroms. And Russian Jewish leaders were able to mitigate the effect of the May Laws considerably. But their lobbying efforts occurred behind the scenes. Most contemporary observers did not have access to this information. It is hardly surprising, then, that the myth of the tsarist government as architect of the pogroms had already emerged in 1881.[23]

Through letters, conversations, and news reports a specific news item spread across the Pale: the Alliance was sending Jews from Brody to Western countries free of charge. Cahan himself mentioned that he wrote letters from Brody to his family and friends, and it is not unlikely that he took a considerable detour via Kiev, not to elude Russian gendarmes but because he too hoped to be dispatched to America. According to Netter and other sources, many Brody refugees were, like Cahan, young, secular, and educated men who had access to news reports and could afford the journey to the border, rather than poor and observant traditional Jewish families from small towns affected by the pogroms.

According to contemporary observers, more than twelve thousand Jewish migrants were stranded in Brody in June 1882, almost as many as the town's inhabitants. In April and May the Alliance evacuated smaller groups, as more migrants were pouring in. In May 1882 the initially sympathetic Austrian government in Vienna expressed concern about a public health crisis and explored "administrative measures to restrict the migration," albeit without ignoring "humanitarian concerns." In the following weeks the pressure on local Jewish leaders and the Alliance increased. Austrian officials stepped up the border controls and refused to admit migrants without papers. Tellingly, leading Jewish representatives did not oppose these measures. Jewish aid associations across Europe and in the United States and the Vienna-based Israelitische Allianz were reluctant to accommodate more migrants. This is understandable considering the cost. During the summer months of 1882 the German Jewish central aid committee spent more than 600,000 Marks, a phenomenal sum at the time. Deprived of alternatives, the Brody committee reached out to Austrian and Russian officials and began repatriating migrants. Only younger men who risked arrest as army deserters or those who had fled Russia for political reasons like Cahan were exempt and received assistance to move to Western Europe and the United States.

In September 1882 a correspondent from Brody informed the readers of Germany's main Jewish weekly about the early phase of the repatriation effort: "Finally, the time has arrived, and we can rid ourselves of our Russian Jewish guests." Thousands had already moved back to their hometowns. The Russian authorities provided the necessary papers for those return migrants who had left without the required passport and assisted the Austrian authorities. Quite a few Brody sojourners, the correspondent pointed out, expressed the explicit wish to go home after they had encountered disillusioned return migrants from America. By the end of 1882 most Jewish newspapers ceased reporting from Brody. The town remained a point of passage for Jewish and other migrants in the following decades, but a similar crisis did not occur again, even after renewed pogroms in Russia's southern provinces between 1903 and 1906.[24]

Without a doubt, as a result of the extensive media coverage in the Jewish and general press, the pogroms, the May Laws, the Kiev expulsions, and the Brody crisis in 1881–1882 were widely *perceived* as part of an ominous attack against the Jews organized by the Russian state. In the Vienna *Neue Freie Presse*, one of the monarchy's main liberal dailies, Jewish journalist and writer Karl Emil Franzos denounced the "excesses" against Jews in Russia in June 1882, comparing the Jewish "mass emigration" to flight from violent pogroms during the crusades and to the expulsion of Jews from Spain in 1492. The repercussions of the crisis were felt beyond the Jewish public, because most major newspapers in Europe picked up and often reprinted articles about the pogroms and the chaotic situation in Brody. The Jewish and general public linked strong Jewish migration with the anti-Jewish violence and the oppressive policies of the Russian authorities. The term "refugees" was widely used for Jewish migrants in contemporary newspaper articles and reports by Jewish aid associations in the following decades, even though authors often conceded most refugees were seeking better economic opportunities. Few authors writing about Brody as a Jewish crisis mention that other Eastern Europeans were on the move as well.[25]

The crisis does mark an important moment in Russian and modern Jewish history. By 1880 migration emerged as an increasingly feasible option for a growing number of Jews in the Russian Empire. Established Jewish businessmen and community leaders in Russia opposed mass emigration, hoping to secure concessions from the state. On the grassroots level, several loosely linked groups promoting different colonization schemes emerged in the early 1880s. One was the Am Olam society, whose members became Cahan's travel companions. The crisis also served as a catalyst for grander resettlement projects. An anonymously published German pamphlet with the programmatic title *Autoemancipation* (1882) by Odessa physician Leon Pinsker demanded concerted Jewish action as a response to the rising antisemitic movement. Pinsker proposed founding a Jewish homeland outside of Russia. He considered various locations besides Palestine, especially in North and South America, and did not oppose Jewish life in the Diaspora after a homeland had been found. This view distinguished him from Herzl. Soon after the publication of his call Pinsker became a leading figure in the

Hibat Tsion (Lovers of Zion) movement, which aimed to establish colonies in Palestine.

Another ambitious colonization scheme can also be traced to the 1881–1882 crisis. Among the Jewish donors who supported the aid effort in Brody was railroad investor and Alliance donor Baron Maurice de Hirsch. After the Russian government rejected his proposal to fund and direct technical schools for Jewish children resembling the schools the Alliance had set up in the Ottoman Empire, Hirsch launched the Jewish Colonization Association in 1891. At the time of the JCA's founding Hirsch boldly promised to permanently resettle more than 3 million Russian Jews in just twenty-five years. In the 1890s the Russian authorities were more forthcoming and allowed JCA to create a network of trade schools and farm colonies in Ukraine. These were designed to prepare future colonists for life on agricultural colonies but also sought to enable local Jews to earn a reliable income from productive jobs. Hirsch, who died in 1896, left much of his fortune to the JCA, which promoted the settlement of thousands of Jews outside of Russia, especially in the Americas. Early on Argentina became a major focus of the JCA. A small group of Jews from Bessarabia and Podolia founded the pioneering colony in Moisés Ville that probably sparked Hirsch's interest in the country. They arrived in 1889 following a call by the Argentinian government inviting Jewish settlers.[26]

The discussion of different well-documented colonization and resettlement plans in the literature overshadows the less visible but rapidly growing movement of average Jews who took their fate into their own hands. They were looking for a better life, especially for their children, not on communal farms in Ukraine, Palestine, or Argentina but in industrial cities in and beyond the Russian Empire. Even those Jews who participated in various agricultural settlement schemes overwhelmingly left for nearby cities, sometimes only weeks after their arrival. Most of these Jews did not hail from the southern provinces but from the economically deprived northern Pale. The pogroms, as Klier and other scholars have demonstrated, really betray the repercussions of an uneven economic transformation in Ukraine and conflicts between new migrants and older settlers.

Among the new residents of southern towns were quite a few Litvaks who had been attracted by economic opportunities. In April 1882 Rülf informed the Alliance that following the 1881 pogroms hundreds had returned to their "overpopulated" and economically deprived northern hometowns. On his visit to one Lithuanian town, crowds of Jews mistook Rülf for a messianic figure who would lead them to Spain. Their assumption was probably based on the rumor that the Spanish government had revoked the 1492 expulsion edict. The episode certainly illustrates the desperation of many Jews, who did not have access to reliable information about the events in the southern provinces. Rülf expected the crisis in Brody would soon be overshadowed by a mass migration from the northern Pale. This prediction was prescient. After 1880 most migrants who moved to overseas destinations and industrial cities in Poland such as Białystok and Warsaw originated in the little-developed northern Russian provinces that were not affected by pogroms.[27]

The chaotic situation in Brody occurred at an inauspicious moment for Jews in Central and Western Europe. In the early 1880s antisemitism made a significant political impact in Germany, Austria, and France. Widespread sympathy and public condemnation of Russian brutality uneasily coexisted with fears of a possible "invasion" of poor Eastern Jews, a staple of antisemitic discourse in Germany and Austria in the following decades. In 1881–1882 Jews in towns and cities across Central and Western Europe raised funds and organized aid committees to find new homes for these migrants, primarily in the United States. Apart from genuine compassion, a major motive was to ensure that no migrant would become a public charge. In 1882 the Alliance and Jewish leaders in France and Germany even hatched a plan to send large groups of Russian Jewish families to the little-known Dominican Republic. This example shows that Western Jewish representatives had not developed a coherent strategy to respond to rising Jewish migration.[28]

The Brody crisis also tested the commitment of American Jews. Initial compassion for pogrom refugees quickly faded when large groups of destitute and ill-equipped Brody migrants arrived. In a May 1882 editorial in the *Chicago Occident*, outraged rabbi Emil G. Hirsch reminded European Jewish communities that America was no "dumping ground" for poor Russian Jews. Another (unrelated) development influenced the ambivalent reaction of established American Jews. In the spring of 1882, the U.S. Congress debated two immigration bills. In May President Chester A. Arthur signed the so-called Chinese Exclusion Act into law, sharply reducing legal immigration from China to the United States. And in early August Congress passed a comprehensive immigration bill that excluded convicts, "lunatics," and persons who were unable to support themselves and would become a "public charge." The main purpose of the second bill was not to reduce immigration from Europe but to provide states, especially New York, overseeing the inspection of a rapidly growing number of immigrants with coherent regulations.[29]

For American Jews the exclusion of Chinese migrants was much more concerning. For the first time members of a specific group that was widely perceived in racial terms and subject to widespread discrimination were targeted by restrictions. All persons born in China (and later Japan) who had legally immigrated were ineligible to be naturalized as American citizens. In a short article with the title "The Chinese To-day: Why Not the Jews To-morrow?" the weekly *American Hebrew* castigated the bill because it violated the spirit of the U.S. Constitution, in particular the Equality Clause. The author expressed concern that Jewish migrants might also be excluded but stressed they were superior to the Chinese because they made a serious attempt to integrate into American society, while the latter were mostly labor migrants. The *Jewish Messenger*, another weekly published in New York, also cited the Constitution. It declared the attempt to exclude Chinese immigrants a "national disgrace." From the pulpit of New York's preeminent Reform congregation, Temple Emanu-El, rabbi Gustav Gottheil condemned the Chinese Exclusion Act in his Passover sermon because it "violated the laws of Liberty."

In 1892, when Congress restricted Chinese immigration further, the *New York Times* observed that Chinese migrants possessed "many of those qualities which have made the 'chosen people of Israel' objects of aversion to less sophisticated Gentiles." During the first decade of the twentieth century, when congressional leaders proposed to categorize Jews as a "race," American Jewish leaders openly worried about the implications of Chinese exclusion. The worst fears of Jewish leaders were vindicated when Congress passed two restrictive immigration bills in 1921 and 1924 that drew on the legacy of Chinese exclusion and reflected racist and antisemitic concepts. The main targets were migrants from Africa and Asia but, not so implicitly, also Jews from Eastern Europe.[30]

The analysis of the events in Brody in the early 1880s reveals a gap between the actual crisis—a large number of migrants expecting support from aid associations—and the public perception of Jewish mass flight from the pogroms. The crisis demonstrated to a broader public that migration was emerging as a major Jewish response to the critical political and economic conditions in the Russian Empire. The older literature linked the strongly growing Jewish migration after the opening salvo of 1881–1882 with a series of calamities in the Russian Empire: mass expulsions of Jews without settlement permits from Moscow and St. Petersburg in 1891, the notorious 1903 Kishinev pogrom, and a wave of violent attacks against Jews between 1903 and 1906, which spread from the southern Russian provinces to several communities in the northern Pale and Russian Poland. In each instance, Jewish migration appeared to reach a new record high. And in each instance, statements in the Jewish press seem to corroborate a link between anti-Jewish Russian government actions and Jewish emigration. Yet Jewish migration to America was driven by strong but uneven demand for cheap immigrant labor in the United States and in a few other places, like Britain and South Africa. The availability of jobs and expanding networks explain the dramatic increase in migration in the 1890s and early 1900s. As more Jews could rely on relatives and acquaintances, an ever-growing number of people with limited means took the decision to leave into their own hands.

3
Jewish Mobilities and the Business of Migration

"I am a traveler. I am on the road eleven months of the year. I go by train, usually in the third class. . . . Oh, what one sees when traveling! What a pity I am not a writer." With these words the narrator of Sholem Aleichem's *Ayznban geshikhtes* (Railroad Stories) introduces himself to his readers. Sholem Aleichem was the pen name of the Yiddish writer Solomon Rabinovitz. Each of the stories Aleichem wrote between 1902 and 1910 focuses on encounters between the narrator, a traveling salesman, and other Jews. The classes of Aleichem's trains betray clearly demarcated social divisions in Imperial Russia. In the first class, as Aleichem's biographer Jeremy Dauber paraphrases the writer, "no one is Jewish, and in the second, no one will admit to it." Aleichem's assumption that most third-class passengers belonged to the Jewish petite bourgeoisie was probably not far off the mark. In contrast to Jewish traveling salesmen, professionals, students, and journalists, few peasants could afford train tickets before 1900. Like other Yiddish and Russian writers at the time, Aleichem portrayed the train as a highly ambivalent harbinger of change.

Aleichem's contemporary Leo Tolstoy famously detested traveling on trains. In his novels, protagonists condemned the railroad as an evil force and a destroyer of the old order. In a strange twist of fate, the elderly Tolstoy died in the apartment of the stationmaster at a small railroad station in 1910, after he had wandered from his large estate and boarded several trains. High fever forced him to interrupt the circuitous journey at Astapovo station. Aleichem almost met a similar fate. In 1908 the financially struggling author went on a reading tour by train through the Pale. After a reading in a packed hall in Baranovich (Baranovichi), a bustling town located between Brest and Minsk, the exhausted Aleichem collapsed. Diagnosed with tuberculosis, he continued to work while recovering in the local hospital. During or shortly after this unintended stopover Aleichem wrote the story "Baranovich Station," in which a Jewish traveler obtains a seat in a full car by grabbing everybody's attention with a riveting tale about a ruthless blackmailer. Just as the story is about to reach its dramatic climax the train approaches Baranovich station and the storyteller makes a hasty exit to catch a connecting train, leaving his stunned audience behind.[1]

None of Aleichem's railroad stories provides the reader with closure. In one story a group of Christians is traveling to participate in a pogrom. By mistake they get on a slow train, giving the Jews at the destination time to prepare for the attack. Unexpectedly the slow train reaches the town early. Disaster is averted when it turns out that the pogrom perpetrators never left the station. Too drunk, they never realized their carriages were not attached to the rest of the train. Like the storyteller of "Baranovich Station," quite a few passengers on Aleichem's trains are slick characters angling for attention but hiding their true intentions. A group of Hasidic Jews turn out to be con men in disguise. Mobility eroded traditional Jewish *Gemeinschaft* and trust. Communities of Jews involved in intense conversations appear fleeting, as passengers disperse after each stop.

In one of the best-known stories, the narrator encounters a jovial and well-dressed "man from Buenos Aires" looking for a young wife. Most contemporary readers of the story would have grasped the man's occupation based on that description. Aleichem added an additional clue at the end of the story. As the narrator steps off the train, he shouts back, " 'What really is your business? What exactly do you deal in?' The man from Buenos Aires: 'What do I deal in? Ha ha! Not in lemons, my friend, not in lemons!' " Aleichem used the Hebrew term *etrogim*, which refers to a lemon as a ritual fruit used during the Sukkot holiday to symbolize purity. By indicating he was not in the "purity" business, the man hinted that he did the very opposite, enticing young Jewish women into prostitution, thus violating their purity. In 1910 about half of the registered prostitutes in Buenos Aires were recently immigrated Jewish women.[2]

Aleichem's railroad stories indicate that Jewish migration was only one, albeit an important facet of an unprecedented mobility revolution that affected Russia later than other parts of Europe. In 1897, when more than 45 percent of the British population clustered in cities and larger towns, almost 90 percent of the Russian population lived in rural communities. This number obscures the beginnings of industrialization and urbanization in the 1880s, especially in the Polish provinces and in towns along the empire's expanding rail network. Jews moved to cities in the Russian Empire earlier and in larger numbers than members of other groups. In most cities and towns in the Pale

Jews represented over half of the population by 1900, far exceeding their share of the overall population. Aleichem's railroad stories, which captured Jewish life literally on the move and in between places, certainly resonated with hundreds of thousands of recent Jewish city migrants in Russia. In fact, these migrants were Aleichem's most devoted readers. Already a celebrity, the writer famously failed to connect with the literary scene and Jewish audiences in New York during an ill-fated sojourn in 1905–1906. After his return he embarked on his reading tour through towns and cities in the Pale.

Among Jewish city migrants in this period were the parents of painter Marc Chagall, who settled in Vitebsk around the time of his birth. In 1897, when Chagall was twelve years old, the expanding industrializing city counted over sixty thousand inhabitants, of whom thirty thousand were Jews, overwhelmingly recent arrivals. Chagall's father worked for a herring merchant, and his mother sold prepared food from the family home. As a teenager the future painter regularly visited his grandparents in nearby Lyozno, a much smaller town that was the birthplace of Shneur Zalman, the founder of a large Hasidic sect.

The myth of the traditional *shtetl* that Chagall and Aleichem helped to popularize reflects the perspective of Jews who had moved to the modern industrial city. Unlike Chagall, Aleichem did not romanticize the *shtetl*. Rather he channeled the growing tensions of Jews trying to strike a balance between both worlds. Rural towns were also experiencing change. Lyozno was already connected to the railroad network before Chagall was born. Baranovich was a quintessential railroad town. In the early 1880s officials decided to locate the intersection of a new rail line from Vilna to Rowno with the Warsaw–Moscow line near the village of Baranovich. The routing of the line resulted in the construction of a second station. The center of the new town developed between the two stations. By 1897, during the early phase of Baranovich's expansion, Jews represented almost half of its forty-seven hundred inhabitants. The history of Baranovich illustrates why location mattered. The intersecting train lines turned an isolated village into a point of passage and thus a destination in its own right.[3]

In the early 1860s few foresaw the transformative impact of railroad expansion. In April 1862 a bridge over the Neman River closed the last gap on the railroad between Berlin and St. Petersburg, coincidentally only a few miles from the home of Bernard Horwich's parents on the outskirts of Kovno. Shortly after Horwich was born in 1861 it was possible to travel from central Lithuania to Königsberg, and from there to Berlin and major port cities on the North Sea. The cost of train tickets was not negligible, but migrants relied on loans from family members and acquaintances at home or at their destination to cover the cost. Thus, already during the 1860s journeys to distant destinations became feasible even for relatively poor Jews (and non-Jews) from the northern Pale of Settlement.[4]

The train cut the travel time from rural towns in Lithuania to Hamburg, Bremen, and Rotterdam from several weeks to a few days. The same steam engine technology that revolutionized transportation by rail also transformed maritime journeys. Unlike the mostly Irish and German migrants who moved to North America before the 1860s, most Eastern Europeans did not have to walk for days to the closest port and were spared the harrowing experience of crossing the Atlantic on sailing vessels. In Southern Europe ports along the Mediterranean with service to North America such as Naples, Palermo, Trieste, and Fiume (Rijeka) had been connected to railroad networks by the early 1880s. Only the Greek port Piraeus lagged behind by over a decade. By 1870 steamships had largely replaced sailing ships on most transatlantic routes. Sailing vessels often required six to eight weeks for the westbound crossing on the northern Atlantic. Steamships cut the time from three weeks around 1870 to a few days by 1910. Information traveled faster too, thanks to the expansion of telegraph lines, more efficient mail services, and increasing literacy rates.

As efficient transportation and communication networks expanded into the hitherto relatively isolated rural regions, globalizing markets reached a growing number of people. The railroad, as Aleichem and Tolstoy observed, was an ambivalent harbinger of change. Industrially manufactured goods, information, and ideas transformed rural economies and societies—in a period of strong population growth. Some nimble Jewish middlemen, artisans, and service providers were able to adapt, finding new markets and economic niches linked to new fashions, often by relocating to expanding towns. Those who could not or did not want to move faced gloomy prospects.

To escape economies barely able to sustain an increasing number of people, younger Jews began looking literally beyond the Pale, especially after early migrants sent back money, reliable information about job opportunities, and prepaid tickets. Horwich was hardly the only Lithuanian Jew who sojourned in East Prussia during the 1870s and then in New York before relocating to Chicago. Individual biographies indicate that migrations to midsize towns like Baranovich, to expanding industrial and commercial centers in the wider vicinity such as Vitebsk, Białystok, Warsaw, and Łódź, and overseas, were frequently related. After several years in South Africa, for example, Liebmann Hersch's father returned to Lithuania. After remarrying he moved with his family to Warsaw, an important destination for Jews from Lithuania.[5]

The pioneering Holocaust historian Raul Hilberg observed that most scholars researching deportations to ghettos, extermination camps, and other killing sites considered railroads as "tools" rather than as "actors in their own right."[6] Hilberg referred to the managers of state-owned railroad companies, especially the German Reichsbahn, which were formed after the merger of privately and smaller state-owned companies. The Reichsbahn was established in 1920, whereas France and the Netherlands nationalized their railroad networks only in the late 1930s. The Belgian state had taken over major railroads already before the 1890s. State ownership obscures the private origins of most European railroads.

Little has been written about the involvement of Jewish entrepreneurs and investors in the construction and management of the European railroad network during the middle decades of the nineteenth century. With the notable exception of Baron Maurice de Hirsch, who devoted much of his fortune to the colonization of Jewish migrants from the Russian Empire, and a few others such as the Rothschilds and American investment banker Jacob Schiff, Jewish railroad investors are conspicuously absent in surveys of modern Jewish history. They were far removed from average migrants like Horwich or Cahan. Only a few were active in Jewish communities. Several converted to Christianity. Most displayed their wealth ostentatiously and donated generously to philanthropic causes. Some lost their fortunes. But several Jewish investors and business executives laid the foundations for mass migration and mobility across Eastern Europe during the second half of the nineteenth century.

Connecting Russia to the World

In Eastern and Southern Europe, the construction of extensive railroad networks began in the late 1850s, when England and Central Europe were already covered by a dense web of tracks. By 1880 the Iberian peninsula, northern and southern Italy, and—to a lesser extent—the Austro-Hungarian Empire, the vast western half of the Russian Empire, and parts of Southeastern Europe were connected to Central and Western Europe. The completion of a railroad did not cause migration, but it redefined the terms of mobility. Railroads linked sparsely developed regions with globalizing markets for labor, goods, services, and information. Few contemporaries grasped the full impact of the economic (and political) transformation that resulted from railroad expansion.

It is often overlooked that military rather than economic considerations drove railroad construction in different parts of Europe during the middle decades of the nineteenth century. Prussia's Ostbahn (eastern railway), a major artery of the European east–west network by 1900, owed its existence to Prussian fears about a possible Russian attack and French railroad expansion in the early 1840s. The Prussian government struggled to raise private capital because the project did not appear economically feasible. In 1847 the Prussian king reluctantly appointed provincial aristocrats and elected representatives of towns and cities to the Landtag (Parliament) to fund the project. Thus, the Ostbahn project contributed to the gradual democratization and modernization of the reactionary Prussian state and, in a curious twist, to Jewish emancipation (and mobility).

The discussions over funding the costly railroad dragged on for months without result. Since the Landtag was in session, it was possible to deal with other business. One matter concerned the status of Jews in different parts of Prussia. In the western provinces Jews enjoyed almost full civil equality, whereas Jews in the eastern provinces, a considerably larger group, still lived under restrictions dating back to medieval times. The partial emancipation bill the Landtag passed in 1847, over the objection of Bismarck and other archconservative landowners, signals Prussia's gradual shift to a more open and mobile society. In the wake of the 1848 Revolution the Landtag was dissolved before a decision on the Ostbahn matter had been reached. After counterrevolutionary forces gained the upper hand, strengthening the position of the Prussian monarch, a newly convened Parliament passed the bill in 1849. In 1857 the first train made the journey from Berlin to Königsberg, twelve years before all Jews in Prussia were fully emancipated.[7]

During the middle decades of the nineteenth century most railroad lines were privately funded and owned. Railroad construction was a lucrative, albeit risky investment opportunity. Investors had to carefully assess the potential profitability of a railroad line, seek permits from officials, sign up and retain other sponsors, and manage intricate, often unpredictable construction projects that depended on complex supply chains. Another challenge was conflict between different state institutions, especially between military leaders and trade officials. The branch line from Vilna to the Prussian border was part of a vast construction project to link St. Petersburg with Warsaw. Two French brothers, Isaac and Emile Pereire, organized a consortium of investors backing the line. They belong to a small group of Western European Jewish investors who helped to expand railroad networks into Eastern Europe.[8]

Several of Eastern Europe's most influential railroad investors were Jews or had Jewish roots. In the Russian Empire, they became known as *shemindeferniks*, a Franco-Yiddish term that is best translated as "railroad men." The most illustrious *shemindefernik* was Samuel Polyakov, the son of a small trader in the Vitebsk region. After making a few successful investments he became a subcontractor for the Baltic-German railroad entrepreneur Karl von Meck. In the 1860s he was awarded lucrative contracts to build several railroads in central and southern Russia. Tsar Alexander II formally recognized his success in the railroad business by ennobling him and his brothers, an honor that was bestowed on very few Russian Jews. Polyakov was also an important philanthropist who supported public education and the small Jewish community in St. Petersburg.

Three other *shemindeferniks* launched the railroad network in Russian Poland. In the mid-1850s Warsaw Jewish businessman Herman Epstein built the Warsaw–Vienna railroad line. The other main railroad lines in Russian Poland were constructed and controlled by Jan Bloch and Leopold Kronenberg during the 1860s and 1870s. Both converted to Christianity. In 1865 Bloch oversaw the construction of the railroad from Warsaw to Łódź. The railroad connection boosted the city's rapid transformation into a bustling hub of Poland's textile industry, attracting tens of thousands of Jewish migrants from the Polish provinces and the Pale. By 1900, 100,000 Jews lived in "the Polish Manchester." Bloch, who married Kronenberg's niece, retained an interest in Jewish life. In the late 1890s he met several times with Theodor Herzl.[9]

Another convert was the Prussian "railway king" Bethel Henry Strousberg, who was born in a small East Prussian town in 1823. As a young man he moved to London to work for a retail business owned by distant relatives. Soon after his arrival he became a member of the Anglican Church. After serving a short jail sentence for embezzling funds from a mortgage bank, he went into journalism and then worked as an insurance broker. When a business rival publicized his past conviction Strousberg dissolved his businesses and settled in Berlin. In the early 1860s he backed the construction of several railroads in Prussia, Hungary, and Romania. To improve Königsberg's access to the Russian grain trade he organized the financing for the construction of a railroad linking East Prussia with the Warsaw–Moscow railroad, which had been partly funded by Bloch and was completed in the late 1860s.

Strousberg's success was short lived, in part because he resorted to increasingly reckless financing schemes to fund highly speculative projects. Following the 1870–1871 Franco-Prussian War Strousberg struggled to pay creditors in different parts of Europe. When he tried to settle his affairs in Moscow in 1875, he was arrested and tried for fraud. During his involuntary absence his properties were sold and several businesses he controlled in Germany and Austria were dissolved. Instead of sentencing him to a lengthy prison term the Russian court ordered his immediate expulsion to Prussia. Deprived of his influence and shunned by former business partners, Strousberg spent his last years in modest circumstances. The spectacular Strousberg affair coincided with a prolonged economic recession and was an early rallying point for the emerging antisemitic movement in Imperial Germany. The scandal also was a catalyst for railroad nationalization. During the 1870s the Prussian state acquired the main rail lines on its territory. Several other European governments also began nationalizing railroad systems before the turn of the century.[10]

Emile and Isaac Pereire were born in Bordeaux in 1800 and 1806, respectively, as descendants of a Sephardi family that had fallen on hard times. In the early 1820s Emile and Isaac moved to Paris, where they joined the household of Isaac Rodrigues, a wealthy relative who belonged to the inner circle of the Saint-Simonists. This social and political movement promoted a vision of an inclusive universal and capitalist society that held a special attraction for upwardly mobile Jews, at a time when the informal social exclusion of Jews in French society was still common. Mobility, the Saint-Simonists predicted, would open the gates to a society of peace and harmony. The Pereire brothers, their relatives, and acquaintances remained beholden to Saint-Simonism long after the movement dissolved in the 1830s. The shift to a constitutional monarchy after the 1830 July Revolution weakened the French aristocracy and benefited upwardly mobile outsiders.[11]

The Pereires' success as entrepreneurs epitomizes mobility. Through employment in the bank of James Mayer de Rothschild in Paris they became familiar with the complex and risky railroad business in its formative phase. Emile and Isaac made their name by completing the first French railroad line from Paris to the suburb of St. Germain in 1837. The brothers invested much of their capital and were able to raise funds from James de Rothschild and others. Unexpectedly the line became a financial success. The influence of the Pereires culminated during the Second Empire under Napoleon III. As property developers, they had a major hand in rebuilding the French capital under Baron Haussmann, especially in the northwestern section of the city. Two imposing train stations, the Gare St. Lazare and the Gare de l'Est, both originally built in the 1840s, still reflect their legacy. Contemporaries perceived the buildings as secular cathedrals of the new age of mass mobility, comparable to massive airport terminals today. The brothers amassed a large art collection and acquired a chateau outside of Paris. Their preferred architect, Alfred Armand, who designed the Gare St. Lazare and several provincial French train stations, oversaw the rebuilding of an eighteenth-century palace into the splendid and opulently decorated Hôtel Pereire.[12]

Like several prominent Jewish business figures in England, Imperial Germany, and Russian Poland, a number of French Jews who rose into the upper bourgeoisie converted or rejected Judaism. For upwardly mobile members of a marginalized group encountering lingering discrimination, conversion frequently was a conscious choice to strike a balance between economic and social mobility. In Paris, several converts were close acquaintances or friends of the Pereires. The banker and French finance minister in the 1860s, Achille Fould (the son of Beer Léon Fould), converted to Protestantism as a middle-aged man in 1858. Adolphe d'Eichthal, a close friend and business partner of Emile and a key figure in the French railroad business, was the son of a Bavarian Jewish banker who converted to Protestantism after moving to Paris. Another Parisian banker and railroad investor was Frédéric Émile d'Erlanger, the son of a Jewish banker from Frankfurt who converted to Protestantism in 1823. It is notable that nouveau-riche converts in Poland and France frequently opted for Protestantism rather than join the Catholic Church, most likely to retain an acceptable degree of difference in those Catholic countries. In Poland Bloch and Kronenberg both became Protestant rather than Catholic. Emile and Isaac did not convert, however. They were freethinkers who socialized with members of the Jewish community and converts. They supported Jewish charitable causes, though apparently not the Alliance Israélite Universelle, even though they were on good personal terms with its founder, Adolphe Cremieux.[13]

In 1852 the Pereires established the aptly named Crédit Mobilier bank. The pioneering investment bank became one of the most important vehicles for funding large infrastructure projects. Initially, the bank invested in steamship lines and public transit projects in Paris. The founding of Crédit Mobilier and a conflict over the control of the Paris–Lyon railroad turned Emile and Isaac into antagonists of their erstwhile mentor James Mayer de Rothschild, who had also emerged as a major investor in the European railroad business. In the 1850s the business ventures of the Pereires reached well beyond France. The brothers oversaw railroad construction in Spain, Austria, and Italy. In 1855 they launched a transatlantic steamship line, the Compagnie Générale Maritime. In 1861, it was reorganized and renamed Compagnie Générale Transatlantique. The line launched a service from Le Havre to New York—and Veracruz, to back the French intervention in Mexico. Compagnie Générale Transatlantique was also involved in the transport of thousands of indentured Chinese and South Asian labor migrants to French colonies in Guadeloupe and Martinique in the 1860s. Isaac brusquely rebuffed contemporaries who criticized the exploitation of these migrants, arguing that they were not slaves and filled an economic need.[14] The episode highlights the global dimension of the mobility business. Less than thirty years after completing the first French railroad, the two brothers had invested huge amounts in infrastructure projects across Europe and were transporting migrants around the globe.

In the mid-1850s French and British railroad investors saw great potential in North America and in European countries lacking railroad networks, notably Spain, Italy, Austria-Hungary, and the Russian Empire. Russia was particularly promising. One of the most backward economies in Europe, it had no railroad network. In the mid-1850s, a single line connected St. Petersburg and Moscow. Hundreds of miles further west Herman Epstein's line linked Warsaw with Vienna. The two lines were divided by hundreds of miles. Construction of a railroad from St. Petersburg to Warsaw began in the 1850s but was interrupted. After the humiliating defeat in the Crimean War, Russia's military leaders acknowledged that a railroad network would be necessary to defend border regions and respond to internal unrest.

Soon after the war the Russian government backed the construction of several rail lines across the western half of the empire. Since the war had depleted Russia's coffers, the only available option was to raise capital abroad. In 1856 Russian banker Baron Alexander von Stieglitz, the son of a German Jewish banker who had converted to Christianity, visited Paris to negotiate with potential investors. Later in the same year James Mayer de Rothschild discussed potential projects in St. Petersburg, but he wisely judged the ventures too risky. Harsh winters, enormous logistical challenges, and the lack of a skilled workforce were the most obvious obstacles. Opponents at the Russian court viewed railroad expansion as an incalculably powerful catalyst for social, economic, and political change. Even business leaders did not hide their skepticism. One demanded that Russians rather than, as he put it, "the Yids and the foreigners," build railroads.[15]

Soon after Rothschild's departure a consortium of French and British investors led by Isaac Pereire reached an agreement with the tsarist government to embark on an ambitious construction project. The Pereire brothers were not interested in making a quick profit. Like the Prussian government, they understood that railroad lines would provide access to Russia's vast resources. The consortium promised to put down thousands of miles of track through hardly developed parts of the empire. Soon after the agreement was signed, construction of the partially built St. Petersburg–Warsaw line resumed. The project included the branch line that linked Vilna and Kovno with the already completed line from Königsberg to the Prussian border at Eydtkuhnen. Several other lines were planned: an eastern line from Moscow to Nizhny Novgorod on the Volga River, a southern line from Moscow to the Crimean Peninsula, and a western line from the central Russian town of Orel (Oryol) to the Baltic port of Libau. Russian observers saw little economic potential in the St. Petersburg–Warsaw line; it served primarily military needs. In contrast, Western investors judged the lines connecting interior Russian cities to be lucrative, especially the railroad from Moscow to Nizhny Novgorod and the southern line because these would link the grain-producing regions along the Volga and near the Black Sea with expanding northern cities.[16]

By 1857 more than fifty thousand workers were involved in the massive construction of the western line. The logistical challenges were significant because much of the equipment and the rails had to be transported over vast distances into thinly developed rural areas. Within five years, more than fifteen hundred miles of track had been laid, and the line from St. Petersburg to Warsaw and the branch from Vilna to the Prussian border were completed. At this point, however, the Russian government had been forced to step in. The project had run into trouble from the start. The Pereires and their partners struggled to raise funds. Most shareholders were Russians who did not understand the risks. As problems with the construction mounted, the Russian government increased the pressure on the Pereire brothers, who already had to deal with unhappy shareholders and antisemitic press coverage. Obstruction by Russian bureaucrats and lower than expected earnings raised questions about the feasibility of the project. The Pereires could not expect support from the French king; to check Prussia's rising influence Napoleon III was unwilling to antagonize Russia. Reluctantly the brothers had to yield control to the Russian government. The "Russian Fiasco" contributed to a severe crisis of Crédit Mobilier in 1866–1867. The brothers lost control of the bank and much of their fortune and political influence. They had to sell their large estate and townhouses, even their beloved art collection. Their downfall mirrored the declining fortunes of the Second Empire in the late 1860s.[17]

Only months after its completion in 1862, the new Russian rail line proved its strategic usefulness. Within days of the January 1863 Polish uprising, Russian troops were dispatched to Warsaw. Polish rail employees were able to slow the advance of Russian forces by destroying telegraph lines and blowing up several bridges. But these were quickly repaired. More controversial was Prussia's response. The new prime minister, Bismarck, allowed Russian troops passage through Prussian territory on the recently completed rail lines. Prussian support contributed to the quick and brutal suppression of the uprising and served as a warning to the large Polish-speaking population in Prussia's eastern provinces. Ironically, the economic impact of the western rail line vindicated the Pereire brothers, even though they were not able to reap the benefits. Apart from boosting trade within the empire and across the western border, the line contributed to the rapid urbanization and industrialization in the Polish provinces. And it became a major pathway for seasonal and other migrants heading to Central and Western Europe and beyond.[18]

Two other Paris railroad investors avoided failure. James Mayer de Rothschild's triumph over the Pereire brothers was short-lived. He passed away in 1868, just when a newcomer, Baron Maurice de Hirsch, was embarking on a remarkable career. Hirsch, who is best remembered as a generous Jewish philanthropist, was born in Munich in 1833 as the grandson of a wealthy court Jew who was ennobled by the Bavarian king in 1818. As a young man Hirsch moved to Brussels, where he married into an affluent Jewish banking family that originated in Frankfurt am Main and Mainz. Hirsch invested his inheritance and his wife's dowry in several railroad projects in the Austro-Hungarian Empire, Southeastern Europe, and the Russian Empire, taking enormous risks. His crowning achievement was the completion of the first railroad line connecting Vienna with Constantinople, which became known as Orient Express and earned him the name "Türkenhirsch." In 1869 he bought concessions for the line from a Brussels banking house, and he successfully lobbied the Ottoman government to grant him permission to build and manage the line. Construction began in the early 1870s and was completed in 1888. The skilled negotiator had to repeatedly rescue the project using his contacts in Constantinople (Istanbul) to overcome opposition at the court and by provincial notables. When he died in 1896 Hirsch was one of the wealthiest men in Europe. He owned an opulent Paris townhouse but spent most of his time in the Austro-Hungarian Empire and Southeastern Europe.[19]

Like Rothschild, Hirsch was an early and generous backer of the Alliance. During the 1870s he increased his donations substantially, supporting Jewish schools and different job-training schemes in the Ottoman Empire and in the Austrian province of Galicia. After tsarist officials foiled his efforts to establish technical schools and agricultural training facilities for young Jews in the Russian Empire Hirsch decided that emigration offered the most promising route to turn Russian Jews into self-sufficient farmers. In 1891 he founded the JCA, which, after his death in 1896, inherited a large part of his fortune and began to resettle Jews from the Russian Empire around the world, in particular in Argentina.

The Business of Migration

The most influential mobility entrepreneur who facilitated the migration of Jews and other Eastern Europeans before 1914 was not a railroad investor but a self-made steamship line executive. Albert Ballin grew up in modest circumstances in the vicinity of Hamburg's port as the thirteenth child of a struggling Jewish ticket agent from Denmark. In 1874 the seventeen-year-old Ballin took over his father's small ticket brokerage. Through contacts and frequent visits in Britain he developed an in-depth understanding of the steamship business in its formative phase. By 1870 steamships had largely replaced sailing vessels on the North Atlantic. Ballin understood that steamships would revolutionize sea journeys just as the railroad had done on land. The use of steel hulls led to the launch of larger and more advanced steamships that could accommodate hundreds of passengers and transport cargo. By 1900 some of the largest ocean liners completed the crossing from British ports to New York in less than a week. Modern steamships were much better equipped than sailing vessels to withstand the rough weather on the North Atlantic. After 1880 ship disasters were rare. Ballin's familiarity with the ticket business explains how he developed a keen sense of shifting passenger markets. Transporting an increasing number of people in the cheapest class on huge ocean liners, which could make more frequent crossings than sailing vessels, he reasoned, would be far more profitable than charging exorbitant prices for a limited number of luxurious first-class cabins.

Ballin was an early pioneer of low-cost travel. Charging rock-bottom prices for basic transportation has been widely associated with airline founders Freddie Laker and Herb Kelleher. Both launched "low-frills" airlines in Britain and the United States in the 1960s and 1970s, making long-distance travel affordable for those with limited incomes. Ballin preceded them by almost a century. In 1881 he formed a partnership with English ship broker Edward Carr to offer a low-cost steamship service from Hamburg to New York. Carr procured two freight steamers, and Ballin installed a large number of bunk beds in the cargo bay for steerage passengers. On journeys with fewer passengers the Carr Line repurposed the ships, loading cargo to make up for unsold passenger berths. Relying on his contacts among ticket brokers, Ballin managed the landside business, underbidding the prices of the dominant Hamburg-America Line (HAPAG). Thanks to rising migration from the Russian Empire the low-cost venture was so successful that HAPAG saw no other choice but to offer a buyout. As part of a complex takeover deal Ballin secured the post of director of HAPAG's passenger division in 1886.[20]

In his new position Ballin decided to retain the first-class quarters, recognizing the importance of luxury for enhancing HAPAG's brand. Ballin is also regarded as a pioneer of the cruise ship business for affluent passengers. In 1891 HAPAG began to offer excursions to the Mediterranean during the winter months, when demand for steamship service between Europe and North America was lagging. Yet the substantial profits HAPAG reaped after the mid-1880s depended in large part on the steerage and cargo business. To fill the berths on HAPAG's large steamers Ballin began to explore growth markets beyond Germany's borders. Before 1880, British and German steamship lines primarily served their respective domestic passenger markets. HAPAG and its main rival, the Bremen-based North German Lloyd (NDL), were founded in 1847 and 1857, respectively, in the wake of strongly increasing migration between different regions in south and north Germany and North America. The transatlantic German migration was still strong in the early 1880s. Yet when Ballin joined HAPAG in 1886, most migrants were Polish speakers from Prussia's little-developed eastern provinces. At the same time migration from the Russian Empire increased substantially. Ballin realized that improving railroad links enabled HAPAG to tap a vast underserved market on Germany's eastern doorstep, just when the transatlantic migration from traditional sending regions in Central Europe was declining. This gave HAPAG and NDL a crucial edge over their British competitors.

The new market appeared so promising that HAPAG and NDL made only halfhearted attempts to compete with British and Danish lines in Scandinavia. Transatlantic migration from Norway and Sweden was also growing strongly after 1880, but both countries had relatively small populations compared to the millions of potential migrants in Eastern Europe. For migrants from the Russian and Austro-Hungarian empires Hamburg and Bremen were closer and easier to reach by rail than other North Sea ports with regular transatlantic service. By 1880 a journey from a small town in the Russian Pale to North America via Hamburg or Bremen took not much more than three weeks. The train journey from Germany's eastern border to Hamburg or Bremen could be completed in less than twenty-four hours. The travel time to Rotterdam and Antwerp was not much longer, and both ports also offered frequent transatlantic service. In the early 1880s British lines advertised cheaper "indirect" passages from Hamburg and other continental ports via Liverpool. Several unrelated developments explain why HAPAG and NDL were able to route most Eastern European migrants to Hamburg and Bremen and ensure that they avoided indirect passages.[21]

Paradoxically, migration restrictions on both sides of the Atlantic enabled the German steamship lines to establish a de facto monopoly over the Eastern European passenger market. In the Russian Empire, all individuals wishing to leave their hometowns had to seek formal permission. An emigration passport was costly and often difficult to obtain. At border checkpoints officials demanded to see the passports of migrants leaving the empire or returning from abroad. Only a few migrants applied for passports, as they could easily cross Russia's sparely guarded land borders with the help of local smugglers. Young men facing lengthy military service were well advised to avoid officials during the journey to the border. The outer borders of the Austro-Hungarian Empire were only loosely controlled. During the second half of the nineteenth century, Austrian and Hungarian authorities pursued a liberal emigration policy. However, young men risked long prison sentences if they were apprehended in the vicinity of the border without the required document proving they were exempt from the draft or had already served.

Shortly after 1900, when migration increased greatly, trade officials in St. Petersburg, Vienna, and Budapest pushed for more liberal migration policies to boost traffic from domestic ports—with limited success. In fact, the Austrian and Hungarian governments increasingly favored a more restrictive approach, especially since a military conflict in Southeastern Europe appeared more likely after 1900. Therefore, most migrants leaving the Russian and Austro-Hungarian empires tended to avoid domestic ports and bypass border checkpoints. Migrants traveled by train to the vicinity of the border, then smugglers took them across. Lacking personnel was not the only reason why state officials did little to prevent the illegal mass movement across borders. Strict migration regimes actually betrayed laissez-faire emigration policies toward unwanted minority groups. Antisemitic narratives about "Jewish" steamship line ticket agents delivering tens of thousands of naive peasants into the hands of ruthless American capitalists should not be taken at face value. It was no secret that leading Russian bureaucrats favored the emigration of Jews. The restrictive 1903 Hungarian emigration law targeted Hungarian speakers. The departure of Croats, Slovaks, Romanians, and Yiddish-speaking Jews from Hungarian territory was tacitly encouraged.[22]

Ballin's early days at HAPAG coincided with a shift to a more restrictive migration regime in Prussia, Germany's largest state, which covered much of the northern half of Imperial Germany. The German emperor and key figures in the government were Prussian, and the government institutions of Prussia and Imperial Germany were closely linked. Like other German states, Prussia retained a significant degree of autonomy over its internal affairs. While the German state conducted negotiations with other governments and maintained embassies outside of Germany, the control of Germany's outer border was largely handled by the respective states, which usually relied on the local police. Prussia shared Germany's border with the Russian Empire and much of the border with the Austro-Hungarian Empire. The Netherlands and Belgium also bordered exclusively on Prussian provinces. Hamburg and Bremen, the two German ports with regular steamship service to overseas destinations, were autonomous city states with their own elected parliaments and governments.

Already before 1880 officials in Prussia viewed the rising migration from the Russian Empire uneasily. Like most states in Europe Prussia guarded its long outer borders only superficially. Yet Prussian officials were alarmed when the United States appeared to take a more restrictive approach to migration in the early 1880s, just when the number of transmigrants was increasing. In 1882 the U.S. Congress passed an immigration bill that excluded convicts, anarchists, persons judged to be mentally ill or suffering from certain diseases, and especially "paupers." In contrast to the Chinese Exclusion Act that was passed a few months earlier, the main goal of the immigration bill was not to slow down migration. America's booming industrial sector depended on cheap European immigrant labor. The 1882 immigration act was primarily an attempt by Congress and the federal government to regulate the admission of arriving migrants by providing uniform criteria that applied in all states and territories of the Union. Like other countries in this period the United States tried to organize increased movement across its outer borders by legally distinguishing between foreign tourists and business travelers, (un)desirable immigrants, and American citizens.[23]

Until 1892 U.S. immigrant inspection remained superficial. But by the mid-1880s New York State officials who examined arriving migrants on behalf of the federal government at the Castle Garden facility on the southern tip of Manhattan began to send more unwanted migrants back to Europe. While the proportionate number of involuntarily returned migrants remained very low, Prussia had to organize the repatriation of hundreds of destitute Russian migrants. Until 1914 Prussia controlled Germany's domestic and foreign policy, including most matters relating to migration. Even before 1880 Prussia had to cover the costs for accommodating and repatriating destitute foreign return migrants. Russian officials often refused to readmit subjects who had left without the required emigration passports, requiring lengthy diplomatic negotiations. As a result, Prussia repeatedly denied passage to Russian return migrants without means, stranding them in such ports as Antwerp, Southampton, and Hamburg.[24]

It is not surprising that news about stricter U.S. admission procedures in the mid-1880s alarmed Prussian officials. In July 1885 the Prussian interior minister informed German and Prussian prime minister Bismarck about the American restrictions against so-called paupers. He suggested applying more stringent controls to prevent the entry of migrants who would potentially face rejection in the United States. In September 1885 the Prussian governor in the port city of Stettin stressed that lacking personnel at the border would make it difficult to prevent poor Russian subjects from crossing Prussian territory. He called on the steamship lines to cover the costs for repatriating unwanted migrants. In late 1885 Prussian officials began checking transmigrants heading to the North Sea ports more systematically, but they could not clearly determine who was a "pauper," because the U.S. immigration bill did not define the term. To clarify this matter, in

1886 the Prussian government required every adult transmigrant to carry at least 400 Marks, plus 100 Marks in cash for each accompanying child, to fund a possible return journey. For average migrants these amounts were astronomical. The real purpose of the not strictly enforced regulation was to allow Prussian officials to reject any migrant they deemed suspicious. The available sources do not indicate that Prussian officials prevented most transmigrants from entering or crossing Prussia, but the announcement of the rule threatened the business of HAPAG and NDL. Just as they were gaining a foothold in the lucrative Eastern European market, the Prussian government appeared to thwart their efforts.[25]

Prussia's harsh line against transmigrants betrays a broader political shift toward migration restrictions. Before 1880 Prussia tolerated foreign labor migration, in part to accommodate influential aristocratic landowners in its eastern provinces. As rural workers and their families left for expanding industrial centers, especially Berlin, on the Ruhr, and in Upper Silesia, and for the United States, landowners increasingly depended on seasonal labor migrants from Russian Poland, Lithuania, and Galicia. Bernard Horwich was one of thousands of Lithuanian Jews who benefited from Prussia's open-door policy in this period. In the early 1880s the Prussian government faced political pressure to decisively contain the "invasion" across the eastern border, not least from the emerging antisemitic movement. German speakers constituted a minority in Prussia's formerly Polish provinces, and rising support for Polish nationalism was a matter of concern.

In 1885, the government responded to widespread fears about uncontrolled mass mobility and social change. Thousands of foreigners from the Russian and Austro-Hungarian empires received deportation orders, even though some had lived in Prussia for decades. The Jewish communities in Memel and Königsberg were particularly hard hit. Protests by Rülf and his colleagues had some effect. The Memel rabbi was able to mobilize support from city leaders and could exempt dozens of families. The relief effort he coordinated with Königsberg rabbi Isaac Bamberger earned Rülf the nickname "Dr. Hülf" (Dr. Help). In Berlin, a quickly organized committee raised funds from leading German Jews like banker Gerson Bleichröder to assist Russian Jews to move to Britain and the United States. Still, thousands were forced to return to the Russian and Austro-Hungarian empires. Between 1885 and 1888 Prussia expelled more than forty thousand foreigners—Poles, Ukrainians, and Jews. It is little known that smaller groups of transmigrants were caught up in the deportations.[26]

Ballin joined HAPAG as director of its passenger division in 1886, just when Prussia stepped up the mass deportations. Anticipating a decline in the German passenger business, the main source of HAPAG's revenue for decades, he decided to focus on the Eastern European market. One of his first moves was to form an alliance with the Bremen-based NDL, a longtime rival of HAPAG. Together with Hamburg and Bremen ticket brokers, HAPAG and NDL built up a network of ticket agencies across the Russian and Austro-Hungarian empires. The two lines loosely divided the market: NDL concentrated on the Austro-Hungarian Empire, while HAPAG directed its marketing efforts primarily at the Russian market, including Russian Poland. The Prussian deportations constituted a serious challenge. However, Ballin sensed an opportunity. He knew that the Prussian government could not effectively police the long land border with the Russian Empire. As his opening move in the negotiations Ballin cleverly adopted the suggestion of the Stettin governor. The steamship lines, he proposed, would fully cover all potential costs for their passengers if they were denied admission by U.S. immigration inspectors and had to return home.

In return, in 1887 Prussia exempted HAPAG and NDL ticket holders from the cash requirement. Passengers of other lines did not enjoy a similar protection, a fact that was not lost on ticket agents marketing HAPAG and NDL passages in Eastern Europe. In 1888 the government also reached a compromise with the large landowners who were hard hit by the deportation of Polish and Ukrainian agricultural laborers. To strike a balance between the landowners and supporters of migration restrictions, Prussia issued standardized identification papers to labor migrants, forcing them return home during the winter months to ensure they did not settle permanently in Prussia. A de facto identification requirement also was the basis of the deal between the steamship lines and the Prussian government. If they were checked during the train journey across Prussian territory, passengers had to prove they were traveling with HAPAG or NDL. Standardized identification papers were (and remain) a much more effective tool to control and contain mobility than costly border fences (or walls).[27]

In the early 1890s HAPAG and NDL reinforced their control of the Eastern European growth market—as a result of stricter U.S. immigration regulations. In 1891 Congress established a federal immigration agency and inspection facilities at major U.S. ports to ensure a more thorough screening of all arriving migrants. The largest station went into operation at Ellis Island in New York harbor in January 1892. The 1891 immigration bill coincided with a renewed (and unrelated) increase in Jewish migration from the Russian Empire. Only weeks after Ellis Island processed its first migrants, in February 1892 several typhus cases were detected on New York's Lower East Side. The outbreak was traced to the *Massilia*, a recently arrived vessel that had taken Russian Jews from Marseilles to New York days earlier. These passengers belonged to a small number of Jews who embarked on their journey to America in Odessa before 1914. The New York City authorities quickly quarantined the affected immigrants, successfully containing the outbreak.

During the summer of 1892 major cholera outbreaks affected central Russia and Hamburg. Unlike its counterpart in New York, the Hamburg city government struggled to respond. It took weeks before the city even acknowledged the outbreak and began to impose quarantine measures, contributing to a high and avoidable death toll among working-class residents. The arrival of Russian migrants from Hamburg with cholera symptoms in the late summer led to a frenzied reaction in New York. Demands for systematic travel bans influenced the presidential election campaign in the fall months. In September 1892 the federal government imposed a three-week quarantine on incoming vessels from all European ports, effectively interrupting the transatlantic passenger traffic and stranding thousands of passengers for months. The Prussian government officially closed its eastern border to stop migration from Russia, with limited effect. Migrants continued to cross the border traveling to other North Sea ports, including Bremen, that did not register cholera cases. After the Hamburg outbreak was contained in early 1893, the United States lifted the quarantine regulations but required all Russian migrants to quarantine for several days in their respective European port of embarkation. Inspectors at Ellis Island and other immigration stations began examining immigrants more carefully for contagious diseases.[28]

On a first glance, the cholera outbreak was a worst-case scenario for HAPAG. Hamburg's port was closed for several months. Increased controls by the United States, especially the quarantine requirement for Russian passengers, was an additional burden. And when transatlantic passenger traffic resumed in early 1893, the Prussian government refused to lift its ineffective border blockade. Prussian officials also rescinded the cash exemption for HAPAG and NDL passengers. Ballin was unfazed. He brashly proposed to privatize Prussia's ineffective border controls. HAPAG and NDL would build and maintain "control stations" along the eastern border. Employees of the steamship lines would screen and disinfect all Russian migrants according to

U.S. immigration regulations. Along the border with the Austro-Hungarian Empire steamship line employees would also examine transmigrants to reduce the chance of another disease outbreak. A local gendarme—the only state official at each checkpoint—would deport inadmissible migrants across the nearby border. Admitted migrants would receive a certificate, a privately issued transit visa, to prove they had passed the control station. HAPAG and NDL would cover the costs for migrants without means who returned to Hamburg or Bremen.

After weeks of negotiations Ballin and his NDL counterpart were able to convince the Prussian interior minister and his top bureaucrats of the advantages of the new system. In September 1894 the public-private partnership deal was sealed. Prussian officials embraced the agreement because it provided substantial cost savings. The steamship lines organized and channeled the transit migration and relieved the Prussian state of a major financial burden. In return the Prussian government allowed HAPAG and NDL to exclude competing steamship lines from the lucrative Eastern European market. All migrants entering the control stations had to buy HAPAG or NDL passages if they did not already possess prepaid HAPAG or NDL tickets.

To hedge against complaints by competing steamship lines Ballin organized a price-fixing cartel, the so-called North Atlantic Steamship Conference, which also became known as the Continental Pool. Similar agreements covered the British Isles and Scandinavia. Ballin won over the main steamship lines serving the European continent—HAPAG's ally NDL (Bremen), the Holland-America Line (Rotterdam), and the Red Star Line (Antwerp)—by offering them symbolic market shares. NDL and HAPAG retained over 70 percent of the market for themselves. Following the deal with the Prussian state the two leading British lines, Cunard and the White Star, reluctantly joined Ballin's Continental Pool to gain a small percentage of the lucrative market. The German and Prussian governments ignored repeated complaints by Western European ambassadors, the Austrian government, and foreign steamship lines criticizing the monopoly of HAPAG and NDL. By the turn of the century HAPAG was the world's largest passenger and cargo line. In 1899 Ballin was promoted to chief executive of HAPAG.[29]

U.S. immigration officials praised the control stations. As U.S. immigration commissioner Herman Stump put it in 1894, Germany was "protecting itself against undesirable immigrants . . . and at the same time protecting us." This is a crucial statement. The United States effectively shifted the control of its outer borders to transit countries (and nonstate actors) in Europe. The main purpose of the control stations was to exclude migrants who did not meet U.S. immigration regulations. Stump anticipated that European and East Asian migrants would try to circumvent controls at American ports by traveling through Canadian ports and cross the little-guarded land border to the United States. Over the explicit objection of the Canadian government, the United States posted immigration inspectors at major Canadian ports in 1894 as part of a private agreement with steamship lines serving these ports. The system was ineffective until Canada overhauled its immigration policy in the late 1890s.[30]

It would be too shortsighted to describe HAPAG and NDL as agents of the U.S. and Prussian governments enforcing restrictive immigration policies. Both lines shared the overarching goals of transporting as many passengers as possible and defending their control of a lucrative growth market. The control stations assuaged American fears linking Russian migrants with the spread of contagious disease. The system also kept the Prussian state in check. Unlike Hamburg and Bremen, Prussia derived only a minor economic benefit from the mass transit migration. Without the involvement of HAPAG and NDL it is quite likely that Prussia would have taken steps to protect its long land border, possibly even interrupting the mass transit migration. The privately managed HAPAG and NDL control stations were the foundation of the de facto monopoly because competing steamship lines were excluded.

Paradoxically, the control station system allowed more Eastern Europeans to move to the United States than would have otherwise been the case because it kept governments on the sidelines. Unlike its counterparts in the Russian and Austro-Hungarian empires, the Prussian government understood that instead of taking ineffective measures to contain mass migration, it made more sense to leave the management to the steamship lines and thus derive some economic benefit from it. In a 1905 newspaper article the executive director of the German Jewish Hilfsverein, Bernhard Kahn, emphasized the immeasurable financial benefit of the public-private partnership for Jewish migrants: passengers of the German steamship lines were exempt from the "strict" Prussian cash requirement. Jewish aid associations could protect migrants and assist them during the journey, but they were not in a position to foot the bill for tens of thousands of transmigrants who were affected by the Prussian requirement to carry large cash amounts.[31]

To date Ballin's achievement of facilitating the mass migration of millions of Eastern Europeans to the United States between the early 1880s and 1914 has not been recognized. Scholars associated with the Leo Baeck Institute, which was founded in 1955 in London to promote the study of German Jewish history, praised Ballin as a far-sighted business leader, highlighting his achievements as a German patriot and as a Jew, but did not discuss the impact of HAPAG beyond Germany's borders. This view continues to resonate with recent German biographers.[32] In contrast, in his memoir Zionist leader Chaim Weizmann characterized Ballin as "more German than the Germans, obsequious, superpatriotic, eagerly anticipating the wishes and plans of the masters of Germany." The editor of a collection of migrant letters describes Ballin as exploiter of Jewish migrants, implicitly echoing Weizmann's criticism.[33]

Ballin's overarching objective was to benefit HAPAG financially. The parallels to the Pereire brothers are striking. Isaac Pereire had no qualms moving thousands of indentured labor migrants from South Asia to the Caribbean. Indeed, HAPAG and NDL also participated in the transportation of indentured laborers between China's Fujian province and Singapore, admittedly as relatively minor players. Both lines also hired hundreds of Chinese men for low wages to undercut attempts to unionize German crews. This practice is still common today. Sailors from the Philippines can be found on most cargo ships plying the world's oceans. Ballin repeatedly laid off striking workers and was a declared opponent of organized labor. HAPAG began providing benefits to its workers much later than other large employers in Hamburg. Like the Pereires, Ballin maintained close ties to government leaders. Kaiser Wilhelm II, a major proponent of German naval expansion, embraced HAPAG's global expansion. Ballin was recognized as one of Imperial Germany's most successful business executives. Yet Hamburg's business elite, which included the respected Warburgs and other established Jewish families, shunned him because of his humble origins.[34]

In a transformative phase during the middle decades of the nineteenth century the railroad business in the Russian Empire and Southeastern Europe attracted several Jewish investors whose parents and grandparents hailed from the proto-capitalist margins of feudal economies. As a new business, it was particularly appealing to outsiders who were willing to take risks and were not daunted by failure. Strousberg belongs to the relatively few Jewish railroad investors who pursued rags-to-riches careers. Most others were descendants of well-to-do entrepreneurs and investors, notably James de Rothschild and Maurice de Hirsch. A wealthy relative provided the Pereire brothers with invaluable social and cultural capital, which they invested skillfully. Albert Ballin stands out as a self-made business executive who recognized the huge potential of the Eastern European market for the steamship business.

The transportation business epitomized high social mobility in rapidly transforming societies and depended on the movement of capital across borders. In the late nineteenth century mobility entrepreneurship served as a catalyst for moving people and goods on a scale that even optimistic boosters could not fathom in the 1850s and 1860s. The same technology that served as a catalyst for economic transformation displacing millions of rural workers and service providers enabled a growing number of people to seek better opportunities elsewhere. Seasonal migration networks that had existed for centuries were transformed as more people moved to nearby cities and to distant destinations and frequently back to their hometowns, where they invested their hard-earned capital. The money migrants sent to family members back home also reshaped local economies. The vast scale of mass mobility between rural areas and newly expanding cities overshadowed movement across borders. For instance, a detailed history of Berlin's railroad system published in 1896 mentioned foreign migrants only in passing, even though their number was so high that a separate train station had been built in 1891 to isolate transmigrants from other travelers.[35]

Moving capital, large numbers of people, goods, and information depended on relatively permeable borders. Connecting underdeveloped regions with a surplus of available labor to urban centers that depended on access to a large pool of unskilled labor created a lucrative business opportunity. The unprecedented economic transformation and uneven business cycles fueled calls for protectionism and immigration restrictions. Critics often resorted to antisemitic stereotypes, blaming Jewish mobility entrepreneurs for having acquired their wealth illicitly and for uprooting and exploiting the rural population. Even respected business journals echoed these views. According to an article published in 1900 in a German railroad journal, Baron de Hirsch belonged to a group of "reckless" businessmen who were exclusively interested in "enriching themselves" and did not show any interest in the "public good." In reality, Hirsch generously supported a wide range of social causes in the Ottoman Empire and various European countries. More important, however, was another point. The author of the article conveniently avoided discussing the enormous cost of large-scale infrastructure projects, not to mention the considerable risks private investors like Hirsch shouldered.[36]

4
Migrant Journeys

On a stifling hot summer day in 1904, a young lawyer, Sammy Gronemann, made a strange discovery in his hometown, Hanover in northern Germany. Unexpectedly, a close friend rushed into his office, visibly agitated. Gronemann's account in his memoirs reflects his complete bewilderment and shock as the young woman dragged Gronemann to a rail yard a few hundred yards from the platforms of Hanover's train station: "There stood a long train, made up of boxcars. Out of the [locked] doors *ostjüdische* (Eastern Jewish) refugees—men, women and children—stretched their arms, pleading for help. . . . What was going on?" As it turned out, the desperate passengers had not received water for hours. After pleading with employees of the rail yard Gronemann and his friend unlocked the doors to allow the passengers to get water at a nearby pump. The ensuing stampede—dozens of desperate migrants fought over access to the single pump—only added to Gronemann's bewilderment.

Conversations with passengers and officials revealed the train was bound for the North Sea port of Rotterdam. It had originated in the Upper Silesian border town of Myslowitz (Mysłowice), almost certainly on the previous day. The passengers were Jewish and Ukrainian migrants from the Austrian province of Galicia. Gronemann was deeply moved by the fate of the Jewish passengers. He obtained schedules from railway officials and learned, to his surprise, that for a limited period during that summer, on some days up to four special emigrant trains bound for Rotterdam passed through Hanover within twenty-four hours, each with several hundred travelers. The purpose of the stop was to load additional coal and water for the engine. Gronemann was the son of the city's senior rabbi. It appears that the Jewish community had no knowledge about these transports. In the following days, Gronemann and his friends organized a support network. Volunteers provided all passengers, regardless of their religion, with water and food during the short stop at the Hanover rail yard.[1]

Most Galician migrants originated in the eastern part of the province. Together with migrants from the Russian Empire who crossed the border near Brody and at other places, they traveled by train to the western Galician town of Oświęcim (better known under its German name Auschwitz) or to nearby Krakow, where most trains terminated. Oświęcim was one of the most important points of passage along the migration route from Galicia to the North Sea ports. Connecting trains traveling across the nearby German border could accommodate only a limited number of passengers. The Austrian authorities did not formally restrict migration but stopped young Austrian men to check whether they had completed their military service. According to observers it was relatively easy to approach smugglers outside the Oświęcim train station who accompanied migrants across the nearby border to Imperial Germany. Austrian officials rarely intervened because they could not muster enough personnel to control the mass movement. A few simple hostels provided accommodation. In small sheds adjacent to the train station building local agents representing different steamship lines sold passages to overseas destinations. During some summer months more migrants congregated in Oświęcim than the town could accommodate. The growing number of seasonal migrants who used the same travel routes only exacerbated the situation.

In early August 1891 a Hamburg police inspector observed hundreds of Jews camping in fields behind the train station in the hamlet of Brzezinka, where Oświęcim rabbi Abraham Schnur tried his best to assist needy families with food and advice. Once migrants had crossed the border, legally by train or with smugglers, they headed to the train station on the German side in the Upper Silesian mining town of Myslowitz. Some walked several miles further to the next larger city, Kattowitz (Katowice). Prussian officials remained on the sidelines because the German steamship lines were responsible for transmigrants.[2]

After 1894 employees of the steamship lines began screening most migrants at checkpoints near the main border crossings. After passing a brief medical check and, if they crossed at the Russian border, undergoing an obligatory washing procedure, migrants had to present their transatlantic ticket or book a passage at a small office maintained by HAPAG and NDL. Migrants who avoided all controls and crossed Germany without a valid steamship ticket and without a *Legitimationskarte,* the de facto transit visa that proved they had passed the health inspection at the border, were subject to deportation during the transit. Migrants traveled independently, or they boarded so-called *Auswandererzüge* (emigrant trains) at the eastern border. These were used for larger groups of migrants and went into service during the 1880s. *Auswandererzüge* were sealed and bypassed regular train stations. The trains went straight from the border to Hamburg or Bremen or to the western border with the Netherlands, from which migrants continued their journey to Rotterdam or Antwerp. During the transit *Auswandererzüge* made a couple of brief logistical stops to load coal and refill water for the engine, like the stop observed by Gronemann in Hanover. Emigrant trains passing Berlin made a single scheduled stop at the Ruhleben *Auswandererbahnhof* (emigrant train station), in a western suburb of the German and Prussian capital. A Berlin journalist characterized Ruhleben in 1900 as the "strangest and in more than one respect most intriguing train station of the Imperial capital."[3]

In 1899 a young Jewish woman published a harrowing account of her Ruhleben experience. Based on Yiddish letters she had written during the journey, Maryashe (Mary) Antin's *From Plotzk to Boston* stands out as one of the few detailed contemporary descriptions of a migrant journey to America. In the spring of 1894, when she was thirteen (or possibly eleven) years old, Maryashe, together with her mother and sisters, left her hometown of Polotzk in the northern Pale to join her father, who had moved to Boston in 1891. The family's journey resembled that of thousands of other Jews. Usually, a young father would follow an acquaintance or relative, find employment, save sufficient funds, secure housing, and send prepaid tickets to his family. After the tickets arrived in early 1894, Maryashe, her sisters, and her mother embarked on the journey. They took the train from Polotsk (Polatsk) to Vilna to visit relatives before heading to the German border, where they boarded an overcrowded *Auswandererzug*. The train passed through Berlin and then came to a halt in a deserted area a few miles west of the city—in Ruhleben.

The conductors rushed the tired and confused passengers off the train. A group of Germans in white overalls, screaming orders, separated men from women and children, throwing the luggage on a big pile. Antin describes a scene of utter chaos as the terrified travelers were driven into a small building. "Here we had been taken to a lonely place.... Our things were taken away, our friends separated from us; a man came to inspect us, as if to ascertain our full value; strange-looking people driving us about like dumb animals, helpless and unresisting; children we could not see crying in a way that suggested terrible things; ourselves driven into a little room." The migrants had to strip naked, were washed with soap, and showered with warm water. The German officials urged the migrants to hurry. "They persist, 'Quick! Quick!—or you'll miss the train!'—Oh, so we really won't be murdered! They are only making us ready for the continuing of our journey, cleaning us of all suspicions of dangerous germs. Thank God!" Antin's mother had to pay 2 Marks for herself and each of her daughters to cover the cost of the cleaning procedure before she was rushed back to the train.[4]

Almost two years before Antin's journey, the cholera outbreak—the "dreadful epidemic"—had claimed the lives of over eight thousand working-class Hamburg residents. Following a simultaneous outbreak in central Russia, German officials and the press blamed Russian and, in particular, Russian Jewish transmigrants for spreading the disease. Yet almost all Russian migrants originated in the empire's western provinces, an area that was not affected by the outbreak. Other North Sea ports did not record an increase of cholera cases during the summer of 1892. The real cause of the high number of casualties was neglect by Hamburg's inept city government, which had done little to improve hygiene in the city's working-class districts. After the outbreak was contained in late 1892 the treatment of migrants in Hamburg and along the main transit routes through Imperial Germany was overhauled. Disinfection procedures were introduced in Ruhleben at some point in 1893. At the same time HAPAG set up a quarantine facility for Russian migrants on the America Quai in the port. In 1896 a tiny makeshift synagogue was dedicated in this facility. And by 1894–1895 physicians employed by HAPAG and NDL closely examined all migrants at control stations near major rail crossings along Germany's eastern border with the Russian Empire. After 1895 Russian migrants had to undergo mandatory washing procedures at the border, in Ruhleben, and at the port of embarkation in Hamburg or Bremen.[5]

When the Antins traversed Germany the fear of another outbreak was still palpable. The police officer who received Antin and her fellow passengers at the platform in Hamburg's train station stayed far away from them. From the train station the migrants were taken in horse-drawn carriages to the HAPAG quarantine facility in the port. Following a thorough search of their luggage and another health inspection they were led to accommodations in the closely guarded port area. Antin felt like a prisoner, but was pleasantly surprised that they were given kosher food. After a quarantine of several days the Antins boarded a HAPAG steamer, and they arrived in Boston two weeks later. Suffice it to say, Antin did not have fond memories of Germany: "Always a call for money, always suspicion of our presence and always rough orders and scowls of disapproval, even at the quickest obedience.... We had to bear it all because we were going to America from a land cursed by the dreadful epidemic."[6]

In 1902 HAPAG opened the *Auswandererhallen* (emigrant halls) on the southern outskirts of Hamburg's huge port. The state-of-the-art complex could accommodate more than a thousand people in clean quarters. Migrants could attend churches and a small synagogue. Hamburg's Jewish community oversaw the provision of kosher food to Jewish passengers. Like Ruhleben and the *Auswandererzüge*, the *Auswandererhallen* were designed to isolate transmigrants, prevent disease outbreaks, and maintain order. Trains took migrants straight to the compound, which was located several miles from the city center. Upon arrival migrants, overwhelmingly Eastern Europeans traveling to North America, had to undergo hygienic and medical checks while their luggage was fumigated. On the clean side of the

Passengers take their meals in the HAPAG dining hall for Jews, c. 1907. This photo is part of a series that Hamburg photographer Johann Hamann took at the *Auswandererhallen*. Some of these images were used by the German Jewish Hilfsverein in its annual report that year. Most of the men and women are young. The features are blurred because some children and adults moved during the long exposure time. Source: Johann Hamann, StaHH, 720-1/343-1/H3001112. *Reprinted with the kind permission of the State Archive Hamburg*

Jewish migrants celebrate at a farewell meal in the HAPAG *Auswandererhallen* complex, c. 1907. The four men on the right are members of the Hamburg Jewish community who provided and prepared the kosher food. The man with the booklet in his hands is almost certainly Paul Laskar, the head of the Hamburg aid association for Jewish migrants. Source: Johann Hamann, StaHH, 720-1/343-1/H3001120. *Reprinted with the kind permission of the State Archive Hamburg*

Auswandererhallen they were accommodated in newly built dormitories that German and American observers praised for their cleanliness. In most other North Sea ports migrants stayed at cheap hotels and hostels that often were notorious for squalor.

Following a smallpox case in March 1910 at a Bremen hostel, an official representing the steamship line NDL assured the city's health officials that all living quarters were regularly inspected and met strict hygiene standards. Once a week, a physician visited the empty quarters and examined migrants' belongings. All migrants had to line up and pass "very slowly" in front of a physician. "Suspicious looking individuals were taken to the side" for a more elaborate check, he wrote. The high-ranking NDL employee remarked that Jewish migrants were prone to disorderly behavior. Many prayed in the morning at a nearby synagogue. In a cynical remark that illustrates antisemitism was a widely shared cultural code in Imperial Germany, the employee stated that unfortunately a "cleansing of the temple" was not allowed.[7]

By 1900 physicians inspected most migrants crossing Imperial Germany several times—at the eastern border, at Ruhleben or at a similar checkpoint at the Leipzig train station, and in Hamburg or Bremen. In December 1904 Julius Kaliski, a journalist writing for Germany's Social Democratic daily *Vorwärts*, a major national newspaper, traveled to East Prussia to investigate rumors about the abuse of migrants by HAPAG employees. Disguised as a Yiddish-speaking migrant named Jossl Kalischer from Russia, he entered the control station in Tilsit that was operated by HAPAG and NDL. After buying a steamship passage he was directed to the men's section of the small building for the obligatory medical examination and washing procedure. Before entering the shower room dozens of naked men waited, pressed against each other in a small room. In his account Kaliski captured the real fears of the migrants, uncertain what would happen to them. Many worried about possible rejection. On the crammed *Auswandererzug* to Hamburg the journalist (who happened to be Jewish) experienced antisemitic verbal abuse by both government officials and HAPAG employees. It is not surprising that migrants resented the washing procedure. In 1895, after disinfection facilities had been installed at the Eydtkuhnen train station, a police official reported, "[M]ost Jews refuse to go into the water." The officials decided to send those migrants to Ruhleben in separate carriages, to ensure they would not mingle with migrants who had already been bathed.[8]

These unsettling examples—Jewish migrants traveling in densely packed boxcars or sealed passenger trains through Germany, large crowds of Jews camping in the fields behind the Oświęcim train station in Brzezinka, only a few hundred yards from where the SS began constructing the vast Auschwitz-Birkenau camp complex in October 1941, intimidating and humiliating cleaning procedures that required men and women to undress in front of strangers, the passing of Jewish migrants in front of German physicians, and antisemitic remarks by German officials—seem eerily familiar in hindsight. In a study of Auschwitz, two respected Holocaust scholars draw a direct line from Antin's Ruhleben experience to the gas chambers in Auschwitz-Birkenau. Deborah Dwork and Robert Jan van Pelt see it as "a blueprint for, and an eerie foreshadowing of, the 'delousing' routine in Auschwitz sixty years later." They include the episode in their study about the history of

Auschwitz to highlight a continuity of the specific German fear and hatred of "*Ostjuden* [who] were lice-ridden."[9]

Other scholars who touch on Antin's description of Ruhleben analyze it more carefully, for instance, by pointing to similar medical checks in other countries at the time, not least in the United States. Dwork and van Pelt do not discuss the fact that *all* migrants originating in the Russian Empire were disinfected and screened during the German transit. Russian Jews were widely blamed for causing the Hamburg cholera outbreak in 1892, but the extensive files of the health administrations in Bremen and Hamburg do not contain any remarks about Jews being more prone to be disease carriers than other Eastern Europeans. The specter of disease outbreaks was a corollary of inter- and transcontinental mass mobility by train and steamship. Health screening procedures for migrants became common in many parts of the world in the last two decades of the nineteenth century.

In the 1880s several states began to coordinate the containment of contagious diseases, especially cholera, at international conferences. In the Suez Canal Zone and in the port city of Jeddah, Muslim pilgrims were carefully screened and isolated. Central neighborhoods in Beirut and Jeddah still carry the name "Karantina." The sanitary stations that opened in the vicinity of the Suez Canal Zone for pilgrims suspected to be disease carriers bear a striking resemblance to the German control stations and to the disinfection facilities that were installed at the U.S.-Mexico border during the First World War. Even within the Russian Empire, internal migrants relocating to western Siberia during the 1890s were screened for contagious diseases and bathed, primarily at a medical checkpoint in the city of Chelyabinsk, the main gateway for settlers moving to Siberia. And medical screenings did not end once Russian and other migrants left German ports.

The United States—*not* the steamship lines or German state authorities—was the main driving force behind the hygienic inspections Eastern European transmigrants had to undergo in Imperial Germany after the Hamburg cholera outbreak. Strict medical checks at Ellis Island and other U.S. ports were introduced in early 1893. American public health officials considered Russian migrants particularly prone to infection with cholera. In the spring of 1893, the U.S. immigration authorities required all Russian subjects to remain in quarantine for several days at European ports of embarkation. The quarantine requirement for Russian subjects was lifted and reimposed several times before 1914. It is well known that migrants worried about the medical exams and possible rejection by U.S. immigration inspectors at Ellis

Island. Soon after 1892 U.S. public health officials and diplomats began to closely monitor migrants for certain contagious diseases, even launching inspections of embarking passengers at ports in Europe and East Asia. In his memoirs, New York mayor Fiorello La Guardia recalled how he inspected thousands of passengers at the Adriatic port of Fiume (Rijeka) as a young U.S. consul between 1904 and 1906.[10]

Sammy Gronemann wrote his memoir during the 1940s in Tel Aviv, more than four decades after the events in Hanover. His depiction of Jewish migrants as "refugees" reflects the use of the term by Jewish aid workers and Jewish newspapers around 1904, even for Jews coming from Galicia who clearly were not fleeing persecution. The use of boxcars for transmigrants crossing Imperial Germany, however, was rare. It is likely that the dramatic growth of migration from Eastern Europe in the summer months of 1904 led to a shortage of passenger carriages. Other sources indicate that passengers had access to food and water during the transit journey. Taken out of context, Kaliski's 1904 article could easily be used as compelling evidence for the abuse and exploitation of Jewish migrants. Yet the *Vorwärts* regularly published acerbic articles about HAPAG and its chief executive, Albert Ballin, who aggressively fought attempts to unionize HAPAG employees. A closer reading of the article shows that Kaliski did not find evidence of severe violations of the existing rules.[11]

The scale of the movement from different regions in Eastern Europe makes it challenging to provide an accurate portrait of individual journey experiences. Routine journeys were not particularly newsworthy. The coverage of train accidents and ship disasters allows a closer perspective on average migrants. Newspapers sometimes recorded names of passengers and details about their journeys. Before 1914 Hamburg officials systematically collected newspaper reports and personal information about the Hamburg-bound victims of train accidents. Occasionally newspapers profiled accident victims, for instance, after a train crash involving an *Auswandererzug* in central Berlin in 1910, in which several migrants were slightly injured. A local newspaper noted the women's strange dress and that each migrant wore a red paper label with the destination "Hamburg" on their clothes. The article noted the names and destinations of the injured passengers.[12]

Some accounts about ship disasters are powerful. In late 1913 staff working for the Hebrew Sheltering and Immigrant Aid Society (HIAS) in New York interviewed David Milstein, a recently arrived Jewish migrant. A few weeks earlier he had boarded the *Volturno* in Rotterdam. The ship regularly served

Halifax and New York and was operated by the small Uranium Line, a low-cost carrier that resembled Ballin's Carr Line and was operated by the Canadian Northern Railway. On that ill-fated October 1913 voyage the *Volturno* soon encountered heavy weather, hardly an unusual occurrence in the fall months on the North Atlantic. In the early hours of October 9 several passengers noticed fire in the cargo hold, close to the front of the ship. An investigation later revealed that the fire was almost certainly caused by a cigarette that was tossed into the cargo hold, which contained highly flammable goods. Soon several explosions rocked the ship in the midst of a budding storm that fanned the flames.

Milstein's account describes the fear and desperation that gripped the passengers: "The roaring flames seemed to be drawing closer and closer. The heat was intense and the smoke was becoming stifling. Everywhere groups were kneeling and praying. Women were tearing their hair. The wind was blowing a gale." In the chaos several crewmembers and passengers piled into lifeboats that were lowered into the water; all of them were crushed against the ship's hull and swallowed by the roaring waves. The ship's captain intervened to protect the remaining boats. Following another explosion around midnight, the fire and the storm became even stronger. Death seemed imminent.

In this apocalyptic moment, "the Jews . . . decided to hold a consultation among themselves to decide whether they would jump overboard or take chances on being burned to death. Finally, they shouted in chorus: 'We'll stick and rely on the will of God.'" Milstein did not touch on a point that was probably obvious to the readers of Jewish papers covering this story: the evening of October 10, 1913, was the beginning of Yom Kippur, the Day of Atonement; the Jews almost certainly spoke the *Unetanah Tokef* prayer ("We shall ascribe holiness to this day"), which refers to the Day of Judgment but offers hope for those who pray, practice charity, and repent. In the morning hours the storm subsided. Several steamers, alerted by the Marconi telegraph operator on the *Volturno*, rescued five hundred Jewish and Polish passengers and crew members. At least 130 passengers and several sailors perished because they had jumped overboard or had ignored the orders not to take the lifeboats down into the stormy sea.[13]

After 1880 ship disasters became less frequent. Standardized journeys of tens of thousands of passengers by train and steamship were a new phenomenon but did not attract much attention. The isolation of migrants during the transit contributed to their low visibility. Newspapers covered accidents

MIGRANT JOURNEYS 85

The front page of the Vienna daily *Volksblatt* on October 19, 1913, depicts a "severe ship disaster on the Atlantic Ocean." The *Volksblatt* supported the antisemitic Christian Social Party and opposed mass emigration. The text underneath the image relates to the supposed exploitation of "poor Austrian emigrants" by the "cartel" of foreign steamship lines. The sensationalistic coverage of the *Volturno* disaster can be read as an implicit warning to readers not to risk a journey across the Atlantic. *Austrian National Library*

and other disruptions of the ordinary flow, not to mention abuse stories, but rarely devoted much attention to the actual migrants.

Routine Journeys

It is tempting to portray steamship lines and their managers, railroad companies, ticket agents, the owners and employees of private hostels, and smugglers as bad actors trying to exploit and cheat migrants. Published sources highlighting abuse, discrimination, and other problems migrants encountered along the way are not difficult to find. In fact, the newspaper coverage of migration in Central and Eastern Europe often reflects the opposition of nationalists and governments to mass emigration after 1880. The few scholars who discuss the journey tend to emphasize obstacles and problems, as historian Zosa Szajkowski does in his frequently referenced article about the "sufferings" of Jewish migrants. The lachrymose approach continues to linger. The author of a detailed study about Jewish migration to Palestine before the 1930s portrays the journey as extremely challenging, as migrants were preyed upon by scheming agents and "suffered a great deal." According to other scholars, Jewish migrants were part of a "wave" and "driven" from their homes, as if they were expelled from Russia. As Irving Howe put it in *World of Our Fathers*, "[B]y the time they reached the Atlantic, many immigrants had been reduced to a state of helpless passivity, unable to make out what was happening to them and why."[14]

But were recorded cases of abuse representative of the actual experiences of migrants? Is every newspaper account about a scheming ticket agent accurate? Analysis of extensive records in Central Europe and Britain shows limited evidence of systematic abuse and exploitation before 1914. Mass migration was a lucrative growth business. Steamship lines, ticket agents, and illegal smugglers shared the same goal, moving more people and keeping governments on the sidelines. Those who cheated migrants did not operate in a vacuum. Migrants sent letters about their travel routes and experiences to relatives and acquaintances back home. By the 1890s journalists began investigating the business practices of steamship lines. American and German officials disguised themselves as migrants to learn more about the journeys. Jewish aid associations publicized information that local representatives collected along the transit routes. Hamburg police officials investigated complaints by migrants about their treatment during the transit journey.

Several German officials, who abused or even punched migrants, were prosecuted. In one case, a Hamburg police officer took two migrants back to the Russian border to determine whether agents representing HAPAG at the border control station had overcharged them.[15]

Although the decision to move to America was momentous, the journey rarely was a sharp rupture. Most migrants carefully planned their migration and knew American streets were not paved with gold. In a 1929 article the Jewish sociologist Jacob Lestschinsky noted the importance of money migrants sent to relatives and acquaintances in Eastern Europe to fund journeys. According to his data, in 1908 60 percent of Jews moving to the United States funded their journey through remittances, but only 32 percent of non-Jewish migrants did so.[16] Those considering whether to move had access to information about America through letters and personal accounts of returning migrants. After settling at their destination, migrants retained close ties to their old homes. A remarkable feature of the Jewish migration from Eastern Europe was the *Landsmanshaftn*, so-called hometown associations. Estimates of the number of *Landsmanshaftn* in New York alone ranged from one thousand to ten thousand before 1914. The disparity covers a large number of informal networks that sometimes existed for only a few years before dissolving or merging with other associations. *Landsmanshaftn* were tied to migrations in both directions. Their representatives regularly visited towns in Eastern Europe, particularly to help with the distribution of money migrants had saved for funding the journeys of relatives and acquaintances. Most *Landsmanshaftn* in the United States were tied to towns in the northwestern part of the Russian Pale.[17]

The decision to migrate cannot be disconnected from the respective social context. Few Jewish men and women were literally driven from their homes in Eastern Europe, but that does not mean they were truly free. The abject economic situation in Galicia, Romania, and the northern Pale, not to mention economic restrictions Jews faced in Russia and Romania, made migration almost the only feasible option for a growing number of young men and women. Younger men had to weigh whether to evade military service. Social obligations to family members who required support or had already moved also came into play. Some younger women and men left to avoid arranged marriages. And some were striving for independence. Migration offered the chance to exercise at least a limited degree of agency.

Those who could not afford the train—a minority—walked to the German border. In 1900 Jewish *Fusgeyer* (walkers) from Romania briefly caught the attention of the Jewish and general public. Romania was one of the least developed countries in Europe. The government refused to emancipate its Jewish population and excluded Jews from the school system. Anti-Jewish violence increased during the first decade of the twentieth century, just when a larger number of Jews began leaving Romania. It is unclear whether discrimination and violence contributed to rising Jewish migration, as research in this area is lacking. In April 1900 an antisemitic German paper reported that a thousand Jews were walking toward the German border. The paper compared the migrants to locusts and warned its readers that they would be begging for support. In May 1900 the German consul in Bucharest expressed doubts about the accuracy of these reports.[18]

In 1900 Abraham Cahan recorded a *Fusgeyer* experience from a recently arrived Jew from Romania. Soon after dusk, his group had reached a rural town. Refused shelter by hostile residents, the weary travelers consulted on where to spend the night. "'In the Jewish cemetery!' shouted a voice. 'That's outside the city limits, and certainly the Gentiles can't forbid us to rest with our dead brethren.'" And that is where they made camp. Through prayer the diverse party, which included atheists and young and old women and men, came together in a safe Jewish space. Cahan was intrigued by the existence of Jewish spaces that offered a degree of protection but also allowed migrants to mingle. During his own journey the largely Jewish town of Brody was such a space, as were Jewish sites he visited when he traveled through Germany in 1882, but also the prayer rooms and kosher dining halls in European port cities and Jewish immigrant neighborhoods, in particular New York's Lower East Side.[19]

Before 1914, a vital part of the journey depended entirely on informal arrangements for the crossing of the Russian and Austrian borders to Germany. Personal recollections and court records provide some background on the smugglers who assisted migrants. During the busy summer of 1891, Wenzel Kilian Kiliszewski, a Hamburg police officer, visited Memel, where more than two hundred Jews were crossing the border every day. He met with rabbi Rülf, who headed the aid committee that covered the cost of sending migrants by ship across the Baltic, the fastest route to Hamburg and Bremen. Kiliszewski described Rülf as "very compassionate." According to Rülf, all the smugglers in the vicinity of Memel were Jewish and colluded with Russian border guards and higher-ranking officers.

Quite a few migrants paid drivers to take them from Kovno across the border. On the outskirts of Memel, Kiliszewski walked across the border and in a single hour counted eighty horse-drawn carriages, each with a dozen passengers, luggage, and a driver. Several Russian border guards ignored him and the carriages. More than forty years later, one of the migrants on those carriages recalled his experience. Boris Bogen left Russia with his wife and infant in 1891. According to his memoir, none other than the Russian governor in the small Latvian port town of Libau introduced him to a smuggler, another Russian official, who organized the illegal crossing for a substantial fee: "[W]e were herded into one of a little string of wagons, piled high with emigrants, their numerous progeny, and their unwieldy baggage. All night we sat cramped in the jolting, rickety cart, that turned into a veritable steam bath from the crowded, hot bodies; when morning came we were dumped out at Palangen, just this side of the [Russian] border." During the following night the smuggler took them across the border to Memel, "with our baby wailing lustily as if to celebrate our escape from our birthland." A study about the journeys of thousands of Belarusian and Ukrainian peasants to Canada hints at only a few cases of smugglers who cheated their clients. Smugglers frequently worked with agents who sold steamship passages to migrants. On the Prussian side of the border smugglers brought the migrants to arranged meeting points where local employees of ticket agencies handed out train tickets and led the migrants to the closest train station.[20]

It is not possible to ascertain how many Russian officials in the western border region assisted smugglers, but in the late 1890s German and Russian observers estimated that up to 90 percent of migrants crossed the border illegally. A movement of this scale depended on the tacit or open collusion of administrators and gendarmes stationed on the border. A biography of the Russian police officer who was in charge of the Kibarty rail crossing checkpoint hints at endemic corruption among higher-ranking Russian officials. Sergei Nicholaevich Miasoedov, born in Vilna, was the son of a well-connected landowner. After a brief military career, he joined the police force, assuming his post on the Kibarty border crossing in 1894, where his main task was to prevent smuggling, register migrants, and check passports.

Located on the St. Petersburg–Berlin railroad, Kibarty-Eydtkuhnen was one of the busiest checkpoints on the western border. Following a promotion in 1901 Miasoedov was the highest-ranking Russian official at the checkpoint. He regularly welcomed prominent travelers, including the tsar himself. On one occasion he joined a hunting party with Kaiser Wilhelm II, who owned an estate a few miles from the border. The Kibarty-Eydtkuhnen crossing was a hotbed of illegal migrant smuggling. Kiliszewski, the Hamburg police officer, reported in 1895 that almost all migrants in this sector crossed the border illegally, usually at night. In 1903 Miasoedov sent a long report about the smuggling to the local governor, identifying the Braunshtein brothers from Kibarty as masterminds of the endeavor. In their offices at Kovno and Eydtkuhnen the ticket agents sold migrants overpriced passages that included informal arrangements to cross the border. Miasoedov's biographer William Fuller presents compelling evidence that his real motive was not to rein in smuggling but to sideline the Braunshteins. Miasoedov had close financial ties to a rival of the Braunshteins, a certain Samuel Freidberg, who had repeatedly been accused of involvement in the illegal migration business.[21]

Opponents of mass emigration and antisemites singled out Jewish ticket agents and smugglers as exploiters who systematically bribed officials. Before 1914 Austrian, Hungarian, and Russian officials regularly accused ticket agents of enticing gullible peasants to migrate, thus robbing them of their meager savings. The Dillingham Commission, which investigated migration in Europe between 1907 and 1910, echoed this perception, reporting that "propaganda conducted by steamship ticket agents [was] undoubtedly the most important immediate cause of emigration from Europe to the United States." Tellingly, the Dillingham Commission could not present compelling evidence to prove the accuracy of this statement. The commission also had to walk back the claim that Jewish aid associations funded the journeys of "paupers" to the United States. U.S. investigators who disguised themselves as migrants could not document a single case proving a violation of U.S. immigration law by Jewish aid associations.[22]

Several scholars take biased government sources at face value. Miasoedov's case, however, demonstrates the pitfalls of uncritically relying on official Russian documents.[23] In her detailed study of emigration from Eastern Europe, Tara Zahra has drawn attention to the antisemitic image of the exploitative ticket agent. She questions the reliability of official sources and argues that officials and newspapers often overrated the influence of travel agents. They were easily identifiable scapegoats for migration opponents.[24]

Attempts by officials to shift the blame for mass emigration on Jewish ticket agents and smugglers betrayed the lack of policies to address the economic malaise in rural regions. Governments in St. Petersburg, Vienna, and Budapest could not muster the personnel to police long land borders. High-ranking civil servants and political leaders openly disagreed about the appropriate migration regime. The Austrian and Hungarian military demanded stricter border controls, while trade officials representing the same governments wanted to wrestle control of the lucrative migration business from the German steamship lines and promote steamship service from underserved domestic ports. Poorly paid officials in remote border posts frequently accepted bribes. Indeed, instead of masterminding an illegal smuggling operation, the Braunshtein brothers were service providers who facilitated the journeys of Russian subjects seeking better economic opportunities elsewhere.

Smuggling was a lucrative business opportunity in Eastern Europe's little-developed borderlands. Court files indicate that many smugglers and ticket agents were not Jewish and did not cheat migrants. The 1889 trial of emigration agents from Oświęcim in the nearby town of Wadowice, the subject of sensationalistic coverage by newspapers in Central Europe, ended with light sentences and acquittals. Court cases against dozens of agents in Galicia in 1913–1914 also resulted in small fines or acquittals. And again, most of the accused were not Jewish. An in-depth investigation of the migration business by the Austrian Trade Ministry in 1913 reiterated some of the widely reported accusations against illegal practices by emigration agents. Yet the same report described migration as a "natural occurrence" that was driven by economic factors. The authors also conceded that the Austrian government could not police its borders effectively. Russian court files on smugglers contain information about their religious affiliation. According to a sample compiled by Börries Kuzmany, the author of a study about Brody, only 14 percent of 1,704 smugglers convicted by the Russian court in Radzivilov between 1885 and 1895 were Jewish. According to several contemporary accounts, Jewish and Christian smugglers worked in teams.[25]

Once migrants reached the German side of the border, they frequently boarded *Auswandererzüge*. In his 1930 memoir Bogen recalled his passage through Germany on such a train in 1891: "At Königsberg we were hustled into a car which I discovered was especially detailed for emigrant transportation. Order . . . regulations . . . maledictions. But there were Russians among us, and Poles . . . a new grouping. . . . [N]o longer were we discriminated against as Jews, thought I, but as emigrants. Again we belonged to a special species. . . . [B]ut the prize will be worth it." *Auswandererzüge* were introduced to better coordinate and regulate the mass migration and protect migrants from swindlers at train stations. In the mid-1880s the French steamship line Compagnie Générale Transatlantique—originally founded by the Pereire brothers—chartered such trains to take migrants from Basel in

Switzerland to the port in Le Havre, sparing them the hassle of having to figure out how to travel with their luggage from the Gare de l'Est to the Gare Saint-Lazare in central Paris. Making such connections in most European railroad hubs and in American cities was challenging because few cities had a central train station. To this day terminus stations are the legacy of privately funded railroad lines. In Paris, London, Vienna, Leipzig, Berlin, and New York exhausted migrants had to use public transportation. They had to watch their belongings carefully and ensure that small children did not get lost. In Britain migrants crossing from North Sea ports such as Hull in Yorkshire to Liverpool or between London and Southampton traveled on regular trains but were accompanied by agents representing the steamship lines or railroad companies. To ensure migrants did not get lost, they pinned to their clothing a piece of paper with the name of the steamship line or their destination. The larger train stations in London had separate waiting facilities for migrants.[26]

By the early 1880s Berlin's train stations were bursting at the seams because midcentury urban planners had not anticipated the dramatic growth of passenger traffic. The first complaints about social disorder caused by transmigrants at Berlin train stations can be traced to this period. In December 1891 the Prussian state railroad administration established the *Auswandererbahnhof* (emigrant train station) in Ruhleben in suburban Berlin, described so hauntingly by Maryashe Antin. Before disinfection facilities were installed in 1893, the main purpose of Ruhleben was simply to relieve congestion at Berlin's train stations. *Auswandererzüge* allowed migrants to reach the ports faster and more efficiently, reducing the costs for food and accommodation along the way. The *Auswandererzüge* also contributed to more efficient capacity management of the steamship lines. In 1905 the journey from Myslowitz to Hamburg usually took a little less than twenty-four hours, from Eydtkuhnen to Ruhleben about twenty-one hours, and from Ruhleben to Hamburg or Bremen eight hours.[27]

Russian and Austrian migrants who traveled from Oświęcim via Prague and Nuremberg to Bremen or Hamburg had to switch train stations in the Saxon city of Leipzig. At Leipzig's Bavarian train station employees of HAPAG and NDL received the arriving migrants. Women and children were dispatched by tram to Leipzig's northern Magdeburg station, while the men had to walk more than a mile through Leipzig's busy center. Kiliszewki noted in a 1905 report that many were hauling large suitcases and boxes. At the northern train station, physicians employed by the steamship lines examined the migrants. The Red Star and Holland-America Line accommodated their passengers in hotels to provide them with some rest before continuing the journey to Antwerp or Rotterdam. Food provisions were included in the passage price. On a day in mid-November 1905, Kiliszewki recorded more than six hundred migrants passing through Leipzig's small registration station.[28]

Migrants from Southeastern Europe usually traveled via Budapest, Vienna, and Leipzig. In the Austrian capital they arrived at one of the southern stations or the large northern station, which served the eastern half of the empire and was located in the Leopoldstadt district, where most Jewish migrants from Galicia settled after 1880. As in other cities, migrants were taken to cheap hostels for the night and were able to settle outstanding balances for the passage at an office representing the steamship line. They were then directed to the train station to catch the appropriate train. During these stopovers in cities on both sides of the Atlantic, pickpockets and conmen preyed on disoriented migrants. The Hamburg State Archive contains extensive material about criminals cheating migrants. New York's Castle Garden facility and the surrounding area were notorious for theft and various schemes to cheat arriving "greenhorns." For this reason, sealed trains and closed facilities like the Hamburg *Auswandererhallen* and Ellis Island were designed to ensure a more orderly flow of larger numbers of people and protect them from abuse in an unfamiliar setting.[29]

The decision to move New York's immigration station offshore relieved Manhattan and Brooklyn of increasing congestion. Before 1910 no bridge or tunnel connected New Jersey and Manhattan, and commuters, travelers, and migrants had to cross the Hudson River by ferry. Several train stations serving points west of the city were located in Jersey City and Hoboken. New York's Penn Station and the railroad tunnels under the Hudson and East rivers connecting Manhattan with New Jersey and Brooklyn—a fraught and controversial construction project—were not completed until 1910. After 1892 many migrants never stepped into Manhattan or Brooklyn; after the registration and examination procedure, they were taken from Ellis Island by ferry to the nearby Central Railroad of New Jersey terminal in Jersey City. The commuter terminal became a major gateway to the American interior for thousands of immigrants.[30]

Canada was a major transit country for European migrants. Before 1900 a majority of Europeans arriving at Canadian ports headed to the United States. Passengers traveling to cities in the Great Lakes region often disembarked in Halifax, Saint John (New Brunswick), Quebec City, or Montreal, continuing by train. Some migrants remained in Canada for weeks or even years before moving on. The number of Polish and Ukrainian migrants settling in Canada increased after 1900, when the Canadian government launched a recruiting drive to boost agricultural settlement in the interior provinces. The recruitment of Eastern Europeans coincided with Canada's shift to Chinese exclusion. During the second half of the nineteenth century the Canadian Pacific Railway (CPR) hired Chinese labor migrants to complete Canada's first transcontinental rail line. Thousands toiled in the Rocky Mountains under extremely challenging conditions for meager pay. In 1881 CPR launched its own steamship line to derive additional profits from the transpacific labor migration.

After its lobbying efforts against Canadian Chinese exclusion bills had failed in 1902–1903, CPR shifted its focus to the European market by acquiring the Beaver Line, which operated services between British and Canadian ports. Steamship services on the Atlantic fed passengers onto CPR's eastern railroad network. A growing number were Polish and Ukrainian peasants traveling to the Canadian interior. In 1912 CPR was drawn into a conflict between Austrian officials over emigration. The Austrian military wanted to prevent the migration of young men from Galicia, opposing efforts by the Trade Ministry to boost traffic from Trieste, the single Austrian overseas port. After CPR steamers began serving Trieste in 1912, supporters of a restrictive emigration policy leaked allegations about a secret conspiracy of Jewish ticket agents representing CPR. Allegedly these agents had assisted thousands of young Galician men to evade military service. In the fall months of 1913, the police searched the CPR office in Vienna and arrested dozens of ticket agents in the capital and in Galicia. The "Canadian Pacific Affair" triggered a more restrictive Austrian policy toward emigrants. Court cases in Galicia in early 1914 showed no evidence for an alleged Jewish conspiracy but indicated that migration resulted from a lack of economic opportunities and widespread poverty. Most of the accused ticket agents, alleged draft dodgers, and smugglers were acquitted; a few who were convicted had to pay small fines.[31]

The journey to America was not a one-way street. Jewish remigration rates from the United States were lower than for Christians from the same regions of origin, but hardly negligible. In 1911 the German embassy in St. Petersburg reported that the return migration from the United States to Russia had increased greatly as the result of a recession in the United States. Those who had left without the required emigration passport relied on smugglers to take them back to Russia. In 1913 HIAS recorded over 126,000 Jewish immigrants and more than 11,000 return migrants. The latter number was an estimate because return migrants were not formally registered. It is doubtful whether HIAS's assessment that most return migrants had failed to adapt to the economic conditions was accurate. In 1913 the booming American economy attracted a record number of migrants. It is likely that many return migrants had not planned to settle permanently in the United States. Others traveled back to look for a partner and visit relatives. The commoditization of long-distance travel made repeat journeys possible, especially between large ports with frequent service. In 1892 Abraham Cahan visited London at least twice to give speeches and meet with Socialist allies. At the time he was still a rising journalist. Later, when he had become a major media entrepreneur, Cahan frequently traveled to Europe.[32]

Meeting Actual Migrants

In 1896 Cahan published a pioneering novella in English about average Jewish immigrants, *Yekl: A Tale of the New York Ghetto*. For the plot Cahan drew on his extensive journalistic work on the Lower East Side. Yekl, the recently arrived protagonist, works in a sweatshop. As "Jake" he quickly adapts to the rapidly transforming city and socializes with his female coworkers. He becomes indifferent to religion. The arrival of his observant wife, Gitl, and their child throws Yekl/Jake into an existential crisis. Unwilling to accept responsibility as a father and husband, he rejects his family. Cahan did not idealize his characters but sketched them as relatable figures. *Yekl* is an ethnographic portrait of an immigrant neighborhood in transition. Cahan reminded his readers of the diverse backgrounds of the Jewish residents of the Lower East Side and provided insights into their living and working conditions.[33] Together with Antin's memoir, *Yekl* is one of a small number of contemporary publications whose authors introduced readers to actual immigrants. Cahan sought to dispel widespread, often crude stereotypes associated with immigrant masses. Likewise, readers could connect with Antin's riveting account of her journey and the emotional stress Yekl and his wife experienced. *From Plotzk to Boston* and *Yekl* enhanced their authors' reputations, but neither book was a bestseller.

With his 1908 play, *The Melting-Pot*, Anglo-Jewish writer Israel Zangwill reached a far wider audience. During the 1880s Zangwill, whose parents hailed from Latvia, developed a genuine interest in the life world of Jewish migrants in London and New York. In 1892 he published *Children of the Ghetto*, an ethnographic novel about Jewish life in London's East End. The successful book clearly inspired Cahan's *Yekl*. Zangwill helped Antin to publish *From Plotzk to Boston*. In a short foreword he noted that Antin provided a rare perspective on the "inner feelings of the people themselves." In Zangwill's *The Melting-Pot* America features as the great redeemer, the place where immigrants shed their past, their hatreds, and their loyalties to form a new society. The play became an instant hit on the Broadway stage. The debate about the melting pot metaphor has obscured one of Zangwill's original intentions, to counter the rising anti-immigrant sentiment and antisemitism in Britain and the United States. *The Melting-Pot* portrayed Jewish and other immigrants as decent and hard-working men and women with great promise—quintessential Americans.[34]

Early literary works and other texts about Jewish (im)migrants reflect a growing interest among urban reformers in the actual background of newly arriving immigrants. The Jewish migration was part of a much larger movement from Europe to the Americas. Most migrants found low-paid industrial jobs and settled in inner-city neighborhoods in proximity to their workplaces. After 1890 urban reformers in the United States and Britain, who belonged overwhelmingly to the Protestant establishment, began to compile social surveys about working-class neighborhoods to address systemic poverty. The surveys reflect the growing commitment of elected officials and reformers on both sides of the Atlantic to employ new scientific methods to better understand the impact of dramatic social and economic changes in industrial cities. Pioneering Progressive social workers like Jane Addams, who cofounded Chicago's Hull House Settlement in 1889, struggled to comprehend the diverse backgrounds and cultural traditions of immigrants. Even established Jews who had immigrated from Central Europe often knew little about their coreligionists hailing from distant parts of Eastern Europe.

The first comprehensive study of Jewish immigration in the United States by a Jewish author, *The Russian Jew in the United States* (1905), reflects the analytical approach of the social surveys. Its editor, Charles S. Bernheimer, the son of Jewish immigrants from southern Germany, grew up in New York and worked at the Jewish Publication Society, which had been founded to help Americanize Jewish immigrants. Even though Bernheimer was part of the establishment, he sought to give a voice to the actual immigrants and provide a more multilayered view of the social and economic conditions in

Jewish immigrant neighborhoods in New York, Chicago, and Philadelphia. Among the authors he recruited were already well-known figures, including publicist Henrietta Szold and Abraham Cahan. Bernheimer based the study on dozens of published statistics, general social surveys, and articles from periodicals and newspapers. Yiddish journalist Peter Wiernik contributed a detailed chapter about Jewish life in the Russian Empire. In his contribution about Russian Jews in America, Cahan rejected widely held stereotypes to show how Jewish immigrants were becoming Americans. He recounted the names of recently arrived Jews who had volunteered for the U.S. Army and died on the battlefield in the war with Spain. He deplored Jewish involvement in New York's notorious machine politics but stressed that it showed that Jews were not isolating themselves from American society, as outside observers often claimed.[35]

In contrast to the large issues of immigrants and immigration, mundane journeys attracted little interest from contemporaries. Among the few exceptions is a reportage that was published in early 1914 in a German Jewish weekly. The author, Jacob Lestschinsky, was a migrant himself, born in 1876 in Horodyshche, a town close to Cherkasy in central Ukraine. Like many young Jewish men and women from this region, he left his observant home in 1896 for the bustling Black Sea port Odessa. There, he completed his secondary school education and became a Zionist. In 1901 he spent a semester studying social sciences and philosophy at the University of Bern before settling in Warsaw. Expelled by the Russian authorities in 1910 for his leftist political activities, he moved to Switzerland, where he attended classes at the University of Zurich but did not earn a diploma. Before leaving Zurich in 1912 he married a fellow Jewish migrant. After the birth of a daughter in his wife's central Ukrainian hometown, the family settled in Vilna in 1913.

Journalism served as Lestschinsky's main source of income, allowing him to publish scholarly articles about Jewish social and economic life. He had a special interest in migration. As a freelance journalist Lestschinsky had to unearth newsworthy material to pique the interest of editors and readers. In 1913 (or possibly in 1912) he traveled to the East Prussian border to interview Jews traveling to America, then followed the migrants to Bremen and Hamburg. "Unsere Emigranten" (Our Emigrants) was serialized in the *Israelitisches Familienblatt*, a German Jewish weekly. To avoid provoking the paper's bourgeois readers, Lestschinsky, a committed Marxist with Zionist sympathies, devoted much space to his actual conversations with migrants.

The title—"*Our* Emigrants"—was an implicit appeal to German Jews to embrace the migrants.[36]

Lestschinsky was struck that he encountered almost as many children, old people, and women as younger men. The available data collected by Liebmann Hersch for his 1913 dissertation corroborate this observation.[37] Lestschinsky had expected to hear complaints about hunger, political repression, and persecution in Russia. Instead, the migrants looked forward to a better life in America. They were seeking economic stability for themselves and their children. Several were aware that by moving from the Russian Pale to the United States they were taking their emancipation into their own hands. In Russia they were subjects of the tsar, deprived of basic rights. In America, the men would be full citizens and able to vote, even, Lestschinsky added, for a Jewish president. A young woman stressed that it mattered greatly to her that she and her children would belong to an inclusive society. Lestschinsky was surprised and moved by these statements. Referring to the exodus of the people of Israel from Egypt, he commented, "A ray of the distant, distant rising sun, and the slaves of yesterday will breathe as free people like faithful children will the love their new fatherland, the land of their children."[38]

Appearances were misleading. Contemporary press reports often highlighted the strange dress and shabby clothes of migrants in stereotypical fashion. Only rarely did observers talk with individual migrants. A party of Jews Lestschinsky encountered near the border in East Prussia looked disheveled and dirty; conversations revealed that the group had just hiked through dense forests with a smuggler to avoid Russian border guards. The individual stories Lestschinsky recorded provide a rare glimpse at the challenges and crises before and during the journey. Most of his interviewees were women, often with small children in their arms or clutching their hands and skirts.

As a recently married father of an infant daughter and as a native Yiddish speaker, Lestschinsky could connect with the migrants. In Bremen he noticed a young woman traveling with a toddler and her fifty-year-old mother. According to the older woman, a widow, they were hoping to join her son-in-law in America, although he had not sent any letters since his departure. They did not even know where he lived. She hoped one of her brothers in America would take them in. But now they were stranded in Bremen for lack of money. The widow, sensing an opportunity, attempted to persuade the journalist—a complete stranger—to marry her daughter. Lestschinsky politely explained to the exasperated woman that he was not drawing up a

Ketubah (a Jewish marriage contract) but taking notes. Even though she did not have many years left, the older woman exclaimed, "Let me go! Let me see America!"[39]

In Deutsch-Eylau (Illawa), an East Prussian border town, he met several Jews who complained bitterly about smugglers overcharging them. A young mother from a town in Volhynia shared her story with Lestschinsky. As a sixteen-year-old she had been matched with an older artisan who struggled to make a living. He left for America when she was pregnant with their second child. No letters came from him, not even to ask about the second child (a daughter). Finally, he sent tickets for herself and the two children. With her children and two young women from her town she boarded a train to Warsaw. In Ivangorod (Deblin) gendarmes arrested her two travel companions—possibly for leaving their hometown without the required official permit. Only after much pleading did they allow her and her children to continue to Warsaw. Overwhelmed by the big city, tired and hungry, she lost her way and failed to locate the agent for the journey across the border. After making the decision to return home the completely exhausted woman fainted at the train station. When she came to, she realized that somebody had stolen her money. Somehow, she and her children made it home.

The Jews in the town raised money for new tickets because she was too embarrassed to ask her husband for help. On her second attempt she found the agent in Warsaw. He assembled a small party of Jewish migrants and took them to a meeting place near the border. After waiting for days, the group set out hiking through the forest toward the border with a local Jewish smuggler. In darkness the drunken smuggler and his Polish helpers rushed the group of frightened women and crying small children through creeks and even a small lake, locking the wet, freezing, and hungry migrants in small huts during the day until they finally reached the Prussian side of the border. The woman was astounded that a small creek was the actual border. "Why did we have to suffer so much, if it was so easy to walk across the border?"[40] The women Lestschinsky interviewed talked openly about their feelings. The extended migration imposed severe strains on young families. Often migrants wrote or talked about their journeys weeks, if not years after the completion of the actual journey, when emotions had faded. Only a few recollections, for instance David Milstein's account of the *Volturno* disaster, evoke similar expressions of existential fear and hope.

For Lestschinky the migrants' experiences contained an important lesson. The expectations migrants attached to citizenship and economic mobility in

America and not least their awareness that they could exercise agency and start a new life elsewhere questioned his deterministic Marxist view of social and economic change. He concluded that migration and migrants were distinct topics. Jewish migration could not exclusively be studied and discussed as an "abstract issue" without taking the actual migrants, their emotions, fears, subjective expectations, and agency, into account.[41] Lestschinsky was hardly the first author who recognized that field research produced unexpected results and added a perspective that statistical analysis of demographic data, the preferred approach of scholars examining migration in this period, did not convey. Lestschinky did not mention non-Jewish migrants, yet his insight to carefully distinguish between migration and migrants transcends the specific experiences and circumstances of Jewish migrants he interviewed. The decisions of individual migrants often do not conform with overarching structural explanations and models that take general economic and political factors into account.

5
Protective Umbrella
The Transnational Jewish Support Network

In early 1894 the Antin family, traveling from their hometown of Polotzk to Boston, reached the same border crossing at Kibarty-Eydtkuhnen that Bernard Horwich had passed almost twenty years earlier. They had carefully planned the long journey. Mary Antin's mother, Esther, had procured Russian passports, sparing her and her children the nighttime hike across the border. Esther's husband, Israel Pinchus, had sent prepaid steamship tickets to his family. But Esther had not anticipated that the legal crossing of the border carried its own risks. In Eydtkuhnen uniformed Prussian officials and a physician boarded the train. After a short discussion they refused passage to the Antins, even though they carried valid third-class steamship tickets issued by HAPAG. The most likely reason for the decision was the subject of intense negotiations between the German steamship lines and the Prussian government at that very moment. In 1892, in the wake of the Hamburg cholera outbreak, the Prussian government officially closed the border with the Russian Empire. This decision voided the 1887 agreement with the steamship lines that exempted HAPAG and NDL passengers from the requirement to carry enough funds in cash for funding an involuntary return journey. Like most migrants, Antin's mother did not have sufficient cash to cover a possible return journey. She was desperate. Her children were scared. Mary Antin wrote, "We were homeless, houseless, and friendless in a strange place. We had hardly money enough to last us through the voyage for which we had hoped and waited for three long years."[1]

There was a ray of hope, however. Esther's pleading moved one of the Prussian officials. He advised her to look for Herr Schidorsky in the small Russian border town of Kibarty. After returning to the Russian side of the border the Antins quickly found his house. Outside, several other migrants were already waiting. Soon Schidorsky arrived. He told the migrants not to worry, he would get them across the border. The next day, the Antins boarded another train and encountered the same Prussian officials. This time Esther stated, as carefully instructed, that they were visiting Herr Schidorsky in Eydtkuhnen, the Prussian border town. The officials, clearly aware that this was a white lie, granted them passage, tacitly acknowledging the protection by the Jewish support network.

Mary Antin recorded the helper's name correctly. Bernhard Schidorsky lived in Eydtkuhnen, where he owned a small carriage business and was a respected member of the small Jewish community. Volunteers like Schidorsky who looked after migrants on a daily basis were an indispensable component of a loosely coordinated global network of Jewish aid workers and volunteers. This decentralized and barely visible network of helpers at the most critical points of passage along major transit routes in and beyond Europe was remarkably effective and benefited all migrants, not just Jews.[2]

Dealing with State Officials

By the 1890s Jewish helpers were stationed at border checkpoints, train stations, ports on both sides of the Atlantic (and beyond) from Ellis Island and other U.S. immigration stations to Buenos Aires and Cape Town, and at the main destinations. Jewish aid associations coordinated their activities, but migrants were usually supported by the local community. This explains why, before 1914, American Jews were not involved in providing assistance in Europe: they primarily cared for arriving Jews. In addition to local communities' efforts, several newly formed national associations began to assist migrants after 1880. In 1903 the U.S. federal government specifically requested that the National Council of Jewish Women (NCJW) address white slavery and protect Jewish women traveling on their own. Two years later NCJW opened a small office on Ellis Island. The New York-based Hebrew Sheltering and Immigrant Aid Society became the most important association overseeing the support for arriving migrants. HIAS started out in 1881 as a shelter on Manhattan's Lower East Side for recently arrived Jews without means. It gradually expanded, following several mergers with other organizations. Whereas NCJW was run by women married to established businessmen, the founders and leaders of HIAS were themselves Jewish migrants from Eastern Europe. HIAS showed great sensitivity in addressing migrants' religious needs. After 1902 a HIAS branch ensured a traditional religious burial for Jews who died on Ellis Island or during the sea journey. HIAS also organized religious services and Passover seders for migrants detained at Ellis Island. In 1904 the organization posted its first permanent representative at Ellis Island, the Yiddish writer and journalist Alexander Harkavy. In 1909 he was replaced by social worker Irving Lipsitch.[3]

The case of a young man who was detained at Ellis Island demonstrates why the presence of Jewish helpers mattered. In the spring of 1913, a young Jewish immigrant from Odessa walked up to an immigration inspector at Ellis Island. He presented a Russian passport and stated that his name was Lebi Zinowoi. The inspector asked him in Yiddish, "You are 22 years old? You came from Odessa? You are a clerk? You paid your own passage? You have $20?" Zinowoi confirmed all this was true. The inspector then accused him of lying, claiming to possess information that Zinowoi was a felon. He nevertheless promised to admit him if he told the truth. Eventually Zinowoi conceded he had served time in prison. He was detained and hauled before the Board of Special Inquiry, which decided to deport him because he was a convict. After the verdict was announced Lipsitch was able to speak with the detainee, who told him that he had deserted from the Russian army and procured the passport of the real Zinowoi to leave the country as quickly as possible. Lipsitch promised to help the migrant. After the board rejected an appeal, Lipsitch brought the case to the attention of the secretary of labor in Washington. An investigation confirmed that the immigrant was not a convict, and after a nine-week detention he was freed.

Why did the migrant not state his real name instead of presenting a passport he needed only to leave Russia? The passport was almost certainly the only identification he possessed, but it had been issued to another person. Carrying any document proving his actual identity would have blown his cover before leaving Russia; therefore, the steamship ticket had probably been issued to Zinowoi. HIAS presented this case to denounce the "questionable methods" used by immigration inspectors, who labeled migrants "convicts" knowing that many young Russian deserters used false passports to avoid draconian punishment. The case of young Jews and others fleeing military recruitment also illustrates why the experiences of migrants frequently transcend simple categorizations. Young men trying to evade recruitment are often not recognized as refugees, but they are also not "economic migrants." HIAS deplored the fact that too many deserving men and women were "barred out, in sight of the Statue of Liberty."[4]

Before 1914 U.S. inspectors often were the first state officials Eastern European migrants encountered. Without a permit to leave their hometown or a document exempting them from military service, young men went to great lengths to avoid the police and other government officials before reaching the German border. During transit, steamship lines and ticket agencies oversaw the transportation and accommodation of migrants. The Zinowoi case was one of dozens that HIAS, the American Jewish Committee, and non-Jewish immigrant associations contested during the second tenure of William Williams as commissioner of Ellis Island between 1909 and 1914. Williams was a capable reformer, but he favored immigration restrictions and took a harsh line against "undesirables," especially those possessing less than the required cash amount. The cases HIAS and other Jewish aid associations litigated show the limits of Williams's power. Fewer than 2 percent of migrants who passed through Ellis Island before 1914 were refused admission.[5]

After 1880 Jewish communities in Germany, especially in Hamburg, Bremen, and Berlin, established a close rapport with the steamship lines and local state officials. Jewish communities often covered the costs for involuntary return migrants. In 1899 the Hamburg police authority went out of its way to praise the Jewish assistance committee for providing kosher food and clothing to Jewish migrants in the port. The authorities would be "sorely disappointed" if the committee dissolved. The provision of support gave Jewish representatives some leverage to lobby on behalf of migrants like the Antins. Adam McKeown, the author of a study about global migration restrictions targeting Chinese migrants, has noted that the Jewish migrant protection system in Europe was aligned with state policies. This is accurate and hardly surprising. Humanitarian organizations and private businesses risk sanctions and even bans if they violate existing legal rules. McKeown underrates the soft power of nonstate actors before 1914. Jewish aid associations and the German steamship lines relieved the Prussian state of a substantial financial burden by ensuring the smooth transit of hundreds of thousands of migrants every year. Public-private partnerships allowed nonstate actors to mitigate the impact of official decisions.[6]

A major reason why state officials embraced Jewish aid associations was related to the rising number of destitute migrants who were stranded along the transit routes after the mid-1880s. While their numbers were negligible in relative terms, thousands of migrants sought financial support from Jewish communities and migrant aid associations in Germany and other transit countries after 1880. In the early 1880s, and again in the early 1890s, the existing support system could barely cope. Jewish aid workers tried to convince those with insufficient funds to return home, usually after providing them with food and a train ticket rather than cash. A persistent problem was professional beggars claiming to be migrants. Aid committees often sent suspicious men and women to local Jewish communities, which maintained and exchanged extensive databases of vagrants. The files of Danzig's Jewish community contain dozens of printed lists with profiles of particularly notorious individuals and their different aliases that were distributed across Prussia. The lists from the decade before 1914 indicate that most vagrants were not Jewish. In 1910 German Jews founded a central office to address vagrancy. American Jewish communities also exchanged information about vagrants. Here too non-Jews tried to take advantage of the extensive Jewish support system for migrants.[7]

Little is known about migrants who were forced to return by state officials or steamship line employees. It is likely that more than a few tried again. In April 1905 a Jewish couple from Russia committed suicide at the Ostrowo control station on the Russian border with Germany, having been turned back because they lacked funds for a possible return journey. This case could easily be cited as an example of the abuse of transmigrants by Prussian officials and steamship line employees. But this appears to have been an isolated incident. The Hamburg emigration authorities carefully collected information about accidents and other disruptions migrants encountered during the journey to the port city. Jewish communities and aid associations usually assisted migrants who found themselves in serious trouble. For instance, in 1891 health officials detained a Jewish woman with three children at the Eydtkuhnen crossing because the family was visibly ill. Two children died in the nearby Insterburg hospital from diphtheria. The Insterburg Jewish community covered the cost of accommodation for the woman and the surviving child for several months, until her husband sent funds for the passage to America. Christian migrants did not enjoy a similar degree of protection. In 1907 Hamburg officials hospitalized a troubled woman from Poland and sent her two children to a local orphanage. The official in charge of the case remarked that the children were Catholic, almost certainly to probe whether a local church or the Jewish community might cover the cost for the return journey.[8]

Jewish aid associations did not support every Jewish migrant, however. In 1897 the London Board of Guardians informed the Hamburg government that it would return destitute women traveling with children, especially if they could not provide the address of their husbands in the United States. The predicaments of young women joining their husbands was a recurring theme in the reports of American Jewish aid associations. Extended periods of separation often led to estrangement and desertion. American Jewish aid associations and Yiddish newspapers frequently reported heart-wrenching stories about recently arrived women and their children who had been deserted by their husbands and fathers. Jewish husbands were no more prone to desert their wives than other migrants. The prominence of this issue demonstrates the importance Jewish communities attached to the protection of families. American Jewish communities and newspapers like the *Forverts* made concerted efforts to locate wife deserters. In the "Galerie fun Farshvundene Mener" (Gallery of Disappeared Husbands) the *Forverts* named and shamed Jewish men who deserted their wives. Locating husbands also mattered because Orthodox women required formal permission from their husbands to obtain a divorce before they could remarry.[9]

Women who traveled on their own often were questioned and even detained because immigration inspectors suspected young women traveling alone of being prostitutes. American and European Jewish aid associations played a prominent role in the fight against "white slavery." Bertha Pappenheim, an Austrian Jewish social worker and pioneering figure of the Jewish women's movement, helped to organize several international conferences to prevent the trafficking of Jewish and other young women. Jewish communities on both sides of the Atlantic exchanged information about suspicious individuals and worked with local police forces.[10]

Jewish aid associations funded the journeys of migrants only in rare cases. To prevent the "dumping" of destitute men and women, the United States made any effort to encourage and finance migration illegal in 1891. Jewish and other migrant aid associations printed fliers explaining this rule. In European ports of embarkation aid workers advised migrants that they would have to prove they could support themselves and prove who had paid for their transportation. American officials suspected Jewish aid societies of covering the cost for steamship passages circumventing the law. When the Dillingham Commission investigated this matter around 1910, U.S. immigration inspectors posing as migrants could not find any evidence for financial assistance provided by Jewish communities or aid associations in Central and Eastern Europe. The only exception was the Jewish Colonization Association, which financed journeys to agricultural colonies in Argentina. And Jewish aid associations frequently *did* fund the cost for involuntary return journeys.

Jewish aid associations supported migrants who had to interrupt their journeys for reasons beyond their control. For instance, in 1911 dozens of Jewish and other return migrants from the Russian Empire were stranded at the Dutch-German border and in Rotterdam because the German authorities refused to admit them for the transit journey. The migrants had traveled with the small British Uranium steamship line, which did not cover the cost of the train ticket. To put pressure on the unwelcome competitor, HAPAG alerted the Prussian government, which ordered border officials to refuse passage to Russian return migrants without tickets. During the involuntary sojourn Rotterdam's Jewish Montefiore Association cared for the stranded migrants. After the Uranium Line agreed to cover the cost and organize the repatriation of its passengers the Prussian government lifted the ban. This example illustrates that Jewish aid associations could act relatively quickly and assist larger groups, especially at major points of passage like Rotterdam, Hamburg, and New York.[11]

What motivated American Jews and their coreligionists in transit countries to spend substantial sums for the assistance and protection of Jewish migrants? Much of the literature emphasizes concerns about antisemitic discrimination and the reputation of the local Jewish community. An efficient support system ensured that no one could blame Jewish communities for problems associated with Jewish migrants. The discussions during the 1869 Berlin conference confirm this view. However, helpers like Schidorsky acted out of genuine compassion and sincere commitment. Rülf's stereotypical view of unproductive Litvaks gave way to a more nuanced understanding of the actual living conditions and aspirations of Lithuanian Jews. Violent attacks and legal restrictions imposed on Jews in the Russian Empire and Romania and reports about extreme poverty in the Austrian province of Galicia contributed to a growing consensus among Western Jews that changes were unlikely. Indeed, many wondered whether Jewish life in the Russian Empire and Romania was viable in the long term. Baron de Hirsch's bold declaration in 1891 to resettle more than 3 million Russian Jews reflects concern about the physical safety of Jews. The view of Jewish representatives in different countries that Jewish migration was not a problem, but a solution, albeit one requiring careful management, influenced a reorganization of the Jewish support system for migrants around the turn of the century.[12]

Changing of the Guard

In the spring of 1891, a decade after the Brody crisis, the decentralized Jewish support system faced a new serious test when Jewish migration from the Russian Empire surged unexpectedly to unprecedented levels. The increase was widely associated with expulsions of Jews from St. Petersburg and Moscow. However, few of the Jews seeking help actually hailed from the imperial cities. As in 1881–1882, news reports and rumors caused a large number of ill-prepared migrants to head to the border, hoping they would receive funds for the journey to Western Europe or America. This time, German Jews were able to carry much of the burden on their own. The Berlin Jewish community led the effort to organize the Deutsches Central-Komitee für die Russischen Juden (German Central Committee for the Russian Jews). The Berlin office coordinated the work of newly formed committees along the border and the main transit routes. The organization successfully raised funds and reached out to the Alliance Israélite Universelle and aid associations in Britain and the United States. The border committees were tasked to examine and move migrants quickly to prevent the erection of visible encampments. Migrants who were unlikely to be admitted by U.S. immigration inspectors or were judged to be vagrants were refused support; instead, they received train tickets to their hometowns. Aid workers accompanied the others from the border to the ports, where local committee members directed them to the steamship line offices.

The number of migrants increased further during the spring and summer of 1892, until a severe recession in the United States led to a gradual decrease in 1893–1894. As in previous years, the majority of Jewish migrants did not require or ask for support. The main factor driving the increase was growing demand for jobs in the United States. A member of the aid committee in the East Prussian town of Insterburg observed that two-thirds of the fifty thousand or so Jews who passed the Kibarty-Eydtkuhnen border crossing in 1892 and 1893 carried enough funds for the journey.[13]

An outbreak of cholera in Hamburg during the summer of 1892 exacerbated the crisis. Prussian attempts to clamp down on transmigration from the Russian Empire had only limited effect, but the closure of Hamburg's port and the American blockade against passenger vessels from Europe stranded thousands of migrants in European ports in late 1892 and early 1893. A major calamity was avoided only because the rate of migration usually declined during the winter months. And thanks to news coverage, an unknown number of migrants delayed their journeys. The cholera outbreak coincided with ominous political developments in Germany. To tap rising support for antisemitism, the influential Conservative Party adopted an openly antisemitic platform in December 1892. The move backfired. In the June 1893 elections the Conservatives registered only modest gains, but radical antisemitic parties increased their share of the vote. The left-of-center Liberal Party, which most German Jewish voters backed, suffered losses. Relatively few German Jews backed the left-wing Social Democratic Party, which also won more seats. The party explicitly opposed antisemitism but appeared too radical for mostly bourgeois German Jews before 1914. The decline of political liberalism and the rise of radical antisemitic parties increased the pressure on German Jewish leaders to coordinate a sustained response. Antisemitic and Conservative politicians demanded the closure of Germany's eastern border and a total ban on Jewish migration. As a result, Jewish communities debated how to handle the crisis.[14]

Jewish migrants from the Russian and Austro-Hungarian empires overwhelmingly moved to the United States; most traveled through Germany. Both countries were home to the largest Jewish communities outside of Eastern Europe and the Ottoman Empire. Yet the provision of aid for transmigrants was largely managed by the metropolitan Jewish communities in Paris and London. Before the turn of the century no other organization could match the Alliance Israélite Universelle. Over four decades the Paris-based organization built a network of contacts to state officials and far-flung Jewish communities and accumulated valuable professional knowledge. The Alliance could tap a large donor base, especially in Germany. Most Jews in Britain and France lived in their respective capital city, where a small number of affluent businessmen coordinated the affairs of the local Jewish community—and transnational aid provision. The much larger and growing Jewish populations in the United States and Germany were more dispersed and less connected. Between the 1840s and 1880s strong internal migration and natural growth boosted Jewish communities in Berlin, Frankfurt, and other German cities. In the United States, mass immigration began to dramatically transform Jewish life after the 1860s. The arrival of new migrants fueled religious and class divisions, hampering efforts to build overarching organizations until the early twentieth century. Shortly after 1900 German and American Jews set up professional organizations that took a more sustained approach to assisting Jewish migrants. They also coordinated effective lobbying strategies to rally political support against migration restrictions in various countries on both sides of the Atlantic. Thanks to a much larger donor base, German and American aid organizations quickly sidelined their French and British predecessors.

Most Jews living in the new German state opposed forming national organizations outside of the religious sphere to avoid raising suspicions that they lacked loyalty. The growing sway of political antisemitism in the early 1890s initiated a rethinking and led to the founding of the Centralverein deutscher Staatsbürger jüdischen Glaubens (Central Association of German Citizens of the Jewish Faith) in March 1893. This professional lobbying organization protected Jews from public attacks and coordinated legal responses. The name reflects an explicit commitment to German citizenship.[15] Among the Centralverein members who expressed support for an organization that would assist Jewish transmigrants was the left-liberal journalist Paul Nathan. He proposed founding a German Jewish association that resembled the Alliance. The Dreyfus Affair in 1894–1895 convinced him to act.

Nathan believed that German Jews, as members of the largest Jewish community outside of Eastern Europe, had special responsibility to protect Jews in Russia, Romania, and the Ottoman Empire against persecution and discrimination. The rise of organized Zionism also influenced Nathan. Like most members of the Jewish establishment in Germany and the United States, Nathan opposed Zionism. But he also saw Herzl and his allies as potential rivals in addressing the social and economic crisis in Russia. A renewed surge of Jewish migration in 1900 raised fears about a dramatic crisis. At a 1901 meeting in Breslau, Jewish community leaders from Germany and Austria expressed concern about the potential of unprecedented Jewish migration from Galicia. A delegate from Lemberg reported that the "misery" in rural areas could not be described in words: "700,000 Galician Jews will one day scream for bread." The fear of another Brody crisis was palpable. Paul Laskar, the head of the Hamburg Unterstützungsverein (a support association), demanded that the delegates tone down the discussion of Jewish emigration because it might encourage thousands of poor Galician Jews to embark on the journey expecting support from Jewish communities in Central Europe.[16]

The founding of the Hilfsverein der Deutschen Juden (Aid Association of the German Jews) in 1901 reflected growing confidence that German Jews should and could resolve seemingly intractable social and political problems. The founding charter emphasized a commitment to German and German Jewish interests. The Hilfsverein declared it would work "hand in hand" with its older sister organizations in Paris, London, and Vienna. This statement was sincere. However, like the Alliance and the Anglo-Jewish Association, the Hilfsverein aligned its projects with the foreign policy agenda of its government. The Alliance focused its work on the Levant and the Maghreb, teaching French to hundreds of Jewish children who lived in French colonies or in territories the French government considered important. The leaders of the Hilfsverein regularly consulted with the German Foreign Office. The main Hilfsverein projects were located in the Russian Empire, Galicia, Romania, Bulgaria, and Palestine. The organization funded, equipped, and managed technical schools and organized job-training schemes in Romania, Bulgaria, and Galicia. Its prestige project was a state-of-the-art technical college in Haifa. Within a few years the Hilfsverein became the main European clearinghouse for Jewish migrants. The organization's membership expanded from two thousand in 1902 to over twenty-seven thousand in 1913, giving the organization considerable financial heft.[17]

During the first decade of the new century American Jews also took steps to overhaul support for arriving migrants. In 1903 alone more than 100,000 Jews immigrated to the United States. At the same time, the anti-immigrant movement gained growing political clout. Rising violence against Jews in Russia and Romania and the likelihood of restrictive immigration legislation required more concerted and professional lobbying efforts. The American Jewish Committee (AJC), founded in 1906, represented primarily members of the affluent business establishment. Like the German Jewish Centralverein, AJC was a lobbying organization, but it also extended financial support to HIAS, whose members hailed overwhelmingly from Eastern Europe. Before 1914 HIAS assisted Jewish immigrants in New York and other American port cities. Beyond the ports hundreds of mutual aid associations, primarily *Landsmanshaftn*, and communal aid organizations supported new arrivals.[18]

Another new player was the Paris-based Jewish Colonization Association (JCA), which was founded in 1891 and linked support for migration with productivization, a long-standing objective of Jewish aid work on the communal level. JCA founder Baron de Hirsch opposed Socialism and Zionism. He sought to relocate Jews from the Russian Empire to safe locations where they would become self-sustaining farmers who over time would return the initial investment for the land and equipment to JCA. The corporate management philosophy of the organization reflects Hirsch's background as a railroad entrepreneur. By 1910 JCA maintained hundreds of small information bureaus across the Pale of Settlement. Its staff examined whether prospective colonists were suitable for farming. Those who were accepted received practical advice, assistance with the procurement of passports, and in a few cases financial support. JCA funded agricultural colonies in the Russian Empire, the United States, Canada, Palestine, and especially Argentina. Early on the Argentinian colonies suffered from a widening gap between Hirsch's vision of flourishing Jewish colonies and the reality on the ground. Already in the 1890s a growing number of colonists drifted to Buenos Aires. By 1920 more than 100,000 Jews lived in the capital city, representing the largest Jewish community in the southern hemisphere.

The Atlantic Rate War

The founding of the Hilfsverein in 1901 signals the shift to a more professional and sustained assistance for Jewish migrants. A major conflict between German and British steamship lines over the control of the passenger market in the Russian and Austro-Hungarian empires in 1904 shows why a professional organization like the Hilfsverein was more effective than behind-the-scenes lobbying by Jewish leaders. In 1903 the British Cunard Line canceled its membership in the North Atlantic Steamship Conference, also known as Continental Pool, which had been launched in January 1892 by HAPAG and NDL. The two lines retained over 70 percent of the continental European passenger market for themselves, yielding smaller shares to competitors in Western Europe. Pool agreements were common practice among transatlantic steamship lines to fix prices and market shares. The Cunard's membership in the Continental Pool gave it a small, largely symbolic share of the transatlantic passenger market from the European continent to North America. Different Pool agreements covered the British Isles and Scandinavia. Eastbound transatlantic traffic was not subject to Pool agreements.[19]

The Eastern European passenger market was large, and it was growing substantially just after 1900. The total number of registered immigrants in the United States increased from 562,000 between July 1, 1900, and June 30, 1901, to 850,000 in 1902–1903, an increase of more than 50 percent. In 1902–1903 slightly more than 200,000 immigrants originated in the Austro-Hungarian Empire (113,000 in 1900–1901) and more than 130,000 in the Russian Empire (85,000 in 1900–1901). Only Italy exceeded these numbers; in 1902–1903 230,000 Italians moved to the United States (135,000 in 1900–1901). Immigrants from these three countries represented almost 70 percent of the total American immigration in 1902–1903. Based on their spoken language, in 1902–1903 76,000 immigrants were registered as "Hebrew," representing close to a tenth of total immigration. Most originated in the Russian and Austro-Hungarian empires and crossed the Atlantic on HAPAG and NDL steamers. The Italian government restricted the business of foreign steamship lines; only steamship lines registered in Italy could transport steerage passengers from Italian ports. Eastern Europe was a different matter. It was no secret that trade officials in Vienna and Budapest tried to erode the German monopoly and were willing to assist steamship lines serving the Adriatic ports of Trieste and Fiume (Rijeka), which belonged to Austria and Hungary, respectively.[20]

The Continental Pool gave Cunard only a token share of the most lucrative passenger market in Europe. Soon after 1900 Cunard faced growing competition. In 1899 the influential American investor J. Pierpont Morgan gained control of several American and British steamship lines. In 1902 he founded a holding company, the International Mercantile Marine Company (IMM), and formed an informal alliance with HAPAG and NDL. After bringing major British lines under IMM's wing, including the esteemed White Star Line, IMM threatened to sideline Cunard in its home market. In 1902 IMM and the German lines took over the Rotterdam-based Holland America Line. And the Red Star Line, which had its main base in Antwerp, became part of IMM. Both lines belonged to the Continental Pool. In the same year Cunard barely averted a hostile takeover by the German lines and IMM. As the only remaining large British steamship line that was not controlled by foreign interests, Cunard reached out to the British government. To modernize its aging fleet—and protect jobs in British shipyards—Cunard secured a large subsidy to launch two giant ocean liners. The *Mauretania* and its sister ship, the ill-fated *Lusitania*, could accommodate more than two thousand passengers each and could make the westbound Atlantic crossing in less than six days.

To fill the berths on these ships Cunard had to find a backdoor into the large Eastern European market. As luck would have it, Hungary offered itself as a willing partner because the government in Budapest wanted to increase passenger and cargo traffic from Fiume (Rijeka) on the Adriatic coast. After failing to convince the German lines to serve Fiume, the Hungarians guaranteed Cunard a minimum of thirty thousand passengers annually. This promise appears puzzling. In 1903 Hungary announced one of the harshest emigration laws in Europe, requiring all men to seek formal permission to leave the country and restricting the business of ticket agents. The implementation was haphazard, however, and it was an open secret that the government in Budapest did not discourage the emigration of Croats, Slovaks, and other non-Hungarian speakers.[21]

In April 1904 Cunard advertised its New York service from Fiume, undercutting the price NDL typically charged for the passage from Bremen. In a letter to London's *Times*, HAPAG chief executive Albert Ballin described the Cunard service from Fiume as an attack on the Continental Pool and, as he freely admitted, on the monopoly of HAPAG and NDL. He accused the Hungarian government of apprehending migrants traveling to the German ports and forcing them to board Cunard steamers in Fiume. HAPAG and its partners would not remain idle but would fight back. Cunard chairman Lord Inverclyde rebuffed Ballin's statement, explaining why the aggressive strategy of its German (and American) competitors left Cunard no other choice. Cunard, as he put it, "had been on the defensive from first to last."[22]

The exchange in the pages of the *Times* in May 1904 was the opening salvo of an unprecedented price war on the North Atlantic passenger market. The conflict provides an intriguing perspective on transatlantic migration from Eastern Europe before 1914. Almost overnight, the prices for transatlantic passages, which had been fixed at high levels for years, fell dramatically, as the competing lines fought over market share. The benefits of the price war for passengers traveling in third-class or steerage, the cheapest class, appeared obvious. The price for a one-way steerage ticket from Bremen to New York on a fast steamer dropped from $40 to $33 and at one point to $16. In 1904 the number of Europeans moving to the United States increased sharply. Yet in contrast to the uneven business cycles of the U.S. economy, fluctuating ticket prices made only a limited impact on the momentous decision of most migrants to move to America. Rather than benefiting from low passage prices, Russian migrants with prepaid Cunard passages became pawns in the increasingly acrimonious conflict.[23]

It is not surprising that HAPAG and NDL aggressively fought any attempt to erode their monopoly. During the summer months of 1904 a quick resolution of the rate war appeared unlikely. Before 1904 holders of prepaid Cunard tickets had been protected by the line's membership in the Continental Pool. In response to the Hungarian government forcing NDL passengers to travel with Cunard via Fiume, HAPAG and NDL began to systematically reject passengers with Cunard tickets crossing Prussia's eastern border. This decision betrays an extraordinary lack of judgment on Ballin's part because the number of these passengers was relatively low, while the stakes in the conflict were high. Following the Japanese attack on Russian bases in Manchuria in early 1904, the Russian authorities began to draft young men to boost its troop contingents in the Far East. At the same time southern Ukraine witnessed an unprecedented rise in anti-Jewish violence following the notorious 1903 Kishinev pogrom. Even a cursory glance at Jewish newspapers in different parts of the world shows almost constant coverage of pogroms in Russia.

In the summer of 1904 left-wing papers in Germany began to blame Ballin for sacrificing the lives of young Russian deserters and Jewish pogrom victims to gain the upper hand in the rate war with Cunard. The Social Democratic daily *Vorwärts*, one of the most widely read German papers, relentlessly attacked the HAPAG chief executive, coining ever more polemic distortions of his name: "Ballin economy" (for the alleged exploitation of migrants), "Ballin press" (for liberal papers not sufficiently critical of HAPAG), and "Ballin bandits" (HAPAG employees on the border). In late August 1904, the *Vorwärts* sharply denounced the "ghastly Tsarist-Prussian-Ballinish emigration policy," claiming that HAPAG, Prussia, and the Russian tsar collaborated to exploit and abuse migrants.[24]

A seemingly unrelated event illustrates Ballin's ruthless side and explains why left-wing critics directed their attacks against him rather than NDL chief executive Heinrich Wiegand. The HAPAG annual report for 1904 provides a clue. Even though the rate war constituted a major "sacrifice," HAPAG announced a profit of 27 million Marks, for which its stockholders received a generous 9 percent dividend. In the same year NDL had to cut its dividend, Cunard ceased paying a dividend altogether, and J. P. Morgan's IMM reported a massive deficit. How could HAPAG not just compensate the losses in the transatlantic passenger division but realize a substantial profit? It was no secret that HAPAG had sold several older steamships to the Russian navy in 1903. The converted ships propped up Russia's Baltic fleet. In 1904 the Russian Admiralty approached HAPAG with an even more intriguing business proposal.[25]

Days after attacking Russian forces in Manchuria in February 1904, Japanese forces obliterated Russia's small Pacific fleet. To relieve the Japanese siege of Port Arthur (Dalian) the Russian Admiralty decided to reposition the Baltic fleet. The extremely risky and costly maneuver hinged on access to coal stations along the route around Africa, through the Indian Ocean, and through the South China Sea. Britain, which controlled most ports on this route, declined a Russian request to deliver coal. Like the German government, Whitehall did not want to be drawn into the conflict. HAPAG, a nonstate actor, maintained its own coal station network for its East Asia services. Through a British seller Ballin procured more than 300,000 tons of coal from Wales. When a London newspaper exposed the deal in August 1904, the governments in Berlin and London were embarrassed. German chancellor Bernhard von Bülow summoned Ballin to his summer retreat, but the HAPAG chief executive had secured the backing of Kaiser Wilhelm II for the controversial deal. Yet to the German and especially the German Jewish public, HAPAG's support of the Russian Admiralty constituted a serious transgression. The struggling tsarist government was widely seen as an oppressive regime that condoned violence against Jews and did little to improve the living conditions of impoverished peasants and workers. German Jewish leaders could not remain idle.[26]

In their contacts with governments and nonstate actors, the Hilfsverein and American Jewish representatives opted for a more proactive strategy than the Alliance and the Anglo-Jewish Association, whose leaders often lobbied behind the scenes. During the early phase of the Russo-Japanese War in the spring of 1904, American investment banker Jacob Schiff secured several loans to back Japan and accelerate the overthrow of the tsar. He tried convincing Morgan and other American business tycoons to boycott Russia. Schiff's advocacy certainly impressed Nathan.[27] Nathan understood that the rejection of passengers with prepaid Cunard tickets violated the informal agreement between Jewish communities and the steamship lines that was based on facilitating journeys. Alliance representatives tried but failed to convince HAPAG and NDL to end the rejection of Cunard passengers.

In early October 1904, after returning from a short journey to the eastern border, Nathan decided to blame Ballin publicly for the rejection of Cunard passengers at the Russian border. Nathan's little-known intervention is one of the relatively few examples of the successful use of soft power by Jewish aid associations on behalf of Jewish migrants. The public attack of a prominent German Jewish figure on a widely respected Jewish business leader, accusing him of sacrificing the lives of Russian Jews to benefit his business, was unprecedented—and effective. Ballin agreed to a meeting with Nathan, Hilfsverein president James Simon, and NDL managers. Confronted with Nathan's "dossier of facts," Ballin promised fair treatment of all transmigrants and, crucially, allowed Hilfsverein committees at the border a continuous presence inside the control stations to prevent arbitrary rejections of migrants. In late October 1904, HAPAG and NDL stopped the rejection of Cunard passengers, satisfying German critics and removing a major stumbling block in the rate war. A closer look at the events shows that Nathan's public attack was better timed than he may have realized.[28]

Mid-October 1904 was a particularly critical moment for Ballin and the Russian Admiralty. On October 15, HAPAG delivered the first shipment of coal to the Baltic fleet off the Danish coast. A few days later the Russians sank several British fishing vessels off Dogger Bank in the North Sea, bizarrely mistaking them for Japanese warships. Three British sailors died. An outraged British government, responding to massive public pressure, demanded the extradition of the responsible Russian officers.[29] Nathan decided to confront Ballin just before he (and the public) learned about the Dogger Bank incident. Yet his step almost certainly contributed to Ballin's willingness to yield to the demands of the Hilfsverein and the liberal critics of the rejections at the border. Suffice to say, the British government, already irritated by Ballin's sale of British coal to the Russian Admiralty, regarded the treatment of Cunard passengers by the two German lines as unacceptable. Ballin could dismiss left-wing critics, but not Germany's liberal bourgeois establishment, represented by openly critical papers like the *Berliner Tageblatt* and the Hilfsverein. The increasingly uncertain outcome of the hugely profitable but precarious Russian deal and growing resentment in Britain forced him to reach out to his critics and to Cunard. At a hastily organized conference in Berlin on November 11 and 12, Ballin, Wiegand, Cunard chairman Lord Inverclyde, and executives of the Continental Pool lines settled their differences and resurrected the North Atlantic Steamship Conference. Foreign member lines were allowed to operate their own ticket offices near the control stations. Cunard retained its Fiume service, but on a reduced basis.[30]

These concessions were only symbolic. Cunard and other lines could not easily penetrate a market that the German lines firmly controlled through a network of ticket agencies. In the years after 1904 more than two-thirds of Hungarian migrants traveled via Bremen, not least because the Hungarian government refused to liberalize its emigration policy. The U.S. consul in Bremen welcomed the restoration of the Continental Pool because higher ticket prices and German hygiene controls ensured that "undesirables" would not reach the United States. After 1904 all Russian migrants were better protected because the Hilfsverein brought more transparency into the handling of transmigrants at the control stations. The Russian Admiralty had less reason to celebrate. In May 1905 Japanese warships inflicted a humiliating defeat on the Russian navy at the Battle of Tsushima. The Japanese sank twenty Russian ships and captured most others. Over four thousand Russian sailors lost their lives, and almost six thousand were taken prisoner. Another thirty thousand Russian soldiers died on the battlefields in Manchuria. After Japan claimed victory, it awarded Schiff its prestigious Order of the Rising Sun.[31]

Bernhard Kahn's Vision

The 1904 Atlantic Rate War illustrates the significant degree of soft power nonstate actors exercised over migration within and beyond Europe before 1914. Critics of the anticompetitive business practices of HAPAG and NDL overlook that, unlike most Western European steamship lines, HAPAG and NDL did not receive government subsidies. Managers of steamship lines had to hedge against high fixed costs because the passenger numbers were fluctuating considerably. Therefore, both lines had to explore new markets and protect reliable sources of revenue. Transporting large numbers of Eastern European steerage passengers to and from North America depended on keeping governments on the sidelines.[32]

It is remarkable that the Hilfsverein could force the mighty HAPAG to make concessions. However, Wischnitzer's claim that the Hilfsverein under Nathan's and Bernhard Kahn's leadership (and later his own) successfully organize[d] the "haphazard" Jewish migration is exaggerated. Unlike the steamship lines, Jewish aid associations were never in a position to control, let alone organize the migration of tens of thousands. Rather the Hilfsverein took the lead to ensure that Jewish migrants were protected from the moment they left their hometowns until they reached their destination. The only comparable aid network at the time was the Catholic St. Raphael Association, which primarily assisted Catholics from Imperial Germany and the Austro-Hungarian Empire traveling to the United States and Canada. It posted aid workers in Hamburg and other European and North American ports, but its reach was limited. During the train journeys to the ports Catholic migrants usually relied on informal support provided by local church members.[33]

Following an international conference of European Jewish aid associations in Frankfurt in late 1904, the Hilfsverein set up the Central Office for

Emigration Affairs, a transnational clearing agency for migration matters in Central and Eastern Europe. From the Hilfsverein main bureau in Berlin the office coordinated the activities of local Jewish communities along the transit routes with the Alliance, JCA, and dozens of aid associations on both sides of the Atlantic. The Central Office relieved the Alliance of a major responsibility. In the following years the Paris-based organization continued to extend support to Jewish communities in the Russian Empire and Romania but concentrated on its school network in the Levant and North Africa. In matters concerning migrants the Hilfsverein collaborated primarily with local Alliance committees in Germany and elsewhere in Western Europe.

Nathan and the leaders of the Hamburg and Bremen aid committees regularly met with government officials in the Russian Empire, Central Europe, Argentina, and the United States. The Central Office closely worked with Jewish aid associations in and beyond Europe and with different steamship lines. The ties between leading German and American Jews were close, not least because members of established American Jewish families like the Warburgs, Loebs, Schiffs, and Seligmans hailed from Central Europe. Nathan and Schiff frequently exchanged letters in German. In 1905 the Hilfsverein began publishing a newsletter that contained extensive tables detailing the prices for steamship passage from different ports and train fares across Europe and at major overseas countries. The newsletter was distributed across Eastern Europe. The data allowed migrants to calculate the cost for the journey from almost any town in Eastern Europe to most cities in Britain, the United States, Canada, Australia, and South Africa.

The newsletter also contained information about support that the Hilfsverein and other Jewish organizations offered at different points along the main transit routes. During the journey migrants could seek professional advice from aid workers affiliated with the emigration office. In port cities and near Germany's eastern border the Hilfsverein provided medical care at select hospitals to treat trachoma, a contagious eye disease that U.S. immigration inspectors considered particularly unacceptable. The organization accommodated close family members of patients during the treatment and often footed the bill. Most patients were cured and passed the screening at Ellis Island and other immigration stations.[34]

The Hilfsverein pursued a sustained approach to coordinating the assistance and protection of migrants. This required the hiring of a permanent staff. Hilfsverein workers began to systematically collect, analyze, and apply information about the social and economic life of Jews in Eastern Europe

Representatives of the Hamburg Jewish aid association bid farewell to Jewish emigrants, c. 1907. This image was reprinted in the 1907 annual report of the Hilfsverein. The man sitting at the table on the right is almost certainly Paul Laskar, the head of the Hamburg Jewish aid association. Source: Johann Hamann, StaHH, 720-1/343-1/H3001165. *Reprinted with the kind permission of the State Archive Hamburg*

and about Jewish migration. The organization was involved in attempts to address trafficking of young Jewish women as prostitutes. These innovations demonstrate the transition from aid associations managed by donors in their spare time and staffed with a limited number of clerical workers to professional organizations with specialized staff members and a clearly defined set of policy goals. Jewish and other communal aid associations in North America and Europe underwent a similar transformation in this period. It was not a coincidence that this shift occurred almost simultaneously with the rise of scholarly attempts to understand social and economic changes—and the causes driving migration.[35]

Paul Nathan was constantly on the road to learn more about the living conditions of Jews in Eastern Europe, organize fundraising drives, and cultivate the growing network of Hilfsverein supporters. The management of the Hilfsverein largely fell to Bernhard Kahn, a key player in the transnational network of Jewish aid associations before and after the First World War. Born in Sweden, the son of stateless Lithuanian Jews, he grew up in Prussia. A promising scholar who acquired two doctoral degrees, he must have realized that obtaining an academic position was not a realistic prospect for a Jew in Germany. Kahn's activities in left-wing circles brought him into contact with Nathan, who recruited him as executive director and first head of the emigration office in 1904. A seemingly paradoxical reason for hiring Kahn may have been his sympathy for the Zionist cause. Although the Hilfsverein board members staunchly opposed Zionism, Kahn may have been hired as a liaison for the Hilfsverein's Palestinian projects. He could not prevent an acrimonious clash between Nathan and leading Zionists in 1913 over the language of instruction of the Haifa Technicum (Technion), the technical institute founded and managed by the Hilfsverein. In 1921 Kahn became the head of the European office of the American Jewish Joint Distribution Committee.[36]

The annual reports of the Hilfsverein and other Jewish aid associations provide a unique perspective on changing migration policies in different parts of the world. The Hilfsverein reports display a growing concern about the unclear legal status of migrants in transit. Several states, including Germany and the United States, passed legislation to protect citizens who emigrated to another country, but the status of foreign transmigrants remained undetermined. The Austrian government intervened repeatedly on behalf of its citizens with German officials and the steamship lines. Yet Jewish (and other) migrants from the Russian Empire were particularly vulnerable because they often had left without required permits. Russian border officials often refused to readmit subjects who had left without formal permission; once they crossed the border these migrants became de facto stateless. In its 1904 annual report the newly established Hilfsverein Emigration Bureau argued the "Jewish collectivity" represented by the Jewish aid associations in different countries had "to do for the protection of Jewish emigrants what usually is the task of the state." According to this passage the transnational network of Jewish aid associations provided a quasi-legal status to Jewish migrants accepted by states and the steamship lines, which also performed tasks usually handled by states. The likely author (or co-author) of this passage was Kahn, who was stateless until he managed to acquire Prussian citizenship in 1908.[37]

Providing migrants with a formal and recognized status while in transit would become a critical issue after 1914, when large numbers of Eastern

Europeans were permanently displaced from their homes, often became stateless, faced migration restrictions, and could not expect much support from nonstate actors. Long before 1914 the leaders of Jewish aid associations were concerned about migration restrictions. After the 1903 Kishinev pogrom and the ensuing violence against Jews in the Russian Empire and Romania, the prospects for Jews living in these countries appeared bleak, and there was little hope that the depressing economic situation in Galicia would improve. It was widely expected that strong Jewish migration would continue for the foreseeable future and possibly increase. In its 1906–1907 edition, the *American Jewish Yearbook* documented the violence in the Russian Empire, the subject of extensive coverage in the Jewish press around the world. A detailed survey listed 254 pogroms in the Russian Empire between 1903 and 1906, with precise numbers of victims and a brief description of the events. A special section dealt with the June 1906 Białystok pogrom, which claimed two hundred Jewish lives. A superficial reading of published reports and speeches seems to leave little doubt that Jewish leaders and the Jewish public genuinely considered the Russian pogroms to be the driving force behind the mass migration.

A closer look, however, betrays more subtle views. In a 1905 essay about Jewish migration that contained grisly images of Jewish pogrom victims Kahn identified industrialization in the United States after 1870 as a major factor behind growing Jewish migration. Most migrants were eager to free themselves from the "tentacles of pauperism." Anti-Jewish violence was a contributing factor, but not the underlying cause. This interpretation echoes the early scholarship on Jewish migration. Frequent references to Russian and Romanian atrocities by Jewish representatives like Kahn reflect genuine compassion and outrage but also were part of a consistent lobbying strategy against immigration restrictions.[38]

In contrast to its laissez-faire attitude toward transmigrants, Prussia pursued a rigid anti-immigration policy. Between 1904 and 1906 hundreds of "illegal" Russian Jewish migrants in Berlin received deportation orders. The Hilfsverein could mitigate the impact by convincing the authorities to allow unwanted Russian Jews to move to Western Europe and the United States. Britain also shifted to a more restrictive immigration policy after 1900. In 1905 Parliament passed the Aliens Act, which required the inspection of arriving migrants traveling in steerage on larger vessels and excluded convicts and "paupers." It was no secret that the bill implicitly targeted Eastern European Jews, the largest group of foreign immigrants. For the opponents of immigration, the passage of the bill after years of discussion was a Pyrrhic victory. Before 1914 different governments chose not to enforce the Aliens Act. The British political establishment and business leaders understood that the empire's economic fortunes depended on relatively permeable borders. Migration restrictions also threatened the British steamship business. The massive subsidies the Cunard Line received in 1902 are an indication of the importance Parliament and the government attached to a major employer and pillar of global British power.[39]

Much more concerning was the likelihood that the U.S. Congress would pass more severe immigration restrictions. After 1900 the view that immigration was a problem found growing support both in Congress and among the public. Should America close its doors, the Hilfsverein agonized in 1911, "a catastrophe would ensue, so terrible, that it will overshadow the persecutions and pogroms." Leading members of the American Jewish establishment also increased their lobbying efforts against restrictions. The founding of the AJC in 1906 was in part influenced by concerns about immigration restrictions. In the same year Nissim Behar, a Sephardi Jewish educator who had long been affiliated with the Alliance school network in the Ottoman Empire, helped to establish the National Liberal Immigration League (NLIL), a group of well-connected American academics and public figures. Through a wide range of publications NLIL promoted factual information about immigration and immigrants. One of the first booklets published under the auspices of NLIL was a short survey about the "immigrant Jew." The lead author was the president of the University of Illinois, Edmund J. James. He focused on a careful discussion of facts to refute widely circulating stereotypes. Jacob Schiff was the main driving force behind an effort to disperse Jewish immigrants into the American interior to reduce their visibility. The Hilfsverein report for 1907 contains photographs of Hilfsverein officials and migrants lined up at the dock in Bremerhaven in front of a ship that was bound for Galveston, Texas, a hub of the dispersion scheme.[40]

Members of the American Jewish business establishment stressed that more was at stake than the protection of Jews facing persecution in Russia

Jewish emigrants line up in Bremerhaven to board a ship to Galveston, Texas. The image was published in the Hilfsverein's 1907 report. Several migrants wear labels on their hats and coats, possibly with information about their destination. The two men standing in the front are almost certainly members of the local Jewish aid association. Source: *Sechster Geschäftsbericht (1907) des Hilfsvereins der deutschen Juden (Berlin: Privately published, 1908), 106*

A local policeman observes as the last Jewish migrants board a steamship to Galveston in Bremerhaven. Closer to the ship stands a well-dressed man, probably a member of the local Jewish aid association. Source: *Sechster Geschäftsbericht (1907) des Hilfsvereins der deutschen Juden (Berlin: Privately published, 1908), 102*

and Romania. In a 1905 speech that was part of the commemoration of the 250th anniversary of Jewish settlement in North America, Chicago judge Julian Mack linked the history of the first Jews who settled in New Amsterdam in 1654 with contemporary Jewish migrants, depicting both as refugees. He dismissed the view popular with those favoring restrictions that too many immigrants coming to America were "paupers." American Jews would take care of their own poor. More important, Mack stressed, was another point: "The doors of the United States shall never be closed to any decent, honest man coming here to settle." He explicitly warned, "[A]ll sorts of qualifications will be enacted as a prerequisite to the admission of future immigrants. It is our duty [as Americans and Jews] . . . to claim for the oppressed of all lands the right under which we ourselves were permitted to come here and become American citizens." Being American and Jewish implicitly carried the obligation to "keep the doors open" for all migrants. By using the door metaphor Mack may have referred to the then obscure poem "The New Colossus" by Emma Lazarus, inspired by the 1881–1882 Russian pogroms. Avoiding references to specific groups, she famously described the Statue of Liberty as "Mother of Exiles" who was welcoming the "huddled masses, yearning to breathe free," lifting her "lamp beside the golden door."[41]

A particularly sensitive issue for established American Jews was the attempt to categorize arriving Jewish immigrants as members of a racial group. In the late 1890s several Jewish representatives lobbied successfully against using the term "race" to distinguish arriving immigrants. A key figure in this campaign was Washington attorney Simon Wolf, an early critic of Chinese exclusion and a close acquaintance of Mack. Wolf was an immigrant himself. He grew up in a small village in the Bavarian Palatinate and moved to Ohio in 1848 as a teenager. After the Civil War the lawyer emerged as a respected lobbyist for Jewish matters in the federal capital. He often testified at congressional hearings. In 1881 he briefly served as U.S. ambassador to Egypt.

Against the background of rising anti-Jewish discrimination and growing popular support for immigration restrictions, established American Jews knew they had to move cautiously to ensure that America's doors remained open for all people seeking to escape economic hardship and political turmoil. The 1882 Chinese Exclusion Act constituted a potential precedent for restricting Jewish immigration. At a congressional hearing in 1902 about the Chinese exclusion laws Wolf opened his statement by pointing out that he represented the Union of American Hebrew Congregations but spoke as "American citizen." In his remarks he stressed that the exclusion of Chinese immigrants violated the universal principles of the U.S. Constitution. He condemned popular stereotypes about Chinese immigrants, declaring, "It is a gross injustice to brand a whole people as scums of the earth."[42]

A close collaborator of Wolf, lawyer Max Kohler, the son of a prominent rabbi, repeatedly took on deportation cases of immigrants from South and East Asia pro bono. In 1903 he litigated the case of a Chinese migrant all the way to the Supreme Court. In a 1909 article titled the "Un-American Character of Race Legislation," Kohler argued that the exclusion laws imposed a "reign of terror for all Chinese or alleged Chinese residents." Kohler's article was part of a concerted effort to fight a renewed attempt by Congress to categorize Jews as a race in the census and on immigration forms. In a 1909 letter Wolf outlined his approach to immigration matters with members of Congress: "[W]hatever we ask we ask as citizens and not as Jews. Immigration laws are made for all and not for any particular class." This remarkable statement betrays a sincere commitment to universalist ideals. Wolf, Mack, and Kohler understood the risks of a Jewish lobbying effort on behalf of immigrant Jews, because the supporters of restrictions were targeting specific groups such as Chinese as undesirable. To undercut racist and antisemitic agitation against immigration it was essential to work across ethnic and religious lines and build coalitions with progressive reformers and employers. The growing political support for immigration restrictions in the 1890s prompted American Jews to coordinate their lobbying strategy with members of other immigrant groups and urban reformers. Leading Jewish figures helped to establish nonsectarian lobbying organizations advocating for a liberal immigration policy such as NLIL and the Immigration Protective League.[43]

Before 1914 a sophisticated but little visible network of Jewish aid workers protected Jewish migrants along the main transit routes from Eastern Europe to distant locations in different parts of the world. At major points of passage such as the North Sea ports but also in remote towns along the western Russian border members of Jewish communities assisted migrants. Jewish representatives lobbied state officials, from low-level bureaucrats in small border towns to high-ranking government ministers on both sides of the Atlantic. Jewish aid associations and local communities usually covered the cost for migrants who required support. This gave them leverage in negotiations with officials. Around 1900 German and American Jews established professional aid organizations that sidelined the older French and Anglo-Jewish associations because they could draw on a large donor base and combined the protection and support of migrants with effective lobbying efforts against migration restrictions.

6
The First World War and Its Aftermath
Displacement and Permanent Transit

In December 1929, a small group of Jewish passengers from the German port of Bremerhaven arrived in New York. They had valid papers and were admitted. Their journey followed a route similar to that traversed by hundreds of thousands of Russian subjects before the First World War. Their migration experience, however, was strikingly different. This group, initially comprising more than twenty men, women, and children, had reached Bremerhaven six years earlier, in 1923. They hailed from the territory of the former Russian Empire and had passed through the Latvian capital of Riga. No information is available about their journey to the new Latvian state. It is quite likely that members of the group had been expelled from or fled their homes during the First World War or in its aftermath. In the early 1920s Riga emerged as a point of passage for displaced Jews from the former Pale. In early 1921 the Soviet representative in Riga announced that repatriation was not an option for those who had left areas that were part of the Soviet Union. In 1922 an American visitor encountered Jews in Riga's streets who "were hungry and in rags." Some had walked hundreds of miles. Jews from the Soviet Union had to stop over in Latvia, Lithuania, or Poland to secure visas and transit permits for the onward journey.[1]

In Bremerhaven, the group faced another layover because the U.S. immigration quota for persons born in the territory of the new Soviet state for the year 1923 had been met. The original plan was to depart during the summer of 1924, following the beginning of the new fiscal year on July 1. Yet in the spring of 1924 Congress passed a new immigration bill that reduced the already low quotas for most Eastern European countries by over 90 percent. Visas that had already been issued were cancelled. The Jews in Bremerhaven were some of the more than seven thousand migrants who were stranded for an indefinite period. Many were stateless and could not return to their former homes. The Hilfsverein used the term *Überlieger* (layover migrants) for the members of this group. The women, men, and children were not officially recognized as refugees, in part because no official refugee status existed. Like most other people on the move, they wished to join family members in the United States and rebuild their lives in a safer place.[2]

During the summer of 1924 Jewish aid associations and representatives frantically lobbied various governments, promising to cover the costs and find alternative solutions for those affected by the sudden closure of America's gates. Aid workers reached out to steamship lines to ensure they did not sell tickets to migrants without a guaranteed quota number. In an internal report HIAS expressed great concern because the U.S. immigration authorities refused to exempt over seven thousand migrants who had received visas before the law took effect and had been stranded in ports like Bremerhaven. A small HIAS delegation traveled to Europe to collect information and coordinate support with other aid associations and local Jewish communities. In Britain, France, and Germany migrants were housed in decent accommodations in port cities. It seemed likely that they would be allowed to stay, perhaps even permanently. In Eastern Europe, however, the situation was far worse. Local Jewish communities struggled to support thousands of destitute Jews who had been displaced during and after the war. The U.S. consulate in the new Lithuanian capital, Kaunas (Kovno), had more than twelve thousand visa applications on file. The annual U.S. immigrant quota for persons born in the territory of the Lithuanian state had been reduced from about 2,600 to a mere 344. At least seven hundred Jews were stuck in the Latvian port of Liepaja (Libau), and six hundred in Riga. The Latvian government threatened to deport them. Because of concerns about potential disease outbreaks in the travelers' housing, many were quarantined and could not receive visitors.

In Warsaw, hundreds of Jews "were left helpless, in the truest sense of the word." In Danzig four hundred Jews were stranded. In Romania thirty-five hundred Jews were waiting to emigrate to the United States. Their prospects were dim. Congress had reduced the annual quota allotted for persons born in Romania from over seven thousand to a little more than six hundred. The quota for those born in the territory of the new Soviet state, the home and birthplace of most stranded Jews and millions of displaced persons, decreased from over twenty-four thousand to about two thousand. HIAS estimated a sum of at least $500,000 had to be raised for short-term assistance. According to its internal report, the only hope was to secure a deal with Congress to exempt the stranded migrants, because otherwise "many will surely perish."[3]

The Bremerhaven aid workers were concerned about the migrants' mental as well as physical health. After several months a few members of the original group pulled out, reducing the group to twenty-three individuals. In the fall of 1929, more than five years later, the U.S. consulate in Bremen announced the Jews would have to wait for an indefinite period, at least another five years. This news apparently broke several of the stranded migrants. The aid workers reported, "[T]hey suffer mentally, because they have been uprooted and separated from their relatives for years. And they suffer physically, for they are condemned to do nothing [but wait] and they do not know what to do with themselves." Why did the members of the group decide to wait instead of moving to another destination or remain in Germany, one of the few countries pursuing a relatively liberal migration policy after 1918? It is unlikely that the stranded migrants had friends or relatives in the few places where they could reasonably expect to be admitted. Returning to the Soviet Union was not possible. Almost certainly their only viable path forward depended on family members in the United States. Without access to a network of acquaintances and relatives, moving to an unknown destination like Brazil or Palestine was risky, especially for families.

The United States had absorbed the lion's share of the pre-1914 Jewish migration. With a large Jewish community and a highly developed industrial sector, it was the only destination where the overwhelming majority of Jewish migrants leaving Eastern Europe could realistically hope to rebuild their lives. In 1929, when all hope had vanished for the Bremerhaven group, New York congressman Samuel Dickstein finally made the impossible possible. The U.S. State Department relented and allowed the group to enter. Dickstein, himself a Jewish immigrant from a town in Lithuania, represented the Lower East Side of New York City and was a prominent critic of immigration restrictions on Capitol Hill who fought for permitting the entry of close family members.[4]

The episode of the Jewish migrants who were stranded in Bremerhaven provides a glimpse at the human toll of the American shift to a restrictive and rigid immigration policy after the First World War. Unable to return to their homes and unable to move to a country of their choice, permanently displaced Jews struggled to rebuild their lives, often lacking legal protection and being subject to forced removal. Those who tried to take their fate into their own hands encountered a maze of bureaucratic obstacles. Few came close to meticulously guarded land borders or ports. Almost insurmountable "paper walls" were a defining characteristic of the postwar migration regime. This

"Nowhere Can One Set a Foot Down" by cartoonist Mitchell Loeb was published in *Der Groyser Kundes,* a New York City Yiddish-language satirical publication, on August 5, 1921. The man resembles a popular image of the Jewish migrant from Eastern Europe that features in several contemporary publications and Marc Chagall paintings, a male figure in simple clothes with a cap, carrying a sack on his back. He is identified as "Jewish refugee." The upright blades refer to destination countries: Poland, Romania, America, Canada, Austria, Latvia, Palestine, and others. *YIVO, Institute for Jewish Research, New York*

term was coined to describe the travails of German Jews trying to enter the United States after 1933, but it aptly portrays the situation of a much larger number of Eastern European Jews and others after 1918, not to mention countless migrants and refugees after World War II. What is unusual about the case of the Jews stranded in Bremerhaven is that they were finally allowed to enter the United States.[5]

The First World War represents a watershed moment in the history of Jewish migrations from and within Eastern Europe and beyond. The war disrupted migration flows globally. In 1915–1916 the Russian military systematically expelled hundreds of thousands of Jews from their homes. In the violent aftermath of the war tens of thousands of Jews fell victim to pogroms instigated by Polish, Russian, and Ukrainian nationalists. In the early phase of the war most participating states imposed strict mobility controls. The requirement to carry standardized identification papers gave rise to the modern passport regime for crossing international borders. Passport and visa requirements betray the lack of trust between states in the "broken world" after 1918. Postwar migration restrictions hit Jews in and from Eastern Europe particularly hard. With the collapse of the multiethnic empires in 1918 an unknown but very large number became stateless. Without valid papers issued by a state, they were deprived of the ability to cross borders legally. Like others who were displaced across Eastern Europe during and after the First World War, notably Armenians who managed to escape the genocide in 1915–1916 and opponents of the Bolshevik regime, Jewish refugees and migrants eluded contested and changing legal categorizations that differed between countries. As a result, many remained stranded in permanent transit for years.[6]

The Long War

The unexpected declarations of war during the summer months of 1914 led to a sudden interruption of most passenger services from continental Europe to the United States and other overseas destinations. In the early phase of the war, European states introduced rigid mobility controls to prevent young men from dodging military service. Millions were drafted or volunteered, among them almost all young Jewish men in the countries involved in the war. Borders that did not become front lines were closed to prevent illegal border crossings and smuggling. While it was still possible to travel to North America from the Netherlands and Britain, both countries were beyond reach for migrants from Central and Eastern Europe. After occupying Belgium, German forces built an electric fence on the border with the neutral Netherlands to prevent civilians and soldiers from leaving. Hundreds died while trying to cross into the Netherlands illegally. A British sea blockade closed Germany's North Sea ports. The German authorities detained transmigrants from the Russian Empire as enemy aliens, together with thousands of permanent residents from Russia. Among the latter were German women who had lost their German citizenship when they married men from the Russian Empire. The German authorities also treated widows and children of Russian subjects as enemy aliens. Similar measures were imposed on formerly British women who had married German or Austrian citizens living in Britain or British dominions such as Australia and Canada. Thousands of civilians were categorized as enemy aliens and detained for lengthy periods because repatriation frequently was not an option.[7]

In November 1914 Paul Nathan, the founder of the German Jewish Hilfsverein, reached out to the American Jewish philanthropist Jacob Schiff. More than sixty thousand Russians were stranded in Germany. Most were Jewish. The Hilfsverein had been able to repatriate more than four thousand people through Sweden. Schiff assured Nathan that American Jews would cooperate with the Hilfsverein to assist Jews in Poland and Palestine. In Britain and throughout the British Empire the government had detained Jewish and other migrants from the Austro-Hungarian Empire in so-called concentration camps along with thousands of German nationals. Many Jews were taken to a makeshift camp on a ship anchored in Portsmouth. Several appealed their confinement to the Board of Deputies of British Jews. The board rejected their request to lobby the government for their release because they "were not under any disability owing to their religion." It ruled that they had been held as citizens of an enemy state, not because they were Jews. Hundreds of Russian transmigrants and sojourners were stranded in neutral Netherlands. Only a few individuals could be repatriated from Dutch ports via Britain and Sweden in the early phase of the war. Together with thousands of Belgian civilians and soldiers who had escaped across a tightly guarded border, most Russian subjects were housed in camps.[8]

In the late summer of 1914 two-thirds of the 15 million Jews around the world lived dispersed in the conflict zone in Eastern Europe and the Ottoman Empire. The war economy deprived Jews in the Russian Pale and in the Austrian province of Galicia of their limited sources of income.

During the first two years of the war the fighting especially affected Galicia. The Jewish communities in Vienna and Budapest went to great lengths to care for thousands of refugees. Jews in the Russian Pale faced an even bigger threat. The Russian army leadership specifically targeted Jews and ethnic Germans as internal enemies. In 1915, German troops launched an offensive into Russian Poland and Lithuania. As a large number of Jewish and other civilians were fleeing the conflict zone, the Russian military forcibly expelled Jews along with smaller numbers of ethnic Germans from the northern Pale. It is estimated that between 1914 and 1917 the Russian military forcibly expelled between 500,000 and 1 million Jews from their homes. Between late April and early May 1915 an estimated 150,000 Jews were expelled from the Kovno district alone. The implementation was chaotic. Most could take only a few personal possessions and were dumped without any provisions in distant towns. In several places Russian troops who were in charge of the expulsions instigated pogroms that claimed hundreds of Jewish lives.

Many expelled Jews headed to larger Russian cities in the hinterland, effectively obliterating the Pale of Settlement. In the summer and fall of 1915, the Russian government announced a relaxation of settlement restrictions in the country's interior for Jews in certain occupations. The Pale was not formally abolished, but such announcements clearly indicated that the authorities were unable to enforce the restrictions. A 1915 Russian decree distinguished between different types of "refugees." *Bezhentsy* had escaped enemy troops by relocating into the Russian interior; *vyselentsy* were those (like Jews and ethnic Germans) who had been "evacuated" by the Russian military; *vykhodtsy* were foreigners who had fled to Russia, for instance Armenian Christians escaping Ottoman persecution. These distinctions highlight the challenge of defining who a refugee is and demonstrate that the Russian authorities differentiated between those they considered deserving and undeserving. Historian Eric Lohr, the author of a detailed study about the Russian expulsions, argues that the worst atrocities against Jews during the Russian Civil War in 1918–1919 took place in provinces that received the largest influx of Jewish expellees in 1915.[9]

The expulsions contributed to a massive social upheaval that prepared the ground for the Russian Revolution in 1917. The decision to forcibly remove hundreds of thousands of people who were considered a potential threat constituted an ominous escalation for another reason. For the first time after the 1492 Spanish expulsion decree a European state specifically selected members of an ethnoreligious group for forced removal on an extensive scale. Almost simultaneously the Ottoman military systematically rounded up Armenian Christians in eastern Anatolia because they were suspected of sympathizing or collaborating with the Russian enemy. It remains contested how many Armenians perished; at least 350,000 escaped to districts under Russian control in the Caucasus region. The U.S. ambassador in Constantinople, Henry Morgenthau Sr., a respected Jewish philanthropist who had grown up in the German city of Mannheim, publicized information about the excesses. Ignored by the Ottoman leaders and frustrated about his lack of leverage in Washington, he then resigned. In a detailed account of his ambassadorship that he published in 1918 Morgenthau explicitly blamed the German government for encouraging the Armenian genocide. According to his estimate, between 600,000 and 1 million Armenians perished.[10]

The war disrupted the sophisticated Jewish transnational aid network. Morgenthau's frantic efforts to publicize and stop the violence against Armenians were influenced by concerns over the physical safety of the Jewish population in Palestine. Many Jewish settlers had refused to become Ottoman subjects and were therefore treated as Russian enemy aliens. British and French Jewish aid associations could not dispatch aid to Palestine, and the Hilfsverein could provide only limited assistance. Therefore the task of taking the initiative and shouldering much of the financial burden fell to American Jewry. The United States was neutral and home to the largest Jewish community outside of Eastern Europe. Yet after decades of strong immigration, no group or organization could yet claim to represent American Jews.

The crisis served as a catalyst bringing together Zionists, Bundists, Orthodox Jews, Socialists, women's organizations, and the business establishment. In October 1914 representatives of more than forty organizations established the American Jewish Joint Distribution Committee (JDC), which quickly emerged as a major Jewish aid association. The first task was to protect and assist the fifty thousand Jews in Palestine. In the early days of the war Morgenthau personally helped to transfer funds raised in the United States to the Yishuv. After launching a fundraising drive, the JDC began sending supplies to Palestine in the spring months of 1915. Packages, letters, and remittances for Jews in German-occupied territories in Eastern Europe were routed through neutral Netherlands. On behalf of the JDC the Hilfsverein handled the distribution of mail and remittances in German-occupied areas in Poland and Lithuania until 1917.[11]

During the war HIAS transformed in ways few could have imagined before 1914. In the first months after the declarations of war the organization continued to assist migrants who were refused entry to the United States. In late 1914 several Jews from the Ottoman Empire who had lived in France were held at Ellis Island. They had left France to avoid detention as enemy aliens but were denied admission because they had not paid for their journey. HIAS successfully prevented their deportation. In May 1915 immigration officials hatched a plan to deport sixty detained Russian subjects from Ellis Island to the isolated northern Russian port of Archangelsk. Apart from six Jews the others were Christians. Most had been denied admission because they were categorized as "insane." HIAS lobbied with the U.S. Department of Labor, which regulated immigration, arguing that these individuals' lives were at risk. The migrants would be dumped in Archangelsk lacking the means to travel to their hometowns in Ukraine. At the last minute—the migrants had already boarded a Russian steamer—the risky venture was abandoned. HIAS covered the cost for the upkeep of the Jewish migrants.[12]

Lobbying on behalf of and supporting recent Jewish and non-Jewish arrivals was HIAS's core task. Yet after July 1914 the number of migrants who managed to reach the United States declined sharply. As news about widespread hunger and Jews' flight from the war zone in Eastern Europe reached the United States in the winter months of 1914–1915 the HIAS board began to rethink its mission. Immigrants from Eastern Europe and their American-born children represented two-thirds of the Jewish population in the United States. Most had family members in the areas affected by the war. In 1915 HIAS set up its own support channel through the Netherlands, enabling relatives to send money and letters to areas occupied by German troops. Jews who were expelled by the Russian military were largely beyond the reach of Jewish aid associations, except those who managed to travel thousands of miles to the Russian Far East. In 1916 HIAS representatives learned that hundreds of Jews who had been displaced by the Russian military from their homes in the Pale were living in appalling conditions in cities along the Amur River, in Vladivostok, and in the Japanese port of Yokohama. In a few cases American relatives funded their passage to Seattle or San Francisco. In late 1917 HIAS dispatched an aid worker to Japan. His reports confirmed that thousands of Jews in the Russian Far East required support. HIAS set up offices in Yokohama and in Vladivostok and managed to send several hundred Jews to the United States from Japan in 1918. But growing obstruction by U.S. diplomats and the Russian Civil War made it difficult to evacuate larger groups.[13]

In the fall of 1918, the Russian Civil War exacerbated the crisis. After the armistice in November 1918 American Jewish organizations were able to route shipments of clothing, food, and money to Poland and adjacent territories through Germany. However, renewed fighting hampered the aid effort. During the Russian Civil War paramilitary nationalist forces and Bolsheviks systematically attacked civilians as enemies and committed atrocious acts of violence. Bolshevik forces did not systematically attack Jews, and even protected them against violence in some places, yet in 1918–1919 alone, White armies and Ukrainian and Polish nationalists killed at least fifty thousand Jews in eastern Poland and Ukraine. An unknown number of Jews perished in Lithuania and adjacent regions.[14] In Siberia and later in Mongolia, the notorious White general Roman von Ungern-Sternberg ordered the systematic killing of every Jew in the sector under his control. Even the farm animals of Jews were slaughtered. Ungern-Sternberg and other White generals considered Jews and Socialists as identical.[15] Some White officers and soldiers who instigated and participated in the attacks against Jews in 1918–1919 had been involved in the mass expulsions of Jews in 1915. Estimates of the number of Jews who perished ranged widely, from 50,000 to well over 300,000. In 1924 Zionist Leo Motzkin opened his speech to the Second Jewish World Aid Conference in Karlsbad by reminding his listeners, "[T]he shadows of hundreds of thousands of murdered Jews stand in our midst."[16]

By late 1918 a large number of Jews were displaced across the constantly shifting war zone in Eastern Europe. JDC representative Boris Bogen described his impressions of a trip to Galicia in 1919: "The road to Lwoff was a Via Dolorosa of hunger and death and sickness and fear. Jewish refugees were tramping on the highways, going God knows where, living in abandoned barns like cattle, crowded often many in a room in houses that gave them shelter." Only a few Jews could leave the region in 1918–1919. Refugees often found shelter in makeshift camps that had been vacated by POWs. Countless families were separated for years, and few prospective migrants had sufficient funds to buy passage. Movement across contested borders in Central and East Central Europe was difficult because wartime restrictions were only gradually lifted. Regular transatlantic steamship service from most continental ports did not resume until 1920.[17]

In early 1919 a British diplomat reported from Prague that Jews had been murdered in several Czech towns because they were seen as traitors loyal to the former Austrian Empire. The fighting in 1919–1920 prevented Galician

Jews from returning to their former homes. The philosopher and Zionist Hugo Bergmann told the diplomat that "no such abominable persecution of their race has been known since the Middle Ages." At least thirty thousand Galician Jews were stranded in the Austrian capital, Vienna. In 1920 the Austrian government threatened to expel them. A Vienna Zionist daily portrayed a few typical "parasites" who had received eviction and deportation orders. Josef Z. was an elderly baker who had been ordered to leave his hometown in Galicia by Austrian officials in 1914. Three sons—whom the paper cynically described as "true Galician [Jewish] shirkers," had died for Austria on the battlefield. The baker's wife had been hospitalized. Josef Z. lived in a tiny apartment with six children, two of whom were employed and provided income for the family. They had to vacate their apartment in less than ten days and leave the country. In the same issue the paper reported that a series of pogroms sowed fear among Jews in the Hungarian capital, Budapest, home to a large Jewish community and a sizable group of displaced Jews. Many Jews had fled the capital in August 1919 when Romanian forces and Hungarian military units brutally crushed the short-lived Hungarian Soviet republic, singling out Jews as enemies.[18]

Most Galician Jews in Austria, Hungary, and Czechoslovakia hailed from areas that became part of the new Polish state in 1918. Some were war refugees, but others had lived in Vienna, Prague, and other European cities for decades. Poland was home to more displaced persons than any other country in Europe and was involved in a massive war with the Soviet Union. In June 1920, when Soviet troops launched an offensive and broke through the Polish front, a German official reported that the Polish government might try to use the war as an excuse to exclude Jews from Polish citizenship and expel Jewish refugees. Since deportation to Poland was not an option, Austrian officials systematically blocked the applications of former Austrian subjects, in particular war refugees, for Austrian citizenship. Applicants often could not produce documents proving their identity and military service because they had been able to take only a few things with them when they fled. The requirement to provide documentation led to Kafkaesque situations. A Jewish merchant from Brody filed an appeal after his citizenship application was rejected. Although the man was a graduate of Brody's German-language high school and argued his case in German, the court raised doubts whether he actually was a German speaker because he could not present formal documentation. Using quotations from a book by the notorious antisemitic author Houston Stewart Chamberlain, the court determined he did not belong to the German "race." Lacking viable alternatives, most Galician Jewish refugees remained in Austria during the interwar period.[19]

Before 1918 the midsize Baltic port of Danzig was a minor point of passage for Jewish and other migrants heading to North Sea ports with direct transatlantic service. To provide the new Polish state with access to port facilities the victorious powers forced Germany to cede control of Danzig and the Vistula delta. In January 1920 the "Free City of Danzig" became a small state with its own currency and government, sharing borders with Poland and Germany. A League of Nations high commissioner oversaw the democratically elected city government. Poland was granted control of the port, backed by a military garrison. In 1919–1920 thousands of migrants from the former Russian Empire congregated in the city, hoping to catch a passage on one of the many American steamers that brought aid to Poland after the end of the war. The city authorities housed migrants in a run-down former POW camp on the outskirts of the city. The Jewish community had to pay for the upkeep of Jewish refugees. Aid officials and journalists who visited the Troyl camp described the conditions as appalling. In late 1920 the U.S. immigration commissioner reported that criminals systematically stole belongings and money from those passing through the Danzig refugee camp. In early 1921 the Polish official representative in Danzig, Maciej Biesiadecki, complained in a letter to the mayor of Danzig that "the rotten and dilapidated barracks" in the Troyl camp violated even the most basic hygienic standards; he accused the city of doing nothing against typhus cases and lice in the camp.[20]

The situation in Danzig escalated when Soviet troops approached the eastern outskirts of Warsaw in August 1920. Thousands who had fled the Bolsheviks feared for their lives and rushed to Danzig hoping to be evacuated from the port. The United States closed its diplomatic mission in Warsaw. Without a declaration issued by the consulate that the migrants met U.S. immigration regulations, it was impossible for the Danzig Jewish community to secure German and Dutch transit visas for those seeking to sail from Rotterdam. Just when Polish troops relieved the siege of Warsaw, passenger steamship service from Danzig to New York, which had commenced in the spring of 1920, was interrupted. Increasing immigration to the United States had overwhelmed the inspections at Ellis Island in the late summer of 1920. In September 1920 the U.S. immigration commissioner briefly halted all immigration. After transatlantic steamship service from Danzig resumed, U.S. diplomats denied boarding to hundreds of migrants because of the appalling hygienic conditions in the Troyl camp. The Danzig Jewish community carried much of the burden. Rabbi Robert Kaelter, who coordinated the support, repeatedly pleaded with JDC representative Boris Bogen in Warsaw. Bogen had grown up in the Russian Empire and had little sympathy for German Jews. He believed the suffering in Galicia was far worse than in Danzig. He was outraged when a desperate Kaelter secured support from the JDC main office in New York behind his back.[21]

In the early 1920s Poland and Romania, the two countries with the largest number of Jewish and other refugees, repeatedly threatened mass expulsions that were averted at the last moment following diplomatic interventions. According to several reports, the Polish government exploited the refugee crisis by either forcing or encouraging larger groups to cross the sparely guarded border to Danzig. The goal was to destabilize Danzig's government and bolster the case for full Polish control. The British Foreign Office expressed concern that Danzig could become a "dumping place for 'undesirables.'" The local Danzig authorities resorted to ruthless methods to stop the influx across the city's borders. Repeatedly Jews were selected for reprisals. In mid-April 1923 a local journalist witnessed the attempted deportation of more than one hundred Russian Jews at Danzig's central train station. The women, men, and children fiercely resisted the deportation. As more spectators tried to get a glimpse of the action, the police aborted the deportation. The group was led back to the Troyl camp, where HIAS cared for them. Since Poland would have refused to admit the migrants, the incident readily illustrates how stateless refugees became pawns in the conflict over the territory's status. An Anglo-Jewish representative, Lucien Wolf, wrote in a letter to the newly created League of Nations refugee office a few months after the incident, "[I]t seems a terrible thing that these poor people should be victimized by the quarrel." The incident betrays the League's inability to intervene and prevent similar deportations.[22]

Particularly concerning was the situation in Romania, where the government considered Jews, Ukrainians, and other groups to be unwanted minorities, even if they had lived for generations in territories that became part of Romania in 1918. Refugees were even less welcome. In 1920–1921, during the final stage of the Russian Civil War, a large number of civilians fled from areas under Bolshevik control in Ukraine across the Dniester River into Bessarabia (contemporary Moldova). The territory became part of Romania in 1918 but was claimed by Russian nationalists and the Soviets. The League of Nations and the JDC dispatched officials to investigate the crisis and organize aid shipments. According to the Romanian government, more than

100,000 Jewish civilians had fled to Bessarabia. The JCA office in Bucharest put the actual number at slightly over 35,000 because the Romanian count included Jewish and other refugees who returned to their homes in Bessarabia.[23]

In November 1921 the Romanian interior minister ordered the immediate resettlement of refugees from Kishinev. According to a local report, officials singled out Jews for abuse. On November 27, the local Jewish aid committee received orders to immediately dispatch sixteen hundred Jews to the Kishinev train station for relocation. Otherwise, Jews would be arrested at random and deported. The destination of the train was not revealed. Many Jews were reluctant to leave because they owned small businesses and did not want to be separated from their relatives. In fact, according to the local correspondent who sent his report to the Jewish World Relief Conference, quite a few probably were Kishinev residents who had fled the city during the war. At the appointed hour 300 Jews assembled outside the train station. After further threats by Romanian general Ioan Popvici, who supervised the deportation, the number increased to 981. A local rabbi (almost certainly the respected Kishinev rabbi Yehuda Leib Tsirelson) read a farewell statement as the military counted the refugees like "parcels." Jews from different Ukrainian towns boarded the train cars in groups. The correspondent lamented that "these evacuated persons represented all that was left of the Jewish Communities formerly well off." The refugees were apparently allowed to return to Kishinev after a delegation representing the League of Nations High Commissioner for Refugees persuaded the Romanian government to reverse the evacuation.[24]

The Dniester River formed the eastern border of Bessarabia. Transnistria, on the eastern, Soviet-controlled side of the Dniester, and western Ukraine were affected by famine and disease outbreaks and, at the end of the decade, by Stalin's forced collectivization policy. Throughout the 1920s and 1930s Romanian soldiers shot a large number of Jews, Ukrainians, and others as they crossed the river to escape the deteriorating economic conditions and political oppression in the Soviet Union. In 1926 a Lieutenant Morarescu, who publicly bragged of killing more than 150 Jewish refugees on the Dniester, was acquitted in a high-profile trial in Bucharest. According to a 1932 report on the trial, Morarescu and his troops lured Jewish migrants to the border, collecting money to smuggle them into Romania, only to kill them as they waded through the river or came ashore. Several guards testified that Morarescu also abused and robbed Christians, but he killed only Jews.

After the acquittal Morarescu associated with Corneliu Zelea Codreanu, who founded the fascist Iron Guard movement in 1927. Jewish aid associations tried to publicize such cases of abuse and murder, but apart from lobbying governments and League of Nations representatives they were powerless.[25]

Closing Gates

Just as Jewish aid associations, communities, and representatives began to rebuild a support network in the early 1920s, the United States closed its doors. Lawmakers and bureaucrats specifically sought to exclude Eastern European Jews, not coincidentally when many were precariously exposed to violent persecution and had few viable alternatives to moving to the United States. Immigration restrictions had enjoyed growing support in Congress since the 1890s. Even before the United States entered the war in April 1917 Congress had passed a more restrictive bill that included a literacy test. This was not the first time that the literacy test passed both houses of Congress, but in early February 1917 Congress overrode the presidential veto of it. Louis Marshall, a respected corporate and civil rights lawyer who served as head of the American Jewish Committee, lobbied for an exemption from the literacy test for those fleeing persecution because of their "religious faith."

Thanks to lobbying efforts by Marshall and other established Jews a brief clause was inserted into the bill ensuring that, upon request, the literacy test would be given in Hebrew or Yiddish so that Jewish immigrants were not rejected because they could not read a text in an unfamiliar language. However, the push by Marshall and immigration lawyer Max Kohler to formally enshrine the right of asylum for religious refugees failed. In a public letter Kohler specifically referred to Jewish and Armenian refugees urgently requiring protection, echoing Henry Morgenthau Sr., whose memoir about the Armenian genocide was published the following year. Long before 1914 Kohler, Marshall, and other Jewish leaders had praised America as a safe haven for persecuted Jews and others. It is noteworthy that American Jewish leaders made the first concerted attempt to guarantee the right of asylum for people being persecuted because they belonged to a specific religious group.[26]

Immigration restrictions were part of Warren Harding's winning platform in the 1920 presidential election. In May 1921, a few months after he was sworn in, Harding signed a temporary immigration bill which became known as the Emergency Quota Act. All countries and other territories such as colonies outside of the Americas were allocated monthly quotas, which were often exhausted after a few days. The quota system favored migrants from Germany, Scandinavia, and the British Isles and limited migration from countries in Eastern and Southern Europe. Immigration from countries and colonial territories in Africa and Asia was almost completely curtailed. The bill established a monthly ceiling for immigrants based on their respective "national origins." The decisive criterion for the quota regime was *not* citizenship or residence in a certain country but the actual location of the birthplace of an applicant. A Russian Jew who had moved to France and naturalized as a French citizen before or after 1914 did not fall under the French quota but under the quota of the country where his or her birthplace was located in or after 1921. If his or her spouse hailed from a nearby town in the Russian Empire that became part of a different state in 1918, she or he had to apply under the quota for that country. Jews from the former Russian Empire or the former Austrian province of Galicia who had settled in France, Germany, or Austria after 1918 had only a remote chance of obtaining a visa in the late 1930s because they fell under the Polish or Russian quota. In contrast, Jews born in Germany would benefit from the relatively generous German quota, albeit only after the United States issued more immigrant visas in the wake of the notorious Kristallnacht pogrom in late November 1938.

In 1921, Marshall realized that it was futile to lobby for an exemption clause for Jewish migrants and refugees. The support for stringent immigration restrictions in both houses of Congress was overwhelming and cut across political divides. A single senator, James Reed, a Democrat from Missouri, voted against the 1921 bill; seventeen other senators abstained. In the House the bill passed by acclamation because the opposition was negligible. The monthly ceilings, which were introduced to reduce migration during the busy summer months, led to chaotic scenes in Ellis Island during the first week of most months. Steamship lines competed to beat the clock, arriving slightly after midnight on the first day of each month to ensure all passengers could enter. On August 31, 1923, for example, four ships clocked in a few minutes before midnight. Since the August quotas for most passengers had already been filled, the steamship lines faced extensive fines. On this occasion, the secretary of labor generously exempted the passengers, but after 1921 thousands were regularly deported from Ellis Island because they arrived a few days too late. Average migrants were not able to time their departure when they booked a passage, and they could not anticipate schedule changes that were the result of weather conditions on the North Atlantic, delays or cancellations resulting from unforeseeable mechanical problems, and the capacity management of the steamship lines.[27]

In May 1924, the Senate passed a modified House bill to permanently adopt the main features of the temporary 1921 bill and address flaws such as the bizarre midnight races. The bill shifted the decision to admit migrants from immigration inspectors at the ports of arrival to the State Department. All migrants had to apply for a visa at a U.S. embassy or consulate in their home country, requiring lengthy waiting periods. Applicants frequently lived far from the closest American diplomatic representative and lacked some of the documents that were required. The bill also included new quota provisions. Observers in Europe were stunned by a drastic reduction in the already low quotas. President Calvin Coolidge swiftly signed the Johnson-Reed Act into law in late May. Only five weeks later, on July 1, 1924, the new quota regime took effect. The new bill did not contain provisions for tens of thousands of migrants with approved visas, such as the Bremerhaven layover migrants who had expected to wait for a few months before entering under the original quota for the 1924–1925 fiscal year. To complicate matters further, most passports and visas were valid for just a couple of months or a year, requiring costly and lengthy applications for extensions and renewals.[28]

Several influential American legislators considered Eastern European Jews to be a particularly unwelcome group. During the 1920 presidential campaign nativists fanned the growing isolationist sentiment by painting Jewish immigrants as Bolshevist agents who would incite a revolution in the United States. In his study of the 1918–1919 pogroms Jeffrey Veidlinger persuasively argues that the association of Jewish migrants and refugees with Bolshevism was in part related to measures taken by Soviet troops to prevent anti-Jewish violence.[29] Eastern European Jews were also widely considered unproductive and a permanent economic burden. A report of the Committee on Immigration and Naturalization submitted to the House of Representatives in 1921 contains an assessment by an unnamed American consular official from Warsaw who warned that large numbers of Jews and Christians would come to the United States from Poland:

> These are not the Europeans of a sturdier day. . . . These are not those who hewed the forests, founded the towns, fought the savages, breasted the storms of wilderness, conquered the wastes, and built America. These are beaten folk, spirits broken, in effect driven from their European habitat into

the west. They have no desire to form and build. They will exist on what has been prepared for them by a better people. They are in search of an easier life.[30]

Based on the rigid provisions of the 1917 immigration act, which had effectively excluded almost all Asians from territories not controlled by the United States, the authors of the 1921 and 1924 bills almost completely curtailed immigration from Africa and Asia. During the First World War, cultural bias among American nativists gave way to overt racism. An early harbinger was the Chinese and Japanese exclusion movement before 1914. Racism and antisemitism were closely intertwined. Already in the early 1880s Jewish observers noted potential pitfalls of the Chinese exclusion legislation for other undesirable "races." The cosponsor of the 1921 and 1924 immigration bills, Congressman Albert Johnson from Washington State, was a longtime proponent of Japanese exclusion and an antisemite. In 1920 he rallied support for restrictive immigration legislation by describing Jews as "unassimilable," "filthy," "un-American," and "dangerous." In a 1927 speech Johnson deplored "the encroachments of the foreign blood" and declared that with the passage of his 1924 bill "the day of unalloyed welcome to all peoples, the day of indiscriminate acceptance of all races has definitely ended."[31]

The 1924 bill actually constituted a compromise because it based the quotas on "national" and not on "racial" origin. During the debates in the House and Senate several speakers pointed out that Jews had been and were strongly overrepresented among Eastern European immigrants. Allotting low quotas to countries like Poland ensured that very few Jews would immigrate. Several lawmakers tried to push further; South Dakota senator Thomas Sterling, for instance, proposed specifically excluding Jews as a "race." This position met with opposition. Pennsylvania senator David A. Reed, the cosponsor of Johnson's House bill, insisted that determining a migrant's actual "racial" origins would be "unworkable" for U.S. consular officers. This comment unwittingly demonstrates the obvious limitations of the pseudoscientific race concept as biologically determined.

The 1921 and 1924 immigration bills reflect the vision of Madison Grant, a well-connected New York socialite and prominent promotor of pseudoscientific racism and eugenics. Scholars disagree over the extent of Grant's influence on the 1924 bill, but the impact of his ideas on several decision-makers in Congress is not contested. In his widely read main work, *The Passing of the Great Race* (1916), Grant presented race as a biologically determined concept and coined the term "Nordic" for the superior race. His reconceptualization constituted a shift from the predominant definition of race as a corollary of cultural traits that bears a certain resemblance to the concept of ethnicity. Like leading Nazi ideologues, Grant was concerned about the supposed biological "threat" of undesirable races to members of the "old-stock" race. He considered Jews to be particularly dangerous because they passed as "white" and could enter social circles reserved for "old-stock" Americans. In one of the most notorious passages of his book he claimed that "Polish Jews" were destroying the American race: "[The] man of the old stock ... is to-day being literally driven off the streets of New York City by the swarms of Polish Jews. These immigrants adopt the language of the native American, they wear his clothes, they steal his name, and they are beginning to take his women." *The Passing of the Great Race* focused on the racial history of Europe and Asia to highlight the threat of unchecked immigration. Educated Americans, including Presidents Harding and Coolidge and leading figures on Capitol Hill, embraced Grant's fundamental opposition to immigration because he cleverly tapped the growing interest in eugenics.[32]

The pitch of the 1924 bill's cosponsor, Senator Reed, betrays Grant's alarmist rhetoric. If the bill failed, he stated, "three million immigrants will come here in the next six months. They will come just as fast as the steamers can bring them." In his view migrants of certain racial backgrounds were a grave threat to American society. However, as Reed put it, "we can easily assimilate 300,000 if they are of the proper racial origins." The 1924 bill passed with overwhelming majorities in both houses of Congress. On the eve of the Senate vote Marshall sharply denounced the backers of the bill and explicitly pointed to the "phrasemonger" Grant as the bill's spiritual author. Congressman Adolph J. Sabath, a Jewish immigrant from Bohemia who represented a Polish and Czech immigrant district in Chicago, observed that the bill was based on a "confusing and unintelligible maze of unsupported statements and bewildering figures." He also warned, "Should the idea of caste ever gain a foothold here, it would unquestionably lead to our undoing." Chicago sociologist Robert Park noted that the bill gave "a sort of sanction to the notion which has been persistently maintained in the case of the Negro, that certain of the racial and national groups in the United States were not only culturally but biologically inferior to others."[33]

Grant's "Nordic" race bears more than a passing resemblance to Hitler's "Aryans." The German-language edition of *The Passing of the Great Race* appeared in 1925, after eugenicist and bestselling author Hans Günther

"If the Statue of Liberty were a living person" by cartoonist Zuni Maud was published in *Der Groyser Kundes*, May 27, 1921. The suicide note on the pedestal reads, "After my friends harassed, betrayed, and deserted me, I no longer have a reason to live in this world." The restrictive Emergency Quota Act, signed by President Warren G. Harding into law on May 19, 1921, drastically reduced immigration and contradicted America's image as a safe haven for persecuted people. The Statue of Liberty had lost its purpose. *YIVO, Institute for Jewish Research, New York*

promoted Grant's work. In the 1930s Günther, who was also known as "Rassengünther," became one of Nazi Germany's most influential race "scientists." Some German readers probably noticed that Grant relied heavily on the German British author Houston Stewart Chamberlain, who popularized the image of the "Aryan" race in his widely read 1899 essay, "The Foundations of the Nineteenth Century." Grant listed the English translation of Chamberlain's book in his bibliography. It is likely that Hitler read the German translation of Grant's book soon after its publication. An American eugenicist claimed that Hitler sent Grant a letter praising the book as "his Bible." This story cannot be proven, but Hitler's personal library included a copy of the German translation, and the Nazi leader repeatedly quoted Grant in campaign speeches, for instance in early 1927, when he praised the American immigration quotas. Heinrich Himmler and the Nazis' "chief ideologue" Alfred Rosenberg also promoted Grant and other American authors, among them white supremacist Lothrop Stoddard and the notorious eugenicist Harry H. Laughlin, who served as expert witness for Johnson's immigration committee in the House, providing the pseudoscientific legitimation for the quotas.[34]

In the early 1930s a *New York Times* reporter came across a copy of Grant's book in the library of the Brown House, the Nazi Party headquarters in Munich, just before interviewing Hitler. The Nazi leader expressed his appreciation of the Johnson-Reed Act: "It was America that taught us that a nation should not open its doors equally to all nations." Hitler's view was hardly isolated. In 1933 Otto Koellreutter, an influential German legal scholar and Nazi sympathizer, praised American immigration restrictions: "The American Union categorically refuses the immigration of physically unhealthy elements, and simply excludes the immigration of certain races. In these respects, America already pays obeisance . . . to the characteristic *völkisch* conception of the state." Koellreutter pointed out that the American immigration restrictions specifically targeted "Ostjuden" as particularly unwelcome. In 1934 Günther described Grant and Stoddard as the real authors of America's immigration bills.[35]

Following the passage of the 1921 and 1924 bills the annual number of Jewish immigrants dropped sharply. In 1921 about 100,000 Jews immigrated, a number that came close to the prewar records. After the first bill was implemented, the number decreased to about 50,000 in each of the three following years. After 1924 about 10,000 Jews immigrated annually until a further decline in the wake of the Great Depression. These numbers include hundreds of immigrants who were exempt from the quotas, notably spouses and minor children of individuals who had legally immigrated before 1924. Little is known about tens of thousands of migrants whose visa applications were turned down. Some managed to reach alternative destinations, and many more delayed their decision to move, gave up, or never tried because of the costs involved to file applications requiring extensive documentation. An estimated 250,000 Jews managed to enter the United States between 1918 and 1924.[36]

The little-disguised features of the restrictive immigration legislation targeting Eastern European Jews reflect the rising influence of antisemitism and biologically determined racism in post-1918 America. Migration scholar Aristide Zolberg has described the post-1918 U.S. immigration policy as a "significant contributory cause to the Holocaust." Zolberg, who survived the Holocaust as the child of stateless Polish Jewish parents in Belgium with false papers, emphasizes the impact of "path dependency." Once an exclusionary immigration policy had been put in place, reformist policymakers had to operate within the confines of the new regulatory system. As Zolberg puts it, "seldom has a scientific formulation encompassed a greater tragedy." In the early 1920s the framers of the restrictive U.S. immigration legislation could not anticipate a genocide that would take place two decades later. Indeed, during the 1930s, when the Nazi regime began to implement its racist and eugenicist policies, a number of prominent American eugenicists (albeit not Grant) had second thoughts and distanced themselves from some of their more extreme ideas. However, throughout the 1920s, 1930s, and 1940s, Congress and the State Department rigidly adhered to the national origins quota system, even as the situation of Jews facing violent persecution became increasingly precarious. This policy ensured that Eastern European Jews and other "undesirables" remained excluded.[37]

Humanitarian Diplomacy

Jewish aid associations were overwhelmed by the scale of the crisis that affected the large center of the Jewish Diaspora in a region stretching from the Baltic to the Black Sea. After the First World War JDC and HIAS remained crucial actors in this region. Both organizations had experienced staff members on the ground and funds at their disposal because they could draw on American Jewish donors. Estimates of the number of afflicted Jews (and others) ranged widely, in part because the fluctuation was high. As some Jews returned to their homes, others were displaced. After 1918 dozens of newly founded local and transnational Jewish aid associations representing Eastern European Jews sought funding from JDC and HIAS. Divisions, primarily between Zionists, Bundists, and other groups from Eastern Europe and members of the Jewish establishment from Britain and the United States, hampered aid efforts.

Among the officials representing the interests of Jewish refugees and minority populations on the international stage after 1918, two figures stand out: Lucien Wolf, a member of the Anglo-Jewish establishment, and Leo

Motzkin, a visionary Zionist. Wolf led the Joint Foreign Committee of London, which represented the Board of Deputies of British Jews and the Anglo-Jewish Association. He had a major hand in shaping the treaties protecting Jewish and other minorities in successor states of the former empires, including Poland and Romania. During the 1920s he served as an unofficial Jewish lobbyist at the League of Nations. His influence in Geneva was enhanced by the absence of American and German Jewish representatives. The United States did not join the League. Apart from raising funds and coordinating support for refugees and local Jewish communities in Poland and other successor states, American Jewish representatives like Marshall kept a low profile on the international stage after the Paris peace conferences. As an American organization the JDC formally decided not to attend meetings at the League. This decision weakened Jewish diplomacy but also reflects the impact of rising antisemitism and nativism in the United States in the aftermath of the war. The JDC withdrawal also reflected internal divisions between different American Jewish groups that resurfaced after the war. Germany was a diminished actor, even after it joined the League in 1926. The war and inflation hit middle-class German Jews hard. Deprived of donations and cut off from its prewar network, the Hilfsverein lost much of its influence.

Motzkin belonged to the Zionist Gegenwartsarbeit faction, whose members called for studying and improving the conditions of Jewish life in the present rather than preparing for Jewish settlement in Palestine in the distant future. He was born in a town near Kiev but completed his secondary school education in Berlin. Motzkin studied mathematics at Berlin's main university but did not graduate. During the early phase of the war, he directed the main office of the World Zionist Organization in neutral Copenhagen. In the 1920s he lived mostly in Paris but kept an apartment in Berlin. Although Motzkin remained active in the World Zionist Organization, during the 1920s his vision of Jewish Diaspora nationalism diverged from the mainstream represented by the new Zionist leader Chaim Weizmann. Motzkin attended the Paris peace conferences together with Wolf as a member of the ad hoc Jewish delegation, the Comité des Delegations Juives. The discussions were marred by conflicts between Zionists and representatives of such establishment organizations as Wolf's Joint Foreign Committee. During the 1920s the Comité was based in Paris and was comprised primarily of Zionist members. As a political organization it claimed to represent all Jews, but its main role was to lobby on behalf of Jewish minorities in and refugees from

Eastern Europe. Nahum Sokolov served as president and Motzkin as general secretary. The Comité became the main predecessor organization of the World Jewish Congress, which was founded in 1936.

During the 1920s Wolf, Motzkin, and several other Jewish representatives lobbied for the protection of Jewish minorities and at the same time managed the provision of aid to Jews in need. The extent of the postwar Jewish refugee crisis, widespread and massive violence, and the uncertain status of Jewish minorities in states such as Romania and Poland forced Jewish aid associations to take a more proactive stance. Officially, both men represented Jewish aid associations; in reality, they were unelected humanitarian advocates who spoke and negotiated with governments on behalf of disenfranchised Jewish minorities and stateless refugees.[38]

The architects of the League did not anticipate the lingering impact of the collapse of the large multiethnic empires, in particular the massive refugee crisis. They were unable to strike a balance between the principle of national self-determination and the protection of religious and national minorities, especially in the Eastern European successor states. Britain, France, Belgium, Japan, the Netherlands, and a few other states represented millions of colonial subjects who were denied the right of national self-determination. The League was charged with overseeing the administration of former German colonies and Ottoman territories as "mandates." Yet powers, including Britain and France, ruled "mandates" such as Palestine and French Cameroon as de facto colonies.[39]

In hindsight, it is easy to portray the League as a misconstrued project doomed to fail. Several scholars have made a compelling case for looking beyond the League's obvious flaws by reassessing it as an underappreciated forerunner of the United Nations. In a curious paradox, at the end of the First World War the triumph of the territorially defined state that was based on the 1648 Westphalian peace treaty coincided with a crisis of the Westphalian system of international diplomacy. The League's main task was to safeguard peace. In addition to providing a permanent platform for diplomatic negotiations, the League and its affiliated bodies served as a forum for international "humanitarianism," represented not least by Jewish aid associations, various nongovernmental organizations like the International Committee of the Red Cross, and other nonstate actors. During the 1920s the League and its affiliated bodies, including the International Labor Organization, brought together experts, business leaders, diplomats, and representatives of nongovernmental organizations to define internationally recognized standards, notably in global trade, transportation, labor relations, and health. The standardized international passport was the product of a series of conferences convened by the League during the 1920s. Establishing basic principles for humanitarian interventions to address refugee crises was of particular importance for Jewish representatives. Jewish organizations had extensive experience in working beyond borders to raise funds and coordinate support with different governments and nonstate actors. Now Jewish representatives were not just overwhelmed by the scale of the post-1918 crisis; they also faced a particular challenge: unlike other groups, for instance German-speaking minorities in Poland and Czechoslovakia, Jews did not have the backing of a state. This made it even more important to lobby for the establishment of universal principles backed by most governments guaranteeing the protection of stateless refugees and minority populations.[40]

The establishment of the League's Office of the High Commissioner for Refugees in June 1921 reflects a shared understanding that the refugee crisis could not be solved in the short term. Jews were disproportionally affected. Yet several other, often disparate groups were also stranded in permanent transit: opponents of the Bolsheviks, large numbers of Armenians, and hundreds of thousands of civilians caught up in dozens of conflicts in Eastern Europe, such as the wars between the Soviet Union and Poland, between Hungary and Romania, and between Turkey and Greece. In the fall of 1920, a few months after the chaotic mass flight from Warsaw to Danzig, Constantinople (Istanbul) emerged as a new hotspot. After the army of the former tsarist general Pyotr Wrangel had been evacuated from Crimea, more than 100,000 Russian refugees of diverse backgrounds, including thousands of Jews, congregated in encampments surrounding Constantinople. Outbreaks of disease claimed hundreds of lives. As the crisis gradually subsided and refugees were repatriated or moved to destinations in Europe and Palestine, the Greco-Turkish War led to renewed mass displacements. No blueprint existed for how to resolve these crises.

According to estimates, more than 3 million Europeans were stateless in the early 1920s. Following the collapse of the large empires, no government was formally responsible for people who had almost literally been fenced out of the system of territorially defined successor states. Many had lost their homes. Frequently repatriation, the preferred solution, was not feasible. Those willing to return were refused entry and risked arrest or even their lives. After 1918 valid passports and visas were required to cross most international borders. Initially, the new passport requirement created niches for stateless migrants. In 1920, for example, a group of stateless Jews from Russia acquired forged passports in Berlin, traveled by ship to Veracruz in Mexico, and presented their passports to enter the United States at El Paso in January 1921. After the authorities were tipped off, several Jews who had remained in the Texas border town were arrested and confessed. El Paso rabbi Martin Zielonka pleaded with JDC chairman and fellow German immigrant Felix Warburg to intervene. Warburg refused. He emphasized the need to obey the law—against the background of overwhelming public support for immigration restrictions, not least for Jews from Eastern Europe. The Jews were deported to Mexico. It was obvious that they required support because the violent civil war had hit Mexico's northern borderlands particularly hard. In the following years Zielonka took an active role in assisting Jewish migrants from Eastern Europe who settled in Mexico.[41]

People without citizenship could not be deported without the prior consent of the receiving country. The case of the stateless Jews who were deported to Mexico, however, was hardly isolated. Stateless people were subject to forced removal, but they lacked agency to cross borders on their own without valid passports. Statelessness was one reason why tens of thousands of displaced Eastern Europeans were permanently stranded on the social margins. Displaced Jews who could not return to their homes had no obvious place where they could go, except to the United States, where many had relatives. Even Zionist leaders conceded that Palestine could accommodate only small groups for the foreseeable future. Statelessness also affected Armenian genocide survivors and "Russian refugees," a huge group that included Jewish refugees, opponents of the Bolsheviks, former Russian POWs, different religious groups, but also veterans of the White armies who often had participated in pogroms against Jews.[42]

Following a meeting convened by the High Commissioner for Refugees with sixteen government representatives in July 1922, the League of Nations persuaded most governments in Europe to issue passports to stateless persons from the territory of the former Russian Empire to address the unprecedented refugee crisis. The passports, which were named after High Commissioner Fridtjof Nansen, the Norwegian explorer, were not real passports but allowed their holders to move to countries recognizing this system. The United States, which did not join the League, did accept the Nansen passports as valid documents. In his semi-autobiographical novel *Pnin*, Vladimir Nabokov, himself a stateless migrant living in Berlin during the 1920s, recalled the hurdles facing stateless migrants and refugees in interwar Europe, "the dreary hell that had been devised by European bureaucrats (to the vast amusement of the Soviets) for holders of that miserable thing, called the Nansen passport (a kind of parolee's card issued to Russian émigrés)." Legal theorists noted that the passports did not confer citizenship but at least confirmed the holder's actual existence and status as a legally displaced person and her or his identity.[43]

The Nansen passport for stateless persons was a pragmatic remedy but not a real solution. Lucien Wolf deserves some credit as one of the passport's initiators. In the summer of 1921, he informed the League that more than 200,000 Jews had been permanently displaced along the western border of the new Soviet state, and perhaps an even larger number had been "slaughtered." Because they were unable to return to their homes, their legal status was undetermined. They had no Russian papers; Poland and Romania had issued quasi-identity papers to some to speed up their departure, but U.S. consular officers refused to accept these documents for visa applications. Wolf realized that the lack of recognized papers greatly exacerbated the affliction of stateless refugees. However, Nabokov's cynical remarks were not far off the mark. Stateless persons had to apply for a Nansen passport for each journey across an international border. The extensive collection of the High Commissioner for Refugees Office contains dozens of applications for Nansen passports and visas to be issued by the Swiss authorities. Unlike Wolf, who was a British subject, the stateless Motzkin had to secure a passport and visa every time he traveled from Berlin or Paris to Geneva—and back. The files of the Zionist office in Berlin contain a thick folder for the "procurement of entry and transit visa[s]" documenting the travails of organizing simple trips across borders, even for holders of valid passports.[44]

During the first half of the 1920s Jewish representatives participated in meetings convened by Nansen's office. Early on, Motzkin challenged Wolf and the traditional leadership of established Western Jewish organizations. His close associate and fellow Zionist, Zevi Aberson, served as the de facto Geneva representative of a network of newly founded Jewish aid associations with close ties to Eastern European Jews and the Comité, the Jewish World Relief Conference. He successfully secured invitations to League meetings. Initially, Wolf refused to accept Aberson's presence, irritating sympathetic League officials. Beyond differing views about Zionism, the conflict betrayed the rising sway of the Zionist World Organization and growing confidence of Jews from Eastern Europe to determine their own destiny. Motzkin's bold project of a formal representation of global Jewry in the international arena challenged Western Jewish leaders like Wolf, who preferred tacit diplomacy. Motzkin also diverged from Zionist leader Weizmann, who considered building the Jewish homeland in Palestine to be the overarching goal.

A particularly unsettling example illustrates why Motzkin's skepticism of the effectiveness of traditional diplomacy was justified. In 1926 Wolf met with the new Romanian foreign minister, Ion Mitilineu, and the Romanian ambassador in Switzerland and permanent League representative, Nicolae Titulescu. Wolf raised the undetermined status of thousands of stateless Jewish refugees living in Romania and suggested that the country provide them with citizenship because they could not move anywhere. An obvious model was Poland, which began naturalizing thousands of Jews from the former Russian Empire in 1926. Three years earlier, following diplomatic pressure by Western powers and after decades of Jewish lobbying, Romania had belatedly emancipated its Jewish population. Wolf had played a major role in drafting the minorities treaties in Paris and lobbying for the emancipation of Romanian Jewry. An ongoing problem was the refusal of the government in Bucharest to extend citizenship to Jewish "refugees," even though many were longtime residents of newly acquired territories such as Bessarabia. Titulescu's stance prompted Wolf to publish a printed report of the meeting through the League. According to Wolf's notes, Titulescu told him that "any pressure would lead to deplorable events." Wolf, as he put it, "declined to discuss this statement."

Titulescu, it is worth noting, was a firm supporter of the Romanian alliance with France; he opposed the fascist Iron Guard and was forced into French exile in the 1930s. Wolf's meetings with Polish diplomats were more cordial but not productive. Wolf was a highly capable diplomat but ultimately he failed to understand that the League had no leverage over governments that discriminated against and oppressed members of unwanted minority populations.[45]

Motzkin pursued a more proactive strategy than Wolf, but he too faced formidable obstacles. One notable success for the Comité, following intense lobbying, was the Lithuanian Parliament's adoption of minority rights in August 1921. Lithuania had even established a ministry for Jewish affairs in 1918, albeit in part to curry favor with the Entente powers to support claims over its contested borders with Poland. Even before the coup by Antanas Smetona in 1926, different governments curtailed Jewish autonomy rights. The ministry for Jewish affairs was abolished in 1924.[46]

The Jewish World Relief Conference (Conference Universelle Juive de Secours) and the affiliated aid association Emigdirect (United Jewish Emigration Committee) were products of a series of "emigration conferences" that Motzkin and several Eastern European Zionists convened in Copenhagen, Karlsbad, and Prague after the war. JDC, JCA, and Wolf's Joint Foreign Committee boycotted most of the conferences. HIAS, whose leaders remained committed to their Eastern European roots, embraced the effort. The main purpose of the conferences was to coordinate relief work for Jewish refugees and issues related to Jewish migration, namely the raising and distribution of funds, vocational training, and political lobbying efforts in and beyond Geneva. Thanks to its enormous endowment, the Paris-based JCA was a much sought-after partner for Jewish aid associations during the interwar period. After 1918, JCA shifted from its focus on Jewish colonization to supporting Jewish refugees and rebuilding Jewish communities in Eastern Europe. Motzkin spent much of the 1920s preserving a brittle coalition among dozens of organizations and political representatives while trying to secure financial support from HIAS, JDC, and JCA. The emergence of dozens of Jewish aid associations with competing politics and interests in the aftermath of the war constituted an additional challenge.[47]

Emigdirect was founded at the Jewish Emigration Conference in Prague in September 1921. The conference proceedings provide a glimpse of the extent of the crisis. Motzkin, who chaired the meeting, stressed that nothing more than a "horrible catastrophe" was taking place. In some countries Jews were at risk of being "exterminated." Following the Soviet announcement that the USSR would issue exit visas to Jewish children and women who wanted to join their fathers and husbands abroad, Motzkin stated that representatives of Emigdirect would negotiate with the governments of Latvia and Lithuania to grant Jewish emigrants the right of safe passage and short-term residency to apply for visas at foreign consulates and embassies in Kaunas/Kovno and Riga. In November 1921 the head of Emigdirect, Meir Kreinin, a Russian-born Zionist, signed an accord on behalf of the organization with the Lithuanian government to protect Jewish transit migrants. Representatives of the Latvian government, HIAS, Emigdirect, and an organization representing Jews from Ukraine signed an almost identical document in August 1922. Small states such as Lithuania and Latvia had limited influence on the international stage and supported the agreements to ensure Jewish refugees would depart.[48]

The little-known treaties are significant because two sovereign governments formally recognized representatives who acted not on behalf of a state but for a transterritorial group. Jewish aid associations did not just lobby on behalf of Jews facing persecution but bypassed diplomatic channels to negotiate formal treaties directly with governments to protect stateless Jewish migrants. The treaties signal Motzkin's vision of securing formal recognition of the Jews as a transterritorial "global people." Such a status would have protected Jews who had been fenced out of the system of territorially defined nation-states. In an undated German-language text he wrote during the mid-1920s titled "The Jewish People and the League of Nations," Motzkin pointed out, "[I]n its current structure the League of Nations treats the Jewish people as an alien organism, as object, never as subject. Only indirectly can we [as Jews] influence consultations and decisions of the League." In a related text titled "The League of Nations and Jewish Policy" Motzkin criticized the Westphalian principle that associated statehood exclusively with sovereignty over a specific territory and its inhabitants. The League of Nations was a misnomer because it really was a "league of states." The Jewish people as "extraterritorial organism" should be allowed to join. Only then would the League become a true "Bund der Völker" (league of nations).[49]

When Motzkin first presented this project in 1918, a British diplomat pointed out practical complications, notably how to handle overlapping claims of sovereignty such as dual citizenship for Jews. Motzkin persisted, in part because the League was unable to enforce the protection of minorities in Eastern Europe. In 1925 he joined forces with Baltic German journalist Paul Schiemann and others to establish the National Minorities Congress (European Nationalities Congress). Populations ruled by European colonial powers outside of Europe were not represented. The Congress met under the auspices of the League to give voice to different minorities in the successor states. It was not a coincidence that the Congress was organized a few months before Germany joined the League in 1926. The Jewish coalition with German minority representatives was controversial, because the German government instrumentalized its advocacy on behalf of minorities to undermine the Versailles Treaty. The Hungarian government, which had passed antisemitic laws to keep the number of Jewish students at low levels, was another strange bedfellow. The membership of the Comité des Delegations Juives in the Congress also raised the question whether Jews in Germany, Britain, and France were ethnic minorities. This was a rather delicate issue after the First World War in the wake of rising antisemitic agitation. Not surprisingly, Wolf as well as leading German and French Jewish representatives opposed the Congress.[50]

Like the League of Nations and many of its most committed leaders, including the head of the International Labor Organization, Albert Thomas, Motzkin remains little known. Even authors of recently published studies about Jewish diplomacy and humanitarian assistance during and after the war largely ignore him—and different organizations he helped to launch, like Emigdirect. His (limited) influence culminated when Jewish aid associations and representatives advocating on behalf of Jewish refugees and minorities were increasingly at odds and losing much of the soft power they had exercised before the war. As a Jewish advocate who moved between borders, Motzkin transcends the artificially narrow purview of scholars beholden to the nation-state (and Zionist) paradigm. Motzkin's visions remain unfulfilled. In contrast, Weizmann's relentless focus on securing the Jewish "homeland" in Palestine was vindicated when in 1948 he became the first president of Israel. The territorially defined Jewish nation-state bore a striking resemblance to the post-1918 Eastern European successor states—and their policies toward unwanted minorities and refugees. In Weizmann's memoir, Motzkin and Aberson, his close friends in the 1890s, make only fleeting appearances.

Motzkin's push for the international recognition and representation of fenced-out stateless groups became even more relevant after 1945 than it was in the interwar period. Decolonization led to the expulsion of unwanted groups across arbitrarily drawn borders in South Asia, the Middle East, and Africa. Most Palestinians living outside of Israel remain stateless, as do the descendants of Muslim Biharis who survived the flight from the new Indian state to East Pakistan in 1947. Since most Biharis were Urdu speakers, they were associated with West Pakistan. They were rendered stateless in 1971, when Bangladesh seceded from Pakistan and declared independence. Bengal nationalists blamed the Biharis for collaborating with (West) Pakistan. Since no country is willing to accept them, most Biharis continue to live in Bangladesh on the social margins as a fenced-out minority. Most recently large numbers of Somalis who fled a collapsing state remain stranded in huge refugee camps in northern Kenya. More than 1 million Rohingya were already stateless before they escaped genocidal killings in Myanmar to neighboring Bangladesh, where they are treated as unwelcome outsiders. In 2020 the Bangladesh government began to relocate the first groups of Rohingya to Bhasan Char, a desolate island in the Bay of Bengal that is precariously exposed to flooding. The plan is to move at least 100,000 Rohingya to the island.[51]

The history of the short-lived aid association Emigdirect mirrors the conflicting visions, challenges, and divisions of the interwar period. The Berlin-based organization partly filled the void left by the Hilfsverein central office for Jewish emigrants. Its complex structure—it was a federation of local organizations—hampered its impact. In the mid-1920s, Emigdirect maintained offices in most Eastern European capitals and even in the Manchurian railroad hub, Harbin, home to a growing Jewish community in the aftermath of the Russian Civil War. Migrants could seek advice and limited assistance from Emigdirect. In 1925 its affiliated staff extended support to more than forty-five thousand Jewish migrants in Poland alone. The Emigdirect office in Harbin complemented the Far Eastern Jewish Central Information Bureau, or DALJEWCIB (its telegraphic address), which owed its existence to the HIAS aid effort in the Far East in 1918–1919. Its files document attempts to reunite thousands of separated Jewish family members in different parts of the world during the 1920s.[52]

Like dozens of smaller and sometimes competing Eastern and Central European aid associations, Emigdirect depended almost completely on support from JCA and other American Jewish organizations. Letters in Motzkin's papers hint at continuous conflicts over control and funding issues. JDC insisted that the organizations it supported adhere to professional standards and become self-sustaining, not least by improving their fundraising operations. HIAS representatives were more sympathetic. The main representatives of Emigdirect resented what they perceived as a patronizing attitude. During the second half of the 1920s, when the crisis of permanently stranded Jewish DPs gradually subsided, JDC turned its attention to economic reconstruction and long-term development, particularly by funding Jewish agricultural colonies in the Soviet Union through the Agro-Joint. This project increased the divisions between its established backers and Zionist leaders who favored colonization in Palestine.[53]

Deprived of reliable access to JDC funds, Emigdirect entered into negotiations with HIAS and JCA to formalize the cooperation. The federation HICEM (HIAS-JCA-Emigdirect), founded in April 1927, benefited from JCA's need to find reliable partners to advance its colonization mission in Eastern Europe. HIAS and JCA provided the lion's share of the budget. In its 1932 report the HIAS board emphasized the need for cooperation and coordination. Global migration restrictions enacted in the wake of the Great Depression made it even harder to assist displaced Jews. In 1933 Emigdirect had to close its main office in Berlin. Unable to provide even a minimal financial contribution Emigdirect left HICEM in 1934 and ceased its activities. Its longtime head, Meir Kreinin, moved to Palestine. HICEM continued to operate and retained its staff, providing crucial assistance from its office in Paris together with JDC until 1940.

Motzkin could not prevent Emigdirect's demise. He died of a heart attack in Paris in November 1933. A few months earlier, when he was already in ill health, he had pulled off one last coup by concocting the successful submission of the Bernheim Petition to the League. Based on little-known protections for minorities in the contested German-Polish borderland in the Paris peace treaties and a complaint procedure first proposed by Wolf, Nazi Germany reluctantly revoked antisemitic laws in Upper Silesia because the territory remained subject to special protections laid down in the Versailles Treaty.[54]

The First World War represents a watershed moment in the history of Jewish migrations from and within Eastern Europe and beyond. The war disrupted migration flows globally. Jews in the Russian Empire were specifically targeted for mass expulsion, and a very large number were displaced during the war. In the violent aftermath of the war tens of thousands of Jews fell victim to pogroms instigated by Polish, Russian, and Ukrainian nationalists. In the early phase of the war most participating states imposed strict mobility controls. The requirement to carry standardized identification papers for crossing international borders gave rise to the modern passport regime. Passport and visa requirements betray lack of trust between states in the "broken world" after 1918. Postwar migration restrictions, especially those passed by the U.S. Congress, hit Jews in and from Eastern Europe particularly hard. With the collapse of the multiethnic empires in 1918 many Jews became stateless and were thus effectively fenced out of the postwar system of territorially defined nation-states.

The expansion of state control over migration and divisions between the successor states of the empires in Eastern Europe reduced the soft power of Jewish aid associations and other nonstate actors. After 1914 Jewish humanitarian diplomats began to advocate on behalf of Jewish refugees stranded between borders. They managed to gain admission to new forums for international diplomacy, especially the League of Nations. However, their impact was limited because the League was unable to enforce the minorities treaties. Internal conflicts between representatives of the Jewish business establishment in Western Europe and the United States and assertive Zionists from Eastern Europe also hampered efforts to effectively lobby on behalf of displaced Jews and Jewish minorities, especially in Poland and Romania.[55]

7
The Interwar Years
Alternative Destinations and Dead Ends

On the eve of the Great Depression, in September 1929, journalist and writer Joseph Roth visited Berlin's narrow Grenadierstraße in the seedy Scheunenviertel (barn quarter) neighborhood, close to the old center of the city. Men in caftans, peddler carts, kosher restaurants, prayer rooms, and Yiddish bookstores gave the street a "Jewish" touch. The Grenadierstraße was the hub of a disparate Jewish transmigrant community that also featured in the 1929 novel *Berlin Alexanderplatz* by the Jewish physician and writer Alfred Döblin. In the same month Roth penned an article about the Kurfürstendamm, the city's upscale entertainment strip, with numerous coffee houses, grand hotels, and cinemas. The dark Grenadierstraße, with its stagnant scenery, appeared far removed in time and space from the restless modern city featuring in the Kurfürstendamm essay. In early September Roth was still coming to terms with the pogrom in Hebron in the previous month. The anti-Jewish violence in Palestine explains the title of the piece—"Contemplations at the Wailing Wall." Roth denounced Zionism as "the return to a primitive form of national existence." Jews, he wrote, "rebel against themselves, by seeking a [permanent] 'home.'" It was the obvious plight of the Jewish transmigrants in the Grenadierstraße that really concerned him: "Not only in Jerusalem stands a Wailing Wall. Many Wailing Walls form the Grenadierstraße."[1]

In the Weimar cultural scene Roth was the quintessential "outsider as insider." He was born in Brody, where he went to school. After wartime service in the Austrian army, he turned to journalism. His biting but beautifully written feuilleton essays were in high demand. By the late 1920s his literary work, especially the novel *Hotel Savoy* (1924), had earned Roth a reputation as a serious writer. He carefully cultivated his outsider status, proudly acknowledging his Galician Jewish origins. He described himself as *Ostjude* (Eastern Jew), a loaded and fraught term in the antisemitic discourse of the Weimar Republic.[2]

It is easy to dismiss Roth as a nostalgic writer who was out of touch with the economic and political struggles of marginalized Jews from Eastern Europe. A successful traveling reporter, he spent the 1920s in plush hotels and coffee houses chasing stories across Europe. A closer look hints at careful research. Roth was a keen observer who did not gloss over the dangers Jews faced in the nationalist atmosphere of the Weimar Republic. His 1923 serialized novel *Das Spinnennetz* (The Spider's Web) about a secret conspiracy of extremist fascists features Hitler as a character and culminates in an antisemitic riot against Jewish transmigrants in Berlin. A powerful illustration for the acute dangers Jews faced is that Roth anticipated this event. The Vienna-based Arbeiter-Zeitung ran the section with Roth's riveting description of a pogrom in central Berlin on October 31. Days later, on November 5, 1923, as hyperinflation gripped German society, right-wing agitators instigated a riot against Jews in Berlin's Scheunenviertel. And on November 9, 1923, Nazi leaders tried to overthrow the Bavarian government in Munich.[3]

In a period when most migration scholars relied on statistical analysis, Roth's texts stood out because he pondered the implications of mass displacement and migration restrictions. Like Jacob Lestschinsky in his 1914 reportage, Roth called on German Jews to embrace Jewish migrants. He deconstructed widespread stereotypes portraying the migrants as decent men and women looking for a better life. Another German critic of the exclusion of Jewish migrants from the East was the Zionist writer and lawyer Sammy Gronemann, who had assisted Jews from Galicia at the Hanover train station in 1904. In his satirical 1923 novel, *Tohuwabohu* (Utter Chaos), Gronemann employed the popular genre of the *Verwechslungskomödie* (comedy of errors) to narrate the encounter of a stereotypically *ostjüdisch* family of migrants with an overly assimilated and hyperpatriotic family of German Jewish converts. Eventually the protagonists realize they belong to the same family.[4]

The postwar refugee crisis, the economic plight of unwanted Jewish minorities in Eastern Europe, and migration restrictions explain the obvious relevance of migration for authors ranging from journalists and writers to aid workers, politicians, and scholars. The American shift to a restrictive immigration policy was devastating because most Jewish (and other migrants) depended on networks of relatives and friends to fund journeys across the Atlantic and to secure employment. Almost all alternative destinations were viable options for only a relatively small number of Jewish migrants. Few Jews had settled in important post-1918 destinations such as France, Germany,

Brazil, or Palestine before 1914. Without support from informal networks the bar for prospective migrants was far higher. And during the 1920s and 1930s hardly any destination offered compelling economic opportunities.

Alternative Destinations

In 1927 Roth devoted a longer essay, *Juden auf Wanderschaft* (Wandering Jews), to Jewish migrants from the East. He did not romanticize their experiences. Jewish life, as he described it, was characterized by the experience of transition and mobility. Roth was interested in the wandering Jews themselves, and in the specific Jewish epistemology of mobility: "Many return. More move on. The Ostjuden have no home anywhere, but graves in every cemetery."[5] The experience of the wandering Jews *in between* who did not really arrive anywhere fascinated Roth because of the relationship between the preservation of a transnational Diaspora identity in time and space with elements of mobility. The subchapters of *Juden auf Wanderschaft* reflect the topography of Jewish migration after 1918. In the East, Jews could not stay. In postwar Vienna, Jews were not welcome. Berlin was the place of passage between East and West. The *Ostjuden* did not come to stay—they came to go.

Berlin had no "ghetto," a space of Jewish life at least partly tolerated and accepted by state and society, because foreign Jews were not welcome. The topography in *Juden auf Wanderschaft* had a temporal dimension too. The *shtetl* was an imagined space in the past; Palestine was a dead end. Three countries, each with an inclusive vision of citizenship—France, the United States, and the Soviet Union—represented the future. Jews could enter if they had valid papers, but they had to leave their Jewish past at the doorstep. Roth devoted only limited attention to the United States, a country he never visited. He did not acknowledge that it was the only feasible destination for most Jews facing economic and political pressure to move because it was the place where they could hope to draw on support from family members and acquaintances.[6]

Most of Roth's readers knew that the situation in Eastern Europe was bleak. Apart from Czechoslovakia, most successor states of the Russian and Austro-Hungarian empires were mired in a prolonged economic crisis. Misguided economic policies exacerbated war-related destruction of vital infrastructure. During the winter of 1925–1926 JDC chairman Felix Warburg visited Poland. He reported that a staggering 83 percent of unskilled Jewish laborers in Warsaw were unemployed. The situation in smaller cities such as Białystok was just as severe.[7] In a 1926 article in the respected *Weltwirtschaftliches Archiv*, Lestschinsky traced growing Jewish poverty in cities to policies of successor state governments that benefited the agricultural sector. In the early 1920s Polish prime minister Władyslaw Grabski announced to a delegation of industrialists from Białystok that the government favored the closure of 60 percent of the city's factories. Laid-off workers should either return to their villages or emigrate.

Lestschinsky did not explicitly mention that Grabski's government backed a boycott of Jewish-owned businesses, nationalized key industries, and dismissed Jewish employees. Younger Jews living in larger cities like Białystok or Warsaw had few realistic choices to improve their condition. The poverty in the rural hometowns of their parents or grandparents was often worse than in the cities. Few friends or relatives could assist them to cover the cost for train tickets and ship passages. The gates to traditional destination countries were closing. In the cities, competition in the few remaining economic niches was fierce. Relocating to France, Germany, or Palestine appeared risky without access to social networks. As a result, tens of thousands of Jews in interwar Polish cities depended on remittances by American relatives and on support from American Jewish aid associations. There can be little doubt that Grabski's economic policies contributed to rising Jewish migration to Palestine in 1925 and 1926.[8]

Some Jews entered the United States illegally after 1921. Migrants who overstayed their tourist visas or somehow managed to cross the southern border with smugglers or used forged papers were well advised to cover their tracks. Illegal migration, however, was an option only for a relatively small number of young men or women with the necessary means and will to take risks.[9] Already in 1921, American Jewish representatives began to explore alternative destinations for Jewish migrants in the Americas. HIAS officials who visited Mexico and Cuba reported that both countries could accommodate few Jewish migrants. The reports of Jewish aid associations from the early 1920s illustrate that the American turn to migration restrictions was part of a global shift. Britain never lifted its wartime restrictions. Canada issued visas almost exclusively to Eastern Europeans with proven farming skills. German-speaking Mennonites from the former Russian Empire who were affected by the U.S. quota regime benefited from the Canadian exemption for farmers. A growing number of Jews participated in agricultural and technical training schemes during the 1920s. Yet those who tried to apply for Canadian visas had little luck. The author of the entry on Canada in a 1923 Yiddish guidebook explicitly advised his readers to avoid the country. In the 1930s it was widely known that Canadian consuls were reluctant to issue visas to Jews, even if they fulfilled all necessary criteria. In 1938 a group of Jewish farmers from Slovakia managed to obtain precious Canadian visas by passing as Christians. They bought farms and regularly attended church to maintain the pretense and avoid deportation. Between 1933 and 1945 Canada admitted a mere five thousand Jewish migrants and refugees.[10]

The most important overseas countries that remained accessible during the 1920s were Argentina, Brazil, Mexico, Cuba, and Palestine. Cuba, home to a small Jewish community before 1914, attracted an estimated seven thousand Jews from Eastern Europe between 1921 and 1924. Most were bound for the United States because the 1921 U.S. quota bill exempted residents of countries in the Western Hemisphere. The bill allowed foreigners to enter the United States as Cuban residents after a waiting period of one year. The 1924 bill closed this gap and the number of Jewish arrivals in Cuba decreased after 1924. A small but unknown number of Jews and others entered Florida on clandestine routes after 1924; others opted to stay in Cuba.[11]

Brazil and Argentina each attracted several thousand Jews annually between 1925 and 1930. Thanks to immigration (and natural growth), Brazil's Jewish population increased from less than 10,000 before 1920 to around 100,000 in the early 1940s. According to estimates, over 50,000 Jews immigrated during the 1920s and to a much lesser extent during the 1930s, primarily from Poland and Germany but also, in smaller numbers, from the Levant. The colonies the JCA had founded in Argentina depended on newly arriving settlers because most pre-1914 migrants had relocated to Buenos Aires. Emigdirect reports from the late 1920s hint at high remigration rates and contain information on disillusioned return migrants from smaller Latin American countries such as Uruguay. Tellingly, Roth did not even mention Latin America in his survey of destinations. In 1926, the New York–based Emergency Committee on Jewish Refugees stressed that Mexico should not be considered a destination for further Jewish immigration because the economic opportunities were limited. Few scholars who work on the emigration of German Jews after 1933 address the extensive research Jewish aid associations conducted in Latin America during the 1920s. Thousands of German Jews who found refuge in Latin America after 1933 benefited from a network of Jewish representatives with access to detailed expertise and contacts, especially in Brazil.[12]

Jewish migration to Palestine increased substantially in the mid-1920s. In 1925, when the annual number of registered Jewish immigrants in the United States dropped from fifty thousand to ten thousand, a record thirty-four thousand Jews moved to Mandate Palestine, primarily from Poland. The numbers decreased in the following years. The focus of the scholarship on the Third and Fourth *Aliyas* as unidirectional movements obscures high remigration rates throughout the interwar period. In 1929 the executive director of the Hilfsverein, Mark Wischnitzer, reported that in the first nine months of 1929 the organization had assisted more than thirty thousand Jewish and other migrants, among them many return migrants, at Berlin's Silesian train station, the city's main eastern gateway. In the wake of the 1929 Hebron massacre the British authorities restricted Jewish settlement in Palestine. Jewish migration to Palestine increased again strongly in 1933. A majority of the more than 160,000 Jews who moved to Palestine between 1933 and 1936 hailed from Poland and Nazi Germany. Palestine remained one of the few viable destinations outside of Europe before new restrictions were imposed in 1937.[13]

The migration restrictions in the United States and the limited opportunities in Latin America sharply reduced the share of Jews from Europe moving to other overseas destinations after 1924. This brief survey indicates that even after the passage of the restrictive quota bill in 1924 the United States remained a major overseas destination, admitting about ten thousand Jews annually during the second half of the 1920s.[14] It is not surprising, then, that in a period of deglobalization after 1914 most Eastern European Jews who had been displaced or decided to relocate after 1918 opted for destinations they could reach with relative ease: Soviet cities, Weimar Germany, and France. The 1915 mass expulsions from the northern Pale marked the beginning of a strong Jewish migration to Russian and Ukrainian cities. The Jewish populations in Moscow and Petrograd/Leningrad soared from a few thousand in 1914 to over 130,000 and 84,000, respectively, in 1926. The numbers increased further in the following decade.

Roth spent several weeks in the Soviet Union in 1926. Although he opposed Communism and Zionism, he clearly sympathized with the Soviet path to modernity. His 1926 trip coincided with a revival of Yiddish cultural life. Like other Western visitors in the 1920s, Roth was beguiled by what he was allowed to see. *Forverts* editor Abraham Cahan, a (moderate) Socialist, was much more critical than Roth when he visited the Soviet Union in 1927. During the 1920s the Soviet authorities stepped up controls at the outer borders and restricted legal emigration and immigration. While loopholes remained, especially in the Far East, illegal crossing ceased to be a viable option. Apart from committed Communists relatively few foreign Jews settled in the Soviet Union before 1939. Many foreign Communists who moved to the Soviet Union fell victim to Stalin's terror after the mid-1930s.[15]

Between 1918 and 1933 most German states pursued relatively liberal migration policies. In 1933 about 100,000 Jews without German citizenship lived in Germany; most hailed from Eastern Europe. This number hides a high degree of fluctuation. Roth's characterization of Berlin as a bleak waiting room did not fully capture the function of the city as a point of passage between East and West. In the early 1920s dozens of Yiddish papers catered to members of overlapping Jewish networks that were literally on the move. Most Jewish artists, writers, and scholars from the former Russian Empire passed through the German capital during the 1920s. Some stopped over on the way to Western Europe and beyond to obtain visas and transit visas at embassies and consulates in Berlin. The waiting period could stretch to many months, even years. As Roth commented, "[H]alf a Jewish life is wasted in the futile struggle for papers." In a society dealing with the repercussions of defeat and economic crisis Jews from "the East" were exposed to antisemitic discrimination and violence. However, as a stronghold of Germany's left-wing parties and hub of a vibrant avant-garde culture, the huge capital city was a relatively safe space, and not just for Jews. Interwar Berlin was a pivotal place for the rise of modern gay culture.[16]

In August 1921 Abraham Cahan, a regular visitor, described Berlin as "the most significant city in the world" for Jewish intellectuals. In the summer of 1921 he personally interviewed candidates for the new *Forverts* Berlin office at one of the city's coffee houses. Cahan picked Jacob Lestschinsky as bureau chief. The journalist had spent the war years in the Russian Empire. In the aftermath of the war Lestschinsky managed to obtain Lithuanian citizenship because he was acquainted with the newly appointed Lithuanian ambassador in Moscow—at a time when Lithuania appeared to be open to granting its Jewish population autonomy. The passport allowed him to travel relatively freely. After Bolshevik forces conquered Kiev in 1920, he relocated to Berlin. His position as *Forverts* bureau chief left him time for scholarly endeavors and research publications.[17]

In 1925 Lestschinsky, linguist Max Weinreich, historian Elias Tcherikover, and several others founded a research institute devoted to Jewish history and culture, the Yidisher Visnshaftlekher Institut (Jewish Scholarly Institute, or YIVO). A major inspirational figure was the respected historian Simon Dubnow, who moved to Berlin in 1922. YIVO coordinated and launched research projects about Jewish culture and history, and especially about the Yiddish language. Another important undertaking was the collection of books, objects, and papers. The historical section, headed by Tcherikover, and the department for demography and economy that Lestschinsky directed, remained in Berlin until 1933. The other YIVO sections were based in Vilna.[18]

A brief look at Lestschinsky's personal network of friends and collaborators illustrates that the spheres of Jewish scholars, aid workers, journalists, and politicians in Berlin overlapped. Lestschinsky recruited Weinreich and Dubnow as contributors for the *Forverts*. Historian Mark Wischnitzer, the executive director of the Hilfsverein during the 1920s, Tcherikover, Lestschinsky, and their families belonged to Dubnow's social circle. During the Russian Civil War, Tcherikover systematically collected material about the pogroms. He took the archived collection to Berlin and later to Paris and New York. In 1927 Leo Motzkin drew on Tcherikover's archive for a study of the 1918–1919 Ukrainian pogroms. His co-author, Joseph B. Schechtman, moved from Kiev to Berlin in 1920 and attended Berlin's main university. In the mid-1920s Schechtman settled in Paris, where he became a close collaborator of the Revisionist Zionist leader Ze'ev (Vladimir) Jabotinsky. After 1918 Motzkin lived mostly in Paris but kept an apartment in Berlin's Wilmersdorf district until 1932. Another acquaintance of Lestschinsky was Ilya Dijour. He grew up in Kiev and fled to Berlin in 1921. Dijour directed the main office of Emigdirect in Berlin and coordinated the cooperation with HIAS and JCA. Motzkin, Tcherikover, and Lestschinsky served on Emigdirect's Berlin board. After Emigdirect ceased its activities in 1934 Dijour represented HICEM in Paris and later Lisbon, where he fled in 1940. Several of these men published work about Jewish migration after escaping to the United States in the early 1940s.[19]

France was one of the few accessible destination countries for Eastern Europeans during the interwar period—and a safe haven for opponents of the Nazi regime and for Jews from Germany after 1933. The French government pursued a generous immigration and naturalization policy during the 1920s. Demand for unskilled labor was high, and Paris offered many economic opportunities. The journey was affordable but required careful planning, especially for Jews without valid papers. In some cases, they relied on smugglers to take them across the French border. Polish Jews clustered in

This group portrait shows several Jewish scholars and their families who belonged to the social circle of historian Simon Dubnow in Berlin, c. 1932. The photo was presented to Elias Tcherikower (first on the left, back row) by Jacob Lestschinsky (second from right, back row). Simon Dubnow and his wife Ida sit on the left in the front row. *Unknown photographer, RG 121, GR 183, YIVO, Institute for Jewish Research, New York*

streets surrounding the Place de la République, not coincidentally in close proximity to the Gare de l'Est and Gare du Nord train stations. According to the Francophile Roth, *Ostjuden* lived in Paris like "Gott in Frankreich," a German expression for life in paradise. The police left them alone. In Paris Jewish migrants were little noticed, in contrast to French colonial subjects from the Maghreb who were frequently harassed by the police. On the eve of the German occupation in 1940 France was home to more than 70,000 Polish Jews, 40,000 German and Austrian Jews, 18,000 Russian Jews, and at least 25,000 Jews from smaller countries such as Romania and Hungary. About 50,000 Eastern European Jews acquired French citizenship before 1938.[20]

Lesser-known stopover destinations for Jewish migrants during the interwar period were the extraterritorial port cities Danzig and Shanghai. Shanghai's small Jewish community was completely transformed in the early 1920s. No visa was required to enter the international settlement that was controlled by Britain, the United States, Japan, and several other powers. Interwar Shanghai's bustling economy and cultural life attracted Europeans and Americans. Most of the fifty-five hundred Jews living in Shanghai in 1936 hailed from the former Russian Empire. Some moved from Harbin to Shanghai after Japanese troops occupied Manchuria in the early 1930s. When most other doors were closing in 1939, lax visa regulations turned Shanghai into a safe haven for over seventeen thousand German and Austrian Jews. However, they had to deal with sharply deteriorating living conditions. In 1937, following the Japanese invasion of China's coastal provinces, more than 400,000 Chinese civilians fled to the international settlement that was already home to over a million Chinese and foreign residents. In December 1941 Japanese troops occupied the international settlement and forced stateless Jews into a crowded area in the Hongkou district. In their memoirs several refugees recall challenging conditions. The local Chinese population fared far worse. Chinese civilians were subject to brutal abuse and random killings by Japanese soldiers.[21]

Jewish representatives in Geneva recognized that Danzig's status as a League mandate represented a unique opportunity to address the unclear status of Jewish (and other) stateless war refugees. Together with groups representing other Russian refugees, Wolf and Motzkin lobbied without success for an inclusive citizenship law that would have applied to all persons residing in the territory. The leader of the Senate, Danzig's democratically elected city government, presented the citizenship law as the last line of defense against Polish encroachment. Thus, only German citizens who had lived in Danzig in January 1920 were granted Danzig citizenship when the law took effect in 1922. Thousands of former Russian subjects who had moved to Danzig in 1918–1919 were excluded. They could apply for citizenship after having resided in Danzig for at least five years after January 1920. The waiting period actually constituted a partial victory for Jewish and other refugee representatives, because initially the Danzig government had proposed a ten-year residency requirement.[22]

After moving to the United States ceased to be an option in 1924, many Jews decided to stay in Danzig. Following negotiations between the League, Danzig and Polish officials, Jewish representatives, and various Russian refugee associations, Poland constructed a better-equipped camp for transmigrants in the nearby town of Wejherowo in 1923. As a result of the influx Danzig's Jewish community increased from about twenty-seven hundred in 1910 to nine thousand in 1924. As a concession to the newcomers the community appointed an Orthodox rabbi (and Zionist), Jakob Sagalowitsch. Several Yiddish publications describe the transformation of Jewish life in the city. Although the Nazi Party gained control of the Danzig Senate in 1933, the League was able to mitigate the effect of antisemitic laws until 1936. Most Jews were able to leave the territory before the German attack against the Polish garrison in Danzig on September 1, 1939.[23]

Another safe haven was the Baltic port of Memel. In 1920 French troops occupied the strategically important district surrounding the city. In 1923 Lithuania thwarted plans to turn Memel into another League mandate by taking control of the territory. To avoid provoking its German neighbor, Lithuania granted almost complete autonomy to the largely German-speaking population. A modest economic boom attracted thousands of Jewish migrants, primarily from the surrounding Lithuanian provinces. After 1933 they were joined by German and foreign Jews who fled Nazi terror in East Prussia. In March 1939 Nazi Germany occupied the Memel district. Almost all Jews were expelled or fled to Lithuania.[24]

Jewish Migration Scholarship

Jewish mass flight, statelessness, and rising "paper walls" in the aftermath of the war drew growing attention to the issue of Jewish migration. The uncertain status of Jewish minorities and antisemitic policies implemented in successor states like Poland and Hungary exacerbated the crisis. During the 1920s Jewish scholars presented different interpretations and solutions. All expressed concern about the implications of postwar migration restrictions for members of unwanted Jewish minorities in Eastern Europe.

In the late 1920s, even Zionist authors did not consider Jewish mass resettlement in Palestine a realistic scenario in the short term. A good example is an informative survey of Jewish migrations after 1900 that targeted members of Jewish communities in Weimar Germany assisting Jewish migrants. The author, German Jewish lawyer Michael Traub, discussed the post-1918 immigration policies in major destination countries and documented which qualifications were required to obtain an immigrant visa. Traub regarded productivization as pivotal. Training Jewish migrants as farmers and skilled workers offered the only viable option to a better life elsewhere, not least in Palestine. Pointing to high remigration rates, Traub made it clear that only smaller groups of well-prepared younger men and women could realistically succeed in Palestine.

In a short historical overview, Traub described the Jews as a wandering people. Before 1800 Jewish migrants were initially welcomed by host societies because they provided specific economic skills but eventually faced persecution and expulsion. In the early twentieth century, a growing number of migrants had managed to escape this vicious cycle. As productive "proletarians" they found better living conditions on agricultural colonies in Argentina and secured jobs in American factories. The war had interrupted this process and deprived most Jews in Eastern Europe of viable economic options. As Traub put it succinctly in a 1924 article, Jewish "migrants became refugees." American immigration restrictions greatly exacerbated the crisis. It was not clear where millions of economically struggling Eastern European Jews would be able to go.[25]

In 1930 the pioneering German Jewish sociologist Arthur Ruppin published his magnum opus, the two-volume study *Soziologie der Juden*, the fruit of decades of research. After a short stint as founding director of a Zionist-oriented statistical research institute in Berlin, Ruppin settled in Palestine in 1908. As a land agent for the Zionist World Organization, he was one of the main architects of early Jewish settlement in Palestine. In 1926 he helped to establish the Sociology Department at the newly founded Hebrew University, where he taught until his death in 1943. In *Soziologie der Juden* Ruppin discussed a wide range of social and economic features of Jewish life based on extensive data. He gleaned some of the statistical information from Lestschinsky's publications. A brief section covered migration. Like other Zionists, Ruppin described the Jews as a *Wandervolk* (wandering people) and noted that industrialization had caused a reversal of Jewish migration patterns during the nineteenth century. Instead of moving to lesser developed territories most Jews were heading to industrializing countries. Ruppin asserted that no other group, not even Italians, had a higher migration rate than Eastern European Jews "leaving their countries of birth" between 1880 and 1929. This statement is debatable, because Ruppin underestimated Jewish return migration before 1914, but the basic point that Jewish migration rates were high is accurate.

Ruppin named four main causes for the strong migration from the Russian Empire, Galicia, and Romania after 1881: the pogroms after 1881, oppressive anti-Jewish policies in Russia and Romania, high Jewish birth rates, and the absence economic opportunities. His analysis left little doubt that he judged demographic and economic factors as decisive. In contrast to other leading Zionists, Ruppin had long viewed Jewish migration to North America as a positive development. In a 1904 publication he pointed out that Jewish migrants were improving their economic condition as industrial workers and their legal status by becoming "free citizens of free states." In his 1930 study he described Jewish emigration as an "emergency valve" that helped to mitigate "extreme economic pressure." Moreover, strong Jewish migration from Russia and Galicia after 1880 had "saved" the shrinking Jewish communities in France and England. Another example for Ruppin's careful approach is his discussion of Jewish migration from parts of Lithuania to South Africa. He noted the importance of networks and chain migration. Ruppin condemned postwar U.S. immigration restrictions as disastrous, characterizing the United States as a "sealed paradise." He also touched on high Jewish remigration rates from Palestine during the second half of the 1920s, conceding that the territory could accommodate only a relatively limited number of Jewish migrants.[26]

Soziologie der Juden displays tension between Ruppin's Zionism and his commitment to critical scholarship. As in his earlier publications he expressed concern about assimilation, especially as millions of Jews migrated to large cities. The available data showed that more than 2 million Jewish migrants had escaped poverty by moving to the United States and England, contradicting the pessimistic predictions of leading Zionists like Max Nordau before 1914. Ruppin pointed to the advantages that bigger cities offered Jewish migrants as individuals, especially better access to education and economic opportunities. Yet overall, he judged urbanization as a "centrifugal" process fostering the disappearance of Jews as a group. In an earlier text he had described cities as "hothouses of assimilation."[27]

Ruppin closely followed new research trends, as his discussion of Louis Wirth's 1928 study *The Ghetto* about Jewish immigrant neighborhoods in Chicago shows. Instead of glossing over a study that questioned his assimilation thesis, Ruppin chose to summarize its findings. Wirth suggested a correlation between settlement patterns and the adaptation of (Jewish) immigrants to American society. Socially mobile Jews who had left the immigrant neighborhood had adopted American cultural norms but preferred to live close to other assimilating Jews. Wirth's finding appeared to indicate that concerns about a dissolution of Jews in mainstream society in the near term were overblown. Ruppin concluded it was too early to predict whether new forms of Jewish *Gemeinschaft* would develop in American cities.[28]

The postwar refugee crisis and the turn to restrictive immigration policies in and beyond Europe put migration on the agenda of international organizations founded at the Paris peace conferences to secure lasting peace and international cooperation. Under the umbrella of the League of Nations, the International Labor Organization (ILO) and the High Commissioner for Refugees, the forerunner of the United Nations Refugee Agency, made a concerted effort to highlight the benefits of coordinating national migration regimes.[29] In the late 1920s ILO funded a massive two-volume survey about migration in different parts of the world to provide political decision-makers and civil servants with objective data and an impartial analysis. For the first volume the Hungarian economist Imre Ferenczi compiled hundreds of statistics about migration. The second volume provided informative background essays about major migrant groups. Most contributors described migration as the norm rather than the exception in human history.

As a migration specialist teaching at the University of Geneva, Liebmann Hersch was an obvious choice for the chapter on Jewish migration. Hersch began by pointing out that Jewish mass migration was a recent phenomenon: "A break in the continuity of the life of the Jewish masses has taken place such as had not been seen for thousands of years, since the Israelites were driven out of their land by the Romans." Like most other authors in the volume, Hersch based his analysis on statistical data. He concentrated on the period before 1914 because it was too early to gauge the impact of mass displacement and immigration restrictions after 1918. Hersch traced the migration to the economic transformation in Eastern Europe after 1850. The pogroms and political instability constituted only "secondary factors." Jews were hit harder by the economic transformation than other groups because they lost their traditional roles as service providers and middlemen, forcing them to seek better opportunities in modernizing urbanizing regions rather than to colonize unsettled regions in the eastern part of the Russian Empire like their Christian neighbors. Hersch considered Jewish settlement and colonization in Palestine to be an aberration.

Two key sentences in his analysis are worthwhile repeating here. Hersch wrote, "It remains true, nevertheless, that among the Jews the occupational structure determined not only the enormous dimensions of the modern migratory movement but also the principal characteristics of the group of emigrants and the direction of their migration." This interpretation contradicted a position popular with Zionist authors in this period, the notion of Jews as a "wandering people." Hersch concluded his piece by stating,

"It seems probable that no people have changed so profoundly as the Jews under the influences of modern world migration." This statement echoes Ruppin's concerns about assimilation. However, the Bundist Hersch opposed Zionism, and his text targeted a primarily non-Jewish readership. His main intention was to reject widespread stereotypes associating Jews with continuous migration. In his careful and detached analysis he pointed to similarities and differences between Jewish and other migrants.[30]

Lestschinsky was the most prolific Jewish migration scholar during the interwar period. The few authors who have written about Lestschinsky concentrate on his YIVO activities and his opposition to Zionism.[31] It is not widely known that Lestschinsky placed articles about Jewish economic life and migration in general journals, just when migration emerged as a topic attracting wider scholarly interest. His goal was to secure a place for scholarship about Jewish migrations and social studies in the emerging field. In 1929 a newly founded German journal focusing on migration, the *Archiv für Wanderungswesen und Auslandskunde*, accepted a longer article about the main causes driving Jewish migration. The text is valuable because of its comparative approach. Like Hersch, Lestschinsky avoided essentializing the Jewish experience by singling out the specific economic profile of Jews as a distinguishing feature. During the 1920s Lestschinsky supported the integration of Jews into the economic fabric of Eastern European societies because migration restrictions had deprived most Jews of other options. He noted the important role of Jewish aid associations for migrants after 1918. JDC and the Hilfsverein supported Lestschinsky's YIVO research projects.[32]

Almost all authors who analyzed Jewish migration during the 1920s drew on social scientific approaches. None regarded anti-Jewish violence as a decisive factor behind the unprecedented Jewish migration from Eastern Europe before 1914. They looked primarily at economic factors and compared Jews with other groups. Zionist and non-Zionist authors viewed Jewish migration as a positive development. Jewish migrants had improved their economic situation and contributed to the economic stability of Jewish communities in Eastern Europe. Jewish historians did not cover the post-1880 Jewish migration in book-length studies during the interwar period, though it is possible to glean some insights from overarching surveys and encyclopedia articles. Unlike social scientists, Jewish historians remained beholden to overarching narratives that were suggestive but did not withstand critical and comparative analysis. During the 1920s the leading specialist of Jewish history and culture in Eastern Europe was Simon Dubnow.

In the tenth and last volume of his *World History of the Jewish People* Dubnow discussed the critical situation in the Russian Empire after 1880. His explanation for the Jewish mass migration is not consistent. He suggested, "[P]ersecutions in Russia and Romania and misery in Austrian Galicia drove out tens of thousands of Jews every year." Yet he also indicated that many migrants from Russia looked for better "economic opportunities" in America. Dubnow's section about the migration to America leaned heavily on Peter Wiernik's 1912 survey of American Jewish history. Wiernik also identified the pogroms as an overarching cause but, almost in the same breath, pointed to the importance of economic opportunities in the United States. In an article about the Diaspora that he contributed to the pioneering *Encyclopedia of the Social Sciences* in 1929 Dubnow traced Jewish migration from Russia exclusively to "pogroms and legal disabilities." However, in the introductory overview he made it clear that the Jewish Diaspora could not be reduced to expulsions and flight. Rather, "the emigration of economically depressed groups [and] the settlement abroad of traders and similar trends" had contributed to the dispersion of Jews.[33]

In the late 1920s a young Jewish historian challenged established colleagues to rethink their interpretation of modern Jewish history. In 1930 Salo Baron began teaching Jewish history at Columbia University. He was only the second Jewish studies scholar appointed to an endowed chair at a major American research university at the time.[34] Baron hailed from Tarnow, a small Polish city in the Austrian province of Galicia. In 1914 he enrolled at the University of Vienna, obtaining three doctoral degrees, in philosophy, political science, and law. In 1920 he was ordained as a rabbi at the Israelitisch-Theologische Lehranstalt in Vienna and began teaching at a Jewish studies seminary in the Austrian capital. In the 1920s American Reform rabbi Stephen S. Wise invited Baron to join the faculty of a newly founded rabbinical school, the Jewish Institute of Religion in New York. In his own research Baron focused on Jewish social and economic history before 1800. Several of his doctoral students pursued research projects that touched on Jewish migrations after 1800. In 1939, Baron cofounded the journal *Jewish Social Studies*, which he edited until his death in the late 1980s. The journal sought to fill the void left by the closure of Jewish research institutes in Germany and East Central Europe after the rise of the Nazi regime. During the 1940s *Jewish Social Studies* served as an important forum for scholarship about Jewish migrations.[35]

Shortly after his arrival in the United States Baron published a polemical essay titled "Ghetto and Emancipation" in which he made a case for reassessing the Jewish experience before and after 1800. Baron rejected a dichotomy that had shaped the view of Jewish history after the destruction of the Second Temple in the year 70. According to this narrative, Jews had faced almost constant persecution. In the 1500s Jews were forced into ghettos and were denied basic rights—until the dawn of emancipation in the nineteenth century, when Jews were "liberated" and became full-fledged citizens. Jews in the Russian Empire and the Middle East continued to be subject to discriminatory laws, violence, and restrictions, if they did not migrate. But was Jewish life before 1800 really uniformly bad? Baron rejected this interpretation as misguided, characterizing it as "lachrymose." Without dismissing anti-Jewish violence and discrimination, Baron pointed out that Jews had often enjoyed autonomy rights and, in some places, had been able to live peacefully for long periods of time. Ironically, certain bans and special taxes imposed on Jews in early modern Europe had been advantageous because they entailed protections. And it was "certainly no evidence of discrimination that the Jews did not have 'equal rights'—no one had them."[36]

Baron was not the first scholar who made a case for a critical analysis of the actual sources and for contextualizing the Jewish experience. Yet his critique questioned a view popular not just with established Jews in countries like Germany, Britain, and the United States who emphasized the benefits of emancipation and citizenship. Baron's essay also cast doubt on Zionist interpretations of Jewish history whose proponents linked Jewish life in the Diaspora with persecution and discrimination. In 1928 Baron could not know that the rise of the Nazi regime, the Holocaust, and the founding of the State of Israel would reinforce the older lachrymose and essentialist view of Jewish history and of Jewish migrations. To better understand the diverging positions on Jewish migration history after 1940 it is necessary to discuss a pioneering study of general migration history whose authors were only loosely linked with the scholarly network of Jewish and Russian-speaking migrants in interwar Berlin.

In 1932 the brothers Alexander and Eugene Kulischer published a survey of migration history that contained a provocative reinterpretation of global history, *Kriegs- und Wanderzüge: Weltgeschichte als Völkerbewegung* (Wars and Other Migrations: Global History as a Movement of Peoples). The Kulischers appear not to have frequented the circles of YIVO scholars or Russian exiles in Berlin. Their research interests were wide-ranging and encompassed penal law, demography, Soviet economics, and politics, but not Jewish studies. Their father, the ethnologist and cultural historian Michael Kulischer, was acquainted with Dubnow. An older brother, the economic historian Josef Kulischer, taught at the University of Leningrad and published on Russian and European economic history in different languages before and after 1914.[37]

Yewgeni Kulischer, as he was known before 1918, was born in St. Petersburg, where he earned his doctoral degree in law in 1906. After being admitted to the bar he worked as a corporate lawyer, serving on the board of a St. Petersburg locomotive company. During and after the war he taught at the universities of Petrograd and Kiev. In 1920, shortly before Bolshevik forces occupied Kiev, Kulischer and his pregnant wife fled to Berlin. As a nontenured teaching fellow at the Institut für Auslands- und Wirtschaftsrecht (Institute for Foreign and Economic Law), which was affiliated with Berlin's Friedrich-Wilhelms University, Kulischer lectured on Soviet economy and law. Like thousands of other Russian-speaking exiles, Kulischer, his wife, Olga, and their infant daughter settled in the bourgeois Wilmersdorf neighborhood.

Kulischer changed his first name twice. In Berlin he adopted the German Eugen. After leaving Germany for Paris in 1934 he used Eugene, a name he retained when he settled in the United States.[38] His brother Alexander was a demographer. After teaching at the University of Petrograd during the war years he too moved to Berlin, where he published a brief text about the Russian Civil War. He portrayed the war as a breakdown of civil order and as a systematic attack by nationalists and Bolsheviks against the people, especially against the small middle class. In the early 1920s Alexander relocated to Paris. He repeatedly applied for academic positions as a demographer in the United States, but without success. Joseph Schechtman mentions Alexander as a fellow revisionist Zionist in Paris.[39]

Kriegs- und Wanderzüge is a groundbreaking account of global migration history and an important contribution to the emerging field of migration studies. According to the authors, their father initiated the study but had completed only a short draft before his death in 1919. The book's ambitious scope and the need to earn income may explain why the brothers published relatively little during the 1920s. The references reflect extensive scholarship in Germany, France, Britain, the Russian Empire, and the United States in social science, geography, economics, demography, global history, and political science. The historical analysis of the correlations between global demographic changes and political, economic, and social transformations illustrated the shortcomings of contemporary historiographies beholden to the nation-state paradigm and a focus on political and intellectual history. The study made only limited use of statistical analysis, an approach demographers favored at the time. Relying on the influential essay on population by Thomas Robert Malthus, and on studies by the German geographer Friedrich Ratzel and the economist and demographer Paul Mombert, the Kulischers claimed that no population was ever truly sedentary. Continuous but uneven migration processes had been shaping human history since its earliest days. The Kulischers did not discuss the "laws" of migration the Anglo-German geographer Ernst Georg Ravenstein had formulated in the 1880s, possibly because they considered Ravenstein's principles too simplistic.[40]

Focusing on Europe and parts of Asia during the second millennium, the Kulischers claimed that all mass migrations followed a similar pattern. Large-scale movements resulted from the unequal distribution of populations and resources as well as different stages of economic development in certain regions. If obstacles blocked the natural movement, overpopulation led to a depletion of resources, fueling wars, which triggered new migrations. Large-scale military movements (*Kriegszüge*) constituted a specific form of mass migration (*Wanderzüge*). Both authors had personally witnessed the rise of Bolshevism and the ensuing Russian Civil War. *Kriegs- und Wanderzüge* offered a sophisticated explanation for the seemingly chaotic and devastating movement of armies and displacement of civilians across East Central Europe between 1914 and the early 1920s—and the ensuing economic collapse.

The view that overpopulation was a major driving force behind migrations to more thinly settled areas that were accompanied by conflicts was widely shared at the time. The Kulischers presented a historical analysis to explore the viability of this hypothesis. They argued that the term "overpopulation" depended on the availability of economic resources and should not be used uncritically. The notion that certain countries were overpopulated was closely related to the already notorious *Lebensraum* concept. The term was coined by Ratzel and popularized by geographer Karl Haushofer. The Kulischers linked the quest for *Lebensraum* with a careful analysis of the availability of resources and population statistics, refuting racist and nationalist claims of exclusive ownership of certain "ancient" lands. As Eugene Kulischer put it poignantly in a later publication, after the collapse of the Roman Empire, "not one German lived in Berlin, not one Russian in Moscow, not one Hungarian in Budapest."[41]

According to the Kulischers, no group or *Volk* (people) could make an exclusive claim to a certain territorial *Raum* (space) for "eternity." Rather than a rejection of Zionism, this statement was a not so implicit critique of one of the most widely read books of the Weimar Republic, Hans Grimm's 1926 novel, *Volk ohne Raum* (People without Space). Grimm, an elitist Conservative writer and nationalist, promoted territorial expansion in overseas colonies as a catch-all solution for Germany's economic and spiritual crisis. Germans had "no space within [Germany] and no rights outside [of Germany]" because the Versailles Peace Treaty had stripped Germany of its colonies. Grimm asserted that the alliance of "pure" German tribes led by "noble" aristocratic leaders during the medieval period had been led astray. In the modern era a coalition of German Social Democrats, Britain, and "the" Jews had been undermining the German nation. The novel was a call to action for members of the "pure" German race to restore their country to its former glory as a leading nation—guided by a strong leader. Even though Grimm opposed the colonization of Eastern Europe and did not use the actual term *Lebensraum*, Hitler repeatedly acknowledged the influence of *Volk ohne Raum* on his ideology and encouraged the members of the Nazi Party to read the book. The Kulischers' critique of Grimm was not lost on several reviewers. Karl Tiander, a Finnish journalist and scholar of Russian history, who almost certainly was acquainted with the Kulischers, read *Kriegs- und Wanderzüge* as a rejection of the "ideal" of "pure races" because mass migrations and ethnic mixing were associated with economic and political changes that had occurred throughout history. In 1934 Tiander did not have to explain to German readers why a critical discussion of the race concept was timely. It is doubtful whether the (German) journal would have printed his sympathetic review after 1934.[42]

The Kulischers refrained from presenting a simplistic Malthusian argument. They conceded that after decades of strong population growth, economically developed states in Western and Central Europe were experiencing demographic decline, a process known as "demographic transition." This widely accepted thesis can be traced to a series of articles Alexander Kulischer wrote for *Poslednie Novosti*, a Russian exile paper published in Paris, between 1928 and 1932. "Demographic transition" also questioned the basic premise of the *Lebensraum* concept and Grimm's novel. The Kulischers predicted another potentially devastating war, not because supposedly overpopulated countries like Germany needed *Lebensraum* but because post-1918 migration restrictions were depriving regions with strongly growing populations and limited resources of a crucial safety valve.

Lestschinsky, Ruppin, and a few other authors grappled with the same question during the 1920s. In their view strong Jewish (and non-Jewish) migration before 1914 had stabilized the economic condition of those Jews (and implicitly their non-Jewish neighbors) who did not migrate. Departing Jewish migrants relieved local job markets and supported their families with remittances. To avoid wars fueled by supposed overpopulation and economic disparities the Kulischers recommended an international system of regulated migration that took imbalances of population and resources into account. Regulated migration was distinct from forced resettlement or population transfers. The Kulischers categorically opposed forced migration and migration restrictions. States had to come together and create conditions for unrestricted migration. They expressed doubts about whether an effective system could be established in the short term.[43]

Jewish migrations feature only in passing in the study, in marked contrast to other nineteenth-century migrations. This was almost certainly a deliberate decision. *Kriegs- und Wanderzüge* targeted members of the academic establishment in and beyond Germany. The Kulischers may have hoped to improve their chances of landing positions at research institutions in Europe and the United States, in a period when antisemitic discrimination in academia was widespread. A short paragraph pointed to the distinct economic profile of the Jewish population as the main reason why Jews left the Russian Empire earlier than other groups and moved in disproportionate numbers to cities in and beyond Eastern Europe after 1880. *Kriegs- und Wanderzüge* contained two implicit statements about Jewish migrations. First, Jewish migrations did not represent an extraordinary movement but were closely related to broader economic and political changes that also affected other groups. And second, post-1918 migration restrictions were disastrous, especially for Eastern European Jewry.[44]

Most scholars at the time considered migration an extraordinary development that resulted from wars, natural disasters, and political decisions. The Kulischers rejected this explanation. They critiqued suggestive but simplistic typologies and divisions, especially between "normal" economic migrations and forced migrations and thus between migrants and refugees. They considered mass displacement and migration restrictions as closely related and potentially precarious developments. A notable weakness was their inability to explain extraordinary political decisions to expel or exterminate a very large number of unwanted people. In their view longue durée demographic and economic forces were the real drivers of mass migrations. This was a likely reason they did not discuss Stalin's forced collectivization policy, not to mention the systematic expulsions that preceded the Armenian genocide in 1915–1916, or the simultaneous Russian "resettlement" of Jews and ethnic Germans.[45]

A 1930 survey of migration history by the Hungarian economist Imre Ferenczi, one of the most prolific migration scholars during the 1920s and 1930s, illustrates why the approach of the Kulischers was innovative. Ferenczi recognized that migrations were not "unique" by highlighting parallels between movements of different groups over time. Instead of considering the implications of this observation, he associated several dominant types of migration with certain time periods in European history. After the collapse of the Roman Empire *Volkswanderungen* (migrations of peoples), large concurrent migrations of supposedly homogeneous ethnic groups, were linked with military conflicts. This type of migration resembled the Kulischers' interpretation of migration history as such. The early modern period witnessed the rise of new types of migration, namely forced migrations of religious groups and the recruitment of settlers by European monarchs like Catherine the Great. Nineteenth-century "proletarian mass migrations" resulted from the collapse of the feudal system and industrialization. Following the First World War European governments adopted a system of "regulated" migration by reaching agreements about seasonal labor migration on a bilateral level. The League of Nations had been tasked to ensure that different states negotiated bilateral agreements to avoid conflicts over migration. Jewish migrants were mentioned only in passing, exclusively as expellees and refugees.

Apart from a short footnote, Ferenczi's Eurocentric and eclectic survey did not address mass displacement and widespread migration restrictions during and after 1918, a blatant omission. He touched on this issue in a 1922 *Weltwirtschaftliches Archiv* article about migration from Hungary after 1918. The article illustrates how pervasive antisemitic views were in academic circles. Ferenczi described Galician Jewish war refugees as "economically undesirable elements" and as *Ostjuden* who derived income from trade and moneylending. In a footnote, the Kulischers dismissed Ferenczi's optimism about the feasibility of international migration regulation in the short term as naive.[46]

Kriegs- und Wanderzüge was widely reviewed. French social historian Maurice Halbwachs criticized the mechanistic understanding of historical change, but like other reviewers he praised the innovative interdisciplinary and global scope of the study. *Kriegs- und Wanderzüge* remains little known, largely because the book was published in German—and in Germany—a few months before the rise of the Nazi regime. In Nazi Germany the critique of the *Lebensraum* concept by two Russian Jewish scholars was hardly welcome. Beyond Germany's borders a densely written study that was rooted in Weimar intellectual discourse found few readers. Eugene Kulischer was able to insert the core thesis of *Kriegs- und Wanderzüge* into his English-language publications, but most authors in the field of historical migration studies have ignored this pioneering study on global migration history.[47]

Forced Emigration and Flight

In 1937, while living in exile in Paris, Roth wrote an introduction for a new edition of *Juden auf Wanderschaft*. He could not resist reminding his (German-language) readers of a sad irony: the Nazi regime had rendered German Jews into *Ostjuden*. Roth associated the term *Ostjuden* with authentic Jewishness but also with migration and a romanticized notion of statelessness. Before 1933 he had called on overly assimilated German Jews to embrace Jews from Eastern Europe and their culture. Now, in a cruel twist of fate, German Jewish emigrants were exposed to the travails of permanent transit and exile. German Jews who had not emigrated were on the move too, either to seek the relative safety of a larger Jewish community or because local Nazis had driven them out. These experiences were only too familiar to *Ostjuden* who had lived through the turmoil of the Russian Civil War and conflicts between successor states trying to rebuild their lives on the social margins of European societies during the 1920s. The text was not published during Roth's lifetime. Following the German annexation of Austria in March 1938 Roth's Vienna publishing house went out of business, and the writer became stateless. Largely deprived of his German-language audience, he died a broken man in the French capital in 1939.[48]

A few weeks after Hitler was sworn in as *Reichskanzler*, Lestschinsky was detained. A Jewish journalist from the former Russian Empire with Lithuanian papers representing a left-leaning New York Yiddish newspaper was an obvious target. According to the *New York Times* Hermann Göring personally ordered his arrest and expulsion because his articles were "unfriendly to German interests." Lestschinsky relocated to Warsaw but feared for his safety when the Polish regime embarked on an aggressive antisemitic policy following the death of longtime ruler Józef Piłsudski in 1935. Even before 1933 the correspondent had pleaded with Cahan to give him a position at the paper's main office in New York. Cahan felt the well-connected Lestschinsky was of much better use in Europe.

In the summer of 1938, following a holiday trip to neighboring Czechoslovakia by Lestschinsky and his family, the Polish authorities refused to readmit them. He, his wife, and adult daughter were waiting for a French entry visa in Geneva when he implored Cahan to assist his application for a U.S. visa because German threats to annex Czechoslovakia would probably cause a European war. He promised to continue reporting for the *Forverts* about Poland, relying on his network of trustworthy contacts. This time Cahan gave in. He provided an affidavit but did not offer his correspondent a salaried position. As a freelancer, Lestschinsky had to find other sources of income, but the move spared him and his family from a worse fate. Many other scholars and authors—Eugene Kulischer, Wischnitzer, Tcherikower, Ilja Dijour, and Joseph Schechtman—moved to Paris during the 1930s. A few went to Palestine, among them Michael Traub. Dubnow settled in Riga in 1934 to be closer to members of his family.[49]

During the 1930s the situation of Jewish minorities in Central and Eastern Europe deteriorated, resembling that of Jews stranded in permanent transit. Facing economic hardship and violence, those who wanted to leave encountered closed gates wherever they turned. During the 1930s Nazi Germany, Poland, and Romania began to confiscate businesses owned by Jews and resorted to violent persecution. Neighboring countries, including Hungary and Yugoslavia, also increased the pressure. In the late 1930s the Polish government openly contemplated the mass resettlement of its Jewish population to Madagascar. In January 1938 Romania revoked the naturalization of more than 270,000 Jews, effectively shredding its commitment to the minority treaties.

Following a wave of violence and public humiliation of the Jewish population in Vienna by German and Austrian Nazis in March 1938, the Roosevelt administration convened an international conference in the French resort of Evian in June 1938 to discuss the Jewish refugee crisis. Several countries, among them South Africa, did not even send delegates to Evian. Apart from the small Dominican Republic, none of the participating countries was willing to admit more than a few German Jews. Australian trade minister Thomas W. White declared that his government was opposed to importing a "racial problem." The United States resisted relaxing its immigration policy for Jews from Germany not least because of fears that Poland, Romania, and other Eastern European countries would try to "dump" their "surplus" Jewish minorities in the United States. American diplomats expressed doubts about the sincerity of the Dominican Republic's offer to admit fifty thousand Jews. In October 1937 the country's dictator Rafael Trujillo had ordered the slaughter of fifteen thousand "illegal" Black Haitian migrants. Trujillo sought to attract "white" migrants to the small island state. Unlike most participating countries, France, the official host of the conference, accommodated a large number of Jews from Germany, Austria, and Eastern Europe as well as Spanish Civil War refugees in its territory. During the 1930s French government officials began exploring colonial territories for resettlement, notably French Guyana, Guinea in West Africa, and even New Caledonia in the Southwest Pacific Ocean. The failure of the Evian conference may have influenced the Nazi regime to take even more aggressive steps.[50]

In October and November 1938 several bizarre incidents in the no man's land between borders in East Central Europe illustrated the legal displacement and de facto statelessness of Jewish minority populations. In April 1938, following the German *Anschluss* of Austria, several dozen Jews from the small Burgenland state were expelled to a small island on the Danube that was part of Czechoslovakia. The Jewish community in Bratislava procured a ship that remained anchored between borders on the Danube for three months, as a Jewish aid association tried to find a solution. After Germany annexed the formerly Czech Sudeten region in October 1938, more than 160,000 Czechs, Jews, and left-wing opponents of the Nazi Party fled to the territory that remained part of the Czech state or were expelled by the Germans. In the following weeks the Czech government deported more than twenty thousand Jews back across the new border, even though they were Czechoslovak citizens. Many were repeatedly stranded between borders as German border guards refused to admit them. The newly created Slovak state pursued a similar policy. After being forced by Germany to cede territory to Hungary the Slovak government expelled two thousand Jews across the new border in early November 1938. The Hungarians pushed them back, stranding three hundred Jews in the no man's land for weeks.[51]

In September 1938 the Polish government announced that Polish Jews living abroad would automatically lose their citizenship if they did not return to Poland by November 1. As the deadline approached, the Nazi regime decided to force out most of the fifty thousand Jews with Polish papers living in Germany and Austria before they would be rendered stateless. On October 27 and 28, the Nazi authorities launched the *Polenaktion* (Polish action), rounding up some seventeen thousand Polish Jews and forcing them across several checkpoints along the border with Poland. At several crossings Polish guards turned back the deportees (who were Polish citizens). At one border post, German officials forced Jews into the river that marked the border; when they emerged on the other side, their Polish counterparts drove them back in. At the Zbąszyń (Bentschen) crossing, on the main rail line between Berlin and Warsaw, hundreds were stranded for hours in no man's land, in chilly and wet weather. Eventually, the Polish authorities admitted most of the women, men, and children, only to detain eight thousand Jews—Polish citizens—in a primitive makeshift camp adjacent to the border. Only a few Jews were allowed to return to Germany. No government volunteered to give them asylum. An attempt by Czech officials to force seventeen hundred Polish Jews across the border to Poland near Ostrava failed. The Polish government refused to admit them, thus stranding them on the Czech side of the border.[52]

On November 7, 1938, Herschel Grynszpan, a young Polish Jew, walked into the German embassy in Paris and shot diplomat Ernst vom Rath in the entry hall. A few days earlier Grynszpan, who was born in Hanover in 1921, had learned that his parents and sister had been taken to the Polish border on October 27. Unable to contact them, Grynszpan feared the worst. His desperate act may have been inspired by Sholom Schwartzbard's assassination of Symon Petlura in Paris in 1926. Schwartzbard blamed the head of the short-lived Ukrainian People's Republic for the slaughter of thousands of Jews, among them his parents. A Paris jury sensationally acquitted Schwartzbard in the fall of 1927. Eleven years later, the Nazi regime used the assassination of vom Rath as justification to unleash an unprecedented attack against Jewish civilians in Germany and Austria. During the night of November 9 and early morning of November 10 almost all synagogues in Germany and Austria were vandalized and set on fire. SA storm troopers and SS men systematically ransacked the private homes of Jews, physically attacking families, even children. Thousands of Jewish-owned businesses were destroyed and looted. Over one hundred Jews perished. Most adult Jewish men were taken to concentration camps, where dozens were murdered.[53]

The Kristallnacht pogrom shocked the world and prompted some countries to loosen migration restrictions—for German and Austrian Jews. In 1939, the United States filled the generous German quota for the first time after President Hoover issued his executive order in 1929. However, the State Department rigidly upheld the extremely low quotas for countries in Eastern Europe, at a time when most other possible destination countries were largely beyond reach. Britain responded by admitting more than ten thousand Jewish children from Germany and Austria to protect them from antisemitic violence. Even Australia belatedly relaxed its restrictive policy toward Jewish refugees, but Canberra's onerous visa application procedure remained in place. In most countries the opposition against admitting unwanted Jews remained strong. Inspired by the British *Kindertransport*, New York's senator Robert Wagner and congresswoman Edith Rogers sponsored a bill to admit twenty thousand refugee children from Germany in early 1939. The American Legion, the Daughters of the Revolution, and other "patriotic" organizations ensured that the bill died in a congressional subcommittee.[54]

The post-1918 refugee crisis, which disproportionally affected Jews in the successor states of the Russian and Austro-Hungarian empires, and desperate attempts by German and Austrian Jews to escape Nazi terror during the 1930s are usually discussed in separate contexts. Yet both crises were closely connected. In the early 1920s Jews who had been displaced during or after the war faced closing doors wherever they turned. Some managed to reach the United States before the restrictive 1924 quota law took effect. In the wake of the Great Depression the few overseas countries that had been accessible severely restricted immigration. Efforts by Jewish aid associations to find alternative destinations beyond Western Europe and Palestine during the 1920s, especially in Latin America, saved many lives after 1933. Jews from Central and Eastern Europe who managed to reach far-flung destinations in Latin America, Africa, and Asia benefited from long-standing contacts established by Jewish aid associations. They had access to detailed and reliable information about travel routes, immigration policies, and job markets and often could rely on support from local Jewish communities.[55]

8
A Not So Typical Journey

On a freezing day in early January 1940 the *De Grasse* steamed into New York harbor. When the French ocean liner left Le Havre almost five hundred berths remained empty, even though, in the fifth month of the war, thousands of refugees were desperate to leave France for the United States. Apart from a few diplomats, business travelers, and crew members, the 528 passengers were overwhelmingly stateless Jews from Central Europe. They were joined by a few dozen stateless "Spaniards" in transit to Mexico. U.S. officials were not allowed to ask arriving migrants for their religion, but all arrivals had to provide information about their "race or people." Most passengers on the *De Grasse* identified as "Hebrew."

The detailed information the ship's captain collected about the passengers and provided to U.S. immigration officials shows the difficulties in distinguishing between Jews of different backgrounds: Jews who had been or were German citizens; stateless Jews from the former Russian and Austro-Hungarian empires who had lived in Germany, France, or elsewhere since the 1920s, and their foreign-born children; Jews with Polish citizenship; Jews whose Polish passports had expired and who were considered stateless by the Polish government, who had fled the country in September 1939; Jews with French citizenship born in France; Jews who had acquired French citizenship after 1918 as immigrants; and Jews who did not identify as "Hebrew." Thanks to the extensive scholarship on the Holocaust much is known about German and Austrian Jews escaping Nazi persecution. Yet surprisingly little has been written about Eastern European Jews trying to leave areas under direct or indirect German control. They faced almost insurmountable obstacles to reach safe havens in the late 1930s.[1]

One of the stateless Jewish passengers on the *De Grasse* was a fifty-four-year-old Russian architect who traveled with her teenage son. Rachel Bernstein was born in 1885 in Minsk in the Russian Empire, the daughter of a timber merchant. After attending high school in Warsaw, she studied architecture and art history in Heidelberg, Brussels, and Paris, where she graduated with a degree in architecture from the Ecole Speciale d'Architecture in 1907. The career prospects for female architects were not bright. She briefly worked for a Paris architect before realizing that her real passion was architectural history. She attended lectures about religious architecture at the University of Munich in 1909–1910 before returning to the Russian Empire. In St. Petersburg she joined a small team headed by Simon Dubnow working on the Russian edition of the *Jewish Encyclopedia*. In 1912 Rachel Bernstein married one of her colleagues, Mark Wischnitzer, who directed the encyclopedia's European history section. A few years older than Rachel, he too hailed from a petit bourgeois family in the Russian Pale. To ensure he received a good education his parents sent him from his hometown, Rowno in Volhynia, to the closest German-language Gymnasium (high school) in nearby Brody, which belonged to the Austrian Empire.

In hindsight, Brody was an intriguing choice for the future migration historian. A decade after thousands of Russian Jews had congregated in the little town in 1881–1882, the young Wischnitzer must have regularly encountered groups of Jewish and Ruthenian migrants heading to Brody's train station. After graduating, Wischnitzer studied history in Vienna and Berlin. In 1906 he defended his doctoral dissertation on German influences on nineteenth-century Russian liberalism at Berlin's respected Friedrich-Wilhelms Universität. In 1909–1910 he served in the Austrian army as a volunteer and was discharged as a reserve officer. It is not clear when Wischnitzer became an Austrian citizen, but he must have been naturalized by the time he entered the army. At the time, women did not have active citizenship rights in most European countries, so by marrying Mark Rachel became an Austrian citizen.

As a Jew, Mark could not hope to secure a permanent university post in a history department in Germany or Austria, not to mention the Russian Empire. As a woman who was Jewish Rachel had no academic career prospects. In St. Petersburg Mark earned income by teaching at a small Jewish studies college. In the summer of 1914, he was called to duty and served as an officer with the Austrian army throughout the war. To avoid detention as an enemy alien Rachel left for Vienna and later Berlin. Mark and Rachel lost their Austrian citizenship in the aftermath of the First World War when they moved to London. In the British capital Mark served as a member of the "English mission" of the short-lived Ukrainian People's Republic, but the collapse of the republic forced him to look for a new job.[2]

In 1921 Mark succeeded Bernhard Kahn as executive director of the Hilfsverein in Berlin. His doctoral degree from the University of Berlin certainly impressed the Hilfsverein board members who hired him. Unlike German Jewish candidates for the position, Mark was fluent in Yiddish, Russian, German, and even English. The Wischnitzers appear not to have been under any pressure to assimilate. They moved among different Jewish milieus in Berlin and mingled with established bourgeois German Jews who ran the Hilfsverein, and with German Jewish historians and art historians. And the couple was a part of the everchanging scene of Jewish intellectuals, writers, and artists from the former Russian Empire who passed through Berlin in the 1920s.[3]

Together with Lestschinsky, Tcherikower, and their families, the Wischnitzers belonged to Dubnow's social circle. Soon after arrival in the early 1920s both emerged as protagonists in Berlin's vibrant Yiddish publishing scene. Together with her husband Rachel launched two beautifully illustrated magazines, *Milgroym* (in Yiddish) and *Rimon* (in Hebrew), publishing texts by several Berlin sojourners, among them writers David Bergelson and Shmuel Agnon, and artwork by Marc Chagall and El Lissitzky. Later the couple joined a team working on an ambitious new encyclopedia project under the auspices of German Jewish historian Ismar Elbogen, the *Encyclopedia Judaica*. The partially completed encyclopedia project was abandoned after 1933 but revived in Israel during the 1960s. Rachel also became an advisor to and briefly a curator of Berlin's new Jewish Museum, which occupied rooms in a building adjacent to the imposing New Synagogue in the center of Berlin. The first exhibition opened its doors in January 1933, only days before Hitler was appointed German chancellor. In 1936 Rachel led Adolf Eichmann through the special exhibition *Unsere Ahnen* (Our Ancestors). In the previous year Eichmann had become a member of the SD (security service) office of the SS, where he covered Jewish affairs. The Gestapo closed the Jewish museum on November 10, 1938, the day after the notorious Kristallnacht pogrom.[4]

Unlike most Jewish scholars from the former Russian Empire, the Wischnitzers remained in Berlin in 1933. Long-standing contacts with Jewish communities and government officials in different parts of the world put Mark Wischnitzer in a unique position to assist German Jews to emigrate—and Jews like him who had settled in Germany only after 1918. Identifying potential safe havens was a challenging task. In the wake of the Great Depression almost all countries had closed their doors to migrants. The United States issued hardly any visas. Until 1936 Palestine served as a major destination for German Jews, but when the Mandate government

Rachel Wischnitzer and Alfred Klee attend the opening of an exhibition showing works by Alexander Oppler and Ernst Oppler at the Jewish Museum Berlin, Oranienburger Strasse, in October 1937. A few months later, Wischnitzer emigrated to Paris. Klee was a leading German Zionist. He died in the Dutch transit camp Westerbork in 1943. The two paintings by Ernst Oppler show the Polish violinist Bronislaw Hubermann and a boxing match. The photo was taken by Abraham Pisarek, who worked for the Berlin Jewish community.
Bildarchiv Pisarek/akg-images

began to restrict Jewish immigration, the Hilfsverein explored new locations. During the summer of 1936 Mark traveled to South and East Africa to meet with Jewish community leaders and government officials. The timing could not have been worse. Shortly after his arrival in Cape Town the South African Union announced a restrictive immigration law that implicitly targeted Jewish refugees. In South Rhodesia (contemporary Zimbabwe) Mark learned of the imminent arrival of the *Stuttgart*, a ship carrying 570 German Jews, days before the restrictive law would take effect. He rushed back to Cape Town to assist the local Jewish aid committee with the initial accommodation and transportation of the arriving migrants. A torrential rainstorm spared the disembarking passengers and Mark from an encounter with a local fascist group, the Greyshirts, who had planned to "welcome" the ship.

Visitors in the waiting room of the emigration advice office of the Hilfsverein, Ludendorffstrasse, Berlin in 1936, await appointments with Mark Wischnitzer or one of his colleagues. The man standing on the left is almost certainly Wischnitzer. The photo is part of a series that Abraham Pisarek took in 1935 and 1936. Pisarek's other images of the Hilfsverein office show crowded rooms with maps of North and South America and large signs asking visitors to refrain from discussing political matters. *Bildarchiv Pisarek/akg-images*

Based on a careful evaluation of the conditions, Mark concluded that only a limited number of Jews could settle in Sub-Saharan Africa. His little-known report serves as an intriguing commentary to several mass resettlement plans for European Jews that European governments and members of the Roosevelt administration proposed in the late 1930s and early 1940s. Several of these plans targeted the same region, in particular the French colony of Madagascar. Mark's report shows that those promoting these schemes knew little about the actual economic conditions and the climate. In early 1938, soon after his return, Mark and Rachel left Germany. Growing pressure by the Nazi regime was not the only reason. Rachel wanted to join her parents, who had moved to Paris after 1918. Mark managed to find a position with the JDC. They almost certainly knew that the French capital would be only a temporary home, as another European war appeared increasingly likely by 1938.[5]

Fleeing Europe

Rachel and Mark Wischnitzer were two of hundreds of thousands of Jewish and other Eastern Europeans who became stateless in 1918, unable to obtain a new citizenship. Their son Leonard James was born stateless in Berlin in 1924 because birth in Germany did not confer German citizenship. In a 1940 letter Rachel mentioned that the small family had obtained German citizenship at some point during the 1920s. If this was the case, the Wischnitzers became stateless in July 1933, when the Nazi regime revoked all naturalizations of foreign Jews granted after 1918 by the various German state governments. During the 1930s the number of stateless Jews in Europe increased. On January 21, 1938, the Romanian government stripped all post-1918 Jewish "immigrants" of Romanian citizenship and required all Jews to produce documentation to prove their citizenship. This policy aimed to denaturalize most Jews living in territories Romania had acquired after the First World War and was widely interpreted as a flagrant violation of the 1919 Minorities Treaty Romania had signed. During the fall of 1938 Romania effectively rendered all Romanian Jews living abroad stateless by refusing to honor their Romanian passports. Denaturalized Jews living in Romania were excluded from most occupations and lost their businesses and property. According to government sources in Bucharest the denaturalization law affected about 300,000 Jews. At least 50,000 were expected to emigrate annually. It was unclear where they would be able to go.

In November 1938 the Polish government made all Polish Jews living abroad stateless. The Hungarian government announced similar measures. During the 1930s the Nazi regime formally stripped some German Jews and left-wing German opposition figures who had managed to emigrate of their German citizenship. Among the figures targeted by this policy were the writers Thomas Mann and Heinrich Mann and the then-little-known philosopher Hannah Arendt. German consular officers often refused to renew the passports of German Jews to ensure they would not return. A few sympathetic diplomats assisted Jews, even issuing them new passports. In October 1938 the Nazi regime forced all German Jews to have their passports stamped with a "J," invalidating all passports without the stamp.[6]

When she arrived in New York in January 1940 and was asked to which "race or people" she belonged, Rachel did not identify as "Hebrew" but as "Russian." It is understandable that following years of humiliation by the Nazi state, German and other Jews without valid passports preferred to identify themselves as stateless and Hebrew rather than as German, but why did Rachel tell the immigration officers she was Russian? As stateless persons Rachel and Mark could apply for a U.S. quota visa, but the quota system was a mixed blessing for them—and for many other Jewish families. Rachel fell under the Russian quota when she submitted her visa application in 1938 in Paris because Minsk belonged to the Soviet Union. Rowno, Mark's birthplace, became part of Poland after 1918, forcing him to apply under the Polish quota. Mark and Rachel were both born in the Russian Empire. In the late 1930s the U.S. quota system separated them and countless other Jewish families, based on seemingly arbitrarily drawn post-1918 borders, often decades after prospective immigrants had left their hometowns.[7]

In 1930, against the background of sharply rising unemployment, President Herbert Hoover signed an executive order to protect American jobs by sharply reducing immigration and rendering the quota system almost meaningless for almost a whole decade. Consular officials were ordered to approve visas only if they were absolutely certain that the applicants had sufficient funds of their own and would not become a "public charge." As a result, hardly any visas were issued. After 1933 a small number of non-quota visas was allocated to a select group of outstanding scholars and clergy and their families. Mark Wischnitzer, who had not taught at a university before 1933, was turned down.

The U.S. State Department rigidly stuck with the quota system, forcing tens of thousands of Jews in Nazi Germany and France who were born in Eastern Europe to apply under the artificially low quotas for Eastern European countries. The chances of obtaining a Polish quota visa were negligible. While the combined annual quota for Germany and Austria was fixed at 27,370 for 1939, the quota for immigrant visas for persons from "Russia" was set at a low 2,712 and the Polish quota at 6,524. Among the applicants for these quotas were also non-Jews who tried to join relatives or had moved to Germany or France in the early 1920s for economic or political reasons. The long shadow of Hoover's executive order partly explains why the relatively generous quota for Germany was fully filled for the first time in 1939. The Polish quota was also exhausted. Only 1,727 persons immigrated under the Russian quota in 1939, including Rachel and her son. It is likely that many "Russians" were rejected because they could not prove that they would be able to support themselves financially in the United States. The national quotas for 1940 were not filled because the German occupation of northern France, Belgium, the Netherlands, Denmark, and Norway closed most escape routes through Western Europe, even for those who had already obtained a U.S. visa. Even those lucky migrants who managed to escape the advancing German troops faced further obstacles. Most passports were valid for only a year and had to be renewed. Once issued, visas expired after a few weeks, forcing emigrants to file additional paperwork for renewal, if they were able to physically walk into a U.S. embassy or consulate. By the late 1930s these were often surrounded by crowds of prospective migrants. The State Department did not relax its rigid admission policy, even after the German occupation of Western Europe in May and June 1940 closed most escape routes.[8]

Obtaining a U.S. visa clearly was exceedingly difficult. Why did Jews trying to leave France not move to alternative destinations, such as Brazil or Canada or countries in the Caribbean, not to mention closer destinations such as French Algeria or Morocco? South Africa was not the only country that closed its gates in the mid-1930s, even before the Nazi regime stepped up its anti-Jewish terror campaign in 1938. Canada admitted a mere five thousand Jewish migrants and refugees between 1933 and 1945. In the wake of the Depression, most other countries around the world restricted migration. Even if prospective migrants successfully navigated the maze of complex visa regulations, an additional obstacle loomed: money. Would it be possible to earn an income sufficient to support a family in distant, little developed countries such as Ecuador, Bolivia, or Uruguay? During the 1920s economic challenges and unfamiliar languages had forced thousands of Jews to leave countries in Latin America after short sojourns.

After the beginning of the war in Europe in September 1939 the U.S. State Department and the British government increased diplomatic pressure on countries in Latin America and the Caribbean to restrict immigration from Central and Western Europe because of concerns about the infiltration of "Nazi spies." One number painfully illustrates the tremendous pressure on Jews to leave Europe on the eve of the war. The 43,450 Jews who legally immigrated to the United States in 1939 (most under the German and Polish quotas) represented 52 percent of all immigrants arriving in the United States—a staggering number for members of a relatively small group. It will never be known how many Jews did not even apply under one of the Eastern European quotas because the effort clearly was hopeless.[9]

The U.S. embassy in Paris issued the Russian quota visa for Rachel and Leonard James Wischnitzer on September 20, 1939, almost three weeks after the beginning of the war increased the pressure on foreign refugees to leave France. After 1918 Paris had emerged as a destination for Eastern and Southern Europeans looking for better economic opportunities. The French government pursued a relatively liberal immigration policy because it could not fully demobilize its army and industrial jobs were plentiful. During the 1930s France accepted more refugees than any other country in the world, a consequence of sharing borders with Nazi Germany and Spain. In March 1938, following the German annexation of Austria, thousands of Jews fled to Paris. In late 1938 an estimated 70,000 Polish Jews and 25,000 German and Austrian Jews lived in France—as did an estimated 500,000 Spanish Civil War refugees. Growing economic pressure, political turmoil, and the mass flight from Spain led to a harsher policy against foreigners in 1938. Several decrees issued by the French government in April and May 1938, shortly after the Wischnitzers arrived in Paris, specifically targeted foreign Jews, excluding them from certain occupations. In April 1939, after the end of the Spanish Civil War, a giant internment camp for members of the International Brigades and political refugees from Spain was constructed in a swamp outside of Gurs, a small town in the foothills of the Pyrenees.[10]

On September 3, 1939, two days after German troops had launched their attack against Poland, France formally declared war against Germany. The conflict brought additional restrictions for foreigners living in France. By 1940 Nazi Germany had not yet stripped all German Jewish emigrants of German citizenship. Those who left Germany by train or on foot still carried German passports. In September 1939, several weeks before the departure of the *De Grasse*, the war interrupted passenger traffic from German ports. The German border with France turned into a military front line. Most German passports expired after a year. German Jews who had moved to France during the 1930s effectively lost their citizenship when they were unable (or unwilling) to renew their passports. On September 1, 1939, Germany closed its embassy and consulates in France. The French government began to detain Germans and Austrian nationals, including Jews, and even stateless Jews, as enemy aliens. Rachel Wischnitzer and her son left France shortly before more than four thousand German Jews were sent to Gurs in early 1940. The war closed down steamship traffic on the North Sea and affected service from French and British ports to North America. The atmosphere was tense. To avoid detention and fight the Nazis some Jews and other Eastern Europeans joined the French army. Among the younger Jews who volunteered was Zosa Szajkowski, a twenty-nine-year-old journalist from Poland, who began publishing about Jewish migration in the early 1940s. Army service was not, however, an option for Mark Wischnitzer, who was fifty-seven years old in 1939.[11]

Most Jews and political exiles in France trying to escape in late 1939 encountered formidable obstacles. The war slowed down transatlantic mail service, increasing wait times for visas and the various documents applicants had to procure. It became even more difficult to determine when a U.S. immigrant visa would be approved. Applicants had to provide extensive documentation to the State Department. The most difficult hurdle was the requirement to secure an affidavit by a relative or acquaintance in the United States who promised to cover all costs for the applicant and her or his family should they be unable to support themselves. Those who applied for an exemption from the quota, rabbis and outstanding scholars, for instance, had to procure sufficient evidence. If their U.S. visa was approved, migrants still had to obtain a French emigration visa and transit visas if their ship departed from a port outside of France.

Migrants without sufficient cash or valuables to cover administrative fees and the cost of the steamship passage depended on the support of friends and Jewish aid organizations. Unlike many others, the Wischnitzers could afford the passage because Mark earned an income from JDC. According to the passenger list Rachel paid for her and her son's steamship tickets. Migrants who had not paid for their own tickets were sometimes detained at Ellis Island under the "LPC" (likely to become a public charge) clause to investigate whether they had sufficient means to support themselves. The migration scholar Eugene Kulischer and his wife, Olga, were held at Ellis Island when they arrived from Lisbon in late June 1941, probably because Olga's father, who had immigrated to the United States during the 1920s, had paid for their passage. After six days the couple was released.[12]

The situation for non-Jews who had fled to France also became much more precarious in the fall of 1939. The Spanish passengers with Rachel and her son on the *De Grasse* belonged to a minority with sufficient means and contacts. In 1939 Mexican president Lázaro Cárdenas offered asylum to Spaniards stranded in France. His government had backed the Republican side during the Spanish Civil War, but the decision to admit thousands of Republican refugees met with widespread criticism from trade unions and right-wing politicians. Like many other countries affected by the Depression,

Mexico had adopted a restrictive immigration policy in 1929. Cárdenas's offer enabled more than twenty thousand Spaniards to move to Mexico until 1945.

Rachel's fellow passengers on the *De Grasse* were lucky because later in 1940 Vichy France made it increasingly difficult for Spaniards to leave. Unlike other refugees and migrants, Spaniards did not have the option to travel through Spain to Lisbon. After the German occupation of northern France, Vichy officials forced many Spaniards into existing camps such as Gurs, where they often were housed together with Jews like Hannah Arendt, who was sent from Paris to Gurs in May 1940. It is estimated that about 200,000 refugees returned to Spain, where the Franco regime detained or murdered an unknown number. Until 1944 thirty thousand Spaniards were deported from France to Nazi Germany for slave labor. An estimated thirty-five hundred perished in the notorious Mauthausen concentration camp outside of Linz in Austria. Cárdenas's offer did not extend to Jews. Only a few were able to move to Mexico from southern France and elsewhere in Europe, including such well-known left-wing figures as Leon Trotsky. For many years the Mexican consul in Marseilles, Gilberto Bosques, was celebrated for having saved thousands of Jewish lives. Actually, Bosques canceled hundreds of visas that had been approved earlier and issued a mere 332 visas to Jewish refugees—not on his own initiative but following instructions from his superiors.[13]

In the late 1930s few people knew more about changing visa regulations and travel routes than Mark Wischnitzer. On behalf of the Hilfsverein and the JDC he had helped thousands of Jews to escape. Now, in late 1939, his own situation was precarious. He could not board the *De Grasse* because he was still waiting for his Polish quota visa, along with thousands of other Jews in France. The information Rachel provided to U.S. immigration officers upon arrival reveals little about her growing fears. Mark almost certainly insisted that his wife and son leave for the United States at once. While she was relieved to have escaped the threat of Nazi persecution, she grew increasingly anxious about the fate of her husband and her elderly father in Paris. Her mother committed suicide in 1939. The most likely reason why her parents did not accompany her was that the Wischnitzers could not procure an affidavit by a person living in the United States promising to support the elderly couple. It is also possible that the parents could not secure the health certificate the U.S. authorities demanded from all immigrants.[14]

Rachel passed away in 1989, at the age of 104. Her papers at the Leo Baeck Institute in New York document a remarkable life. She saved letters from museum curators and artists such as Chagall, who belonged to her generation, shared her urban middle-class background in the northern Russian Pale, and crossed her path in Berlin in the 1920s and again in New York in the 1940s. Only a few documents in her papers originated before 1940, almost certainly because she had to leave them behind when she departed from Paris. The pre-1940 documents relate almost exclusively to her husband and fit in a small folder: Mark's high school diploma from Brody, his doctoral certificate from the University of Berlin, a few letters he received from scholars, friends, and family members. However, after she arrived in New York Rachel meticulously saved copies of most letters she wrote on a typewriter. She frantically pleaded with the JDC, the U.S. State Department, and several friends to rescue her husband. The letters provide a rare glimpse at the fears and travails many Jewish (and other) refugees experienced, even after they reached safe havens like New York.[15]

During the spring months of 1940 it was increasingly likely that the *drôle de guerre* (phony or funny war) on the French-German border would turn into a serious military conflict. Unlike most other Jewish refugees Mark Wischnitzer was well connected. One of his contacts was Joseph A. Rosen, who had managed the Agro-Joint colonization projects in the Soviet Union on behalf of the JDC during the 1920s. In the late 1930s Rosen directed a settlement scheme for German and Austrian Jews in Sosúa in the Dominican Republic, coincidentally one of the few countries willing to issue visas to Jewish refugees. In early 1940 Rosen arranged a Dominican visa for Mark, but the document never reached Paris. On May 10, 1940, German troops launched a major offensive against France, Belgium, and the Netherlands. Four weeks later German troops entered Paris. A few days earlier Rachel had received a letter from the State Department informing her that Mark would "have to wait for a considerable period" for his Polish quota visa. He would not be considered for "the classes of aliens for whom the immigration laws provide preference." In other words, the State Department refused to grant Mark one of the few special visas that were available for outstanding scholars.[16]

Following the German occupation of Paris Rachel feared the worst. The letters from her husband stopped, and she found out that the French authorities had interned him. Ilja Dijour, an acquaintance of Mark and the former Berlin director of Emigdirect, was luckier. He and his family had escaped to Bordeaux. For most refugees that city was a dead end because occupying the strategically important port was a major objective of the German invasion. Days before the Wehrmacht reached Bordeaux after the June 22 armistice Portuguese consul Aristides de Sousa Mendes issued thirty thousand Portuguese visas to refugees, among them ten thousand Jews, including Dijour and his family. The Portuguese government honored the visas but dismissed Sousa Mendes, who died poor in 1954. Throughout June 1940 Rachel did not hear from her husband. Now, several months after her arrival in New York, she faced increasing hardship. The limited income she earned from lecturing and publishing was not sufficient to support herself and her son. In a letter to a friend, she admitted that she had reached "a very tragic moment of my life."[17]

In early July she finally received news that Mark had escaped to the unoccupied southern part of France and was in Marseilles. With Rosen's help he managed to renew the expired Dominican visa. Rachel wrote to the head of the visa division in the State Department imploring him to grant Mark a transit visa so that he could reach the Dominican Republic. The response informed her that her husband would have to personally apply for a U.S. transit visa. He also needed to procure transit visas for Spain and Portugal because the German occupation of the Netherlands, Belgium, and the French Atlantic coast had closed most overseas escape routes.[18]

On June 14, 1940, the Franco regime took advantage of the impending French defeat, sending troops to the international zone of the northern Moroccan port of Tangier, thus closing the city and the surrounding hinterland to Jewish and other transmigrants and refugees. Just one major port with regular transatlantic service remained:Lisbon. For the long journey to the Portuguese capital and from there to the Dominican Republic Mark had to obtain transit visas for Spain, Portugal, and the United States—and a French exit visa. According to another desperate letter Rachel wrote to an immigration lawyer she had hired to assist her husband, the Spanish authorities refused to stamp a transit visa into a passport with a French exit visa. One explanation for this Kafkaesque measure was the declared Spanish policy of preventing Republican refugees from returning home.

Generally, it was more difficult to leave France than to travel through Spain. Spain usually tolerated foreign transit migrants, even if officials were aware that they had crossed the border illegally. However, hundreds were detained in the concentration camp Miranda de Ebro in northern Spain. It was the largest of two hundred camps the Franco regime set up for political

Captioned "The door of hope," this photo was published in HIAS's 1939 Annual Message and Reports. American Jews came to the HIAS main office in New York seeking advice on how to help family members trapped in Nazi-occupied Europe. Since obtaining a U.S. immigrant visa was almost impossible, much of the work of Jewish aid associations focused on disbursing financial assistance in Eastern Europe. *YIVO Library—015006626, YIVO, Institute for Jewish Research, New York*

prisoners across Spain and the only camp where foreign nationals were held. Some refugees were released quickly, especially if they were not de jure or de facto stateless and could claim diplomatic support. Others spent the rest of the war in Miranda de Ebro. Refugees in Marseilles were not in a position to distinguish reliable information from rumors to consider the risks involved. They knew Nazi Germany had supported Franco during the Spanish Civil War. And it was no secret that the Franco regime had murdered thousands of left-wing opponents, among them returning Spanish leftists. On several occasions, Spain deported refugees back across the border, where they faced almost certain detention by Vichy officials.[19]

In her autobiographical 1944 novel, *Transit*, the German Jewish writer and Communist Anna Seghers evoked the surreal atmosphere Jewish and left-wing opponents of the Nazis encountered in Marseilles in 1940–1941. The novel's protagonists face a maze of visa regulations, waiting many hours in front of different consulates, hit by conflicting rumors, barely making ends meet. Most diplomats were indifferent, some were corrupt, but a few, including U.S. Vice Consul Henry Bingham IV, went out of their way to help refugees. Seghers belonged to a small group who managed to escape by boat via North Africa and Martinique to Mexico. Like other Jewish refugees, including Chagall and his wife, Mark Wischnitzer almost certainly hiked across the Pyrenees into Spain. The journey was risky because the migrants traversed a legal no man's land. Could the smugglers be trusted, or did they work for the Germans? Would the Spanish police arrest them or return them to Vichy France? In early November 1940 Mark resurfaced in Lisbon, the main port for European Jewish refugees moving to the Americas after 1940.[20]

In December 1940 Mark arrived in New York. To identify potential "Nazi spies" the State Department detained most migrants from Germany and Austria heading to the Dominican Republic at Ellis Island while they waited for the departure of their ship to the Caribbean. Mark was spared detention and even received permission to reunite with Rachel and Leonard for a few days. On December 19 he left for the Dominican Republic. In Ciudad Trujillo (Santo Domingo) he resubmitted his U.S. visa application. He did not have to wait long. The most obvious reason for the speedy approval was the low number of applications for Polish quota visas. By early 1941 most prospective Jewish (and non-Jewish) applicants could not reach the closest U.S. consulate or embassy. And traveling to the United States was almost impossible. An unknown number were already dead. Even the ones who had avoided detention in one of the several French detention camps and managed to reach Marseilles struggled to organize the required transit visa and obtain a ship passage. That was not a problem for Mark and a few other lucky migrants in Santo Domingo. On May 5, 1941, he returned to New York, this time as an official immigrant. In 1944 Rachel learned that her father, eighty-one-year-old Vladimir Bernstein, had been taken to the notorious transit camp in the Paris suburb of Drancy. He was deported several weeks before the French capital was liberated. He died almost certainly in Auschwitz.[21]

Making Sense of Jewish Migrations

The experiences of the Wischnitzer family resemble those of thousands of other Jews trying to escape from Europe to the United States during the 1930s and early 1940s. An unknown but very large number were not in a position to escape because they lacked the means. Those who tried were forced to travel separately and leave elderly relatives and children behind. Others failed to reach their intended destination and were stranded along the way. Eugene Kulischer's brother and co-author Alexander was apprehended by Vichy officials on his way to Marseilles. According to an unconfirmed report he died in a French transit camp in 1942. Seghers describes how Jews and political refugees in Marseilles tried to navigate the surreal bureaucratic maze that was constantly shifting. It was widely expected that the Germans would take full control of the city in a matter of weeks or months. Visa applicants waited in vain for documents or they missed appointments because the French police had detained them. Many could not arrange or afford steamship passages. Not all ships actually departed. Others did not want to leave close relatives, children, and partners behind. In November 1942 German and Italian troops entered the unoccupied part of France, closing down the escape route from Marseilles. The State Department processed some visas long after the applicants had been deported to extermination camps and ghettos in "the East."[22]

The journey of Rachel and Mark Wischnitzer and their son was unusual because they belonged to the small number of Jews from Eastern Europe who reached the United States during the 1930s and 1940s. It is doubtful whether Mark would have been able to escape southern France without a Dominican visa. Foreign-born Jews and their French-born children made up over 70 percent of Jews deported from Vichy France to ghettos and extermination camps. The repeated moves of the Wischnitzers from Russia to Germany and then to France and the Americas also illustrate that flight and migration to seek better opportunities were frequently related. Several scholars, notably Jacob Lestschinsky, Joseph Schechtman, the Kulischer brothers, Ilya Dijour, and others, left Kiev in 1919–1920, when the city repeatedly changed hands before falling fully under Bolshevik control. They chose to move to Berlin to seek employment or (in Schechtman's case) attend university. The Wischnitzers initially headed to London before opting for Berlin after Mark secured his position as Hilfsverein executive director. Movements that are tied to the quest for better opportunities elsewhere and flight from violent persecution often overlap. The experiences of the scholars reflect those of a much larger group of Jews and others.[23]

The repeated moves of Rachel and Mark Wischnitzer hauntingly show how closely the story of Jewish migrations was interwoven with the personal journeys of the men and women who tried to make sense of this subject. After settling in Paris Mark turned to Jewish migration history as an academic topic. In 1940 he was among the first and regular contributors to Salo Baron's

Jewish Social Studies. The second volume of the journal contains his article about Jewish emigration from Nazi Germany, one of the first scholarly texts on this topic. After reaching the Dominican Republic in 1941 he contributed an article about an earlier, failed attempt to direct Jewish migrants to the island state in 1881–1882. Shortly after reaching New York, he began working on a manuscript about Jewish migrations, which he published in 1948. The study, *To Dwell in Safety*, remains the most comprehensive overview of this subject. It is not an optimistic book. His own journey offers clues to why he linked Jewish migrations after 1800 almost exclusively with persecution and expulsion. In contrast, Lestschinsky and Eugene Kulischer, who reached New York on similarly protracted paths, judged Jewish migrations differently, before and after the Holocaust.

The journey of the Wischnitzers thus raises a profound question that occupied much of Mark's professional career as an aid worker and migration historian, namely, how to make sense of Jewish migrations and of migration more generally. Were Jewish migrations a distinctive phenomenon because Jews could look back on a long history of enforced marginalization, discrimination, systematic expulsion, and eventually genocide, as he argued? Or did Jewish statelessness and permanent displacement betray a much larger unsolved problem of unwanted minorities that was a product of the post-1918 system of successor states of the multiethnic empires? Did the experience of permanently displaced Jews contain important lessons for designing a system of internationally guaranteed protections for permanently displaced people who were legally or de facto stateless? Before the founding of the State of Israel in 1948 these were existential and political rather than academic questions.[24]

9

Jewish Migrations or Wandering Jews?

Shortly after he and his wife were released from detention on Ellis Island in July 1941, Eugene Kulischer began looking for a job. Following in the footsteps of other European refugee scholars seeking employment, he went to an office building on 45th Street in Manhattan, just off Fifth Avenue. On the floor of the offices of the Institute for International Education he knocked on the door of Elizabeth ("Betty") Drury, who worked for the Emergency Committee in Aid of Displaced Foreign Scholars. The organization was set up in 1933 to assist refugee scholars from Nazi Germany. In 1938, following the German annexation of Austria, the committee widened its scope to scholars from all countries under German control. Kulischer did not seek financial support but expressed interest in an academic position. On a small notecard Drury scribbled a few initial impressions. He appeared friendly, was relaxed, and had a strong Russian accent. Kulischer indicated his willingness to give lessons in German or Russian to earn some income. He presented references from the well-known French sociologists Marcel Mauss and Maurice Halbwachs.

Kulischer's job search turned out to be frustrating, an experience shared by most émigré scholars who reached the United States after 1933. Three sociology departments at well-regarded research universities turned him down, even though the Rockefeller Foundation had indicated it would support him if he secured a teaching post. A demographer whom Drury recruited to write a reference sat down with Kulischer for several hours in the fall of 1941. He described him as an impressive researcher who "tends to work on a broad canvas." Kulischer did not suffer from "persecution psychology" and he had no "political phobias." In other words, he was willing to make sacrifices to accommodate to the American setting, and he was not a Communist. But his written English was poor.

The committee closed the file in December 1942 after Kulischer stopped visiting the office. By then he had managed to secure a commission for a book-length study about displacement in Europe after 1939 from the ILO. In the fall of 1942 and spring of 1943 Kulischer compiled the manuscript at the small ILO office in Montreal. He was also working on a short survey about Jewish migration history for a pamphlet series published by the AJC. *Jewish Migrations* was the only text Kulischer devoted to a Jewish topic during his career, apart from two short articles he contributed to a HIAS newsletter in the late 1940s. It is not far-fetched to assume that he accepted the commission because he needed the income.[1]

AJC's decision to recruit a generalist rather than a specialist in Jewish history was made by Max Gottschalk, the head of the newly founded AJC Research Institute on Peace and Post-War Problems. He met Kulischer in June 1942 at a conference about postwar population resettlement. Before the war Gottschalk was a high-ranking Belgian civil servant who was affiliated with the ILO and belonged to the leadership of the Belgian Jewish community. After 1933 he coordinated support for German and other Jewish refugees with the JDC and the Belgian government. In the wake of the German invasion of Belgium in 1940 he and his family managed to escape to Lisbon. After he reached New York, Gottschalk's contacts in the JDC helped him to secure the directorship of the newly founded AJC Research Institute. As one of its first projects the institute launched the pamphlet series "Jews and the Post-War World," designed for Jewish public and government officials. The purpose was to prepare the ground for an informed discussion about Jewish rights and resettlement after the war.[2]

Kulischer's *Jewish Migrations* is of particular interest for this study because he largely avoided discussing Jews in his other publications, before and after 1942–1943. A short bio in *Jewish Migrations* is the only one he ever provided for a publication hinting at his own Jewish background; following a brief description of his teaching appointments and publications he added that he had served as "vice-president of the Jewish Anti-Pogrom Committee, Kiev" in 1919–1920.

It is not surprising that Kulischer approached the topic from a general perspective. He began by dismissing the thesis that migration was an inherently Jewish experience. The narrative of the "everlasting Jewish wanderings," he wrote, deliberately or inadvertently confirmed the traditional Christian stereotype of the Wandering Jew. Jewish migrations were not an exceptional phenomenon because "the story of the whole of mankind is a history of migrations." Without ignoring anti-Jewish persecutions and violence, Kulischer identified economic factors as decisive in the history of Jewish migrations. The Russian pogroms of 1881–1882 were merely a trigger but not an underlying cause. In the Austrian province of Galicia anti-Jewish incidents were isolated but Jewish migration rates were high. Jewish economic deprivation was only in part a consequence of restrictions imposed on Jews in the Russian Empire. Industrialization, Kulischer wrote, had displaced Jewish artisans and traders from their traditional roles in the rural economy.

Kulischer judged the "new great Trans-Atlantic migration of the Jews to the West" after 1880 not as a distinctive movement but rather as "part of an enormous world-wide movement of people." As in his earlier publications, Kulischer criticized migration restrictions and highlighted the economic and cultural contributions refugees such as the Huguenots had made to their host societies. The United States would benefit greatly from the flight of European Jews. He could not resist the caustic remark that "Nazi 'science'" had clearly shown to the rest of the world that "German culture in all its aspects from the department store to the Nobel Prize Winner, was, in fact not German, but German-Jewish." He was not entirely off the mark. Before 1933 Jews represented about 1 percent of Germany's population. Of the thirty-one men born in Germany or a German state who were awarded a Nobel Prize in the sciences before 1933, eleven were of Jewish descent.[3]

Instead of emphasizing persecution and discrimination Kulischer pointed out that Jews in Europe had prospered after 1800, more so than most other Europeans, especially if they had migrated. Rapid industrialization was beneficial for Jews who decided to relocate. In nearby cities and in North America unskilled Jewish peddlers from Eastern Europe became wage earners who could feed their families. Jewish city migrants generally had managed to uplift themselves, especially in the United States. Remittances by Jewish and Italian migrants from the United States were significant. In short, Jewish migration was a success story.

To emphasize the benefits of migration Kulischer shifted from a differentiated discussion of economic factors to crude stereotypical images. This perhaps quickly written section provides a rare glimpse at Kulischer's personal view of Jewish life and betrays Zionist influences. He argued that Jewish migrants and their children in the United States, Palestine, and Soviet cities differed from the "Ghetto type" of Jews in Eastern Europe, who were "weak, servile," and clung to religion. In contrast, the migrant's "body is straight, his muscles strong, his expression free and straightforward." The migrants' descendants had spent their "childhood in the open air and in modern schools, not in the stifling heder (the old-style Hebrew school)." The migrant "earns his living from manual labor, and competes in sports." He did not mention female migrants, whose role had been transformed even more impressively because they too had overwhelmingly become wage earners. The dichotomy between *Luftmenschen* and *Muskeljuden* was, of course, a staple of Zionist discourse, but also a vision shared by other adherents of agricultural and imperialist colonization schemes. Max Nordau popularized the terms at the 1898 and 1901 Zionist congresses by contrasting images of marginalized, unproductive, and physically weak Jewish men (and women) in Eastern Europe with idealized Zionist settlers. Unlike Zionist authors, Kulischer did not promote agricultural colonization as a catch-all solution. Rather, he considered Jewish settlement in industrial cities to be a beneficial development. His intention was to show that Jewish migrants had escaped a hopeless existence on the margins of economically backward societies unable to sustain a growing number of people.[4]

The final paragraph of *Jewish Migrations* linked the history of Jewish flight from persecution with the unfolding genocide and the postwar settlement. Jewish mass migration from Eastern Europe before 1914, Kulischer argued, had saved millions of Jews from slaughter by the Germans and their local collaborators after 1939. In late 1942, when Kulischer completed the manuscript, news of the systematic killings of Jews in Poland and the Soviet Union had reached the American public: "Throughout their history migrations have saved the Jewish people and Judaism from extermination. Migrations have always opened up new horizons for persecuted and destitute Jews. At the present time millions of Jews are being murdered by the Germans. But in three new centers, Palestine, the cross-roads of the British Empire, America and the Soviet Union—the fate of the Jews is linked with that of the three great nations under whose blows the Germany of Hitler will disappear."[5]

Before and after 1942, Kulischer repeatedly and explicitly voiced his opposition to migration restrictions, not least those passed by the U.S. Congress in the early 1920s. Yet in *Jewish Migrations* he did not discuss the severe impact of post-1918 migration restrictions specifically on Eastern European Jews. These restrictions had closed migration routes and exposed many to discrimination and persecution years before the Holocaust. This omission is even more striking considering Kulischer's own precarious flight, first from Kiev to Berlin, then, after the rise of the Nazi regime, from Berlin via Paris, Marseilles, and Lisbon to New York. A study course Gottschalk and his assistant Abraham Duker compiled almost simultaneously for the AJC Research Institute explicitly stated that Jews were the "chief victims of the closed-door policy" after 1918. Instead, Kulischer reminded his readers not to lose sight of the fate of other refugees and victims of German persecution and of the powers who would ultimately determine the postwar order: "The question of post-war migration is especially vital for the Jewish people. We must remember, however, that it is not an exclusively Jewish question, and should therefore not be treated as such."[6]

In a short preface, written in April 1943, Gottschalk summarized the essence of the *Jewish Migrations*. Kulischer, he said, was an "optimist" surrounded by pessimists who expected that the Nazi regime would destroy Jewish life in Europe for generations to come and that Palestine would remain closed to Jewish settlement. Kulischer reminded the pessimists of the successful side of Jewish migration history. There might even be a resettlement of surviving Jews that would "satisfy both the countries of emigration and immigration," an implicit hint that Jewish settlement in Palestine remained a viable option. Migration offered hope in dark times.[7]

In hindsight, Kulischer's stereotypical view of "Ghetto-type" Jews and his nonchalant attitude about the unfolding mass murder appear difficult to fathom. However, the full extent of the Nazi genocide was not known when he submitted his manuscript to Gottschalk. And in late 1942 there was still hope that many Jews could perhaps be saved. Moreover, *Jewish Migrations* was not a major departure from the scholarship of the 1920s, which had highlighted the importance of economic factors as a major cause for Jewish migration before 1914. Kulischer's insistence that postwar Jewish migrations would have to be part of a larger political settlement in Europe can be read as an implicit criticism of other Jewish scholars whose paths he had already crossed after his arrival in New York.

Kulischer may have declined a request to write a longer study of Jewish migrations for the AJC, if it was actually made. Almost simultaneously with *Jewish Migrations* he published *The Displacement of Population in Europe* on behalf of the ILO. This study enhanced his reputation as a migration specialist. It was the first systematic overview of forced migration in German-controlled areas before and during the war. He estimated that 30 million civilians had been displaced after the beginning of the war in 1939. The "permanent resettlement" of millions of displaced persons would constitute "one of the most urgent tasks of post-war reconstruction." Kulischer opposed forced resettlement. Ideally policymakers should assist refugees to return to their homes. He did not address possible options for those refugees who could not go back. He also ignored mass deportations in Stalin's Soviet Union before and after 1941. The displacement study was widely reviewed; for instance, Hannah Arendt, writing in *Jewish Social Studies*, praised Kulischer's "careful and expert analysis." Kulischer did not provide specific definitions for the terms "refugee" and "displacement." Therefore, he was probably surprised that the book's title "displacement of population" became a crucial catch phrase for the European refugee crisis. The *New York Times* published a short notice about the book in 1943. In the following months the usage of the term "displaced person" and "displaced people" increased sharply. In a 1949 article Kulischer claimed ownership of the term "displaced persons." His obituary in the *New York Times* confirmed his authorship.[8]

By 1940, it was clear that the war was a fateful pivot point for Jews in Eastern Europe. Jews who had not managed to escape from territories under German control were largely deprived of agency. Kulischer was one of a number of Jewish émigré scholars from the former Russian Empire who reached New York in 1940–1941. These men and a few women, including Arendt, grappled with the implications of an unprecedented crisis. Unlike Kulischer's relatively obscure *Jewish Migrations* essay, several book-length studies that he and other Jewish émigré scholars in New York published in the 1940s laid the conceptual foundations for the general field of migration and refugee studies. Jews do not feature prominently in some of these. Yet authors like Kulischer tried to make sense of (their own) Jewish migrations. A key question was whether Jewish migrations were a distinct phenomenon throughout history or whether the situation of unwanted Jewish minorities and displaced Jews betrayed a larger crisis that was tied to the breakup of the multiethnic empires in Eastern Europe and the Middle East in 1918. This crisis was exacerbated during the late 1930s when several countries began to forcibly push out unwanted Jewish populations.

The M Project

In 1939 John Hope Simpson, a high-ranking British civil servant, published a comprehensive study on refugees; it was a revised version of a report he had prepared for the Evian conference. He noted that the status of refugees was undefined and undetermined, describing the refugee as the "unwanted inhabitant of the world, unwanted in the country of his origin, unwanted in any other country." The League of Nations had provided definitions only for specific groups of refugees it had formally recognized, but had not settled on a general definition. Thus a large and growing number of people had effectively been pushed into a legal no man's land. Refugees were, as he noted, de jure or de facto stateless and lacked almost any legal protection. Simpson did not explore the questions of how to distinguish between different refugees, such as those requiring immediate protection and those who had been permanently displaced, and how to define "normal" migrants. A related issue hovering over the text was the question of which institution would determine whether a person was a refugee and which rights a formal recognition would entail.[9]

The post-1918 refugee crisis in Europe and the Middle East was a product of the breakup of the multiethnic empires and of the triumph of such nation-states as Poland, Romania, and Turkey. A crucial and unresolved question was where permanently displaced refugees and unwanted minorities could actually go or, as some suggested, should be taken against their will. The situation of Jews who were in some cases literally stranded between East Central European borders in late 1938 showed the pressing need for an international solution. Simpson's report provided a wealth of information about major refugee groups, with a long discussion of the acute problems faced by German *and* Eastern European Jews, different crisis regions, nongovernmental aid associations, and the main destination countries that were (or might be) accommodating refugees for "final resettlement." Even though Jews were one of the largest refugee groups, Simpson did not devote a specific chapter to them but subsumed Jews under migration from the former Russian Empire and individual states such as Germany.

Simpson, who in 1929 had conducted a formal investigation of the violent clashes between Arabs, Jewish settlers, and British troops in Mandate Palestine, did not consider the small territory suitable for mass Jewish resettlement. He presented four general solutions: a better protection of minorities, repatriation, relocation to countries where refugees could settle permanently, and "absorption" by the countries where refugees were living in permanent transit. That was, we now know, wishful thinking. In 1939 no institution existed that could oversee the implementation of these policies and ensure they were not violated, except the much-weakened League of Nations and the Intergovernmental Committee on Refugees that had been set up at Evian.[10]

In the aftermath of the Evian conference the Roosevelt administration began to explore potential territories for Jewish resettlement. In early 1939 Roosevelt observed that "the larger Eastern European problem is basically a Jewish problem." Echoing ideas proposed by a wide range of authors during the interwar years, he suggested that removing young men and women through "organized emigration" from overpopulated Eastern Europe would lead to a "decrease in economic pressure." In 1939 geographer Isaiah Bowman, who advised Roosevelt in refugee matters, began drawing up plans for potential Jewish mass resettlement in sparsely inhabited territories around the globe. A memorandum the president received from the State Department in late November 1938 identified the former German colony of Tanganyika in East Africa as the only realistic option. Bowman, who made no secret of his antisemitic views, favored Peru, where he had conducted research. The only area in North America he deemed suitable for Jewish resettlement was Alaska because it offered vast unsettled spaces. In 1940 Harry Slattery, the undersecretary of the interior, proposed that European refugees could provide a boost to Alaska's economy. Slattery was quite aware of the challenging conditions in the territory. Refugees would be able to apply for a visa for the American mainland only after working at least five years in Alaska. Meanwhile the British government explored resettlement in British Guiana, while French and Polish officials discussed Madagascar. Tara Zahra has pointed out the bizarre nature of plans developed by armchair strategists about the suitability of urban Jews for agricultural settlement in remote and barely developed territories with harsh climates—just as governments in Poland, Romania, and Nazi Germany were resorting to violence against unwanted Jewish populations.[11]

After the beginning of the war in Europe in September 1939 the Roosevelt administration began to make preparations for a much more far-reaching "migration project"—the so-called M Project. The planners envisaged that the United States would oversee a vast global resettlement and economic development effort to address the postwar refugee crisis and at the same time cultivate supposedly "vacant" territories in different parts of Europe, the Middle East, North Africa, and South and East Asia. In contrast to the violent resettlement schemes pursued by Nazi Germany and the Soviet Union at the same time, the M Project authors considered mass resettlement as a voluntary option. At least that was the plan. FDR may have pursued the project in part to appease the strong nativist faction in Congress because territories in the United States were excluded from the resettlement plan. Another goal was to boost U.S. exports of technology and consumer goods to regions that were selected for redevelopment and resettlement.

Several studies about the origins of the refugee crisis and likely solutions that were published in the 1940s remain the project's most important legacy. The expectation of a postwar refugee crisis was based on a sound analysis of the likely outcomes of the war. The same cannot be said about the vast social engineering plans and neocolonial schemes that the project envisioned. In a conversation with anthropologist Henry Field, one of M Project's lead managers, Roosevelt sketched his vision of turning North Africa "into the granary of Europe, just as it was in the Roman days." Desalination would open up vast spaces in Australia, northern India, and the Middle East for millions of settlers from Europe and Southeast Asia.[12]

The M Project was formally launched in the summer of 1942, coincidentally just when the Nazi "resettlement"—one of the camouflage terms the regime used for the genocidal killing of Jews—reached a decisive phase with mass deportations from the Warsaw Ghetto and other parts of Europe to the Aktion Reinhard extermination camps. It is not known whether the "Final Solution" was part of a far-reaching genocidal resettlement plan, the General Plan Ost (General Plan East). This scheme originated in the spring of 1940, when the office in charge of the Strengthening of German Volkstum (Peoplehood) in occupied Poland directed by SS leader Heinrich Himmler began to draw up strategies for mass expulsions of Polish civilians to make room for German settlers. These plans were overhauled at some point in early 1941 when Hitler issued directives for the invasion of the Soviet Union. Agronomist and SS officer Konrad Meyer, the lead author, drew on the expertise of demographers and infrastructure specialists who may have encountered some of the Russian Jewish émigré scholars later affiliated with the M Project in Weimar Germany during the 1920s. In July 1941, during the early phase of the German invasion of the Soviet Union, Meyer presented the first draft of the General Plan East. No copy of the actual document has been located, but other sources indicate that Meyer sought to remove or exterminate between 30 million and 40 million "racially undesirable" people, primarily Jews and Slavs, move several million German settlers to state-of-the-art agricultural colonies, and enslave over 10 million Slavs as forced laborers.

After Himmler issued a ban on Jewish emigration from territories under German control on October 18, 1941, an amendment to the German citizenship law in November stripped all German (and Austrian) Jews living abroad of German citizenship. Apart from a few Jewish emigrants who had managed to acquire new citizenship and those who had already been formally stripped of their German citizenship—including Arendt—this measure rendered the overwhelming majority of German and Austrian Jews who had left Germany (and Austria) stateless. However, the amended law primarily applied to Jews who would be leaving Germany *after* November 1941—on trains to ghettos and extermination sites in "the East." The amended citizenship law legally erased German and Austrian Jews as they were deported across an invisible border enabling the German state to confiscate their remaining property before they were murdered.

Apart from the "resettlement" of ethnic Germans and the forced removal of Jews, Poles, and others in several locations in occupied Poland and Ukraine, it remains contested whether the Holocaust and the mass killings of Soviet civilians under the guise of "partisan warfare," especially in the area of contemporary Belarus, were actually related to the General Plan East. At first glance, the M Project and its German counterpart could not be more different. Meyer's plan envisioned the removal, enslavement, and killing of millions of "surplus" Eastern Europeans to create "living space" for German settlers. The M Project was conceived as a long-term strategy to address supposed overpopulation and permanent displacement in and beyond Europe. However, the two plans did share several features. The lead authors were academics versed in agriculture, demography, geography, and infrastructure planning. The plans covered vast spaces and were based on resettlement projections involving millions of people. Like late nineteenth-century Jewish colonization projects, which had mostly failed by the 1930s, both plans betray romantic notions attached to subsistence farming in the preindustrial era at a time when employment in the farming sector was declining due to the impact of scientific research, the adoption of technology to agriculture, and the emergence of an urban consumer society. And both plans put emphasis on Jewish "resettlement" from Eastern Europe, a question that had been debated widely in the 1930s. The architects of the "Final Solution," of course, used the term "resettlement" as a cipher for the systematic extermination of Jews.[13]

Under the auspices of the M Project, more than 660 studies about migration, refugees, and the economic and climatic conditions in potential settlement areas were produced between 1943 and 1945. The project's bold agenda bears a striking resemblance to the vision Eugene and Alexander Kulischer had sketched in *Kriegs- und Wanderzüge*. An international clearinghouse would address growing disparities between areas with increasing populations and lacking resources by "resettling" millions of people to reduce supposed overpopulation and prevent future conflicts. Europe in particular would be relieved of "surplus" populations. In 1945, weeks after Roosevelt's death, the M Project was mothballed. Because of its secret status, most files remained restricted until 1960. The international migration office that would have coordinated the resettlement of refugees and regulated global migration flows remained a lofty vision, even though the founding of the United Nations in 1945 would have provided an opportunity.

The resemblance of the M Project's vision to the premise of *Kriegs- und Wanderzüge* is not coincidental. Eugene Kulischer was formally affiliated with the project. Other contributors were Max Gottschalk, Ilya Dijour, Joseph Schechtman, Nahum Goldmann, who cofounded the World Jewish Congress in 1936, and Joseph Rosen, who helped Mark Wischnitzer to escape to the Dominican Republic and had coordinated Jewish agricultural colonization projects in the Soviet Union on behalf of JDC during the 1920s. According to Henry Field, who directed the M Project, Kulischer and Schechtman were "assigned" by the Office for Strategic Services (OSS), the forerunner of the CIA. He credited both for making significant contributions. Among the organizations that had assisted the M Project, Field listed the New York office of YIVO and more than a dozen Jewish aid associations, including HIAS, JDC, JCA, the defunct Hilfsverein, and HICEM, which operated from Lisbon with JDC support during the war.[14] The input of Jewish associations reflects their unrivaled expertise based on a long track record of working with migrants and agricultural colonization schemes. Few nonstate organizations could draw on a comparable degree of institutional knowledge, represented not least by contributors like Dijour and Rosen. The studies Kulischer and Schechtman published on mass displacement and "population transfers" in the 1940s are part of the M Project's legacy. Both decided to treat Jewish migrations only in passing but presented conflicting views about migration policy. Both books influenced policymakers and continue to serve as reference points for scholars in migration and refugee studies.[15]

The Jewish Refugee

Even before the first reports about systematic mass killings of Jews reached the United States, Jewish representatives and aid associations frantically focused on last-minute efforts to evacuate displaced Jews. They also began devoting more attention to preparing the ground for postwar resettlement. The AJC Research Institute on Peace and Post-War Problems competed with a rival Jewish think tank, the Institute for Jewish Affairs (IJA), which was also founded in 1941 in New York and also solicited papers by scholars and other specialists about Jewish migration. Its head was Jacob Robinson, a Jewish legal scholar from Lithuania. Between 1925 and 1933 he represented Jewish minorities in Lithuania at the National Minorities Congress and became a close collaborator of Leo Motzkin.[16]

IJA was set up as the research arm of the World Jewish Congress and its close affiliate, the American Jewish Congress. The WJC was founded in 1936 as the successor to Motzkin's Comité des Delegations Juives, not coincidentally just as the failure of the minority protection system had become apparent and a new Jewish refugee crisis loomed following the rise of the Nazi regime. The WJC sought to overcome the division of dozens of different national Jewish organizations by representing all Jews, regardless of where they lived. Motzkin and fellow Zionist Nahum Goldmann envisioned the WJC not as a humanitarian aid association but as a representative political body of global Jewry. The other major figure driving the founding of the WJC was Rabbi Stephen S. Wise. A charismatic figure and an early advocate of Zionism, he had long felt the established AJC did not represent recently immigrated working-class Jews who made up the majority of the American Jewish population. In 1918 he and other American Zionists established the American Jewish Congress as a separate organization that took a more proactive and public stance than AJC. Wise first proposed founding the WJC in the aftermath of the war and continued to promote the WJC throughout the 1920s.

The WJC struggled to overcome deep-seated divisions. The AJC, the Alliance Israélite Universelle, and other establishment organizations turned down invitations to attend the founding ceremony because they regarded the new body as a Zionist project. These divisions persisted throughout the 1930s and 1940s. Gottschalk's institute firmly moved within the orbit of the AJC. Robinson and Wise put great emphasis on maintaining a safe distance from the establishment organization. Therefore, it is noteworthy that Gottschalk and Robinson regularly corresponded about their respective (and overlapping) agendas and exchanged unpublished manuscripts.[17]

Schechtman and Lestschinsky both worked for IJA in 1942 and 1943. In this period Robinson and Schechtman met several times with Kulischer, who was collecting data for his displacement study. In 1942 demographer Arieh Tartakower joined IJA. Tartakower was born in Brody. After completing his doctoral dissertation at the University of Vienna in 1922 he became a prominent Labor Zionist in Poland and served on the Łódź city council in the late 1930s. After reaching New York he quickly emerged as a leading figure in efforts to find a solution to the unprecedented Jewish refugee crisis. During the war Tartakower headed the WJC relief and rehabilitation section. In this role he became one of the leading Jewish advocates seeking formal Jewish recognition in intergovernmental discussions about the postwar resettlement and reconstruction planning. In 1943 Tartakower attended meetings of the newly founded United Nations Relief and Rehabilitation Administration (UNRRA) on behalf of WJC. UNRRA represented a concerted effort by the Allies to prepare a postwar settlement for refugees and other victims of German and Japanese aggression. The organization became affiliated with the United Nations only when the UN was established in 1945 as successor to the League of Nations. Like Motzkin in the 1920s, Tartakower tried but failed to gain recognition for Jewish refugees as a separate nationality and secure a promise for resettlement to a safe territory.[18]

In 1944 Tartakower and Kurt Grossmann published *The Jewish Refugee*, the most comprehensive survey of Jewish displacement and migration written during the Holocaust. Grossmann was a left-wing journalist who fled Berlin in early 1933. In Prague and later Paris, he led efforts to assist other Jewish refugees before he moved to the United States in 1939. He worked with Tartakower at WJC and regularly contributed to émigré newspapers. The seven-hundred-page survey was among the first IJA book publications. The authors pursued three goals: presenting detailed information about the extent of the crisis, gaining international recognition for Jewish refugees as a specific group, and securing an agreement about the resettlement for surviving Jews in Europe, ideally in Palestine. *The Jewish Refugee* was designed as a factual survey for political decision-makers, filling a striking gap. Simpson did not devote a separate chapter to Jewish refugees, even though, as he conceded, by the end of 1937 a mere 15,000 of the 150,000 refugees from Germany were not Jewish. This example demonstrates why Jewish organizations went to great lengths to publish information and data about the Jewish refugee problem and push for a formal acknowledgment of Jewish displacement as an international problem that had to be addressed. *The Jewish Refugee* contained a carefully researched bibliography with almost nine hundred titles, including dozens of newspaper and magazine articles. It was the first systematic attempt to document publications on Jewish migrations.[19]

In a short preface Robinson criticized Simpson because he did not devote sufficient attention to the specific plight of Jewish refugees: "The Jewish refugee is not always identified as such and very often refugees are not classed as Jews." *The Jewish Refugee* was one of the first publications that featured

Kulischer's term "displacement of population." Tartakower and Grossmann diverged from Kulischer by linking the history of Jewish migrations almost entirely to persecution. They did not approach Jewish migrations and displacement as a scholarly topic but as a political issue. Both authors advocated on behalf of millions of Jews under German control whose lives were at stake. In December 1942 reports about mass killings of Jews in Europe were published in the American press. The American, British, and ten other governments denounced the attempt by Nazi Germany to systematically murder Jews in Europe.

On March 1, 1943, Wise's American Jewish Congress organized a large protest rally in New York. A few weeks later, in April 1943, American and British government representatives met on the island of Bermuda to discuss the refugee issue. Jewish representatives were not invited. In fact, the location was carefully chosen to exclude potential protesters, journalists, and lobby groups. In a notorious (and confidential) memorandum that was drafted for the conference in January 1943, the British government expressed concern that Nazi Germany might stop the killings of Jews: "There is a possibility that the Germans or their satellites may change over from the policy of extermination to one of extrusion, and aim as they did before the war at embarrassing other countries by flooding them with alien immigrants." The Bermuda conference produced no tangible results. Britain refused to lift the settlement ban for Jews trying to move to Mandate Palestine. American representatives declined to change the restrictive immigration quotas. *The Jewish Refugee* was part of a concerted lobbying strategy to stop the genocide and marshal support for the resettlement of surviving Jewish refugees. Copies of the book were sent to Albert Einstein, Eleanor Roosevelt, and other influential figures.

In the introductory chapter Tartakower and Grossmann distinguished among three forms of migration that were associated with the "displacement of population": emigrants who moved voluntarily to a different place, usually permanently; refugees who were forced to move or fled as the result of a military conflict but retained some agency over choosing their destination; and deportees who were "deprived altogether of their personal freedom and driven like slaves or cattle from place to place" depending on the whims of the deporting authorities. No binding definition of the status of refugees existed. It was unclear when refugees ceased to be refugees, and under which circumstances they would be in a position to claim compensation for lost property. In the first section Tartakower and Grossmann emphasized "the glaring disproportion between the extent of the problem and the prospects of solving it." They also identified the degree of agency a person can apply as a means to distinguish between different types of migration—a crucial insight.[20]

The brief historical overview betrays a familiar Zionist view of Jewish migrations and echoes Yiddish articles Tartakower had written about Jewish migration in the late 1930s. Jews had "a special inclination for wandering; they have been driven from country to country either by actual violence or by fear of violence. Voluntary migration prompted mainly by economic motives is, among them, the rare exception." Indeed, Jewish migrations were almost by default the result of violence: "In large measure, therefore, the history of Jewish migration is a history of refugees. Jewish flight has been more or less continuous for thousands of years." The three most prominent cases were the Jewish flight after the Roman destruction of the Second Temple in the year 70, the expulsion of Jews from Spain in 1492, and, not least, Jewish "flight" from Eastern Europe after 1881.

Like other authors Tartakower and Grossmann expressed the hope that an international agency would provide a solution, possibly under the auspices of a reformed League of Nations: "The miracle of Babylon and of Plymouth may yet be repeated. Refugees have built the future and glory of many nations; they may do this once again in Jewish life after the war.... [A] glorious revival will follow the martyrdom of the past." The references to the end of Jewish exile in Babylon and the arrival of the Puritans in colonial America referred to distinct visions. Jewish refugees would perhaps be allowed to "return" to Palestine and rebuild a Jewish state, or they would be allowed to settle in a country that was conceived as a reincarnation of the "Promised Land" by religious refugees (who, unbeknownst to Grossmann and Tartakower, did not tolerate Jewish settlers in their midst). When *The Jewish Refugee* was published in 1944, another author had just begun compiling an ambitious historical survey of Jewish migrations that targeted a similar group of Jewish leaders and political decision-makers.[21]

To Dwell in Safety

Today, Salo Baron's polemical critique of Jewish historiography has been vindicated. However, during the Holocaust a darker view of Jewish history emerged that would shape popular accounts of the Jewish migration from Eastern Europe for decades. One of the most influential advocates was historian Mark Wischnitzer. In the brief foreword to his 1948 survey of Jewish migration history, *To Dwell in Safety: The Story of Jewish Migration since 1800*, Wischnitzer referred to his hands-on experience with "practical migrant-aid activities" between 1921 and 1940 but not to his own flight from Europe in 1939–1940, let alone the deportation of his father-in-law from Paris in 1944 and the loss of relatives and friends like Dubnow in the Holocaust. He stated that the study had been "prepared at the request of the Research Institute on Peace and Post-War Problems of the American Jewish Committee." This statement raises the question why the AJC commissioned the study and why Wischnitzer was chosen as its author.[22]

It is doubtful whether Wischnitzer would have written the survey had the AJC not approached him in late 1942. In a 1942 report Gottschalk pointed out that Wischnitzer was a respected historian. He could have stated that few authors could claim to have a similarly detailed understanding of the multifaceted Jewish migration crisis. In 1935, when he was still working for the Hilfsverein, Wischnitzer had compiled an encyclopedic survey about Jewish history in countries around the world. It was a model for the better known 1938 "Philo Atlas"—a guidebook with maps and basic information about potential destination countries for German Jews planning their emigration. A short introductory chapter covered the "migrations of the Jews." Jewish migration would "lose its significance" only if almost all the 16 million Jews were able to relocate to Palestine. This was not a realistic goal in the short term. After he had lived and worked for two years under Nazi rule, Wischnitzer's critical view of Zionism clearly had shifted. Moreover, between 1933 and 1936 Palestine was among the few destinations where Jews from Europe could realistically expect to get a visa. Wischnitzer encouraged his readers not to be afraid of distant countries. Wherever German (and Eastern European) Jews decided to go, they would be able to connect with other Jews and draw on a well-established support network. Wischnitzer included detailed information about distant territories such as Angola and the Dominican Republic.[23]

In New York Wischnitzer found a position with a major Jewish welfare organization. In late 1943 Gottschalk informed the AJC board that Wischnitzer was still working on the study, which would be part of an effort to secure new homes for Jews after the war.[24] Wischnitzer finally managed to complete the manuscript in May 1948. Unlike other scholars, he earned income from a job that left him time to write only on the weekends. As an independent scholar he had to conduct much of the substantial research on his own. He also had to take into account a dramatically shifting landscape of Jewish migrations between 1943 and 1947. The manuscript Wischnitzer submitted to the publisher differed from Gottschalk's brief outline and reflected the postwar challenges and changes. In early 1948 the United States still pursued a restrictive immigration policy, and the future status of Palestine was not yet determined. Wischnitzer compiled detailed information about Jewish postwar migrations, carefully documenting the names of ships that brought Jewish refugees to Palestine between 1945 and 1947. James Grover McDonald, who had served as the League of Nations high commissioner for Jewish refugees between 1933 and 1935, contributed a short foreword. In 1935 he had resigned from his position because he felt the League ignored the violent persecution of German Jews by the Nazi state. In 1948 President Harry S. Truman dispatched McDonald as his representative to Israel; in early 1949 he became the first U.S. ambassador to the Jewish state.

To Dwell in Safety can best be characterized as encyclopedic. Wischnitzer offered no overarching thesis other than highlighting the impact of anti-Jewish persecution and violence on Jewish migrations after 1800. Almost every chapter begins with a reference to "oppression" and violent anti-Jewish persecution. He linked economic factors with exclusion and discrimination. Wischnitzer provided more background than the brief historical section in *The Jewish Refugee*, but the basic interpretation is almost identical. For Wischnitzer the predicament of Jewish Holocaust survivors stranded in DP camps in occupied Germany was an outrage and only the latest chapter in a long history of Jewish persecution and marginalization. He added three short sentences to an otherwise pessimistic foreword: "As this is being written the radio announces that the State of Israel has been proclaimed. The problems of migration will assume a different aspect. We are at a new turn of history." The founding of the Jewish state constituted indeed a decisive turning point. For the first time in the modern era, persecuted and displaced Jews could move to a safe place where they did not depend on the goodwill of others.[25]

Wischnitzer's survey remains the most comprehensive historical study of Jewish migrations to date and is still widely cited. In the 1980s migration historian Lloyd Gartner critiqued the accuracy of Wischnitzer's statistical section and dismissed the book, perhaps a little too harshly, as "not very good." *To Dwell in Safety* clearly was designed to appeal to a wider, mostly Jewish readership. Several striking gaps are noteworthy. Wischnitzer completely ignored non-Jewish migrants. He also avoided discussing the First World War, possibly because key sources were not accessible. He almost certainly decided not to treat Jewish migration from Galicia before 1914 because it was not related to violence or persecution and would have called his main thesis into question.[26]

To Dwell in Safety represented an important professional milestone for Wischnitzer. In 1948, when the study was published, he was appointed to a professorship at Yeshiva University. None other than Eugene Kulischer reviewed *To Dwell in Safety* for *Jewish Social Studies*. He applauded Wischnitzer for presenting the first extensive survey of the topic and for drawing on primary sources. He could not refrain from criticizing Wischnitzer's focus on "factors specific for the Jewish population" and his neglect of "those general factors which make the Jewish migration part of the European migration."[27]

Europe on the Move

Kulischer's 1943 displacement study, several essays he contributed to the M Project about migration in Europe, and passages he drafted with his brother during the 1930s formed the basis for a study about migration after 1918 in Europe that he placed with Columbia University Press in 1948, *Europe on the Move: War and Population Changes 1917–47*. In a short preface he wrote in Washington, D.C., in January 1948, several months before the State of Israel was founded, Kulischer revealed a few personal details. After discussing his father's research and the 1932 book *Kriegs- und Wanderzüge*, he explained that he and his brother Alexander had begun working on a study about post-1918 migration in Europe during the 1930s, when he was affiliated with the French National Center for Scientific Research. Following the German occupation of Paris, he sent a copy of the draft on an underground route to southern France, from where it was dispatched to Martinique. After reaching the United States he resumed work on the draft that he was able to retrieve from his unnamed contact in Martinique.

In the acknowledgments he devoted one sentence to his brother and longtime collaborator Alexander: "My brother, when crossing the demarcation line, was arrested by Petain's gendarmes and died in a concentration camp." It is notable that Kulischer shared this story with his readers. He did not disclose that he and his brother had left Paris because they were stateless Jews fleeing the Germans. The list of colleagues in the acknowledgments is short. Kulischer omitted the AJC or other Jewish bodies. Absent are the sociologists

Marcel Mauss and Maurice Halbwachs, who had provided references for him. After the German occupation in 1940, Mauss, who was Jewish, had to give up the prestigious chair in sociology he held at the Collège de France but was not deported. Halbwachs, who was not Jewish, kept his position at the Collège de France. He was detained by the Gestapo days before the Americans liberated Paris because he protested against the brutal killing of his wife's elderly Jewish parents. He was deported to the Buchenwald concentration camp, where he died in early 1945. Kulischer's close collaborator Schechtman and other Jewish émigré scholars are also absent. Kulischer thanked his wife and nine men, among them a law professor and an economics historian at Columbia University, who almost certainly had helped him to place the book with the university's press, several demographers, an assistant, the Social Science Research Council for modest funding, and Arnold D. Margolin.[28]

More than a few contemporary Jewish readers stumbled over this last name. Kulischer's association with Margolin requires a short excursion because it provides background about his own biography and the 1918–1919 pogroms in Ukraine. Arnold D. Margolin was Kulischer's father-in-law. He became known to a wider Jewish public in 1913 as Mendel Beilis's defense counsel in a blood libel trial in Kiev that made headlines around the world. In 1918–1919 he was appointed deputy foreign minister of the short-lived Ukrainian People's Republic and attended the Paris peace conferences. He immigrated to the United States in 1923. Margolin's association with the Ukrainian People's Republic made him a despised figure in Jewish circles. The leader of the People's Republic, Ukrainian nationalist Symon Petlura, was blamed for pogroms that claimed thousands of Jewish lives in 1918–1919. In the United States, Margolin worked toward a better understanding between Jewish and Ukrainian representatives, in particular after a young Jew whose parents had perished in a pogrom fatally shot Petlura in central Paris in 1926. A jury sensationally acquitted the shooter, Sholom Schwartzbard, the following year, corroborating the view that he had avenged Ukrainian Jewish pogrom victims.

Even though Petlura's responsibility for the pogroms remains contested, he figured prominently as a villain in popular Jewish memory decades after his death. In *Jewish Migrations* and *Europe on the Move* Kulischer did not downplay the atrocious violence Petlura's armies had inflicted upon Jewish civilians. He compared the troops of Petlura and the White Russian general Anton Denikin with marauding armies during the Thirty Years War. In *Europe in the Move* Kulischer added a footnote to stress that Petlura had "dealt severely with these criminals"—his commanders responsible for the pogroms. This remark clearly betrays Margolin's influence but also indicates that Kulischer was striving for accuracy. In *To Dwell in Safety* Wischnitzer devoted a single sentence to the 1918–1919 pogroms without naming Petlura or Denikin. A possible reason is Wischnitzer's own affiliation with the Ukrainian People's Republic in 1919.[29]

Quite a few Jewish scholars had passed through Kiev in 1918–1919, among them Lestschinky and Schechtman. Initially many Russian Jews had attached high hopes to the new Ukrainian state. In 1919, a small lobby group, the Friends of Ukraine in Washington, D.C., published a pamphlet to address the pogrom issue and shore up support for the new state. In a letter to several American and American Jewish papers, Julian Batchinsky, the Ukrainian representative in the United States, pointed out that the main instigators of the pogroms were groups and forces sympathetic to the old tsarist regime. Troops of the Ukrainian People's Republic involved in pogroms had ignored Petlura's instructions. Batchinsky quoted an order signed by Petlura on August 26, 1919, that accused sympathizers of the old regime of "defiling our struggle for liberty" and called on his troops to fight against those perpetrating pogroms and bring them to the courts where they would be tried as "enemies of the State."[30]

The pamphlet reprinted an interview that Margolin—at this time still a member of the Ukrainian government—had given to the London *Jewish Chronicle*. Margolin revealed that Petlura had persuaded him not to tender his resignation. None other than Wischnitzer, who served as a member of the informal Ukrainian mission in London in 1919, provided a short declaration of support for an independent Ukrainian state. Its parliament had granted autonomy rights to Jewish, Russian, Polish, and other minorities. The alternative, a division of Ukrainian territory by Poland, Russia, and Romania, would be a grave threat to Jews. The Friends of Ukraine even secured a short note from an elderly Israel Zangwill, who deplored the pogroms and praised the decision to provide Jews in Ukraine with autonomy.[31]

In an ironic twist, Denikin ultimately found a safe haven in New York. Denikin's responsibility for the slaughter of thousands of Jewish civilians was never contested. In fact, none other than Schechtman had published one of the first detailed accounts of the Ukrainian pogroms in 1923. In 1920 Denikin moved from Constantinople to Paris. In 1940 he was briefly interrogated by the Germans but left alone for the remainder of the war. Fearing that the postwar French government would deport him to Stalin's Soviet Union,

Denikin applied for a U.S. immigration visa and settled in New York in 1945. Nobody could deny the former general's anti-Communist credentials. The same State Department officials who swiftly approved Denikin's visa application turned down those of thousands of Jews stranded in DP camps in Germany and Austria. The charge of "crimes against humanity" at the Nuremberg Trials was applied only to the period of World War II and did not cover the systematic atrocities perpetrated in the aftermath of the First World War. Instead of keeping a low profile the elderly Denikin shrewdly exploited the growing anti-Communist sentiment in the United States. In 1946 he gave a public speech in Manhattan condemning the global threat of Communism. Several left-wing protesters picketed the venue. They carried posters with the demand "Expel Denikin—Murderer of the Jews." Denikin died in 1947 during a vacation trip to Michigan, several months before Kulischer's *Europe on the Move* was published.[32]

In that book Kulischer presented the same argument as in *Kriegs- und Wanderzüge*, namely that migrations had defined global history. He expressed strong opposition to forced population transfers as a policy solution, predicting that closed borders and forced migrations in the aftermath of World War II would cause new military conflicts. He reiterated his case for international regulation of migration and a fair redistribution and repatriation of expellees and refugees, not least of Germans, to prevent another European war. Kulischer avoided unnecessary jargon and provided factual information about little-known European countries, clearly with the intention of helping decision-makers in the United States to get a better understanding of the demographic upheaval in Europe. *Europe on the Move* offered one of the best-informed discussions of forced migration during the Russian Civil War.[33]

However, the study contains curious gaps. Kulischer touched on Stalin's collectivization policy in the late 1920s but gave only cursory attention to forced resettlement in the Soviet Union during World War II. Stalin's name features twice in passing, in contrast to frequent references to Hitler. Ultimately, Kulischer was interested in the big picture of global migrations and the longue durée. As in *Kriegs- und Wanderzüge* he refused to discuss at length that certain governments and rulers pursued forced migration as a calculated policy to expel, marginalize, and even exterminate unwanted groups. In his view, not dictators or regimes but demographic factors and economic disparities were driving migration processes, peacefully or through military conflicts.

Even though he had personally lived through the Russian Civil War, Kulischer did not link the post-1917 refugee crisis with the collapse of the multiethnic (and colonial) empires that exposed members of dispersed minorities—Jews, Greeks, Armenians, ethnic Germans, and other unwanted groups—to persecution by nationalist regimes. He did, however, express strong opposition to forced migration, singling out the population transfer of Germans in the aftermath of World War II as a disastrous mistake. Millions had been sent to an overpopulated country struggling to rebuild its economy. Germany would remain a source of instability hampering efforts to contain the Soviet Union. Younger Germans should be allowed to emigrate to more promising destinations to reduce the economic and political pressure during the rebuilding process. Several influential decision-makers in Washington shared this view. The 1948 Displaced Persons Act explicitly favored ethnic Germans for resettlement in the United States but implicitly excluded Jewish and Polish DPs.[34]

Kulischer's collaborator Joseph Schechtman took a strikingly different view of forced migration in his 1946 study, *European Population Transfers*. Like Kulischer, whom he thanked for providing valuable feedback, Schechtman drew on the reports he had written for the OSS (and the M Project) during the war years. *European Population Transfers* contains an implicit political statement about the question of Jewish resettlement. Under certain conditions, Schechtman considered "population transfers" to be legitimate. The League of Nations had failed to protect minorities in interwar Europe. The obvious model for population transfers was the 1923 Lausanne Treaty between Greece and Turkey. Schechtman discussed the background and implementation of the treaty without ignoring the difficulties, notably the forced removal of Muslims from Greece and the excessive cost.

Regardless of these challenges, he promoted the Lausanne Treaty as a model, not least for the resolution of the "Arab-Jewish conflict in Palestine." Schechtman used a rather ill-suited metaphor comparing problematic minorities with a cancer that had to be surgically removed to save a patient's life. "Any serious and responsible physician would consider every other possible means of effecting a cure and would have recourse to the scalpel only as a last resort. And so it is with the drastic remedy of population transfer." As examples for successful transfers he cited the Nazi "repatriation" of ethnic Germans from territories under Soviet control between 1939 and 1941 and the mass flight and systematic expulsion of Germans from Eastern Europe during the final phase of the war and in its aftermath. As a result, a major source of instability had been removed from Eastern Europe. Schechtman did touch on the deportations of Jews from different parts of Europe but not on the Holocaust. Considering genocide (another recently coined term) an extreme form of population transfer obviously would have undermined his case. While hinting at the darker side of population transfers, especially the economic disadvantages for members of transferred groups, he strenuously avoided discussing the violent nature of population transfers in detail.[35]

Schechtman was a close associate of Ze'ev (Vladimir) Jabotinsky, who broke with the Zionist World Organization in 1935. In 1936 he sent a memorandum to the Polish government asking for support for moving over 1 million Jews to Palestine. This plan reflects Jabotinsky's concern that Polish Jewry was threatened and had to be rescued. In the late 1930s Schechtman conducted talks on behalf of Jabotinsky with Polish officials. In 1939 the openly antisemitic Polish government tried without success to persuade its British counterpart to let Polish Jews move to Mandate Palestine. At the same time Warsaw explored the feasibility of Jewish resettlement in Madagascar. The Polish resettlement plans were still being discussed in the United States in the early 1940s and influenced Roosevelt's decision to launch the M Project.

Schechtman clearly favored Jewish settlement in Palestine and a transfer of the Palestinian population, but he had to move carefully. In 1946 the founding of a Jewish state was by no means certain. Like Kulischer, he knew that touching on the travails of Jewish refugees and survivors would weaken his case because his intended readers—leading academics, top bureaucrats, and elected representatives in Washington and London—moved in circles where antisemitic discrimination was rife. Schechtman provided a few clues. The Arab population of Palestine, he said, could stay—or leave. In passing he noted that leading British politicians had repeatedly considered resettlement of Palestinian Arabs to other Arab countries such as Iraq.[36]

Kulischer certainly sympathized with Jewish settlement in Palestine. But unlike Schechtman he opposed forced resettlement. And he did not pursue a covert political agenda. Kulischer's overarching goal was to provide policymakers and scholars with a detailed analysis of the seemingly confusing refugee crisis in the wake of the two major European wars—based on the model he and his brother had first presented in their 1932 study. In *Europe on the Move* Kulischer paid even less attention to Jewish migrations than Schechtman did. He briefly touched on the pogroms in Ukraine in 1918–1919 but not on Jewish mass displacement in and beyond Eastern

Europe after 1918. A short subchapter covered the emigration of German Jews between 1933 and 1939. Palestine was mentioned three times, once in a footnote and twice in a short parenthesis, even though it was an important destination for Jews from Eastern Europe and Germany during the interwar period and after 1945. A mere two sentences summarize the Holocaust: "Up to the end of the war more than 5,000,000 Jews were deported to extermination camps in Poland and elsewhere. Almost all perished."[37]

The Final Solution and Jewish mass displacement during and after the two world wars were hardly footnotes in the history of mid-twentieth-century European migrations. Kulischer's startling omission stands in stark contrast to Wischnitzer's treatment of the "Campaign of Extermination." In *To Dwell in Safety*, Wischnitzer quoted at length from the protocol of the 1942 Wannsee Conference, a document that had surfaced only in March 1947. Wischnitzer did not mince words: "[M]illions of Jews were slaughtered, burned or buried alive in many parts of Europe." He expressed outrage over the unwillingness of Western powers, singling out the United States and Britain, to take steps to intervene, even though they possessed concrete information about the systematic murder of Jews. Wischnitzer also devoted a lengthy paragraph to the "conspicuous role" of the Mufti of Jerusalem in the Final Solution.[38]

Why did Kulischer touch on the Holocaust only in passing? Political explanations for (forced) migrations questioned his basic theory about global migrations driven by long-term economic and demographic changes.[39] The main reason for the brief discussion of Jewish persecution is related to the readers Kulischer was targeting. His intended audience differed markedly from that of Wischnitzer. Like Schechtman Kulischer understood that dwelling on his own background and Jewish suffering would hurt his goal to be taken seriously in the circles of established academics and political decision-makers in the United States. A prominent example is geographer Isaiah Bowman, the official head of the M Project, who almost certainly read earlier drafts of Schechtman's and Kulischer's studies. As president of Johns Hopkins University he introduced an anti-Jewish quota in 1945, at a time when other universities began gradually to relax their admission criteria for Jewish students.

A few years after Kulischer, Arendt based her pathbreaking study *The Origins of Totalitarianism* explicitly on the experience of Jews in the modern period and the Holocaust. Arendt was younger than Kulischer and cherished her role as independent and provocative public intellectual. Wischnitzer moved in a relatively sheltered Jewish sphere. He worked for Jewish organizations and institutions for most of his life. His publications focused almost exclusively on Jewish history. *To Dwell in Safety* was published by the Jewish Publication Society. In 1948 he began teaching at Yeshiva University, a private Jewish university. Wischnitzer's publications were hardly noticed outside of the small Jewish studies field during his lifetime. Suffice to say, Kulischer's decision to downplay the experience of Jewish migrants paid dividends. *Europe on the Move* was positively reviewed and became a standard work that is still referenced.[40]

One of the first reviewers was Wischnitzer. In the *Journal of Economic History*, he praised *Europe on the Move* as an "indispensable handbook" but wondered why Kulischer had not discussed attempts to regulate international migration, for instance, the 1938 Evian Conference, which focused on the question of Jewish refugees. Strangely, Wischnitzer emphasized that Kulischer had "devoted much attention to the Jewish populations." Of course, he had not. This comment can only be read as an implicit critique. Ilja Dijour, who was affiliated with HIAS and YIVO after reaching New York and also had contributed material to the M Project, wrote a positive review for *Jewish Social Studies*. He recommended *Europe on the Move* as "'must' reading" and pointed out—perhaps to defend Kulischer's extremely brief discussion of the Holocaust—that "no political and no demographic theory can offer an explanation for the unprecedented slaughter of 6,000,000 Jews in four years."[41]

On the eve of the founding of the Jewish state, Lestschinsky produced a short survey in English about Jewish migrations for a multivolume handbook about Jewish life and history. The handbook addressed primarily Jewish readers. Among the thirty-five contributors was Rachel Wischnitzer, an indication of her rising reputation as a specialist in Jewish art history. She and historian Anita Libman Lebeson were the only female authors. Lestschinsky's chapter has no overarching thesis but contains important insights. In his opening remarks he referenced Kulischer without naming him, emphasizing that mass migrations had perhaps not defined but certainly had shaped human history. This indirect reference is intriguing because the papers of IJA contain a scathing (unpublished) review Lestschinsky wrote in 1943 of Kulischer's *Jewish Migrations* essay. Lestschinsky's main critique was that Kulischer ignored the specific factors that distinguished Jews from other groups, particularly the lack of a territorial homeland. He reluctantly conceded, though, that Kulischer's broad view of the subject constituted a significant achievement.

In the 1949 survey Lestschinsky traced the Jewish mass migration from Eastern Europe to economic factors, as he had before the Holocaust. Like Kulischer he noted the transformative impact of Jewish mass migration in the United States. American Jews belonged to a society that was more inclusive of Jews than any other after 1800. Unlike Wischnitzer, who emphasized the long history of anti-Jewish violence on migration, Lestschinsky identified the First World War as a crucial turning point. Following the unprecedented antisemitic violence in the aftermath of the war, successor states like Poland treated Jews as unwanted minorities, marginalizing them economically to "encourage" Jewish emigration. After 1933 the antisemitic policy of the Nazi regime, which pursued the same goal, emboldened Eastern European governments to force out their respective Jewish populations, albeit with limited success because of widespread migration restrictions. "Jews did try to find some corner in the world where they might live in peace, but, as is well known, they were not very successful."[42]

Lestschinsky did not want to discuss the "Hitler Gehenna." As he put it, "To dwell on the result of Hitler's triumph in Germany and the occupied countries is superfluous. Even in Jewish life this is an unprecedented experience." Lestschinsky's observation that antisemitic policies marginalized and impoverished Jews in Eastern Europe after 1918, while migration restrictions prevented them from relocating, deserves more attention in the burgeoning research about the Holocaust. Kulischer was aware of this point but decided to downplay it, while Wischnitzer did not regard it as particularly important because, as he saw it, Jews had been fleeing persecution throughout history.[43]

Beyond New York

Mark Wischnitzer died during a short visit in Tel Aviv in 1955, just after having completed a commissioned history of HIAS. Rachel Wischnitzer became a respected scholar of Jewish art history who specialized in synagogue architecture. During the war she attended New York University and wrote a master's thesis on the paintings in the Dura synagogue in Syria. In 1956, when she was seventy-one years old, she was appointed to a professorship at the Stern College for women at Yeshiva University. She retired in 1968.[44]

After the war Kulischer moved to Washington, probably because he hoped to secure a permanent position within the massively expanding federal bureaucracy. But although there was no shortage of positions, as a Russian exile and a Jew who had spent years in Berlin and Paris before the war, he was suspected of having Communist sympathies. In 1946, when he taught at American University, the FBI briefly investigated him, probably without his knowledge, as a suspected member of a Soviet spy ring. The investigation confirms that Kulischer and Schechtman worked for the OSS in 1943–1944. Kulischer's main task, as a demographer, was to provide estimates about the expected manpower of Soviet forces. The FBI file covers his desperate search for employment in the summer of 1946, after American University did not renew his teaching contract. Kulischer shifted through several positions. In 1947 he worked for the Bureau of the Census; in 1948 he was employed by the Department of Defense; eventually, in 1949, when he was sixty-eight years old, the Library of Congress gave him a position as a demographer. Kulischer died in 1956, before he could begin to write a study about global migration history in English. His contribution on migration in the 1952 edition of the *Encyclopedia Britannica* was an outline of the envisaged study. In his relatively concise article Kulischer devoted more attention to Jewish migration and the Holocaust.[45]

Wischnitzer and Kulischer struggled for decades to find a position at a university or respected research institution commensurate with their academic reputations. Their prolific publication activity in the last fifteen years of their lives was a result of their freelance work and their attempt to find a more secure academic position. Their involuntary moves, the relatively limited income they earned, and the lack of a pension explain why they could not retire but had to seek employment when they were in their late sixties. Although he published widely on forced migration in Europe until his death in 1956, Kulischer was a relatively obscure figure during his lifetime. His early emphasis on "general factors" and global history differentiates him from most other scholars who wrote about the immigration experience of specific groups. Kulischer was an outsider throughout his career, as a Jewish lawyer in the Russian Empire and as a Russian Jewish émigré scholar in Berlin, Paris, New York, and Washington.[46]

The older Lestschinsky outlived Wischnitzer and Kulischer by a decade. After initially retiring in Miami Beach, he settled in Israel in 1959. He published several surveys with smaller presses in Yiddish and Hebrew. Unlike Wischnitzer and Kulischer he did not produce an academic monograph in German or English about the two main subjects he researched: Jewish economic life and Jewish migration. His journalistic work left him limited time for research and writing. Reports that Lestschinsky compiled for IJA in the 1940s indicate his preference to write in Yiddish. Without university degrees he could not pursue an academic career. For a second edition of the handbook *The Jews* that was published in 1955, when he was eighty years old, Lestschinsky added a few paragraphs to his 1949 handbook essay. The essay was reprinted for a third edition in 1960, where edition Lestschinsky still cited the *Daily Jewish Forward*, the Anglicized name of the *Forverts*, as his affiliation. He died in Jerusalem in 1966, six months before his ninetieth birthday.[47]

Arieh Tartakower moved to the Hebrew University of Jerusalem in 1946. As Arthur Ruppin's successor he trained a generation of Israel's sociologists. In his 1983 obituary sociologist Daniel Elazar recognized him together with Lestschinsky and Ruppin as the "triumvirate of founders of modern Jewish social science." In his later years, as Elazar put it diplomatically, Tartakower increasingly clashed with younger colleagues "who did not share his sense of Jewish nationalism and who saw the Jews integrating into the society to which they had migrated."[48]

10
Migrants Become Immigrants

On February 28, 1949, a group of almost five hundred Jews, most of them stateless, arrived on Ellis Island en route to Israel. They had disembarked from a ship in San Francisco a week earlier together with smaller groups of non-Jewish Eastern Europeans and Jews with valid U.S. immigrant visas. The group had departed from Shanghai as Communist forces were advancing toward the city where thousands of Europeans were still stranded. The transport was organized by the International Refugee Organization of the United Nations, the successor to the interwar Nansen office of the League of Nations. The original plan to sail for Haifa had to be abandoned after Egypt refused the ship passage through the Suez Canal. In San Francisco a reporter for the German Jewish emigrant newspaper *Aufbau* learned from several passengers that they would have preferred to move to the United States but had failed to obtain visas.

Shortly after its arrival the group boarded a "liberty train," a name derived from its destination, Jersey City, which was adjacent to the Statue of Liberty. The train's route was carefully planned to include stops in Los Angeles, Dallas, Atlanta, Washington, D.C., and other cities. Jewish communities arranged impromptu receptions at these train stations, allowing the passengers to meet family members they had not seen for over a decade. A second transport with Israel-bound Jews from Shanghai reached San Francisco in March 1949 and followed the same route. The *Aufbau* noted the actual treatment of the Jews was "not exactly an example for American hospitality." The "liberty trains" were sealed, accompanied by guards, and resembled prisoner transports. The actual destination was not the Statue of Liberty but Ellis Island, a major detention and deportation facility for unwanted migrants. During scheduled stops the passengers could talk to visitors only through the windows of their carriage; they could not step onto the platform. These measures were taken to ensure that they did not illegally enter the United States. After a short stay at Ellis Island, the migrants departed on a steamer bound for Genoa. The "liberty trains" were hardly a new feature. The U.S. immigration authorities had used sealed trains and carriages since 1919 to ferry detained migrants across the country to the main deportation centers in Ellis Island and San Francisco. The routes of the trains varied, depending on the number of unwanted migrants designated for deportation in towns and cities in the American interior.[1]

Other Jews also passed through Ellis Island during the 1940s without formally entering the United States. In 1940–1941 Jews from Austria and Germany traveling to Sosúa, an agricultural settlement designed for Jewish refugees from Europe in the Dominican Republic, were regularly detained at Ellis Island while waiting for the steamship to Ciudad Trujillo (Santo Domingo). Since the only viable route from Europe required a stopover in New York, all migrants with Dominican visas had to apply for an American transit visa. This allowed the State Department to exert control over the settlement scheme. Fewer than eight hundred Jews were able to leave from ports in Europe before Germany declared war against the United States in December 1941. Over a thousand never received an American transit visa. Even more remained excluded, because initially the Dominican Republic had indicated that a much larger number of Jews would be allowed to enter the country. State Department officials led by Assistant Secretary of State Breckinridge Long justified the sluggish transit visa policy and the detention at Ellis Island by pointing to the need to identify and exclude "Nazi spies" among the Jewish refugees. Long systematically obstructed other rescue attempts. In internal communications he depicted Jewish refugees from Europe as undesirable because they supposedly were inassimilable and treacherous.[2]

Long retired in 1944, but he was surrounded by likeminded officials in the State Department and in other government offices. And few members of Congress supported an open-door immigration policy. In the aftermath of the war the United States and other countries refused to lift migration restrictions for Jewish and other displaced Eastern Europeans. When Congress did not show any inclination to admit Holocaust survivors, President Truman issued an executive order in December 1945 to apply unused national quotas. He ordered the State Department to speed up the approval of visas. More than forty thousand refugees, most of them Jewish, benefited from this measure. Even though polls indicated that American voters overwhelmingly opposed a more liberal policy toward Jewish and other refugees, Truman continued to pressure Congress to act.

The concerns Kulischer and other migration scholars expressed about overpopulation in postwar Germany found support in Congress and led to the passage of the Displaced Persons Act of 1948. The main goal was to alleviate the refugee crisis in Europe, not coincidentally when tensions with the Soviet Union over the control of Germany were mounting. But instead of allowing 400,000 DPs to enter, as initially envisaged, the bill provided 200,000 visas for two years. To Truman's consternation Congress apportioned the visas to the low existing quotas to ensure that only a few Eastern Europeans would be able to immigrate in the foreseeable future. Truman reluctantly signed the bill but continued to push for an open-door policy.

The final version of the bill was tweaked to favor groups that had benefited from the German occupation in Eastern Europe but could claim to be victims of Communist aggression, namely ethnic Germans, Ukrainians, Lithuanians, and Latvians. Thus Jews and Poles were effectively excluded. Allegedly, West Virginia senator William C. Revercombe declared, "We could solve this DP problem all right if we could work out some bill that would keep out the Jews." This opinion was hardly isolated. Several legislators openly emphasized the importance of excluding undesirable "racial" groups. Nevada senator Pat McCarran, the powerful chair of the Senate Judiciary Committee after the 1948 elections, was known for his antisemitic views. For two years he blocked attempts to amend the bill, prompting New York House member Emanuel Celler to describe the bill as "America's first Nuremberg law." Celler, the descendant of Jewish immigrants from Central Europe, was an outspoken opponent of racist and antisemitic immigration legislation. During his first term he was one of the few members of Congress who voted against the 1924 immigration bill.[3]

In the spring of 1950 Congress debated an extension of the DP Act, just as another transport was leaving Shanghai. The ship that reached San Francisco on May 25, 1950, carried more than a hundred stateless Jews who refused to move to Israel or to a DP camp in West Germany, the only other options. Almost all had filed applications for a U.S. immigrant visa. In May 1950, after almost a century of foreign occupation, Shanghai had been fully under Chinese control for a year. Just before Communist forces reached the city in May 1949 the United States closed its consulate. At the last minute, a U.S. steamer evacuated more than fifteen hundred Western nationals and refugees, including Jews bound for Israel. The United Nations refugee organization struggled to find a new home for Jews who did not want to move to Israel because few countries were willing to admit more than a few stateless Jewish refugees. As a result, at least fifteen hundred Jews were left behind. After a long siege during which Nationalist troops regularly executed alleged Communists in the streets of the city, Communist troops entered

"Jedziemy Na Zachod!" (We are going to the West!). American photographer John Vachon, who later worked for *Life* and *Look* magazines, took this picture for the Joint Distribution Committee in October 1946 in Lower Silesia (possibly near the train station in Wrocław/Breslau). The unidentified women and children were Polish Jews who had survived the Holocaust in the Soviet Union. Lower Silesia was a major point of passage for Jews returning from Soviet exile. Most left for DP camps in occupied Germany after a few months. *NY 07699, Joint Distribution Committee Archives*

Shanghai on May 25, 1949. The residents were relieved that there was only sporadic looting and violence. But in the following weeks and months the Communists systematically purged tens of thousands of internal enemies. Some disappeared; others were publicly executed. However, the remaining European refugees were not harmed. The Communist government indicated that it would tolerate European refugees if they were evacuated within the foreseeable future.

Shanghai's changing status deprived stateless refugees of one of the last remaining relatively safe spaces where they could reside without papers. During the journey of the train from San Francisco to Jersey City in May 1950, Celler, New York senator Herbert H. Lehman, and New York congressman Jacob Javits succeeded in delaying the deportation of the over one hundred Jews for almost three weeks. They sensed an opportunity. Since more generous provisions for Jewish refugees had already been secured, they tried to negotiate an exemption for the passengers on the "liberty train." Truman supported the effort, declaring that "everybody with a heart would permit these people to stay." Yet on June 20 the *New York Times* reported that the group would be deported to West Germany. Truman announced a compromise that ensured a speedy processing of the visa applications. In an editorial titled "Odyssey of the 106" the *New York Times* deplored the "cold logic of the immigration laws," observing the irony that Jews who had fled Nazism and Communism were locked up and waiting for their deportation in close proximity to the Statue of Liberty. "Valuable as visitors, they will be still more valuable as citizens." After a few months in West Germany most returned to the United States as legal immigrants.[4]

The *New York Times* described the Jews from Shanghai as both "refugees" and "displaced persons." In the postwar transition these terms were now being tied to formal legal status. In *Origins of Totalitarianism* Hannah Arendt argued that "displaced person" was formalized to avoid recognizing statelessness and to make it possible to repatriate unwanted persons or pressure them to return, even if they risked arrest and punishment. In 1946 the International Refugee Organization (IRO), which was part of the newly founded United Nations, published a formal definition recognizing that "genuine refugees and displaced persons constitute an urgent problem which is international in scope and character." The document then provided definitions of both terms. A refugee was "a person who has left, or who is outside of, his country of nationality or of former habitual residence," if this person was a victim of Nazi or another fascist regime, including the Franco regime in Spain, or if this person had become a refugee before World War II "for reasons of race, religion, nationality or political opinion." A displaced person was defined as a person who "has been deported from, or has been obliged to leave his country of nationality or of former habitual residence." Apart from ignoring women, the authors did not mention victims of Communist persecution because the Soviet Union was a founding member of the United Nations. However, these opaque definitions provided protection to millions who had lost their homes during the war and were admitted to DP camps in occupied Germany, Austria, and Italy. The IRO recognized European Jews in Shanghai as refugees and covered the cost for their transportation.[5]

Even though the 1948 DP bill was deeply flawed, it marks a milestone. The United States formally recognized certain refugees and displaced persons as "eligible" for immigration. "Eligible displaced persons" would be approved for a U.S. immigration visa and would be exempt from the usual waiting period based on the quota system. Congress embraced the IRO definition but included persons fleeing Communist persecution. Yet the rigid national origins quota immigration system remained in place. Each refugee or displaced person was "charged" to a quota number for his or her country of birth. If the annual ceiling for a quota was reached, quotas for future years were used. This scheme became known as "mortgaging" quotas. The 1948 bill illustrates Aristide Zolberg's observation about the impact of "path dependency." Reformers had to operate within a system designed to exclude migrants. Zolberg noted that the allocation of quotas for future years extended the waiting period for Greek applicants for an immigrant visa for such a long time that Greeks were effectively excluded for decades from immigrating to the United States. Greece stands out because the country had been allocated an annual quota of a mere one hundred immigrant visas and was embroiled in a civil war between 1946 and 1949. In this period over 100,000 people fled the country, and many more were displaced internally. The admission of two thousand Greek DPs would have filled the Greek quota for twenty years.[6]

The Greek case is extreme because the country had been assigned a very low quota. Thanks to the lobbying efforts of Jewish representatives and of members of other immigrant groups, the 1950 DP bill watered down the "mortgaging" system. In hindsight, Congress's acceptance of "refugees and displaced persons" as "eligible" signifies an important shift for another reason. During the postwar period the terms "deserving refugee" and "economic migrant" diverged in regard to receiving formal permission to enter countries in (and beyond) Europe and the United States. Kulischer's term "displaced person" was now tied to a legal status. Yet the confusion over the exact meaning of the terms "refugee," "migrant," and "displaced person" persisted.[7]

The last camp for Jewish DPs in Germany, in Föhrenwald in the vicinity of Munich, closed only in 1957, years after the United States had gradually relaxed admission criteria for "eligible" DPs and almost a decade after the founding of the State of Israel. A study by Ori Yehudai about a little-known chapter of Israel's early history sheds light on the causes. In the early 1950s the number of Jews expressing a wish to leave Israel greatly increased. Many were Holocaust survivors from Eastern Europe who had lost family members and were permanently displaced at the end of the war, often after lengthy and complicated journeys that led through Nazi camps and the Soviet Union. Jewish aid organizations assisted them in reaching Palestine/Israel, where some initially received public assistance.

The challenging economic conditions in the young state, the uncertain security situation in the region, the wish to reunite with family members living elsewhere, and possibly overly optimistic expectations about life in Canada and the United States convinced many to leave. The U.S. consulate in Haifa could barely cope with the visa applications. During the summer of 1949 alone more than four thousand applications were filed; only twenty-seven visas were granted. The others faced a waiting time of many years because they had to file under the low quotas for countries in Eastern Europe at a time when tens of thousands of non-Jewish Eastern European refugees also submitted applications. As a result, many disillusioned migrants opted for Canadian visas. In 1947 Canada had relaxed its notoriously rigid immigration policy and opened the doors to European DPs. Several onerous requirements remained in place, however. All visa applicants had to reside at least two years in the country where a Canadian consulate was located. In the early 1950s Canada maintained consulates in several European countries but not in Israel.

The Israeli government tried to slow down the rate of emigration by demanding repayments of health and welfare benefits. Yet between 1951 and 1953 more than thirty-five thousand Jews left Israel. Hundreds decided to return to DP camps in West Germany. But they could not reclaim their DP status, and Jewish communities and aid associations like the JDC and HIAS were torn whether to extend support. As a result, several groups were stranded in Italy and Austria. Repeatedly migrants circumvented formal restrictions, for instance by illegally moving from France to West Germany or by staging sit-in strikes to receive support from Jewish communities and German government bodies. Some migrants hired smugglers who brought them from Paris to Föhrenwald. By 1953, fourteen hundred of the two thousand Föhrenwald inhabitants were Israeli emigrants. As rumors were circulating that up to five thousand more were heading to the camp, the Bavarian government announced it would cease welfare payments to the inhabitants and close the camp. The Bavarian junior minister for refugees, who led the negotiations with Jewish associations and Israeli diplomats, was Theodor Oberländer, a notorious Nazi scholar who was suspected of war crimes and involvement in the Holocaust in Ukraine. Ultimately, a compromise allowed migrants with pending visa applications to stay.[8]

The experience of Föhrenwald migrants illustrates the challenges of applying the correct term to people on the move. Most migrants from Israel were former refugees who were seeking better opportunities in Canada. In hindsight, understandable concerns about a mass departure of disappointed new settlers from Israel were overblown. As the economic and political situation stabilized, emigration declined. The Föhrenwald DP camp was closed in 1957. Apart from the complicated status of Jews remaining in several countries in the Middle East, Jewish migration ceased to be a matter of concern for Jewish aid associations and international bodies after the early 1950s—until the issue of Soviet refuseniks emerged in the 1960s. The situation of the refuseniks differed from that of permanently displaced Jews or of members of unwanted minorities facing expulsion before the early 1950s. The crucial issue was not where these Jews would be able to settle but whether they would be allowed to leave the Soviet Union.

The territorially defined sovereign Jewish state (largely) solved the problem of stateless and fenced-out Jewish subjects of the former multiethnic empires. Like members of most other minorities during the interwar period, Jews now had the option to move to a national "homeland" if they fulfilled the requirements of the 1950 Law of Return and the 1952 Israeli citizenship law. The Law of Return gives every Jew the right to move to and settle in Israel, realizing a major goal of the Zionist movement. The citizenship law defined how Israeli citizenship can be acquired. Neither law provided a precise definition of what constituted Jewish descent, but the state and the courts applied religious law (Halakah), which bases Jewishness on matrilineal descent.

Both laws bear a striking resemblance to the descent-based citizenship laws of successor states such as Poland during the interwar period because they privileged members of the ethnic majority. Quite a few members of the Knesset who were involved in drafting the laws had lived in Poland in the early 1920s as members of what Arendt characterized as a "de facto stateless" minority. Israel's status as a territorial nation-state with a descent-based citizenship law put Jewish aid associations in a tough spot. In November 1948 the World Jewish Congress pointed out (in an internal memorandum) that Israel would very likely pursue the same selective immigration policy as many other countries. Government officials in South American countries could justify refusing to admit Jewish DPs by pointing to Israel's similarly selective immigration policy, which explicitly favored the Jewish majority population of the state. As a result, it would become very difficult to find destinations for Jews who did not want to settle in Israel.[9]

In 1948, when Congress appeared unwilling to admit more than a few Jewish refugees stranded in Europe, the concerns of the World Jewish Congress were justified because it was already apparent that some Jewish refugees did not want to settle in Israel, which became independent a few weeks before Truman signed the DP Act. Yet after 1948 the United States and Canada began relaxing their migration policies toward Jews who had been displaced during World War II. The Jews from Shanghai who explicitly refused to move to Israel were allowed to officially immigrate to the United States in 1950, albeit only after they had spent a brief period in a DP camp in West Germany. The Israeli emigrants who passed through the Föhrenwald camp in the early 1950s were able to settle in Canada and other countries.

During the 1950s the interest of social scientists and historians shifted from researching the causes of Jewish migration and the implications of permanent transit and statelessness to newly relevant and more rewarding topics, primarily that of Jewish immigration. In the aftermath of the Holocaust, the United States, Israel, and the Soviet Union had emerged as the new centers of the Jewish Diaspora, as envisaged by Kulischer in his 1942–1943 essay about Jewish migrations. In 1950, most American Jews and Jewish Israelis were immigrants or children of immigrants. The rise of ethnic and immigration studies in the United States during the 1960s helped to sustain the lachrymose interpretation of Jewish migrations as a distinct experience marked by continuous persecution. The conceptual foundations of ethnic and immigration studies were laid by American Jewish scholars, who often were immigrants or children of immigrants from Central and Eastern

Europe. The informal constraints Kulischer and Schechtman faced as Jewish refugee scholars also affected a small number of American-educated Jewish social scientists who managed to obtain positions at research universities during the 1930s and 1940s. In this period, scholars such as Horace Kallen, Louis Wirth, and Melville Herskovitz conceptualized America as a diverse and inclusive society because they were exposed to informal discrimination and exclusion but also because they were committed to maintaining cultural difference.[10]

Conclusion

Migrants *and* Refugees

Were Jews leaving Eastern Europe migrants or refugees? Did (and do) Jews have a special proclivity to migrate? A study with the title "Refugees or Migrants" about Jewish "population movements" in medieval Europe and in areas under Muslim rule addresses these questions. Historian Robert Chazan, a student of Salo Baron, distinguishes between Jewish refugees who were expelled or fled violent persecution and a much larger number of Jews who "relocated voluntarily." As members of a dispersed minority occupying economic niches, he argues, voluntary Jewish migrants were more mobile than others. Chazan's carefully researched study is committed to Baron's critique of the lachrymose interpretation of Jewish history.[1]

Distinguishing between Jewish "refugees *or* migrants" is suggestive but misleading. Arieh Tartakower and Kurt Grossmann proposed in 1944 to use the degree of agency individuals can exercise to differentiate among migrants, refugees, and deportees. This criterion sidesteps artificial divisions as well as the contested and shifting meanings of categories that cannot sufficiently capture a wide range of overlapping experiences that depend(ed) on a complex set of specific circumstances. Evidence for Jews who fled actual violence in the Russian Empire and Romania to neighboring countries and beyond before 1914 is surprisingly scant. Anti-Jewish violence occurred in both states, and both governments appeared to do little to stem it, let alone improve the legal and economic situation of the respective Jewish populations.

Even though few Jews fled actual pogroms all the way to America, growing insecurity and fear cannot be dismissed as factors influencing the decisions of prospective migrants seeking better economic opportunities. In hindsight, memories of cursed Russia but also nostalgic images of life in the *shtetl* shaped the self-perception of those who had "escaped" and their descendants. Jewish collective memory of the pogroms continues to cast a long shadow over the scholarship to this day. However, the concept of the "voluntary migrant" is also problematic. Few migrants were and are truly "free" in their decision to move; instead they are bound by a web of social obligations and economic constraints. Some flee personal responsibilities to start a new life elsewhere, for instance, young women trying to avoid arranged marriages. Many more move to provide urgently needed support for family members.[2]

Even for the period between 1914 and 1948 the term "refugee" often does not sufficiently capture the actual experiences of Jews (and others) who were fleeing or had fled violent persecution. Like other DPs, Jews who managed to retain a degree of agency were trying to gain entry to the most favorable place to rebuild their lives. The return of Jews from Israel in the early 1950s to DP camps in West Germany to secure Canadian immigration permits illustrates the gap between legal categories and personal aspirations. Most had survived the Holocaust in hiding or in Soviet exile and spent years in DP camps before settling in Israel.

The formal recognition of refugees raised the protracted question whether certain refugees were more "deserving" than others. In a 1989 editorial the *New York Times* backed the admission of more Soviet Jewish refuseniks but emphasized that Vietnamese who were also fleeing Communist oppression and others were "equally deserving migrants." The paper noted that a very large number of people fell between the existing categories: "The gateway is packed: many more foreigners want admission to the United States than can be accommodated. Most are immigrants who seek a better life. Some are refugees fleeing persecution. But suddenly, many are not exactly either." The paper advised policymakers to open the doors: "Yes, admit many more Soviet migrants, but extend the same generosity to people from around the world. The country's economy can stand it; the country's sense of fairness compels it." The editorial, which was written in April 1989, a few months before the collapse of Communist regimes in Eastern Europe, reflects the growing consensus among American policymakers that refugees from Communist countries were not more deserving than those fleeing other authoritarian regimes and often were not white Europeans.[3]

The status given to Jews from the (former) Soviet Union in Germany after the collapse of the Berlin Wall in November 1989 also illustrates the pitfalls of differentiating between refugees and migrants. In the spring of 1990, the first and only democratically elected government of East Germany offered Soviet Jews asylum. After reunification in October 1990 the German federal government continued to honor this policy. Jews from the (former) Soviet Union were formally recognized as refugees upon arrival and given permanent resident status, based on a policy applied to Vietnamese refugees admitted by West Germany in the 1970s. Although antisemitic discrimination was widespread in the early 1990s in the Soviet Union and its successor states, few Jews who moved to Germany were fleeing persecution. In contrast, others who moved to Germany in the early 1990s, for instance those fleeing "ethnic cleansing" during the violent collapse of Yugoslavia, had to undergo a lengthy review process before being granted political asylum— or not. Refugees from the Bosnian conflict were granted only temporary asylum status. After the Dayton peace agreement was signed in late 1995 Germany repatriated Bosnian refugees in 1996–1997. A substantial number moved to the United States, where they were recognized as refugees. German policymakers justified the privileged treatment of Jews from the (former) Soviet Union by pointing to the special responsibility of the German state to protect Jews from persecution after the Holocaust.[4]

The fraught thesis that Jews had a "proclivity" to migrate, often as a result of persecution, distinguishing them from others, remains influential.[5] Based on the definition of mobilized diasporas by political scientist John Armstrong, some Jews in medieval Spain and in the Ottoman Empire can indeed be described as members of highly mobilized and small diasporic communities who occupied specific economic niches and carefully enforced social and religious boundaries. Members of other ethnoreligious groups pursued similar strategies, such as Armenians and Greeks in the Ottoman and Russian empires, Parsees in Mughal India, and migrants from South China in Southeast Asia, to name but a few. And disparities between Jewish populations in different regions were (and remain) significant—a point Chazan recognizes. Instead of essentializing the Jewish experience, it is necessary to carefully assess different cases within their respective settings and time periods.

The proclivity argument is problematic for two other reasons. First, the view of Jews as a migrating or wandering people betrays a notorious stereotype with a checkered history. Second, migration is not a recent phenomenon and not limited to small, highly mobile diaspora populations. Following in the footsteps of Alexander and Eugene Kulischer, migration historians have shown that before and after 1800 few people were truly sedentary. Seasonal migrations, even over extended distances, have comprised large numbers of people in different parts of the world for millennia. During the nineteenth century technological innovations enabled a rapidly growing number of people to cover enormous distances within relatively short periods. The intercontinental migrations of millions represented a genuinely new phenomenon. Some migration patterns illustrate continuity even for long-distance migrants. After 1900 well over 50 percent of the mostly male migrants from the Italian South in the United States were return migrants. Some moved repeatedly across the Atlantic for work on construction sites in American cities.[6]

It is true that about a third of the Jewish population left Eastern Europe for North America and a few other far-flung destinations between 1870 and the early 1920s. Yet the proportion of migrants leaving Norway and Ireland at the same period was even higher. The economic conditions in both countries resembled that of the northern Russian Pale. The opportunities in little-developed rural societies experiencing strong population growth were limited, forcing younger men and women to join other members of social networks and migrate elsewhere to find employment. Most men, women, and children leaving Eastern Europe between 1860 and 1914 did not move because they were Jews, Christians, Poles, or Lithuanians but because they were looking for a better life for themselves and their families elsewhere. The artificial constraints imposed by the ethnicity paradigm can all too easily essentialize and distort the experiences of actual migrants.[7]

The history of Jewish migrations from Eastern Europe after the 1860s falls into two distinct phases. Before 1914 the overwhelming majority of Jews (and Christians) moving within and beyond the Russian and Austro-Hungarian empires and Romania were looking for better economic opportunities. The available sources do not show a causal link between pogroms and large-scale Jewish migration. The northern Pale was notorious for widespread poverty and economic decline and experienced strong population growth, just like the Austrian province of Galicia, where all Jews had been fully emancipated in 1867. Fear from violent persecution cannot be dismissed as a factor. In the Russian Empire and in Romania most Jews were subject to restrictions limiting their mobility and economic activity. And after 1870 Jews in Russia and Romania faced growing hostility and violent attacks, albeit not constantly and not everywhere.[8]

The Jewish migration from Eastern Europe before 1914 was one facet of an unprecedented mobility revolution. Railroad lines and steamship lines were ambivalent harbingers of change. Expanding globalizing markets for labor and industrially manufactured goods displaced Jews from their traditional economic roles in rural societies earlier than Christian peasants. The same railroads that fueled economic transformation threw open the gates to better opportunities elsewhere, especially for younger women and men, like

Mary Antin's parents. Before 1914 Europeans who moved abroad, regardless of their background or origin, faced few legal obstacles—in marked contrast to Chinese migrants. Already in the 1890s members of the American Jewish business establishment lobbied against Chinese exclusion laws because they understood the potential ramifications of a racist immigration policy for other groups.

Networks and the quest for economic opportunities were the main drivers of the migration. This pattern has been characteristic for many other groups on the move. After the 1850s a growing number of Jews and others moved to industrializing cities at home and abroad, in Europe, North America, and beyond. Most migrants kept links to their homes, and some returned. Bernard Horwich, for instance, who left a small village in Lithuania for East Prussia in 1875 and later moved to Chicago, regularly sent money to his family. A relative provided funds for his journey to the United States. His four brothers all followed him to Chicago within a few years after he had settled there in the early 1880s. Like their Christian fellow migrants, Jews sought economic stability for themselves and their children in relatively inclusive societies. The women Jacob Lestschinsky interviewed shortly before the First World War during their transit through Germany were aware that they literally emancipated themselves by moving from Russia to America.

By 1900 newly arriving migrants were transforming Jewish life even in far-flung corners of the world. New communities emerged in places where few or no Jews had lived before 1880, for instance in Buenos Aires and Johannesburg. Nonstate actors, ranging from railroad investors to smugglers, the German steamship lines, and Jewish aid associations facilitated the journeys of millions of Jews and Christians leaving the Russian and Austro-Hungarian empires. An efficient transnational Jewish support network—a distinctive feature of Jewish migration—protected Jewish but often also other migrants during the journey, even at remote points of passage and at far-flung destinations.

The inability of governments in the Russian and Austro-Hungarian empires to liberalize their migration regimes enabled the German steamship lines to establish a monopoly over the Eastern European passenger market. HAPAG and NDL fixed the passage prices at relatively high levels but also paid much attention to hygiene and comfort. By keeping the Prussian state on the sidelines and satisfying American immigration officials, the German steamship lines facilitated the journeys of millions of Eastern Europeans, admittedly for a price.

The First World War was a watershed moment in the history of Jewish migrations from and within Europe. In the Russian Empire Jewish civilians were specifically targeted as potential enemies, even though over 300,000 Jewish men served in the Russian army. The Russian deportations of over 500,000 Jews between 1914 and 1917 constituted an ominous escalation. For the first time since 1492 a European government forcibly removed a large number of its Jewish subjects from their homes, rendering them destitute and exposing them to violent persecution. During the Russian Civil War and the wars between different successor states large numbers of Jews were systematically attacked and slaughtered—by Polish, Ukrainian, Romanian, Hungarian, Russian, and German nationalists. Many more were permanently displaced. About 250,000 Jews managed to enter the United States between 1920 and 1925, but a far greater number was excluded by the 1924 national origins quota bill.

Those who failed to settle in the United States were stranded in permanent transit, often living on the margins of societies in Central and Eastern Europe, unable to return to their homes or move to a destination of their choice. As states began to fortify their outer borders and implement restrictive migration regimes, nonstate actors lost much of their soft power and were relegated to the sidelines. At the League of Nations leaders of Jewish aid associations like Leo Motzkin and Lucien Wolf advocated on behalf of stateless refugees. The Nansen passport was a pragmatic solution, but it was (and remains), as Vladimir Nabokov so poignantly observed, not a real passport.

After the First World War most governments were reluctant to admit displaced Jews from Eastern Europe, who were widely associated with Bolshevism. It was no secret that Eastern European Jews were a specific target of the restrictive immigration bills passed by Congress in 1921 and 1924. After the Kristallnacht pogrom the United States relaxed the admission criteria for German and Austrian Jews, but the rigid restrictions for Jews born on the territory of the successor states of the Russian and Austro-Hungarian empires—a much larger group—remained in place.

Little is known about the fate of Eastern European Jews trying to escape Nazi Germany and from countries like Poland, Hungary, and Romania pursuing antisemitic policies during the 1920s and 1930s. The travails of Jews caught in the no man's land between borders in East Central Europe in 1938 and 1939 illustrate that Jews had literally been fenced out of the fragile "order" of territorial successor states of the multiethnic empires.

The Nazi regime and Vichy France formally rendered German and French Jews stateless before deporting them to ghettos and extermination camps.[9]

In 1940 the Vichy regime detained Arendt as a stateless Jewish refugee. After escaping from the Gurs detention camp but *before* she secured a U.S. visa in Marseilles, she wrote a brief essay that was not published until 2007. In the text she wrestled with the "conundrum" of the Jews as a transterritorial people. In a play on the well-known Zionist maxim, she described them as "a people without land in search of a land without people." Such a land of course did not exist, except, as she sarcastically pointed out, on the moon. Arendt in 1940 was thinking along similar lines as the German Jewish Hilfsverein in 1905 and Leo Motzkin during the 1920s. If members of a group, whether they belong to a minority or have been displaced, cannot establish or move to their "own" state or to a state that does not treat them as an unwanted minority, they require some form of internationally recognized status that provides the same protection as the citizenship of a territorially defined state. Arendt's "commonwealth of European nations with a parliament of its own" bears a strong resemblance *not* to the European Union as it emerged during the second half of the twentieth century but to the system of transterritorially defined group rights in the multiethnic empires that collapsed in 1918. Like Motzkin, Arendt proposed to decouple nations and territorialism. National groups rather than territorial states would have formed her European commonwealth. It remained a utopia.[10]

In his 1939 survey John Hope Simpson described the refugee as the "unwanted inhabitant of the world, unwanted in the country of his origin, unwanted in any other country." According to the 1951 United Nations Convention relating to the Status of Refugees, the term "refugee" applies if a person can prove a "well-founded fear of being persecuted for reasons of race, religion, nationality, membership of a particular social group or political opinion." In addition, the definition covers persons who are outside of the country whose nationals they are but who do not receive protection or who are unwilling to return to their former country of residence for fear of persecution. The Convention has obvious shortcomings. Terms like "persecution" are just as vague as the term "refugee" itself. Who determines when the "fear of being persecuted" is "well-founded"? Women fleeing arranged marriages or sexual violence, or those women, men, and children fleeing failing states and criminal gangs are often not recognized as refugees but treated as unwanted "economic" migrants.[11]

The international recognition of refugees after World War II—a project to which Jewish legal scholars like Jacob Robinson made important contributions—constituted a step forward compared to the inability of the League of Nations to resolve the refugee crisis after the First World War.[12] Yet legal definitions separated deserving "political" refugees seeking asylum from supposedly undeserving and unwanted "economic" migrants. In the mid-1950s the United States provided access to political refugees from Communist dictatorships in Europe but continued to exclude "economic" migrants from non-Communist countries in Latin America.

The 1965 Hart-Celler Act abolished the racist national origins system but maintained ceilings for all countries, effectively controlling the number of "economic" migrants. President Lyndon B. Johnson signed the act at the foot of the Statue of Liberty. As a member of Congress Johnson, like most Southern Democrats, had supported immigration restrictions. Yet during the 1930s he lobbied behind the scenes for the admission of Jewish refugees and personally arranged visas for several Jews from Europe. The choice of the Statue of Liberty as symbolic backdrop illustrates that the intended beneficiaries of the bill were those facing political oppression, especially in Communist Eastern Europe. Some policymakers in Congress continued to express reservations about admitting nonwhite migrants as the legal immigration from Latin America and Asia increased after 1965. The laudable effort to formally recognize refugees has separated a small number of privileged asylum seekers and legal (often highly skilled) immigrants from wealthy countries from a large number of labor migrants from less-developed countries in the Global South with an uncertain status who often were trying to escape failing states, natural disasters, and crime-ridden societies.[13]

Migrants from West Africa, Vietnam, Afghanistan, or Pakistan seeking a way into Europe today or those leaving Central America for the United States resemble young men and women from the Russian Empire and Italy moving to the United States before 1914. While the latter faced hardly any legal obstacles and quickly secured citizenship, the former have to borrow huge amounts of money and risk their lives to reach their intended destinations. Many are stranded in permanent transit along the main migration routes; some are enslaved by paramilitary groups in transit countries like Libya or Colombia. Those who manage to reach their intended destination often fill essential niches in the service sector but are subject to exploitation and live on the social margins in a legal gray zone trying to avoid detention and deportation. Even legal immigrants from less-developed countries face lengthy waiting periods before they can acquire citizenship. The situation of those seeking better economic opportunities today often resembles that of unwanted and stateless refugees after 1918.[14]

The harrowing experiences of Jewish migrants and refugees between 1914 and 1948 reinforce the case for protecting permanently displaced stateless persons such as Rohingya and Biharis in Bangladesh or Somalis who have fled to Kenya who exist in a state of legal limbo and are often detained in camps in close proximity to the border. Yet the much celebrated immigration of Jews, Italians, Poles, and others who moved to the United States before 1914, not least at symbolic sites like Ellis Island, also questions the categorization of children, women, and men who are fleeing failing states, ecological disasters, and economic insecurity as unwelcome "economic migrants." The history of Jewish migrants and Jewish migrations from Eastern Europe before and after 1914 serves as a reminder that individuals on the move straddle the artificial and shifting divide between the flight from persecution and the quest for a better life.

Notes

Introduction

1. Joseph Jacobs, "Migration," in *The Jewish Encyclopedia*, ed. Isidore Singer (New York: Funk and Wagnalls, 1906), 8:523; Thomas Sowell, *Migrations and Cultures: A World View* (New York: Basic Books, 1996), 234.
2. Howard M. Sachar, *Course of Modern Jewish History* (New York: Vintage Books, 1990), 365; Philipp Ther, *The Outsiders: Refugees in Europe since 1492* (Princeton, NJ: Princeton University Press, 2019), 44; Paul Hohenberg and Lynn Hollen Lees, *The Making of Urban Europe 1000–1994* (Cambridge, MA: Harvard University Press, 1996), 252.
3. Derek Penslar, *Theodor Herzl: The Charismatic Leader* (New Haven, CT: Yale University Press, 2020), 109; Eugène Sue, *Le Juif Errant* (Paris: Meline, 1844).
4. Roger Daniels, *Coming to America: A History of Immigration and Ethnicity in American Life* (New York: Harper Collins, 1991), 127, 164, 189; Mark Choate, *Emigrant Nation: The Making of Italy Abroad* (Cambridge, MA: Harvard University Press, 2008); Briant Lindsay Lowell, *Scandinavian Exodus: Demography and Social Development of 19th Century Rural Communities* (Boulder, CO: Westview Press, 1987), 159–211; Jonathan Sarna, "The Myth of No Return: Jewish Return Migration from Eastern Europe 1881–1914," *American Jewish History* 71, no. 2 (1981): 256–268.
5. *Annual Report of the Commissioner General of Immigration (1904)* (Washington, D.C.: GPO, 1904), 9; Jacobs, "Migration."
6. Charles King, *Gods of the Upper Air: How a Circle of Renegade Anthropologists Reinvented Race, Sex, and Gender in the Twentieth Century* (New York: Doubleday, 2020), 96–106; Katherine Benton-Cohen, *Inventing the Immigration Problem: The Dillingham Commission and Its Legacy* (Cambridge, MA: Harvard University Press, 2018), 168–199.
7. Eli Lederhendler, "The Interrupted Chain: Traditional Receiver Countries, Migration Regimes, and the East European Jewish Diaspora 1918–39," *East European Jewish Affairs* 44, nos. 2–3 (2014): 171–186.
8. On Jewish immigration, see, for instance, Jeffrey Lesser, "The Immigration and Integration of Polish Jews in Brazil, 1924–1934," *The Americas* 51, no. 2 (1994): 173–191; Víctor A. Mirelman, *Jewish Buenos Aires, 1890–1930: In Search of an Identity* (Detroit, MI: Wayne State University Press, 1990); Annie Polland and Daniel Soyer, *Emerging Metropolis: New York Jews in the Age of Immigration, 1840–1920* (New York: NYU Press, 2012); Susan L. Tanabaum, *Jewish Immigrants in London 1880–1939* (London: Routledge, 2015).

9. Eli Lederhendler, *Jewish Immigrants and American Capitalism, 1880–1920: From Caste to Class* (Cambridge: Cambridge University Press, 2009).
10. Irving Howe, *World of Our Fathers: The Journey of the East European Jews to America and the Life They Found and Made* (New York: Harcourt Brace Jovanovich, 1976), 5, 26.
11. Gur Alroey, *An Unpromising Land: Jewish Migration to Palestine in the Early Twentieth Century* (Stanford: Stanford University Press, 2014), 1–3.
12. Notable exceptions are studies that discuss the process of migration: Michael R. Marrus, *The Unwanted: European Refugees in the Twentieth Century* (Oxford: Oxford University Press, 1985); Gur Alroey, *Bread to Eat and Clothes to Wear: Letters from Jewish Migrants in the Early Twentieth Century* (Detroit, MI: Wayne State Press, 2011); Tobias Brinkmann, ed., *Points of Passage: Jewish Transmigrants from Eastern Europe in Scandinavia, Germany, and Britain 1880–1914* (New York: Berghahn, 2013); Alroey, *An Unpromising Land*, 127–156; Libby Garland, *After They Closed the Gates: Jewish Illegal Immigration to the United States, 1921–1965* (Chicago: University of Chicago Press, 2014); Devi Mays, *Forging Ties, Forging Passports: Migration and the Modern Sephardi Diaspora* (Stanford: Stanford University Press, 2020); Nancy L. Green, *The Limits of Transnationalism* (Chicago: University of Chicago Press, 2019).
13. Important exceptions: Tara Zahra, *The Great Departure: Mass Migration from Eastern Europe and the Making of the Free World* (New York: Norton, 2016); Ewa Morawska, "Polish-Jewish Relations in North America, 1880–1940: Old Elements, New Configurations," in *Polish-Jewish Relations in North America*, ed. M. B. Biskupski and Anthony Polonsky (Oxford: Littman, 2007), 71–86.
14. Jonathan Dekel-Chen, "East European Jewish Migration: Inside and Outside," *East European Jewish Affairs* 44, nos. 2–3 (2014): 154–170.
15. David S. Wyman, *Paper Walls; America and the Refugee Crisis, 1938–1941* (Amherst: University of Massachusetts Press, 1968); Eric T. Jennings, *Escape from Vichy: The Refugee Exodus to the French Caribbean* (Cambridge, MA: Harvard University Press, 2018); Allen Wells, *Tropical Zion: General Trujillo, FDR, and the Jews of Sosúa* (Durham, NC: Duke University Press, 2009); Laura Jockusch, *Collect and Record! Jewish Holocaust Documentation in Early Postwar Europe* (New York: Oxford University Press, 2012); Eliyana Adler, *Survival on the Margins: Polish Jewish Refugees in the Wartime Soviet Union* (Cambridge, MA: Harvard University Press, 2020); Marcia Reynders Ristaino, *Port of Last Resort: The Diaspora Communities of Shanghai* (Stanford: Stanford University Press, 2001); Atina Grossmann, *Jews, Germans, and Allies: Close Encounters in Occupied Germany* (Princeton, NJ: Princeton University Press, 2007); Daniel Mendelsohn, *The Lost: A Search for Six of Six Million* (New York: HarperCollins, 2006).
16. Simone Gigliotti, *The Train Journey: Transit, Captivity, and Witnessing in the Holocaust* (New York: Berghahn, 2009); Raul Hilberg, Christopher Browning, and Peter Hayes, *German Railroads, Jewish Souls: The Reichsbahn, Bureaucracy, and the Final Solution* (New York: Berghahn, 2019); Sarah Federman, *Last Train to Auschwitz: The*

French National Railway and the Journey to Accountability (Madison: University of Wisconsin Press, 2021).
17. Mays, *Forging Ties, Forging Passports*; Sarah Abrevaya Stein, *Plumes: Ostrich Feathers, Jews, and a Lost World of Global Commerce* (New Haven, CT: Yale University Press, 2008).
18. Mae M. Ngai, *Impossible Subjects: Illegal Aliens and the Making of Modern America* (Princeton, NJ: Princeton University Press, 2003); Nandita Sharma, *Home Rule: National Sovereignty and the Separation of Natives and Migrants* (Durham, NC: Duke University Press, 2020).
19. Jessica Reinisch and Matthew Frank, "Introduction: Refugees and the Nation-State in Europe, 1919–59," *Journal of Contemporary History* 49, no. 3 (2014): 477–490; Adam M. McKeown, *Melancholy Order: Asian Migration and the Globalization of Borders* (New York: Columbia University Press, 2008); Aristide R. Zolberg, "The Great Wall against China: Responses to the First Immigration Crisis, 1885–1925," in *Migration, Migration History, History*, ed. Leo Lucassen and Jan Lucassen (Berne: Peter Lang, 1997), 291–315.
20. Aron Rodrigue, *French Jews, Turkish Jews: The Alliance Israélite Universelle and the Politics of Jewish Schooling in Turkey, 1860–1925* (Bloomington: Indiana University Press, 1990).
21. Helen M. Davies, *Emile and Isaac Pereire: Bankers, Socialists and Sephardic Jews in Nineteenth-Century France* (Manchester: Manchester University Press, 2015).
22. Gennady Estraikh, "Jacob Lestschinsky: A Yiddishist Dreamer and Social Scientist," *Science in Context* 20, no. 2 (2007): 215–237; Gennady Estraikh, *Transatlantic Russian Jewishness: Ideological Voyages of the Yiddish Daily* Forverts *in the First Half of the Twentieth Century* (Boston: Academic Studies Press, 2020); Anne-Christin Saß, *Berliner Luftmenschen: Osteuropäischen-jüdische Migranten in der Weimarer Republik* (Göttingen: Wallstein, 2012); Cecile Esther Kuznitz, *YIVO and the Making of Modern Jewish Culture: Scholarship for the Yiddish Nation* (New York: Cambridge University Press, 2014); Mark Volovici, *German as a Jewish Problem: The Language Politics of Jewish Nationalism* (Stanford: Stanford University Press, 2020); World Jewish Congress, Meetings, Geneva, 1939–1940, American Jewish Archives, Cincinnati (AJA), WJC Records, MS Coll. 361, Box A7, Folder 2.
23. A note on place names: The term "Eastern Europe" refers to the Russian and Austro-Hungarian empires as well as Romania before 1918 and the different successor states after the First World War. Place names in this region changed during the twentieth century, in some cases repeatedly. Often new names are relatively similar; for instance, after the First World War the Silesian mining center Kattowitz became Katowice. Other changes are less obvious. Since 1945 Königsberg has been Kaliningrad, Tilsit was renamed Sovetsk, and Memel is Klaipeda today. To avoid confusion, I decided to use the official name of towns and cities that applied at the respective time. Two maps will help readers locate smaller towns and unfamiliar places.

Chapter 1

1. Ruth Leiserowitz, *Sabbatleuchter und Kriegerverein: Juden in der ostpreußisch-litauischen Grenzregion 1812-1942* (Osnabrück: fibre, 2010), 118, 221-240; Isaak Rülf, "Zur Geschichte der Juden in Memel," in *Erster Bericht der Israelitischen Religionsschule zu Memel*, ed. Emanuel Carlebach (Memel: Siebert, 1900), 18. On Rülf, see Leon Scheinhaus, "Zwei Hundertjährige," *Jüdische Rundschau* (Berlin), February 10, 1931, 69-70; Albert Kahn, *Isaak Rülf—Ein Gedenkblatt zu seinem Geburtstag am 10. Februar 1901* (Bonn: Privately published, 1901).
2. Werner Mosse, *Alexander II and the Modernization of Russia* (London: Tauris, 1992), 29; Leiserowitz, *Sabbatleuchter*, 118, 221-240; Rülf, "Zur Geschichte der Juden in Memel," 13, 18; Frithjof Benjamin Schenk, "Travel, Railroads and Identity Formation in the Russian Empire," in *Shatterzone of Empires: Coexistence and Violence in the German, Habsburg, Russian, and Ottoman Borderlands*, ed. Omer Bartov and Eric D. Weitz (Bloomington: Indiana University Press, 2013), 136-151.
3. Leiserowitz, *Sabbatleuchter*, 226-232; Dieter Gosewinkel, *Einbürgern und Ausschließen: Die Nationalisierung der Staatsangehörigkeit vom Deutschen Bund bis zur Bundesrepublik Deutschland* (Göttingen: Vandenhoeck & Ruprecht, 2003), 263-277.
4. Leiserowitz, *Sabbatleuchter*, 226-232; Stefanie Schüler-Springorum, *Die jüdische Minderheit in Königsberg, Preussen 1871-1945* (Göttingen: Vandenhoeck & Ruprecht, 1996), 164, 174, 367.
5. Josef Reinhold, "Die Entstehung einer jüdischen Großgemeinde," *Sächsische Heimatblätter* 43 (1997): 117-141.
6. Rülf, "Zur Geschichte der Juden in Memel," 7-12, 20; Kaiserliches Statistisches Amt, *Zur Eisenbahn- und Bevölkerungs-Statistik der Deutschen Städte: Insbesondere der Deutschen Kleinstädte und Landstädte in der Periode 1867 bis 1875* (Berlin: Puttkammer & Mühlbrecht, 1878), 52; Leiserowitz, *Sabbatleuchter und Kriegerverein*, 235; Immanuel Etkes, *Rabbi Israel Salanter and the Musar Movement* (Philadelphia: Jewish Publication Society, 1993).
7. Leiserowitz, *Sabbatleuchter*, 234; David I. Kertzer, *The Kidnapping of Edgaro Mortara* (New York: Alfred A. Knopf, 1997); Lisa Moses Leff, *Sacred Bonds of Solidarity: The Rise of Jewish Internationalism in Nineteenth Century France* (Stanford: Stanford University Press, 2006); Abigail Green, "Intervening in the Jewish Question 1840-1878," in *Humanitarian Intervention: A History*, ed. Brendan Simms and D. J. B. Trim (Cambridge: Cambridge University Press, 2011), 139-158.
8. *Jewish Chronicle* (London), October 11, 1867; Isaak Rülf, *Jankel Widutzky, der den Händen der Judenbekehrungsmission entzogene Knabe* (Memel: Ed. Schnee, 1867).
9. Isaak Rülf, "Mein Lebensgang," December 1897, handwritten CV, in Leo Baeck Institute—New York [LBI—New York], Isaak Rülf Collection 1858-1987, AR 3179; Rülf, "Zur Geschichte der Juden in Memel."
10. *Allgemeine Zeitung des Judenthums* [AZ], February 4, 1868, 101-103.
11. Isaak Rülf, *Meine Reise nach Kowno um die Uebersiedelung nothleidender Glaubensgenossen aus den Grenzbezirken nach dem Innern Russlands zu ordnen, sowie*

die in der dortigen Synagoge gehaltene Predigt von Dr. Ruelf (Memel: Goldschmidt, 1869), 4, 12–13.
12. *AZ*, June 15, 1869, 469; Rülf, *Meine Reise nach Kowno*, 27–28, 42–43.
13. H. Simon, "Der Flecktyphus in seiner hygienischen und sanitätspolizeilichen Bedeutung," *Deutsche Vierteljahrsschrift für öffentliche Gesundheitspflege* 20, no. 3 (1888): 472–514.
14. *AZ*, February 4, 1868, 101–103; May 4, 1869, 355–356; February 2, 1869, 90–91; *Die Noth unserer Glaubensbrüder in Rußland* (Berlin, March 1869), Central Archive for the History of the Jewish People, Jerusalem [CAHJP], Berlin Collection, D/Be4/86.
15. *AZ*, July 27, 1846; London Committee of Deputies of the British Jews, *The First Annual Report for Nisan, 5647—April 1887* (London: Wertheimer, 1887), 21 ("deter paupers from coming to this country").
16. Otto von Bismarck, "Stellung der Juden im christlichen Staate" (June 15, 1847), in *Die politischen Reden des Fürsten Bismarck: Historisch-kritische Gesamtausgabe*, ed. Horst Kohl (Stuttgart: Cotta, 1892), 1:26, 30; Jack Wertheimer, *Unwelcome Strangers: East European Jews in Imperial Germany* (New York: Oxford University Press, 1987), 24. For the text of the law, see *AZ*, August 16, 1847, 509–517.
17. *AZ*, May 19, 1868, 577; May 11, 1869, 369; July 20, 1869; Steven Aschheim, *Brothers and Strangers: The East European Jew in German and German Jewish Consciousness 1800–1923* (Madison: University of Wisconsin Press 1982).
18. *AZ*, May 18, 1869, 386; *AZ*, August 3, 1869; Steven M. Lowenstein, "Die Gemeinde," in *Deutsch-jüdische Geschichte in der Neuzeit*, ed. Michael A. Meyer (Munich: C. H. Beck, 1996), 3:137.
19. *AZ*, May 25, 1869, 407; July 6, 1869, 536; August 17, 1869, 657; Rülf, *Meine Reise nach Kowno*.
20. *AZ*, June 1, 1869, 425; July 27, 1846, 448–449.
21. *AZ*, June 1, 1869; October 5, 1869, 801.
22. *AZ*, October 12, 1869, 820; May 7, 1872, 367; *Bulletin de L'Alliance Israelite Universelle, Mai 1862* (Paris: Wittersheim, 1885), 81–112.
23. *AZ*, October 19, 1869, 840; Michael Graetz, *The Jews in Nineteenth-Century France: From the French Revolution to the Alliance Israélite Universelle* (Stanford: Stanford University Press, 1996), 103–110.
24. *AZ*, October 19, 1869, 841; November 9, 1869, 897–898, February 27, 1872, 162; "Liste der Untergebrachten," March 6, 1870, CAHJP, Königsberg Collection, D/Ko1/594; Mark Wischnitzer, *To Dwell in Safety: The Story of Jewish Migration since 1800* (Philadelphia: Jewish Publication Society, 1948), 28–36. The short-lived Hebrew Emigration Aid Society had no connection with the Hebrew Immigrant Aid Society that was founded in New York in 1881.
25. Lowenstein, "Die Gemeinde," 136–7; *AZ*, November 12, 1872, 906.
26. Derek Penslar, *Shylock's Children: Economics and Jewish Identity in Modern Europe* (Berkeley: University of California Press, 2001), 198.
27. *The Statutes at Large of the United States of America, Dec. 1881 to March 1883* (Washington, D.C.: GPO, 1883), 22:214–5 (47th Congress, Session I, Ch. 376, August 3, 1882).

28. *Report of the Anglo-Jewish Association—In Connection with the Alliance Israelite Universelle for the Year 1873-1874* (London: S. Meldola, 1874), 9.
29. *Fifth Annual Report of the United Hebrew Relief Association of Chicago* (Chicago: Privately published, 1864); Hyman Meites, *History of the Jews of Chicago* (Chicago: Privately published, 1924), 489.
30. Bernard Horwich, *My First Eighty Years* (Chicago: Argus Books, 1939), 1-81, quote on 79.
31. Schüler-Springorum, *Königsberg*, 48; *Sammlung der Drucksachen des Preußischen Hauses der Abgeordneten, 19. Legislaturperiode, V. Session* (Berlin: W. Moeser, 1903), vol. 4, Drucksache zu Nr. 115: 2143, 2151-2153.
32. Horwich, *My First Eighty Years*, 79.
33. Horwich, *My First Eighty Years*, 102-122; Jonathan Z. S. Pollack, "Success from Scrap and Secondhand Goods: Jewish Businessmen in the Midwest, 1890-1930," in *Chosen Capital: The Jewish Encounter with American Capitalism*, ed. Rebecca Kobrin (New Brunswick, NJ: Rutgers University Press, 2012), 93-112.
34. Horwich, *My First Eighty Years*, 78-104, 175; *American Jewish Yearbook* 51 (1950): 521 (obituary).
35. Exceptions are Joel Perlmann, "The Local Geographic Origins of Russian-Jewish Immigrants, circa 1900," Working Paper No. 465, August 2006, Levy Economics Institute of Bard College, http://www.levyinstitute.org/publications/the-local-geographic-origins-of-russian-jewish-immigrants-circa-1900; Saul Stampfer, "The Geographic Background of East European Jewish Migration to the United States before World War I," in *Migration across Time and Nations: Population Mobility in Historical Contexts*, ed. Ira A. Glazier and Luigi de Rosa (New York: Holmes & Meyer, 1986), 220-230; Carl Henrik Carlson, "Immigrants or Transmigrants? Eastern European Jews in Sweden, 1860-1914," in Brinkmann, *Points of Passage*, 47-62.
36. Jeffrey A. Marx and Walter B. Miller, *A History of the Breakstone/Bregstein Family* (Los Angeles: Privately published, 2009), 49-83; Meites, *History of the Jews in Chicago*, 489; Carlsson, "Immigrants or Transmigrants," 53; Gideon Shimoni, "From One Frontier to Another: Jewish Identity and Political Orientations in Lithuania and South Africa, 1890-1939," in *Jewries at the Frontier: Accommodation, Identity, Conflict*, ed. Sander L. Gilman and Milton Shain (Urbana: University of Illinois Press, 1999), 129-154; Anne Kershen, *Uniting the Tailors: Trade Unionism amongst the Tailors of London and Leeds 1870-1939* (London: Frank Cass, 1995), 128; Cormac Ó Gráda, *Jewish Ireland in the Age of Joyce: A Socioeconomic History* (Princeton, NJ: Princeton University Press, 2006), 13-17; Moses Rischin, *The Promised City: New York's Jews 1870-1914* (Cambridge, MA: Harvard University Press, 1962), 116; Jonathan Sarna, "The Jews of Boston in Historical Perspective," in *The Jews of Boston*, ed. Jonathan Sarna and Ellen Smith (Boston: Northeastern University Press, 1995), 6; *Eleventh Annual Report of the Anglo-Jewish Association for the Year 1881-1882* (London: Wertheimer, 1882), 24; London Committee of Deputies of the British Jews, *49th Annual Report for Nisan, 5660—April 1900* (London: Wertheimer 1900), 27-30.
37. Perlmann, "The Local Geographic Origins"; Charles Tilly, "Transplanted Networks," in *Immigration Reconsidered: History, Society and Politics*, ed. Virginia Yans-McLaughlin (New York: Oxford University Press, 1990), 78-95.

38. Jacob Toury, *Soziale und politische Geschichte der Juden in Deutschland, 1848–1871* (Düsseldorf: Droste, 1977), 30.

Chapter 2

1. Abraham Cahan, *Bleter fun mein Lebn* [Yiddish] (New York: Forverts, 1926), 1:11–30, 264–382.
2. Cahan, *Bleter fun mein Lebn*, 2:9–24.
3. Cahan, *Bleter fun mein Lebn*, 2:24–65; Nachweisbüro der Auswanderungsbehörde, May 23, 1882 (Brody family), p. 160, Staatsarchiv Hamburg, Auswanderungsamt I, 373–377 I [abbreviated as Auswanderungsamt HH], Überwachung des Rückwandererverkehrs über Hamburg durch die Polizeibehörden bis 1902/03, II B I 3; Leo Goldenstein, *Brody und die russisch-jüdische Emigration* (Frankfurt am Main: Kauffmann, 1882), 10; Börries Kuzmany, *Brody: Eine galizische Grenzstadt im langen 19. Jahrhundert* (Vienna: Böhlau, 2011), 238.
4. "Abraham Cahan, Editor, 91, Is Dead," *New York Times*, September 1, 1951; Ezra Glinter, "Looking Back at *The Forward*: 'The Rise of Abraham Cahan,'" *Los Angeles Review of Books*, October 14, 2013; Beverly Schwartzberg, "'Lots of Them Did That': Desertion, Bigamy, and Marital Fluidity in Late-Nineteenth Century America," *Journal of Social History* 37, no. 3 (2004): 573–600; Howe, *World of Our Fathers*, 528–530.
5. "Albert Vorspan, Who Rallied Reform Judaism for Social Justice, Is Dead at 95," *New York Times*, February 20, 2019; "Louis Sokoloff, Pioneer of Pet Scan, Dies at 93," *New York Times*, August 6, 2015; "Robert B. Sherman, a Songwriter for Disney and Others, Dies at 86," *New York Times*, March 7, 2012; "Jeremy Morris, 99 ½; Proved Exercise Is Heart-Healthy," *New York Times*, November 8, 2009; "Arthur Zinn, 90, Celebrity Photographer," *New York Times*, March 21, 2003; "Mary Bodne, Ex-Owner of Algonquin Hotel, Dies at 93," *New York Times*, March 2, 2000. See also "Outpost on Pampas," *New York Times*, June 10, 2013; "Chicago Is the Second-Biggest Lithuanian City," *Economist*, August, 23, 2018; Molly Crabapple, "My Great-Grandfather the Bundist," *New York Review of Books*, October 6, 2018; Darius Staliūnas, *Enemies for a Day: Antisemitism and Anti-Jewish Violence in Lithuania under the Tsars* (Budapest: Central European University Press, 2015).
6. Dirk Hoerder, *Cultures in Contact: World Migrations in the Second Millennium* (Durham, NC: Duke University Press, 2002), 326–327, 341; Susan F. Martin, *International Migration: Evolving Trends from the Early Twentieth Century to the Present* (Cambridge: Cambridge University Press, 2014), 29; Benton-Cohen, *Inventing the Immigration Problem*, 76.
7. Colin Holmes, *John Bull's Island: Immigration and British Society 1871–1971* (London: Routledge, 2015); *AZ*, April 13, 1906, 170 (around sixty-five hundred Jews were deported from Berlin); Wertheimer, *Unwelcome Strangers*, 61; Philip Cowen, *Memories of an American Jew* (New York: International Press, 1932), 243–245.

8. Benton-Cohen, *Inventing the Immigration Problem*, 9. *Geschäftsbericht (1910) des Hilfsvereins der deutschen Juden* (Berlin: Privately published, 1911), 140.
9. Bernhard Kahn, "Die jüdische Auswanderung," *Ost und West* (Berlin), July and August 1905, 457–480.
10. Holmes, *John Bull's Island*; John Higham, *Strangers in the Land: Patterns of American Nativism 1860–1925* (1955; New York: Atheneum, 1977), 66–67.
11. Jacobs, "Migration," 584.
12. Liebmann Hersch, *Le Juif Errant d'Aujord Hui: Etude sur l'Emigration des Israelites de l'Europe Orientale aux Etats-Unis de L'Amerique du Nord* (Paris: M. Girard & E. Briere, 1913). See also Samuel Joseph, "Jewish Immigration to the United States: From 1881 to 1910" (PhD diss., Columbia University, 1914); *New York Times*, June 11, 1955 (Hersch obituary); Gur Alroey, "Demographers in the Service of the Nation: Liebmann Hersch, Jacob Lestschinsky, and the Early Study of Jewish Migration," *Jewish History* 20, nos. 3–4 (2006): 265–282.
13. Hersch, *Le Juif Errant d'Aujord Hui*, 166–168.
14. Wladimir Wolf Kaplun-Kogan, *Die Wanderbewegungen der Juden* (Bonn: Marcus & Webers, 1913), 115.
15. Kaplun-Kogan, *Die Wanderbewegungen der Juden*, 148; Wladimir Wolf Kaplun-Kogan, *Die jüdischen Wanderbewegungen der neuesten Zeit* (Bonn: Marcus & Webers, 1919), 3, 5–17.
16. Zwi Avraami, *Die jüdische Wirklichkeit und der Zionismus: Eine sozial-ökonomische Studie* (Zurich: Ostheim, 1905), 45–62.
17. U.S. Senate, *Reports of the Emigration Commission, Presented by Mr. Dillingham: Emigration Conditions in Europe* (Washington, D.C.: GPO, 1911), 271–336; see also 56, 65. For background, see Benton-Cohen, *Inventing the Immigration Problem*.
18. Zosa Szajkowski, "How the Mass Migration to America Began," *Jewish Social Studies* 4, no. 4 (1942): 291–310.
19. Wischnitzer, *To Dwell in Safety*, 37–39, 66.
20. Mark Wischnitzer, "Die Stellung der Brodyer Juden im internationalen Handel in der zweiten Hälfte des 18. Jahrhunderts," in *Festschrift zu Simon Dubnows 70. Geburtstag*, ed. Mark Wischnitzer, Ismar Elbogen, and Josef Meisl (Berlin: Jüdischer Verlag, 1930), 113–123; Wischnitzer, *To Dwell in Safety*, 98; Daniel Unowsky, *The Plunder: The 1898 Anti-Jewish Riots in Habsburg Galicia* (Stanford: Stanford University Press, 2018), 1–2, 174; Arthur Ruppin, *Soziologie der Juden* (Berlin: Jüdischer Verlag, 1930), 1:133; Annemarie Steidl, *On Many Routes: Internal, European, and Transatlantic Migration in the Late Habsburg Empire* (West Lafayette, IN: Purdue University Press, 2021).
21. David Vital, *A People Apart: The Jews in Europe 1789–1939* (Oxford: Oxford University Press, 1999), 124.
22. Kuzmany, *Brody*, 110, 253–258; Paulus Adelsgruber, Laurie R. Cohen, and Börries Kuzmany, *Getrennt und Doch Verbunden: Grenzstädte zwischen Österreich und Russland 1772–1918* (Vienna: Böhlau, 2011), 144–148.
23. John Klier, *Russians, Jews, and the Pogroms of 1881–1882* (Cambridge: Cambridge University Press, 2011), 3, 56–57, 365–371, 384–414; Kuzmany, *Brody*, 234–246;

NOTES TO PAGES 44-49   261

Aschheim, *Brothers and Strangers*, 36; Jonathan Frankel, "The Crisis of 1881-82 as a Turning Point in Modern Jewish History," in *The Legacy of Jewish Migration: 1881 and Its Impact*, ed. David Berger (New York: Brooklyn College Press, 1983), 9-22.

24. Kuzmany, *Brody*, 234-246; Goldenstein, *Brody und die russisch-jüdische Emigration*, 19-28; "Die Judenverfolgungen in Rußland III," *Neue Freie Presse* (Vienna), June 1, 1882; "Lemberg, 7. September," *Neue Freie Presse*, September 8, 1882; "Berlin Konferenz," *AZ*, May 2, 1882; "Brody," *AZ*, September 5, 1882; Aschheim, *Brothers and Strangers*, 34.

25. "Die Judenverfolgungen in Rußland III," *Neue Freie Presse*, June 1, 1882.

26. Frankel, "The Crisis of 1881-82"; Leon Pinsker, *Autoemancipation! Mahnruf an seine Stammesgenossen von einem russischen Juden* (Berlin: Issleib, 1882); Dimitry Shumsky, "Leon Pinsker and 'Autoemancipation!': A Reevaluation," *Jewish Social Studies* 18, no. 1 (2011): 33-62; Penslar, *Shylock's Children*, 241; Yehuda Levin, "Labor and Land at the Start of Jewish Settlement in Argentina," *Jewish History* 21, nos. 3-4 (2007): 341-359; Lea Literat-Golombek, *Moisés Ville: Crónica de un shtetl argentino* (Jerusalem: La Semana Publicaciones, 1982).

27. Isaak Rülf (for Ständiges Hilfskomitee für die Notstände Russischer Israeliten) to Alliance, April 19, 1882, in Central Zionist Archive, Jerusalem [CZA], Isaak Rülf Papers, A1/3-3.

28. *Eleventh Annual Report of the Anglo Jewish Association for the Year 1881-1882* (London: Wertheimer, 1882), 14, 24; *Elfter Jahresbericht der Israelitischen Allianz zu Wien, 27. April 1884* (Vienna: Waizner, 1884), iii-iv; Nachweisbüro der Auswanderer-Behörde, March 21, 1882, 72 (Dominican Republic), Auswanderungsamt HH, Überwachung des Rückwandererverkehrs über Hamburg durch die Polizeibehörden bis 1902/03, II B I 3; Mark Wischnitzer, "The Historical Background of the Settlement of Jewish Refugees in Santo Domingo," *Jewish Social Studies* 4, no. 1 (1942): 45-58; Peter Pulzer, *The Rise of Political Anti-Semitism in Germany and Austria*, revised edition (Cambridge, MA: Harvard University Press, 1988), 142-148; Aschheim, *Brothers and Strangers*, 34.

29. *Chicago Occident*, June 3, 1881; *Illinois Staatszeitung* (Chicago), December 4 and 5, 1881; Emil G. Hirsch, "Was nun?," *Der Zeitgeist* (Milwaukee), July 20, 1882; *24th Annual Report of the United Hebrew Relief Association of Chicago* (Chicago: Privately published, 1883); *1st Annual Report of the United Hebrew Charities of Chicago* (Chicago: Privately published, 1889); Daniel J. Tichenor, *Dividing Lines: The Politics of Immigration Control in America* (Princeton, NJ: Princeton University Press 2002), 69, 106-108.

30. "The Chinese To-day: Why Not the Jews To-morrow?," *American Hebrew* (New York), March 24, 1882 (Nissan 4, 5642); "Temple Emanu El," April 7, 1882 (Nissan 18, 5642); "The Veto," *Jewish Messenger* (New York), April 7, 1882; "How John Views the Bill," *New York Times*, June 13, 1892; Eric Goldstein, *The Price of Whiteness: Jews, Race, and American Identity* (Princeton, NJ: Princeton University Press, 2006), 103.

Chapter 3

1. Sholem Aleichem, "Zu die Leser," in *Ale Verk von Sholom Aleichem* [Yiddish] (New York: Folks-Fond Oysgabe, 1923), 11–13, quote on 11; Jeremy Dauber, *The Worlds of Sholem Aleichem* (New York: Schocken, 2013), 212, 228–231, quote on 228; Boris B. Gorshkov, "Serfs on the Move: Peasant Seasonal Migration in Pre-Reform Russia, 1800–61," *Kritika: Exploration in Russian and Eurasian History* 1, no. 4 (2000): 627–656; Leah Garrett, *Journeys beyond the Pale: Yiddish Travel Writing in the Modern World* (Madison: University of Wisconsin Press, 2003), 90–122; Sidra DeKoven Ezrahi, *Booking Passage: Exile and Homecoming in the Modern Jewish Imagination* (Berkeley: University of California Press, 2000), 109–115; Schenk, "Travel, Railroads and Identity."
2. Aleichem, "A Mentsch von Buenos Aires," in *Ale Verk von Sholom Aleichem*, 69–88, quotes on 11, 88; Dauber, *The Worlds of Sholem Aleichem*, 230; Mir Yarfitz, *Impure Migration: Jews and Sex Work in Golden Age Argentina* (New Brunswick, NJ: Rutgers University Press, 2019), 41, 166n.
3. Benjamin Harshav, *Marc Chagall and His Times: A Documentary Narrative* (Stanford: Stanford University Press, 2004), 23, 41–43; Yehuda Slutsky, "Baranovichi," in *Encyclopedia Judaica*, 2nd edition, ed. Michael Berenbaum and Fred Skolnik (New York: Macmillan, 2007), 3:133.
4. *Bradshaw's Shareholders' Guide, Railway Manual and Directory for 1862* (Manchester, UK: Bradshaw & Blacklock, 1862), 336; *American Railroad Journal* (New York), April 18, 1868, 376–377.
5. Perlmann, "Local Geographic Origins"; Eli Lederhendler, "The New Filiopietism, or Toward a New History of Jewish Immigration to America," *American Jewish History* 93, no. 1 (2007): 1–20; Vadim Kukushkin, *From Peasants to Labourers: Ukrainian and Belarusan Immigration from the Russian Empire to Canada* (Montreal: McGill-Queen's University Press, 2007), 12–49.
6. Hilberg, *German Railroads, Jewish Souls*, 19–20.
7. Jan Musekamp, "The Royal Prussian Eastern Railway (Ostbahn) and Its Importance for East-West Transportation," in *Eastern European Railways in Transition. 19th to 21st Centuries*, ed. Ralf Roth and Henry Jacolin (Aldershot: Ashgate, 2013), 117–127; Stefi Jersch-Wenzel, "Rechtslage und Emanzipation," in *Deutsch-jüdische Geschichte in der Neuzeit*, ed. Michael A. Meyer (Munich: C. H. Beck, 1996), 3:35–36.
8. *Bradshaw's Shareholders' Guide*, 336; *American Railroad Journal* (New York), April 18, 1868, 376–377.
9. Thomas C. Owen, *Dilemmas of Russian Capitalism: Fedor Chizhov and Corporate Enterprise in the Railroad Age* (Cambridge, MA: Harvard University Press, 2005), 172; Benjamin Nathans, *Beyond the Pale: The Jewish Encounter with Late Imperial Russia* (Berkeley: University of California Press, 2002), 129; Joseph Marcus, *Social and Political History of the Jews in Poland, 1919–1939* (Berlin: De Gruyter, 1983), 81–83; Ela Bauer, "Jan Gottlieb Bloch: Polish Cosmopolitism versus Jewish Universalism," *European Review of History/Revue Européenne d'Histoire* 17, no. 3 (2010): 415–429.

10. Ralf Roth, "Difficulties of International Railway Investments in Germany: The Example of the 'Railway King' Bethel Henry Strousberg 1855–1875," in *Across the Borders: Financing the World's Railways in the Nineteenth and Twentieth Centuries*, ed. Ralf Roth and Günther Dinhobl (Aldershot: Ashgate, 2013), 33–47; Wolfgang Klee, *Preußische Eisenbahngeschichte* (Stuttgart: Kohlhammer, 1982), 148–156, 179–190; Joachim Borchart, *Der europäische Eisenbahnkönig Bethel Henry Strousberg* (Munich: C. H. Beck, 1991).
11. Davies, *Emile and Isaac Pereire*; Penslar, *Shylock's Children*, 148; Todd Endelman, *Leaving the Jewish Fold: Conversion and Radical Assimilation in Modern Jewish History* (Princeton, NJ: Princeton University Press, 2016), 280.
12. Davies, *Emile and Isaac Pereire*; Niall Ferguson, *The House of Rothschild: Money's Prophets 1798–1848* (New York: Viking, 1998), 1:416–424; Wolfgang Schivelbusch, *Geschichte der Eisenbahnreise: Zur Industrialisierung von Raum und Zeit im 19. Jahrhundert* (Munich: Carl Hanser, 1977).
13. Davies, *Emile and Isaac Pereire*, 75, 100; Endelman, *Leaving the Jewish Fold*, 144–146.
14. Davies, *Emile and Isaac Pereire*, 125–128, 200–202.
15. Alfred Rieber, "The Formation of La Grande Société des Chemins de Fer Russes," *Jahrbücher für Geschichte Osteuropas* 21, no. 3 (1973): 375–391, quote by A. Vonjlarjarskij after Rieber on 387; Owen, *Dilemmas of Russian Capitalism*, 66–67.
16. Rieber, "Formation," 380; Schenk, "Travel, Railroads and Identity," 139.
17. Rieber, "Formation," 380–388; Davies, *Emile and Isaac Pereire*, 201; Rondo E. Cameron, *France and the Economic Development of Europe 1800–1914: Conquests of Peace and Seeds of War* (Princeton, NJ: Princeton University Press, 1961), 114–119, 190–195; Endelman, *Leaving the Jewish Fold*, 280–281; Fredric Bedoire and Robert Tanner, *The Jewish Contribution to Modern Architecture, 1830–1930* (Jersey City, NJ: KTAV, 2004), 163–174; Christophe Bouneau, "The Pereires' International Strategy for Railway Construction in the 1850s and 1860s," in Roth and Dinhobl, *Across the Borders*, 13–24; Victor Perera, *The Cross and the Pear Tree: A Sephardic Journey* (New York: Alfred A. Knopf, 1995), 129–136.
18. Rieber, "Formation," 375–391; Frithjof Benjamin Schenk, *Russlands Fahrt in die Moderne: Mobilität und sozialer Raum im Eisenbahnzeitalter* (Stuttgart: Steiner, 2014), 327–330.
19. Matthias Lehmann, *The Baron: Maurice de Hirsch and the Jewish Nineteenth Century* (Stanford: Stanford University Press, 2022); Bülent Bilmez, "European Investments in the Ottoman Railways, 1850–1914," in Roth and Dinhobl, *Across the Borders*, 183–206; Werner E. Mosse, *The German-Jewish Economic Elite 1820–1935: A Socio-Cultural Profile* (Oxford: Oxford University Press, 1989), 170.
20. Bernhard Huldermann, *Albert Ballin* (London: Cassell, 1922), 12–5; Lamar Cecil, *Albert Ballin: Business and Politics in Imperial Germany 1888–1918* (Princeton, NJ: Princeton University Press, 1967), 19–20.
21. Huldermann, *Albert Ballin*, 70–72; Bernhard Karlsberg, *History and Importance of the German Control of Emigrants in Transit* (Hamburg: Gebrüder Enoch, 1922); Michael Just, *Ost- und südosteuropäische Amerikawanderung: 1881–1914. Transitprobleme in Deutschland und Aufnahme in den Vereinigten Staaten* (Stuttgart: Steiner, 1988),

23–27; Birgit Ottmüller-Wetzel, "Auswanderung über Hamburg: Die HAPAG und die Auswanderung nach Nordamerika 1870–1914" (PhD diss., Free University Berlin, 1986), 99–101; Wertheimer, *Unwelcome Strangers*, 75–119.
22. Hans Rogger, "Tsarist Policy on Jewish Emigration," *Soviet Jewish Affairs* 3, no. 1 (1973): 26–36; Eric Lohr, *Russian Citizenship: From Empire to Soviet Union* (Cambridge, MA: Harvard University Press, 2012), 83–114; Zahra, *Great Departure*, 30, 38. For a biased and flawed account whose author depicts steamship lines and ticket agents as "villains" based on an uncritical reading of official sources, see Martin Pollack, *Der Kaiser von America: Die Große Flucht aus Galizien* (Vienna: Paul Zsolnay, 2010).
23. *The Statutes at Large of the United States of America, Dec. 1881 to March 1883* (Washington, D.C.: GPO, 1883), 22:214–215 (47th Congress, Session I, Ch. 376, August 3, 1882); Tichenor: *Dividing Lines*, 69; McKeown, *Melancholy Order*, 107–112.
24. Vincent Cannato, *American Passage: A History of Ellis Island* (New York: HarperCollins, 2009), 42–49; Tony Kushner, "The Boys and Girls Not from Brazil: From Russia to Rio and Back Again via Southampton and Hamburg, 1878–1880," in Brinkmann, *Points of Passage*, 148–162.
25. Prussian Minister of the Interior and Prussian Minister of Trade and Commerce to Count Bismarck, July 21, 1885, Geheimes Staatsarchiv Berlin, Preußisches Ministerium für Handel und Gewerbe, Bestimmungen zum Schutze und zur Fürsorge für die Auswanderung und Kolonisation, XIII, 20, 1, vol. 13, [GeSta Berlin Auswanderung und Kolonisation]; *Hamburger Correspondent*, September 4, 1885; Karlsberg, *German Control of Emigrants*, 10–44, esp. 25.
26. Leiserowitz, *Sabbatleuchter*, 238; Ulrich Herbert, *Geschichte der Ausländerpolitik in Deutschland* (Munich: C. H. Beck, 2001), 14–44; Comitee zur Unterstützung der Ausgewiesenen, 1885, CAHJP, Königsberg Collection, D/Ko1/580.
27. Albert Ballin to Hamburg Emigration Authority, April 29, 1887; Report, Hanseatic Embassy, Berlin, July 6, 1887, Auswanderungsamt HH, Grenzkontrollstationen und Registrierstationen, II E I 1; Karlsberg, *German Control of Emigrants*, 32; Herbert, *Geschichte der Ausländerpolitik*, 14–44.
28. Richard Evans, *Death in Hamburg: Society and Politics in the Cholera Years 1830–1910* (Oxford: Oxford University Press, 1987), 279–284; Howard Markel, *Quarantine! East European Jewish Immigrants and the New York City Epidemics of 1892* (Baltimore: Johns Hopkins University Press, 1997), 15–59, 85–134.
29. Ballin to Senator Dr. Hachmann, May 30, 1894; Memo Prussian Minister of the Interior, Berlin September 18, 1894, Auswanderungsamt HH, Grenzsperre, II E I 1a 7; Red Star Line to Regierung Oppeln (Silesia), July 27, 1898, GeSta Berlin Auswanderung und Kolonisation, XIII, 20, 1, vol. 16; Ambassador Buchanan (Britain) to Baron v. Richthofen, December 18, 1903, GeSta Berlin Auswanderung und Kolonisation, XIII, 20, 1, vol. 16; Ambassador Austria-Hungary to Auswärtiges Amt, November 24, 1906, GeSta Berlin Auswanderung und Kolonisation, XIII, 20, 1, vol. 17.
30. *Annual Report of the Commissioner General of Immigration for the Fiscal Year Ended June 30th 1894* (Washington, D.C.: GPO, 1894), 13–14; McKeown, *Melancholy*

Order, 112; Zolberg, "The Great Wall against China"; Dorothee Schneider, *Crossing Borders: Migration and Citizenship in the Twentieth-Century United States* (Cambridge, MA: Harvard University Press, 2011), 89–90; "Immigration through Canada," *New York Times*, September 10, 1894.

31. Bernhard Kahn, "Der jüdische Auswanderer in Deutschland," *Jüdische Presse* (Berlin), October 6, 1905.
32. Eduard Rosenbaum, "Albert Ballin: A Note on the Style of His Economic and Political Activities," *Leo Baeck Institute Yearbook* 3 (1958): 257–299; Eberhard Straub, *Albert Ballin: Der Reeder des Kaisers* (Berlin: Siedler, 2001), 153–156.
33. Chaim Weizmann, *Trial and Error: The Autobiography of Chaim Weizmann* (New York: Harper, 1949), 183–184; Alroey, *Bread to Eat*, 55–57.
34. Straub, *Ballin*, 153–156; Lars Amenda, *China in Hamburg* (Hamburg: Ellert & Richter, 2011); Sebastian Conrad, *Globalisierung und Nation im Deutschen Kaiserreich* (Munich: C. H. Beck, 2006), 206–212; Michael Grüttner, *Arbeitswelt an der Wasserkante: Sozialgeschichte der Hamburger Hafenarbeiter 1886–1914* (Göttingen: Vandenhoeck & Ruprecht, 1984); "The Lonely and Dangerous Life of the Filipino Seafarer," *New York Times*, November 13, 2019; Yves Boquet, *The Philippine Archipelago* (Cham, Switzerland: Springer, 2017), 367–404.
35. For an excellent discussion about the mobility concept, see Valeska Huber, *Channelling Mobilities: Migration and Globalisation in the Suez Canal Region and Beyond, 1869–1914* (Cambridge: Cambridge University Press, 2013), 1–30; Valeska Huber, "Multiple Mobilities: Über den Umgang mit verschiedenen Mobilitätsformen um 1900," *Geschichte und Gesellschaft* 36, no. 2 (2010): 317–341; *Berlin und seine Eisenbahnen 1846–1896* (Berlin: Julius Springer, 1896), 1:52–3, 2:402.
36. "Von Berlin nach Konstantinopel," *Zeitung des Vereins Deutscher Eisenbahn-Verwaltungen* (Berlin), August 22, 1900.

Chapter 4

1. Sammy Gronemann, *Erinnerungen* (1947; Berlin: Philo, 2002), 294–297.
2. Dziedzice, 10. Bericht, August 3, 1891, Auswanderungsamt HH, Registrier- und Kontrollstationen, II E I 1b Beiheft 1; Kukushkin, *From Peasants to Labourers*, 49–54.
3. Besichtigung der Auswandererkontrollstationen an der russischen Grenze (Myslowitz, May 4 1906), Staatsarchiv Bremen, Auswanderung 3-A., 4,21–506; "Legitimationskarte" for Hersch C. from Jassy, Ratibor, June 14, 1901, Auswanderungsamt HH, Israelitischer Unterstützungsverein für Obdachlose, II E III 23; "Moderne Auswanderer," *Berliner Illustrirte Zeitung* 39 (1900): 612; Elisabeth Janik-Freis, "Grenzregime am Dreikaisereck: Galizische Auswanderung in die Amerikas," in *Galizien in Bewegung: Wahrnehmungen—Begegnungen—Verflechtungen*, eds. Magdalena Baran-Szołtys, Olena Dvoretska, Nino Gude, and Elisabeth Janik-Freis. (Vienna: V&R Unipress, 2018), 171–185.
4. Mary Antin, *From Plotzk to Boston*, foreword by Israel Zangwill (Boston: W. B. Clarke, 1899), 41–43.

5. Evans, *Death in Hamburg*, 279–284; Markel, *Quarantine*, 28–74; Programm zur Einweihung der Synagoge, September 3, 1896, Auswanderungsamt HH, Synagoge, I II E III P 27 (2–3).
6. Antin, *From Plotzk to Boston*, 51.
7. Walter Sthamer, *Die Auswanderer-Hallen in Hamburg* (Hamburg: HAPAG, 1900); Letter Plettenberg, Abt. Zwischendeckpassage, Norddeutscher Lloyd to Gesundheitsrat Tjaden, June 7, 1910, Staatsarchiv Bremen, Auswanderung 3-A, 4,21–507, vol. 1; Shulamit Volkov, "Antisemitism as a Cultural Code: Reflections on the History and Historiography of Antisemitism in Imperial Germany," *Leo Baeck Institute Year Book* 23, no. 1 (1978): 25–46.
8. *Vorwärts* (Berlin), December 23, 1904 ("Unterwegs mit Ballin"); Eydtkuhnen, 12. Bericht, October 1, 1895, Auswanderungsamt HH, Beiheft 1, Registrier- und Kontrollstationen, Dienstreisen, Reiseberichte, II E I 1b; "Der Redakteur des Vorwärts, Julius Kaliski," December 1904, Auswanderungsamt Hamburg, II E III P 45.
9. Deborah Dwork and Robert Jan van Pelt, *Auschwitz. 1270 to the Present* (New York: Norton, 1996), 53–54.
10. Paul Weindling, *Epidemics and Genocide in Eastern Europe 1890–1945* (Oxford: Oxford University Press, 2000), 69–71; Wertheimer, *Unwelcome Strangers*, 50–51; Howe, *World of Our Fathers*, 37; Huber, *Channelling Mobilities*, 245–263; Ulrike Freitag, *A History of Jeddah: The Gate to Mecca in the Nineteenth and Twentieth Centuries* (Cambridge: Cambridge University Press, 2020); Alexandra Minna Stern, "Buildings, Boundaries, and Blood: Medicalization and Nation-Building on the U.S.-Mexico Border, 1910–1930," *Hispanic American Historical Review* 79, no. 1 (1999): 41–81; Lewis H. Siegelbaum and Leslie Page Moch, *Broad Is My Native Land: Repertoires and Regimes of Migration in Russia's Twentieth Century* (Ithaca, NY: Cornell University Press, 2015), 38; Markel, *Quarantine*; Amy L. Fairchild, *Science at the Borders: Immigrant Medical Inspection and the Shaping of the Modern Industrial Labor Force* (Baltimore: Johns Hopkins University Press, 2003), 57–58; Fiorello La Guardia, *The Making of an Insurgent: An Autobiography, 1882–1919* (Philadelphia: J. B. Lippincott, 1948), 54–61.
11. "Der Redakteur des Vorwärts, Julius Kaliski," December 1904, Auswanderungsamt Hamburg, II E III P 45.
12. See Unglücksfälle von Auswanderern auf der Eisenbahn, Auswanderungsamt Hamburg, I E I 3, vol. 1; *Berliner Lokalanzeiger*, August 2, 1910.
13. "Thrilling Story of Rescue," *New York Times*, October 12, 1913; Milstein's report to HIAS: "The Volturno Disaster," *American Hebrew and Messenger* (New York), October 17, 1913; "Volturno Disaster," *Morning Chronicle* (Halifax, NS), October 13, 1913; "Charter of Canadian Northern Steamships Limited," October 21, 1909, Library and Archives Canada, Ottawa, Canadian Northern Railway (CNR), Deposit No. 56, Secretary's Office, RG 30, Vol. 10258.
14. Zosa Szajkowski, "Sufferings of Jewish Emigrants to America in Transit through Germany," *Jewish Social Studies* 39, nos. 1–2 (1977): 105–116; Alroey, *An Unpromising Land*, 134–141; Gur Alroey, "Bureaucracy, Agents and Swindlers: Hardships Faced by

Russian Jewish Emigrants in the Early Twentieth Century," *Studies in Contemporary Jewry* 19 (2003): 214–231; Howe, *World of Our Fathers*, 39, 52.

15. Benton-Cohen, *Inventing the Immigration Problem*, 148–151; Schneider, *Crossing Borders*, 29–31; Georg Halpern, "Bade bei Ballin," *Freistatt, Süddeutsche Zeitschrift fuer Politik, Literatur und Kunst* (Munich), October 8, 1904. For sensationalistic undercover reportage of the steerage journey, see "Steerage to Canada—The Truth about the Horrors of Emigration to the 'Land of Promise,'" *Reynold's Newspaper* (London), September 18 and 25, 1910; HAPAG to Behörde für Auswanderungswesen Hamburg, November 30, 1907 (includes report by Kiliszewki, November 28, 1907), Auswanderungsamt HH, Registrier- und Kontrollstationen, II E I 1b Beiheft 2; see also "Misshandlung russischer und galizischer Auswanderer," *Berliner Tageblatt*, May 27, 1907 (a doctor employed by NDL denounced a police official who had beaten migrants). For an account of a clandestine journey to Russia in 1906 on behalf of the U.S. immigration commissioner, see Cowen, *Memories of an American Jew*, 189–253. For an investigative report by a declared supporter of immigration restrictions, see Broughton Brandenberg, *Imported Americans: The Story of the Experiences of a Disguised American and His Wife Studying the Immigration Question* (New York: Frederick A. Stokes, 1904); Louis Anthes, *Lawyers and Immigrants, 1870–1914: A Cultural History* (El Paso, TX: LFB Scholarly Publishing, 2003), 59–66.

16. Jakob Lestschinsky, "Die jüdische Wanderung, ihre Ursachen und ihre Regelung (1. Fortsetzung)," *Archiv für Wanderungswesen und Auslandskunde* 1, no. 4 (1929): 168–172.

17. Daniel Soyer, *Jewish Immigrant Associations and American Identity in New York 1880–1939* (Cambridge, MA: Harvard University Press, 1997); Stampfer, "The Geographic Background."

18. Senat to Polizeibehörde, May 28 and November 7, 1900, Auswanderungsamt HH, Rumänische Juden, II E III P 28; "Ein Wort zur Auswanderungsfrage rumänischer Juden," *Die Neuzeit* (Vienna), June 22, 1900; "Berlin, Aufgepaßt!" Staatsbürger-Zeitung (Berlin), April 25, 1900.

19. Abraham Cahan, "The Rumanian Exodus" (1900), in *Grandma Never Lived in America: The New Journalism of Abraham Cahan*, ed. Moses Rischin (Bloomington: Indiana University Press, 1985), 129–132; *Sechster Geschäftsbericht (1907) des Hilfsvereins der Deutschen Juden* (Berlin: Privately published, 1907), 77–92.

20. Königsberg, 2. Bericht, July 22, 1891, Auswanderungsamt HH, Registrier- und Kontrollstationen, II E I 1b Beiheft 1; Boris Bogen, *Born a Jew* (New York: Macmillan, 1930), 31; Kukushkin, *From Peasants to Laborers*, 49–54.

21. Eydtkuhnen, 12. Bericht, October 1, 1895, Auswanderungsamt HH, Registrier- und Kontrollstationen, II E I 1b Beiheft 1; William C. Fuller, *The Foe Within: Fantasies of Treason and the End of Imperial Russia* (Ithaca, NY: Cornell University Press, 2006), 13–25; Lohr, *Russian Citizenship*, 95.

22. U.S. Senate, *Emigration Conditions in Europe*, 61–67; Zahra, *Great Departure*, 23–63.

23. Pollack, *Kaiser von Amerika*; Eugene M. Avrutin, *Jews and the Imperial State: Identification Politics in Tsarist Russia* (Ithaca, NY: Cornell University Press,

2012), 138–140; Ivan Light, "The Migration Industry in the United States, 1882–1924," *Migration Studies* 1, no. 3 (2013): 258–275, see esp. 262.
24. Zahra, *Great Departure*, 23–63.
25. Nordamerika, March 31–April 2, 1914, No. 495, Austrian State Archive, Vienna [OeStA/AVA], Justiz JM Allgemein Sig 6 VZ 18, carton 3326; *Bericht über die vorläufigen Ergebnisse des vom k.k. Handelsministerium durchgeführten Untersuchung über die Organisation der Auswanderung in Österreich* (Vienna: Hof- und Staatsdruckerei, 1913), 4; Kuzmany, *Brody*, 253–258.
26. Bogen, *Born a Jew*, 31–32; Nicholas Evans, "Aliens en Route: European Transmigration through Britain 1836–1914" (PhD diss., University of Hull, 2006), 120–133.
27. "Personenwagen für Auswanderer," *Organ für die Fortschritte des Eisenbahnwesens* 23 (1886): 37; "Ein Auswandererzug in Berlin," *Vom Fels zum Meer: Spemans Illustrierte Zeitschrift für das Deutsche Haus* (Stuttgart), 1889: 286–288; *Spandauer Anzeiger für das Havelland*, October 15, 1882 ("disorder"), November 8, 1882 ("fisticuff"); *Centralblatt der Bauverwaltung* (Berlin), April 8, 1893: 142; Hamburg Polizeibehörde, Abt. IV, May 13, 1905, Auswanderungsamt HH, Überwachung des Rückwandererverkehrs, II B I 3; Ratibor, 3. Bericht, November 4, 1905, Auswanderungsamt HH, Registrier- und Kontrollstationen, II E I 1b Beiheft 1.
28. Leipzig, 14. Bericht, November 15, 1905, Auswanderungsamt HH, Registrier- und Kontrollstationen, Dienstreisen, Reiseberichte, II E I 1b Beiheft 2.
29. Markian Prokopovych, "Urban History of Overseas Migration in Habsburg Central Europe: Vienna and Budapest in the Late Nineteenth Century," *Journal of Migration History* 2, no. 2 (2016): 330–351. For a detailed list of instructions for migrants traveling from Galicia and Hungary to Rotterdam via Vienna, see *Reiseführer für Zwischendeck-Reisende aus Ungarn und Galizien nach Nordamerika über Rotterdam mittelst der Holland-Amerika-Linie* (Vienna: Holland-Amerika-Line, 1897), 41–60.
30. "Bigger Penna. Station," *New York Times*, February 11, 1907; Jill Jonnes, *Conquering Gotham: Building Penn Station and Its Tunnels* (New York: Viking, 2007).
31. "Chinese Exclusion Urged," *New York Times*, January 26, 1902; "Konzession der Canadian Pacific," *Neue Freie Presse*, December 2, 1913; Gordon H. Chang and Shelley Fisher Fishkin, eds., *The Chinese and the Iron Road: Building the Transcontinental Railroad* (Stanford: Stanford University Press, 2019); Ninette Kelley and Michael Trebilcock, *The Making of the Mosaic: A History of Canadian Immigration Policy* (Toronto: University of Toronto Press, 1998), 63; *Bericht über Auswanderung in Österreich*, 18–22; McKeown, *Melancholy Order*, 200; "Nordamerika," April 21–23, 1914, No. 521, OeStA/AVA, Justiz JM Allgemein Sig 6 VZ 18, carton 3326.
32. Sarna, "The Myth of No Return"; *HIAS Annual Report 1913* (New York: Privately published, 1914), 9; Trautmann (German Embassy, St. Petersburg) to Bethmann Hollweg (Reich Chancellor), May 15, 1911, Auswanderungsamt HH, Auswanderung aus Russland, II C I 8; Seth Lipsky, *The Rise of Abraham Cahan* (New York: Schocken, 2013), 51–54.
33. Abraham Cahan, *Yekl: A Tale of the New York Ghetto* (New York: D. Appleton, 1896).
34. Israel Zangwill, foreword, in Antin, *From Plotzk to Boston*, 7; Israel Zangwill, *Children of the Ghetto: Being Pictures of a Peculiar People* (Philadelphia: Jewish Publication

Society, 1892); Israel Zangwill, *The Melting-Pot* (New York: Macmillan, 1909); Steven J. Zipperstein, *Pogrom: Kishinev and the Tilt of History* (New York: Norton, 2018), 204.
35. Charles Zeublin, "The Chicago Ghetto," in *Hull House Maps and Papers: A Presentation of Nationalities and Wages in a Congested District of Chicago*, ed. Residents of Hull House (New York: Thomas Crowell, 1895), 91–114; Ewa Morawska, *For Bread with Butter: Life-Worlds of East Central Europeans in Johnstown, Pennsylvania* (Cambridge: Cambridge University Press, 1985); Kukushkin, *From Peasants to Labourers*; Kathryn Sklar Kish, "Hull House Maps and Papers: Social Science as Women's Work in the 1890s," in *The Social Survey in Historical Perspective 1880–1940*, ed. Martin Bulmer, Kevin Bales, and Kathryn Sklar Kish (Cambridge: Cambridge University Press, 1991), 111–147; Charles Seligman Bernheimer, ed., *The Russian Jew in the United States* (Philadelphia: John C. Winston, 1905), 26.
36. Jacob Leschtchynski [Lestschinsky], "Unsere Emigranten," *Israelitisches Familienblatt* (Hamburg), January 15 and 22, 1914. See also Jacob Lestschinsky, "Hashkafot Kalkaliot," *Ha-Olam*, January 12, 1912 [Hebrew]. For background on Lestschinsky, see Estraikh, "Jacob Lestschinsky," 215–237; Jacob Lestschinsky, Petition for Naturalization, Petition no. 21042, November 21, 1958, Florida Naturalization Records, 1880–1991, Records of the District Courts of the United States, 1685–2004, Record Group 21, National Archives, Atlanta, Georgia.
37. Liebmann Hersch, "International Migration of the Jews," in *International Migrations*, ed. Walter Willcox (New York: National Bureau of Economic Research, 1931), 2:471–521; Wertheimer, *Unwelcome Strangers*, 162–175.
38. Leschtchynski [Lestschinsky], "Unsere Emigranten."
39. Leschtchynski [Lestschinsky], "Unsere Emigranten."
40. Leschtchynski [Lestschinsky], "Unsere Emigranten."
41. Leschtchynski [Lestschinsky], "Unsere Emigranten."

Chapter 5

1. Antin, *From Plotzk to Boston*, 22–35, quote on 26; Esther Antin (and children), Ship Manifest, SS Polynesia, Hamburg, April 21, 1894, Auswanderungsamt HH, Hamburger Passagierlisten, VIII A 1, Band 087 B, Page 254, Microfilm No. K 1751.
2. Antin, *From Plotzk to Boston*, 27–35; Marthi Pritzker-Ehrlich, *Gestörte Bürgerlichkeit: Zeugnisse einer jüdisch-christlichen Familie in Briefen, Dokumenten und Bildern* (Brugg, Switzerland: Munda, 2007), 1:17, 64.
3. *3. Geschäftsbericht (1904) des Hilfsvereins der Deutschen Juden* (Berlin: Privately published, 1905), 38–39; Mark Wischnitzer, *Visas to Freedom: The History of HIAS* (Cleveland, OH: World Publishing, 1955), 35–74; Thomas M. Pitkin, *Keepers of the Gate: A History of Ellis Island* (New York: NYU Press, 1975), 45; Faith Rogow, *Gone to Another Meeting: The National Council of Jewish Women 1893–1993* (Tuscaloosa: University of Alabama Press, 1993), 130–165.
4. *HIAS Annual Report 1913*, 22–23.
5. Pitkin, *Keepers of the Gate*, 53–58; Zahra, *Great Departure*, 6–9.

6. Torsten Feys, *The Battle for the Migrants: Introduction of Steamshipping on the North Atlantic and Its Impact on the European Exodus* (St. John's: International Maritime Economic Association, 2013), 175; Memorandum, Hamburger Polizeibehörde, April 18, 1899, Auswanderungsamt HH, Israelitischer Unterstützungsverein für Obdachlose, II E III P 23; McKeown, *Melancholy Order*, 110.

7. Deutsches Central-Komitee für die Russischen Juden, *Instructionen für die Beförderung*, January 1892, CAHJP, Danzig Collection, Da/552; List with profiles of wandering beggars, Danzig Gemeinde, 1900–1909, CAHJP, Danzig Collection, Da/920; Penslar, *Shylock's Children*, 203; *25th Annual Report of the United Hebrew Relief Association of Chicago 1883/84* (Chicago: Privately published, 1884); *Chicago Occident*, July 2, 1886.

8. *Vorwärts*, May 1, 1905; Hermann Elösser, "Chronik der Synagogengemeinde Insterburg" (handwritten ms., 1905), 42, CAHJP, Insterburg Collection, D/In1/13; Bericht Vogel, Auswandererhallen, November 19, 1907, Auswanderungsamt HH, Rückwanderung Mittellose, II E III P 34.

9. Board of Guardians (London) to Hamburg Auswandererbehörde, August 10, 1897, Auswanderungsamt HH, Israelitischer Unterstützungsverein fuer Obdachlose, II E III P 23; Reena Sigman Friedman, "'Send Me My Husband Who Is in New York City': Husband Desertion in the American Jewish Immigrant Community 1900–1926," *Jewish Social Studies* 44, no. 1 (1982): 1–18.

10. Lloyd P. Gartner, "Anglo-Jewry and the Jewish International Traffic in Prostitution, 1885–1914," *AJS Review*, nos. 7–8 (1982–1983): 129–178; Elizabeth Loentz, *Let Me Continue to Speak the Truth: Bertha Pappenheim as Author and Activist* (Cincinnati, OH: HUC Press, 2007), 123–156; Benton-Cohen, *Inventing the Immigration Problem*, 151–158. A biased contemporary account is Clifford Griffith Roe, *Horrors of the White Slave Trade: The Mighty Crusade to Protect the Purity of Our Homes* (London: Privately published, 1911), 102.

11. U.S. Senate, *Emigration Conditions in Europe*, 271–336, see also 56, 65; *The Statutes at Large of the United States of America, Dec. 1889 to March 1891* (Washington, D.C.: GPO, 1891), 26:1084 (51st Congress, Session II, Ch. 551, March 3, 1891); Paul Laskar, *Über, Aus- und Rückwanderung; Erster Bericht des Deutschen Central-Komitee für die Russischen Juden* (Berlin: Privately published, July 1891), 14; Königliche preußische Gesandtschaft to Bürgermeister Hamburg, March 16, 1911, Auswanderungsamt HH, II B I 3, Überwachung des Rückwanderwandererverkehrs über Hamburg durch die Polizeibeh. 1902/03—1918; "Landverhuizersverkeer door Pruisen," *Nieuwe Rotterdamsche Courant*, February 25, 1911 (evening edition); "Landverhuizers," *Rotterdamsch Nieuwsblad*, February 28, 1911; E. M. J. van Schip, "Montefiore Vereeniging tot ondersteuning van behoeftige passanten: Een onderzoek naar het functioneren in de periode van 1883 tot 1914," *Rotterdams Jaarboekje* 4 (1996): 389–453.

12. Penslar, *Shylock's Children*, 199, 202, 241.

13. Penslar, *Shylock's Children*, 198; *Berliner Tageblatt*, May 27 and 31, 1891; Deutsches Central-Komitee für die Russischen Juden, *Erster Bericht* (Berlin: Hermann, 1891); *Erster Bericht des ständigen Hülfscomites für die Notstände Russischer Israeliten*

(Memel: Privately published, 1891); Instructionen für die Beförderung, Deutsches Central-Komitee für die Russischen Juden [DCKfRJ] January 1892; Letter DCKRJ to Danzig Committee, January 22, 1895, CAHJP, Russische Juden, Danzig Collection, Da/552. On Hamburg committee, see Laskar, *Über, Aus- und Rückwanderung*. On Eydtkuhnen committee, see Elösser, *Chronik der Synagogengemeinde Insterburg*, CAHJP, Insterburg Collection, D/In1/13.

14. Pulzer, *Rise of Political Anti-Semitism*, 111–119.
15. Wertheimer, *Unwelcome Strangers*, 32–33, Avraham Barkai, *"Wehr dich!" Der Centralverein deutscher Staatsbürger jüdischen Glaubens (C.V.) 1893–1938* (Munich: C. H. Beck, 2002).
16. *Jüdisches Volksblatt* (Breslau), November 8, 1901; *Israelitisches Familienblatt*, November 18, 1901; Ottmüller-Wetzel, *Auswanderung über Hamburg*, 125–129.
17. *1. Geschäftsbericht (1901–1902) des Hilfsvereins der deutschen Juden* (Berlin: Privately published, 1902), 6; Christoph Jahr, *Paul Nathan: Publizist, Politiker und Philanthrop 1857–1927* (Göttingen: Wallstein, 2018), 104, 178.
18. Wischnitzer, *Visas to Freedom*, 35–74; HIAS, *Third Annual Report 1911* (New York: Privately published, 1911), 49–54; Naomi W. Cohen, *Not Free to Desist: The American Jewish Committee, 1906–1966* (Philadelphia: Jewish Publication Society, 1972).
19. Drew Keeling, *The Business of Migration between Europe and the United States, 1900–1914* (Zurich: Chronos, 2012), 33–142.
20. *Annual Report of the Commissioner-General of Immigration for the Fiscal Year Ended June 30th, 1902* (Washington, D.C.: GPO, 1902), 4; *Annual Report of the Commissioner-General of Immigration for the Fiscal Year Ended June 30th, 1903* (Washington, D.C.: GPO, 1903), 1–7; Choate, *Emigrant Nation*, 21–56.
21. Keeling, *Business of Migration*, 61–105; Feys, *The Battle for the Migrants*, 163–210; Erich Murken, *Die großen transatlantischen Linienreederei-Verbände, Pools und Interessengemeinschaften bis zum Ausbruch des Weltkrieges. Ihre Entstehung, Organisation und Wirksamkeit* (Jena: G. Fischer, 1922), 24–60; Zahra, *Great Departure*, 30, 38.
22. *The Times* (London), April 14, May 16, and May 23, 1904.
23. Keeling, *Business of Migration*, 107–142; Henry Diederich, "Emigration to the United States via Bremen," *Monthly Consular Reports*, no. 295 (April 1905): 42–48.
24. *Protokoll über die Verhandlungen des Parteitages der Sozialdemokratischen Partei Deutschlands, Abgehalten zu Bremen* (Berlin: Vorwärts, 1904), 137, 322–324; *Israelitisches Familienblatt*, September 29, 1904; *Vorwärts*, August 3 and 30, December 1, 1904.
25. *Jahresbericht der HAPAG, Achtundfünfzigstes Geschäftsjahr 1904* (Hamburg: Persiehl, 1905); Murken, *Linienreederei-Verbände*, 278.
26. Lamar Cecil, "Coal for the Fleet That Had to Die," *American Historical Review* 69, no. 4 (1964): 990–1005.
27. Naomi W. Cohen, *Jacob Schiff: A Study in American Jewish Leadership* (Hanover, NH: Brandeis University Press), 33–34, 134–137.

28. *3. Geschäftsbericht (1904) des Hilfsvereins der Deutschen Juden*, 20–32; *Berliner Tageblatt*, September 27, October 4, 8, and 28, 1904; *Vorwärts*, November 30, 1904; *AZ*, October 7, 1904; *Israelitisches Familienblatt*, October 6, 13, and 27, 1904; Karlsberg, *German Control of Emigrants*, 111–114.
29. Cecil, "Coal for the Fleet That Had to Die," 996; *North Sea Incident (21–22 October, 1904) Reports Thereon by the Commissioners Appointed by the Board of Trade* (London: Wyman & Sons, 1905).
30. *Berliner Zeitung*, October 28, 1904; Karlsberg, *German Control of Emigrants*, 116–119; Murken, *Linienreederei-Verbände*, 268–281; *New York Times*, November 13 and 14, 1904.
31. Murken, *Linienreederei-Verbände*, 278–325; Diederich, "Emigration to the United States via Bremen," 46; Cohen, *Jacob H. Schiff*, 134–137.
32. Keeling, *Business of Migration*, 63–64.
33. Wischnitzer, *To Dwell in Safety*, 99–105; Deirdre M. Moloney, *American Catholic Lay Groups and Transatlantic Social Reform in the Progressive Era* (Chapel Hill: UNC Press, 2003), 100–102.
34. *Bulletin de L'Alliance Israelite Universelle, 1907* (Paris: Privately published, 1907), 9–104; *3. Geschäftsbericht (1904) des Hilfsvereins der Deutschen Juden*, 20–31; *Sechster Geschäftsbericht (1907) des Hilfsvereins der Deutschen Juden* (Berlin: Privately published, 1907), 121; *Korrespondenzblatt des Centralbureaus für jüdische Auswanderungsangelegenheiten*, July 15, 1906, September 23, 1909; Ron Chernow, *The Warburgs: The Twentieth Century Odyssey of a Remarkable Jewish Family* (New York: Vintage Books, 1994).
35. Tobias Brinkmann, "The Road from Damascus: Transnational Jewish Philanthropic Organizations and the Jewish Mass Migration from Eastern Europe 1860–1914," in *Shaping the Transnational Sphere: Experts, Networks, and Issues from the 1840s to the 1930s*, ed. Davide Rodogno, Jakob Vogel, and Bernhard Struck (New York: Berghahn Books, 2015), 152–172; Gartner, "Anglo-Jewry and the Jewish International Traffic in Prostitution."
36. Jahr, *Nathan*, 175–176, 198–199; Biographische Notizen, LBI—New York, Bernhard Kahn Papers, AR 416, Box 2, Folder 11; C. Jacobowsky, "Bernhard Kahn," *Nordisk Judaistik/Scandinavian Jewish Studies* 3, no. 1 (1979): 21–31; *Festschrift anlässlich der Feier des 25jährigen Bestehens des Hilfsvereins der Deutschen Juden, gegr. am 28. Mai 1901* (Berlin: Marx & Co., 1926); Cowen, *Memories of an American Jew*, 252; *Korrespondenzblatt des "Centralbureaus für jüdische Auswanderungsangelegenheiten,"* September 23, 1909; Tobias Brinkmann, "Why Paul Nathan Attacked Albert Ballin: The Transatlantic Mass Migration and the Privatization of Prussia's Eastern Border Inspection, 1886–1914," *Central European History* 43, no. 1 (2010): 47–83.
37. *Vierter Geschäftsbericht (1905) des Hilfsvereins der deutschen Juden* (Berlin: Privately published, 1906), 78–79; Jahr, *Nathan*, 175; *Die Neuzeit* (Vienna), June 22, 1900; McKeown, *Melancholy Order*.
38. *American Jewish Yearbook* 8 (1906–1907), 34–89 ("From Kishineff to Bialystok"); Bernhard Kahn, "Die jüdische Auswanderung."

39. Hannah Ewence, *The Alien Jew in the British Imagination 1881–1905* (London: Palgrave, 2019); Bernard Gainer, *The Alien Invasion: The Origins of the Aliens Act of 1905* (London: Pearson, 1972); *AZ*, April 13, 1906 (about sixty-five hundred Jews were deported from Berlin); Wertheimer, *Unwelcome Strangers*, 61.

40. Cowen, *Memories of an American Jew*, 243–245; *Neunter Geschäftsbericht (1910) des Hilfsvereins der deutschen Juden* (Berlin: Privately published, 1911), 140; Edmund J. James, Oscar R. Flynn, J. R. Paulding, Charlotte Kimball, and Walter Scott Andrews, *The Immigrant Jew in America* (New York: B. F. Buck, 1906); Maddalena Marinari, *The Unwanted: Italian and Jewish Mobilization against Restrictive Immigration Laws 1882–1965* (Chapel Hill: University of North Carolina Press, 2020), 24–26; Jack Glazier, *Dispersing the Ghetto: The Relocation of Jewish Immigrants across America* (Ithaca, NY: Cornell University Press, 1998); *Sechster Geschäftsbericht (1907) des Hilfsvereins der deutschen Juden* (Berlin: Privately published, 1908), 106.

41. *The Two Hundred and Fiftieth Anniversary of the Settlement of the Jews in the United States* (New York: New York Co-Operative Society, 1905), 146–147; John Higham, *Send These to Me: Immigrants in Urban America*, revised edition (Baltimore: Johns Hopkins University Press, 1984), 71–80 (Lazarus's poem is quoted on 70).

42. Goldstein, *The Price of Whiteness*, 96–97, 103–108; U.S. Senate, *Chinese Exclusion: Testimony Taken before the Committee on Immigration* (Washington, D.C.: GPO, 1902), 398, 427; "Simon Wolf at 84 Years," *New York Times*, October 23, 1921.

43. Goldstein, *The Price of Whiteness*, 96–97, 103–108; Leon Huhner, "Max James Kohler," *Publications of the American Jewish Historical Society* 34 (1937): 295–301; Max J. Kohler, "Un-American character of Race Legislation," *Annals of the American Academy of Political and Social Science* 34, no. 2 (1909): 275–291, quote on 283; Wolf quoted in Benton-Cohen, *Inventing the Immigration Problem*, 102; Joel Perlmann, *America Classifies the Immigrants: From Ellis Island to the 2020 Census* (Cambridge, MA: Harvard University Press, 2018), 109–132; Marinari, *The Unwanted*, 14–36.

Chapter 6

1. *Hilfsverein Jahresbericht für 1929* (Berlin: Hilfsverein der Deutschen Juden, 1930), 24; *American Israelite* (Cincinnati), August 31, 1922. See also "Jews Fleeing from Russia," *New York Times*, March 10, 1921.

2. *Hilfsverein Jahresbericht für 1929*, 24; "7.100 Aliens Stranded," *New York Times*, December 19, 1924.

3. Undated HIAS Report (c. 1924), CZA, Leo Motzkin Papers, A126/705; Samuel Altman, *Geschichte der Wanderung: Verfasst für die Royal Mail Steam Packet Company* (Vienna: Hermes, 1924), 270–272.

4. *Hilfsverein Jahresbericht für 1928* (Berlin: Hilfsverein der Deutschen Juden, 1929), 30; *Hilfsverein Jahresbericht für 1929*, 24; *American Jewish Yearbook* 30 (1928–1929): 259; "Backs Smith on Aliens," *New York Times*, August 26, 1928; Ruppin, *Soziologie der Juden*, 1:138.

5. Wyman, *Paper Walls*.
6. Raymond J. Sontag, *A Broken World 1919–1939* (New York: Harper & Row, 1971).
7. Matthew Stibbe, "Civilian Internment and Civilian Internees in Europe, 1914–1920," *Immigrants and Minorities* 26, nos. 1–2 (2008): 49–81; Daniela L. Caglioti, *War and Citizenship: Enemy Aliens and National Belonging from the French Revolution to the First World War* (Cambridge: Cambridge University Press, 2021); Bohdan S. Kordan, *No Free Man: Canada, the Great War, and the Enemy Alien Experience* (Montreal: McGill-Queen's University Press, 2016).
8. Nathan to Schiff, September 11, 1914; Schiff to Nathan, February 16, 1915, AJA, Jacob Schiff Papers, Box 439, Folder 9; London Committee of Deputies of the British Jews, *63rd Annual Report for Tebet, 5675—December 1914* (London: Wertheimer, 1915), 22–25; Caglioti, *War and Citizenship*, 146–147; Evelyn De Roodt, *Oorlogsgasten: Vluchtelingen en Krijgsgevangenen in Nederland Tijdens de Eerste Wereldoorlog* (Zaltbommel: Europese Bibliotheek, 2000), 258–267.
9. David Rechter, *The Jews of Vienna and the First World War* (Oxford: Littman, 2001); Peter Gatrell, *A Whole Empire Walking: Refugees in Russia during World War I* (Bloomington: Indiana University Press, 2005), 12–13, 18, 22–26, 200; Eric Lohr, *Nationalizing the Russian Empire: The Campaign against Enemy Aliens during World War I* (Cambridge, MA: Harvard University Press, 2003), 137–150, 159; Semion Goldin, *The Russian Army and the Jewish Population, 1914–17: Libel, Persecution, Reaction* (Cham, Switzerland: Palgrave, 2022), 109–144; Mark Levene, "The Forty Years' Crisis: The Jewish Dimension," in *Refugees in Europe, 1919–1959: A Forty Years' Crisis?*, ed. Matthew Frank and Jessica Reinisch (London: Bloomsbury Academic, 2017), 85–100; Irina Belova, "'Human Waves': Refugees in Russia, 1914–18," in *Europe on the Move: Refugees in the Era of the Great War*, ed. Peter Gatrell and Liubov Zhvanko (Manchester: Manchester University Press, 2017), 88–107; *American Jewish Yearbook* 18 (1916–1917): 157–158.
10. Henry Morgenthau, *Ambassador Morgenthau's Story* (New York: Doubleday, 1918), 322.
11. Barbara Tuchman, "The Assimilationist Dilemma: Ambassador Morgenthau's Story," in *Practicing History: Selected Essays* (New York: Alfred A. Knopf, 1981), 208–217; Jaclyn Granick, *International Jewish Humanitarianism in the Age of the Great War* (Cambridge: Cambridge University Press, 2021); Yehuda Bauer, *My Brother's Keeper: A History of the American Jewish Joint Distribution Committee 1929–1939* (Philadelphia: Jewish Publication Society, 1974), 3–10; Simon (The Hague) to Hantke (Berlin), October 10, 1917, CZA, Central Zionist Office Berlin, Z3/139.
12. HIAS, *Sixth Annual Report 1914* (New York: Pinski and Massel, 1915); HIAS, *Eighth Annual Report 1916* (New York: Privately published, 1917); "Deportation in Time of War," May 28, 1915, and "Insane Aliens to Remain," *American Hebrew & Jewish Messenger* (New York), July 16, 1915.
13. Wischnitzer, *Visas to Freedom*, 78–88; "Flight of Galician Jews" and "Many Jews Killed during Invasion," *American Hebrew & Jewish Messenger*, December 4, 1914; HIAS, *Ninth Annual Report 1917* (New York: Privately published, 1918); Giuseppe Motta, *The Great War against Eastern European Jewry, 1914–1920* (Cambridge, UK: Cambridge Scholars, 2018), 123–135.

14. Oleg Budnitskii, *Russian Jews between the Reds and the Whites 1917–1920*, trans. Timothy J. Portice (Philadelphia: University of Pennsylvania Press, 2012), 216–274; Jeffrey Veidlinger, *In the Midst of Civilized Europe: The Pogroms of 1918–1921 and the Onset of the Holocaust* (New York: HarperCollins, 2021).
15. Willard Sunderland, *The Baron's Cloak: A History of the Russian Empire in War and Revolution* (Ithaca, NY: Cornell University Press, 2014), 174–176.
16. Lohr, *Nationalizing the Russian Empire*, 137–150; Reichskommissar to Reichsminister des Inneren, November 30, 1920, Staatsarchiv Bremen, Auswanderung 3-A.4, Berichte des Reichskomissars fuer das Auswanderungswesen, No. 438; Leo Motzkin, "Eröffnungsrede," Zweite Jüdische Welthilfskonferenz, Karlsbad, Bulletin No. 4, August 22, 1924, AJA, WJC Records, MS Coll. 361, Box 8, Folder 7.
17. Bogen, *Born a Jew*, 190. For a detailed treatment of Bogen's activities, see Granick, *International Jewish Humanitarianism*.
18. Cecil Gosling to Lord Balfour, January 21, 1919 (position of Jews in Bohemia and Poland), National Archives, Kew, FO 608/16/11; Sir J. Tilley to Sir E. Crowe, September 23, 1919, National Archives, Kew, FO 608/16/12; "Zarenrußland in Wien," *Wiener Morgenzeitung*, October 9, 1920; the *Morgenzeitung* article was reprinted in French translation in *Bulletin du Comité des Delegations Juives* (Paris), May 30, 1921.
19. Reichswanderungsamt to Reichsminister des Inneren, June 9, 1920, Staatsarchiv Bremen, Auswanderung 3-A.4., Jüdische Auswanderung aus Polen, No. 432; Beatrix Hoffmann-Holter, *"Abreisemachung": Jüdische Kriegsflüchtlinge in Wien 1914 bis 1923* (Vienna: Böhlau 1995), 225–271.
20. Wischnitzer, *To Dwell in Safety*, 148–150; M. Biesiadecki to H. Sahm, February 24, 1921, League of Nations Archive, Geneva [LNA], Russian Refugees, Section 45, Box 133, Doc. No. 11258; "Immigrants Robbed at Journey's Start," *New York Times*, October 24, 1920. For a detailed (and biased) account of Jews in the Troyl camp by an American antisemite and immigration opponent, see Kenneth Roberts, *Why Europe Leaves Home* (New York: Bobbs Merrill, 1922), 88–94.
21. Ruth Ollendorf, ed., *Robert Kaelter: Ein Lebensbild* (Berlin: Philo Verlag, 1927), 57; "Ellis Island Jam Halts Immigration," *New York Times*, September 24, 1920; Kaelter to Bogen, November 6, 1920; Bogen to "Kelter," November 13, 1920, CAHJP, Danzig Collection, Da/2083, Jüdische Auswanderung 1920–1924.
22. Senatspräsident Sahm to Oberkommissar des Völkerbunds, April 12, 1922; Paul E. Evans (Foreign Office) to P. Baker (Nansen Office, League), May 31, 1922; Lucien Wolf to Mayor T. F. Johnson, June 28, 1923, LNA, Russian Refugees, Section 45, Box 1736, Doc. No. 17362; *Gesetzblatt für die Freie Stadt Danzig*, June 15, 1922; "Heimatlos," *Danziger Zeitung*, April 16, 1923.
23. Bruno Cabanes, *The Great War and the Origins of Humanitarianism 1918–1924* (Cambridge: Cambridge University Press, 2014), 143; John Hope Simpson, *The Refugee Problem: Report of a Survey* (London: Oxford University Press, 1939), 77, 413.
24. "How the Evacuation of the Ukrainian Refugees from Bessarabia Was Begun," *Bulletin of the Executive Committee of the Jewish World Relief Conference* 3 (February 6, 1922): 5–7.
25. "League of Human Rights Protests against Acquittal of Morarescu," January 18, 1926, and "Wholesale Murder of Jews by Roumanian Border Guards," January 14,

1932, *Jewish Telegraphic Agency*; Panait Istrati, "Unhappy Rumania," *The Index* (New York), May 1926, 3; *Detroit Jewish Chronicle*, December 31, 1926 ("The Events in Roumania").

26. Mae M. Ngai, *Impossible Subjects: Illegal Aliens and the Making of Modern America* (Princeton, NJ: Princeton University Press, 2003), 19–23; John Higham, *Strangers in the Land: Patterns of American Nativism 1860-1925* (1955; New York: Atheneum, 1977), 277–285, 309; Marinari, *The Unwanted*, 14–42; Daniel Okrent, *The Guarded Gate: Bigotry, Eugenics, and the Law That Kept Two Generations of Jews, Italians, and Other European Immigrants Out of America* (New York: Scribner, 2019), 226, 287; U.S. Department of Labor, *Immigration Laws: Rules of May 1, 1917*, 7th edition (Washington, D.C.: GPO, August 1922), 6; Max Kohler, "The Right of Asylum," *New York Times*, February 1, 1917.

27. Higham, *Strangers in the Land*; Roger Daniels, *Guarding the Golden Door: American Immigration Policy and Immigrants since 1882* (New York: Macmillan, 2005), 55; *New York Times*, September 6, 1923 ("Fines Ships $600,000 for Surplus Aliens"); Craig Robertson, *The Passport in America: The History of a Document* (New York: Oxford University Press, 2010), 205; Okrent, *The Guarded Gate*, 287; U.S. Department of Labor, *Immigration Laws*, 6.

28. "7.100 Aliens Stranded," *New York Times*, December 19, 1924; Marinari, *The Unwanted*, 59–69.

29. Veidlinger, *In the Midst of Civilized Europe*.

30. Higham, *Strangers in the Land*, 272–274, 309; Report by "Officer of the United States Government" in Warsaw, quoted in "House of Representatives, Report No. 4, Restriction of Immigration," in *House Reports, Vol. 1, 67th Congress, 1st Session* (Washington, D.C.: GPO, 1921), 11. For similarly biased descriptions of Jews in Poland, see Roberts, *Why Europe Leaves Home*.

31. Ngai, *Impossible Subjects*, 21–55; Johnson quoted in Higham, *Strangers in the Land*, 309; Johnson quoted in Daniels, *Guarding the Golden Door*, 55.

32. Jonathan Spiro, *Defending the Master Race: Conservation, Eugenics, and the Legacy of Madison Grant* (Lebanon, NH: University of Vermont Press, 2009), 220–230, 356–374; Madison Grant, *The Passing of the Great Race or the Basis of European History* (New York: Charles Scribner's Sons, 1916), 81; Perlmann, *America Classifies the Immigrants*, 205–211, 223.

33. "Predict Close Vote," *New York Times*, April 14, 1924; *Immigration: Speeches of Hon. Adolph J. Sabath of Illinois in the House of Representatives, April 4 to May 15, 1924* (Washington, D.C.: GPO, 1924), 18–19; Park quoted in Aristide R. Zolberg, *A Nation by Design: Immigration Policy in the Fashioning of America* (Cambridge, MA: Harvard University Press, 2006), 260.

34. Madison Grant, *Der Untergang der großen Rasse: Die Rassen als Grundlage der Geschichte Europas* (Munich: Lehmann, 1925); Hans Günther, *Rassenkunde des deutschen Volkes* (Munich: Lehmann, 1924), 4, 412; Geoffrey G. Field, *Evangelist of Race: The Germanic Vision of Houston Stewart Chamberlain* (New York: Columbia University Press, 1981); Stefan Kühl, *The Nazi Connection: Eugenics, American Racism, and German National Socialism* (New York: Oxford University Press, 2002), 38, 85; James Q. Whitman, *Hitler's American Model: The United States and the Making*

of *Nazi Race Law* (Princeton, NJ: Princeton University Press, 2017), 50–53; Okrent, *The Guarded Gate*, 276–278, 361; Tymothy W. Ryback, *Hitler's Private Library: The Books That Shaped His Life* (New York: Alfred A. Knopf, 2008), 98–110.

35. Harold Callender, "The Nazi Mind: A Study in Nationalism," *New York Times Magazine*, January 3, 1932, 21; Koellreutter quoted in Whitman, *Hitler's American Model*, 46; for the original, see Otto Koellreutter, *Grundriss der allgemeinen Staatsrechtslehre* (Tübingen: J. C. B. Mohr, 1933), 48, 51–52.

36. *American Jewish Yearbook* 42 (1940–1941): 618.

37. Higham, *Strangers in the Land*, 156–157; Leonard Dinnerstein, *Antisemitism in America* (New York: Oxford University Press, 1994), 66–68, 79, 95; Zolberg, *A Nation by Design*, 270–272; Okrent, *The Guarded Gate*, 355–371.

38. Carole Fink, *Defending the Rights of Others: The Great Powers, the Jews, and International Minority Protection, 1878–1938* (Cambridge: Cambridge University Press, 2004), 283–289, 319–320; Mark Levene, *War, Jews and the New Europe: Diplomacy of Lucien Wolf, 1914–19* (Oxford: Oxford University Press, 1992), 1; Granick, *International Jewish Humanitarianism*, 145; Hannah Arendt, "The Minority Question," in *Hannah Arendt—The Jewish Writings*, ed. Jerome Kohn and Ron H. Feldman (New York: Schocken, 2007), 125–132; "Dr. Motzkin Dead; A Pioneer Zionist," *New York Times*, November 8, 1933.

39. Mark Mazower, "Minorities and the League of Nations in Interwar Europe," *Daedalus* 126, no. 2 (1997): 47–63; Susan Pedersen, *The Guardians: The League of Nations and the Crisis of Empire* (New York: Oxford University Press, 2015).

40. Cabanes, *The Great War*, 80, 106–107, 137; Mark Mazower, *No Enchanted Palace: The End of Empire and the Ideological Origins of the United Nations* (Princeton, NJ: Princeton University Press, 2009), 104–113; Barbara Metzger, "The League of Nations, Refugees and Individual Rights," in Frank and Reinisch, *Refugees in Europe*, 101–120; League of Nations, Organization for Communication and Transit, *Passport Conference, Geneva May 12th to 18th, 1926, 1926 VIII 4* (Geneva: Publications of the League of Nations, 1926).

41. Maurice Hexter, *The Jews in Mexico* (New York: Emergency Committee on Jewish Refugees, 1926), 4–5; Hollace Weiner, *Jewish Stars in Texas: Rabbis and Their Work* (College Station: Texas A&M University Press, 1999), 102–105. On statelessness, see Mira L. Siegelberg, *Statelessness: A Modern History* (Princeton, NJ: Princeton University Press, 2020).

42. Wischnitzer, *To Dwell in Safety*, 151; Simpson, *Refugee Problem*, 73–74, 371.

43. Cabanes, *The Great War*, 136–140, 170–172; Vladimir Nabokov, *Pnin* (Garden City, NY: Doubleday, 1957), 46; Martin, *International Migration*, 52.

44. Cabanes, *The Great War*, 136–137, 156–173; L. Wolf to Secretary General, August 15, 1921 (and attached memo, August 17), LNA, Russian Refugees, Section 45, Box R-1726, Doc. No. 14817 and 14598; Aberson to Johnson, August 19, 1926, LNA, Dossiers du Bureau International de Travail (BIT), Section C, Reg. 1379–1467, Box C1410/306, Folder R 404/3/59/1; "Beschaffung von Einreise- und Durchreisevisen," CZA, Central Zionist Office Berlin, Z3/209–212.

45. Frank Nesemann, "Minderheitendiplomatie: Leo Motzkin zwischen Imperien und Nationen," in *Synchrone Welten: Zeiträume jüdischer Geschichte*, ed. Dan Diner

(Göttingen: V&R, 2005), 147–171; Fink, *Defending the Rights of Others*, 283–290, quote on 290; Granick, *International Jewish Humanitarianism*, 148; Wlodzimierz Borodziej, *Geschichte Polens im 20. Jahrhundert* (Munich: C. H. Beck, 2010), 165; Lucien Wolf to Edouard Frick, September 20, 1921, LNA, Russian Refugees, Section 45, Box R-1732, Doc. No. 16223; *Report of the Secretary and Special Delegate of the Joint Foreign Committee Presented to the Board of Deputies and the Council of the Anglo-Jewish Association November 1926* (Geneva: League of Nations, 1926), 34 (Doc. No. 16); Keith Hitchens, *Rumania, 1866–1947* (Oxford: Oxford University Press, 1994), 437–438.

46. *Bulletin du Comité des Delegations Juives*, August 13, 1921; Anthony Polonsky, "The New Jewish Politics and Its Discontents," in *The Emergence of Modern Jewish Politics: Bundism and Zionism in Eastern Europe*, ed. Zvi Gitelman (Pittsburgh: University of Pittsburgh Press, 2003), 35–53.

47. Nesemann, "Minderheitendiplomatie," 155–165; Penslar, *Shylock's Children*, 245.

48. *Wiener Morgenzeitung*, September 28, 29, 30, and October 2, 1921 ("Die jüdische Emigrationskonferenz"); "Executive Committee of the Jewish World Relief Conference," No. 2, November 17, 1921, LNA, Russian Refugees, Section 45, Box R 1737, Doc. No. 17799; Aberson to Nansen, November 29, 1921, LNA, Russian Refugees, Section 45, Box 1736, Doc. Nos. 17796 and 17102; "Agreement between the Latvian Government and Various Jewish Organizations," LNA, Russian Refugees, Section 45, Box 1748, Doc. No. 24916.

49. Leo Motzkin, "Das jüdische Volk und der Völkerbund," undated ms., and Leo Motzkin, "Völkerbund und Judenpolitik," 1930, CZA, Leo Motzkin Papers, A 126/659.

50. Jehuda Reinharz, *Chaim Weizmann* (New York: Oxford University Press, 1993), 321; Levene, *War, Jews and the New Europe*, 159, 218; Fink, *Defending the Rights of Others*, 318–319.

51. Peter Gatrell, *The Making of the Modern Refugee* (Oxford: Oxford University Press, 2013), 129–145, 171, 242; Sunil Amrith, *Crossing the Bay of Bengal: The Furies of Nature and the Crossings of Migrants* (Cambridge, MA: Harvard University Press, 2013), 212–234; UNHCR, *The State of the World's Refugees: Fifty Years of Humanitarian Action* (Oxford: Oxford University Press, 2000), 74; "From Crowded Camps to a Remote Island: Rohingya Refugees Move Again," *New York Times*, December 4, 2020.

52. 1924 HIAS Report (typescript), CZA, Leo Motzkin Papers, A126/705; Far Eastern Jewish Central Information Bureau, DALJEWCIB Harbin, CAHJP, Far East Collection, RI-41 DAL.

53. Jonathan Dekel-Chen, *Farming the Red Land: Jewish Agricultural Colonization and Local Soviet Power, 1924–1941* (New Haven, CT: Yale University Press, 2008); Penslar, *Shylock's Children*, 242.

54. Anne-Christin Saß, *Berliner Luftmenschen: Osteuropäisch-jüdische Migranten in der Weimarer Republik* (Göttingen: Wallstein, 2012), 215–224; Motzkin to Oskar Cohn (Berlin), March 13, 1927, CZA, Leo Motzkin Papers, A 126/661; Protokoll—Sitzung der Exekutive der Hias-JCA-Emigdirect, March 11, 1928 (Paris), June 18, 1928 (Berlin), CZA, Leo Motzkin Papers, A 126/711; HIAS, *23rd Annual Report 1931* (New York: Privately published, 1932); Bauer, *My Brother's Keeper*, 19–25; Fink,

Defending the Rights of Others, 331; Rakefet Zalashik, "Jewish American Philanthropy and the Crisis of 1929: The Case of OZE-TDC and the JDC," in *1929: Mapping the Jewish World*, ed. Hasia Diner and Gennady Estraikh (New York: NYU Press, 2013), 93–106.
55. Raymond J. Sontag, *A Broken World 1919–1939* (New York: Harper & Row, 1971).

Chapter 7

1. Joseph Roth, "Betrachtung an der Klagemauer," in *Joseph Roth, Werke*, ed. Klaus Westermann (Cologne: Kiepenheuer & Witsch, 1990), 3:86–89, quote on 88), first published in *Das Tagebuch*, September 14, 1929; Joseph Roth, "Der Kurfürstendamm," in Westermann, *Joseph Roth, Werke*, 3:913.
2. Peter Gay, *Weimar Culture: The Outsider as Insider* (New York: Harper & Row, 1968).
3. "Das Spinnennetz" was serialized in the Vienna *Arbeiter-Zeitung*; the first installment appeared in the October 7, 1923 issue, the installment about the riot was published on October 31, 1923. Joseph Roth, *Das Spinnennetz* (1923; Cologne: Kiepenheuer & Witsch, 1967). On the antisemitic riot in the Berlin Scheunenviertel, see David Clay Large, "'Out with the Ostjuden:' The Scheunenviertel Riots in Berlin, November 1923," in *Exclusionary Violence: Antisemitic Riots in Modern German History*, ed. Christhard Hoffmann, Helmut Walser Smith, and Werner Bergmann (Ann Arbor: University of Michigan Press, 2002), 123–140. For an in-depth analysis of the "Ostjude" stereotype, see Aschheim, *Brothers and Strangers*.
4. Sammy Gronemann, *Utter Chaos*, foreword by Joachim Schlör, trans. Penny Milbouer (Bloomington: Indiana University Press, 2016).
5. Joseph Roth, *Juden auf Wanderschaft* (Berlin: Die Schmiede, 1927), 14.
6. Roth, *Juden auf Wanderschaft*, 65–68.
7. Bauer, *My Brother's Keeper*, 18; Rebecca Kobrin, *Jewish Bialystok and Its Diaspora* (Bloomington: Indiana University Press, 2010), 135–145.
8. Jakob Lestschinsky, "Die soziale und wirtschaftliche Entwicklung der Ostjuden nach dem Kriege," *Weltwirtschaftliches Archiv* 24 (1926): 39–62; Kobrin, *Jewish Bialystok*, 26; Marrus, *The Unwanted*, 117.
9. Garland, *After They Closed the Gates*.
10. Saß, *Berliner Luftmenschen*, 275–278; Jochen Oltmer, *Migration und Politik in der Weimarer Republik* (Göttingen: Vandenhoek & Ruprecht, 2005), 196; *Annual Message Presented by John Bernstein, the President, at the 13th Annual Meeting, HIAS*, March 12, 1922 (New York: Privately published, 1922); Irving Abella and Harold Martin Troper, *None Is Too Many Canada and the Jews of Europe, 1933–1948* (New York: Random House, 1982), 1–2.
11. Kathleen Lopez, "Gatekeeping in the Tropics: US Immigration Policy and the Cuban Connection," in *A Nation of Immigrants Reconsidered: US Society in an Age of Restriction 1924–1965*, ed. Maddalena Marinari, Madeline Y. Hsu, and Maria Christina Garcia (Urbana: University of Illinois Press, 2019), 50–52.

12. Report Ilja Dijour, HICEM, May 3, 1928, *Nachrichtenblatt der Emigrationsvereinigung HIAS-JCA-EMIGDIRECT*, June 1928, CZA, Leo Motzkin Papers, A126/705; Morton D. Winsberg, "Jewish Agricultural Colonization in Argentina," *Geographical Review* 54, no. 4 (1964): 487–501; Jeffrey Lesser and Raanan Rein, "Introduction," in *Rethinking Jewish-Latin Americans*, ed. Jeffrey Lesser and Raanan Rein (Albuquerque: University of New Mexico Press, 2008), 11; Jeffrey Lesser, "The Immigration and Integration of Polish Jews in Brazil, 1924–1934," *The Americas* 51, no. 2 (1994): 173–191; Jeffrey Lesser, "In Search of Home Abroad: German Jews in Brazil, 1933–1945," in *The Heimat Abroad: The Boundaries of Germanness*, ed. Krista O'Donnell, Renate Bridenthal, and Nancy Reagin (Ann Arbor: University of Michigan Press, 2005), 167–184; *American Jewish Yearbook* 46 (1944–1945): 513; *American Jewish Yearbook* 50 (1948–1949): 694; Hexter, *The Jews in Mexico*, 18–21; Bauer, *My Brother's Keeper*, 288.
13. *American Jewish Yearbook* 42 (1940–1941): 632; Ruppin, *Soziologie der Juden*, 1:118–129; Mark Wischnitzer, "Programm und Werk des Hilfsvereins der Deutschen Juden," *CV-Zeitung* (Berlin), November 8, 1929.
14. Lederhendler, "The Interrupted Chain."
15. Gabriele Freitag, *Nächstes Jahr in Moskau! Die Zuwanderung von Juden in die sowjetische Metropole 1917–1932* (Göttingen: Vandenhoek & Ruprecht, 2004); Simpson, *Refugee Problem*, 84; Estraikh, *Transatlantic Russian Jewishness*, 193–199.
16. Tobias Brinkmann, "Zwischenstation: Berlin als Schnittstelle der jüdischen Migration nach 1918," in *Transit und Transformation: Osteuropäisch-jüdische Migranten in Berlin, 1918 bis 1939*, ed. Verena Dohrn and Gertrud Pickhan (Göttingen: Wallstein, 2010), 25–44; Roth, *Juden auf Wanderschaft*, 65; Robert Beachy, *Gay Berlin: Birthplace of a Modern Identity* (New York: Alfred A. Knopf, 2014).
17. Estraikh, *Transatlantic Russian Jewishness*, 150–152.
18. Saß, *Berliner Luftmenschen*; Kuznitz, *YIVO and the Making of Modern Jewish Culture*; Esra Bennathan, "Die demographische und wirtschaftliche Struktur der Juden," in *Entscheidungsjahr 1932*, ed. Werner Mosse (Tübingen: J. C. B. Mohr, 1966), 98.
19. Michael Brenner, *The Renaissance of Jewish Culture in Weimar Germany* (New Haven, CT: Yale University Press, 1995), 195–196; A. Linden [pseudonym used by Leo Motzkin], *Die Judenpogrome in Russland* (Köln: Jüdischer Verlag, 1910); Elias Tcherikover, *Antisemitizm un pogromen in Ukrayne, 1917–1918* (Berlin: Yidisher Literarisher Ferlag, 1923) [Yiddish]; Joseph B. Schechtman, *The Life and Times of Vladimir Jabotinsky: Fighter and Prophet. The Last Years* (Silver Spring, MD: Eshel Books, 1986), 2:29, 287, 549; Committee of Jewish Delegations, *The Pogroms in the Ukraine under the Ukrainian Governments (1917–1920)* (London: Bale, 1927); Joseph B. Schechtman, *Pogromy Dobrovolcheskoi Armii na Ukraine* (Berlin: Ostjüdisches Historisches Archiv, 1932) [Russian]; Mazower, *No Enchanted Palace*, 115–123; *Amtliches Fernsprechbuch für Berlin und Umgegend, 1932* (Berlin: Oberpostdirektion, 1932), 759, 880; Saß, *Berliner Luftmenschen*, 46, 222. On Dijour, see Ilya Dijour Papers, YIVO Archive, Center for Jewish History, New York [YIVO], RG 589.
20. Roth, *Juden auf Wanderschaft*, 75; Mary Dewhurst Lewis, *The Boundaries of the Republic: Migrant Rights and the Limits of Universalism in France 1918–1940*

(Stanford: Stanford University Press, 2007); Clifford Rosenberg, *Policing Paris: The Origins of Modern Immigration Control between the Wars* (Ithaca, NY: Cornell University Press, 2006), 101–103; Patrick Weil, "The Return of Jews in the Nationality or in the Territory of France," in *The Jews Are Coming Back: The Return of the Jews to Their Countries of Origin after WWII*, ed. David Bankier (New York: Berghahn Books, 2005), 58–59; Jonathan Boyarin, *Polish Jews in Paris: The Ethnography of Memory* (Bloomington: Indiana University Press, 1991), 46–53.

21. Marcia Reynders Ristaino, *Port of Last Resort: The Diaspora Communities of Shanghai* (Stanford: Stanford University Press, 2001), 21–53; Anna Ginsbourg, *Jewish Refugees in Shanghai* (Shanghai: China Weekly Review, 1940); *American Jewish Yearbook* 38 (1936–1937): 562.

22. "Mémoire concernant la situations des Juifs à Dantzig," Comité des Delegations Juives, Geneva, December 13, 1920, LNA, Administrative Commissions and Minorities Section, Registry Files, Subseries 4 Danzig, Box R-140/4/9663 (Situation of Jews in Danzig), Doc. No. 9663 (7-9); *Gesetzblatt für die Freie Stadt Danzig*, June 15, 1922.

23. "Jewish life in Zoppot," *Danziger Lebn* [Yiddish], June 1, 1922; *American Jewish Yearbook* 1930–1931, 249–251; Samuel Echt, *Die Geschichte der Juden in Danzig* (Leer: Rautenberg, 1972), 96.

24. Leiserowitz, *Sabbatleuchter*, 289–312.

25. Michael Traub, "Moderne jüdische Wanderungsbewegungen (1915–1923)," *Zeitschrift für Demographie und Statistik der Juden* 1 (1924): 115–122; Michael Traub, *Jüdische Wanderbewegungen vor und nach dem Weltkriege* (Berlin: Jüdischer Verlag, 1930), 11, 14, 96.

26. Ruppin, *Soziologie der Juden*, 1:130–33, 142, 158.

27. Ruppin, *Soziologie der Juden*, 1:118–29; Arthur Ruppin, *Die Juden der Gegenwart: Eine sozialwissenschaftliche Studie* (Berlin: S. Calvary, 1904), 267; Arthur Ruppin, *Die Juden der Gegenwart*, 3rd edition (Berlin: Jüdischer Verlag, 1920), 85.

28. Ruppin, *Soziologie der Juden*, 1:118–29; Louis Wirth, *The Ghetto* (Chicago: University of Chicago Press, 1928). In August 1933 Ruppin met with the Nazi race "scientist" Hans Günther during a visit to Germany. For a critical discussion that highlights substantial differences between Günther and Ruppin regarding their conception of race, see Amos Morris-Reich, "Arthur Ruppin's Concept of Race," *Israel Studies* 11, no. 3 (2006): 1–30.

29. Gatrell, *Making of the Modern Refugee*, 55–56; Cabanes, *The Great War*, 133–188.

30. Hersch, "International Migration of the Jews," 520, 571; Alexander Kulischer and Eugen Kulischer, *Kriegs- und Wanderzüge: Weltgeschichte als Völkerbewegung* (Berlin: De Gruyter, 1932); Kuznitz, *YIVO and the Making of Modern Jewish Culture*, 176.

31. Kuznitz, *YIVO and the Making of Modern Jewish Culture*; Estraikh, "Jacob Lestschinsky"; Alroey, "Demographers."

32. Jakob Lestschinsky, "Die jüdische Wanderung, ihre Ursachen und ihre Regelung," *Archiv für Wanderungswesen und Auslandskunde* 1, no. 3 (1929): 127–131; Jakob Lestschinsky, "Die jüdische Wanderung, ihre Ursachen und ihre Regelung

(1. Fortsetzung)," *Archiv für Wanderungswesen und Auslandskunde* 1, no. 4 (1929): 168–172; Jakob Lestschinsky, "Die jüdische Wanderung, ihre Ursachen und ihre Regelung (Schluß)," *Archiv für Wanderungswesen und Auslandskunde* 2, no. 1 (1930): 20–26; Kuznitz, *YIVO and the Making of Modern Jewish Culture*; Estraikh, "Jacob Lestschinsky," 226, 238; Jakob Lestschinsky, *Probleme bei der Bevölkerungsbewegung bei den Juden* (Berlin: Privately published, 1926).

33. Simon Dubnow, *Weltgeschichte des jüdischen Volkes: Von seinen Uranfängen bis zur Gegenwart* (Berlin: Jüdischer Verlag, 1929), 10:190, 275, quote on 276–283; Peter Wiernik, *History of the Jews in America* (New York: Jewish Press, 1912), 261–269; Simon Dubnow, "Assimilation," in *Encyclopedia of the Social Sciences*, ed. Edwin R. A. Seligman (New York: Macmillan, 1931), 5:126–130; Michael Brenner, *Prophets of the Past: Interpreters of Jewish History* (Princeton, NJ: Princeton University Press, 2010), 124.

34. In 1925 Harvard appointed the Lithuanian-born philosopher Harry Wolfson to an endowed position; see Lewis S. Feuer, "Recollections of Harry Austryn Wolfson," *American Jewish Archives Journal* 28, no. 1 (1976): 25–50.

35. *New York Times*, November 26, 1989 (Baron obituary); Lila Corwin Berman, *Speaking of Jews: Rabbis, Intellectuals, and the Creation of an American Public Identity* (Berkeley: University of California Press, 2009), 48; Robert Liberles, *Salo Wittmayer Baron: Architect of Jewish History* (New York: NYU Press, 1995).

36. Salo Baron, "Ghetto and Emancipation," *Menorah Journal* 14 (1928): 515–526, quotes on 517, 522. For a careful analysis, see Robert Chazan, *Refugees or Migrants: Pre-Modern Jewish Population Movement* (New Haven, CT: Yale University Press, 2018), 57–77; Max Nordau, *Das Judentum im 19. und 20. Jahrhundert. Vortrag, gehalten in Hamburg am 29. Dezember 1909* (Cologne: Jüdischer Verlag, 1911), 16.

37. Kulischer and Kulischer, *Kriegs- und Wanderzüge*, 3–35, 202; Avraami, *Die jüdische Wirklichkeit*. On Michael Kulischer, see Abraham Duker, "Evraiskaia Starina: A Bibliography of the Russian-Jewish Historical Periodical," *Hebrew Union College Annual*, nos. 8–9 (1931–1932): 525–603; Sophie Dubnov-Erlich, *The Life and Work of S. M. Dubnov: Diaspora Nationalism and Jewish History* (Bloomington: Indiana University Press, 1991), 179; Karl Tiander, "Review of *Kriegs- und Wanderzüge, Weltgeschichte als Völkerbewegung*," *Zeitschrift für Politik* 23 (1934): 337–340.

38. *New York Times*, April 4, 1956 (Kulischer obituary); Friedrich Wilhelms-Universität to Städtisches Zentralamt für Wohnungswesen, July 11, 1923, Universitätsarchiv, Humboldt Universität, Berlin, Personalakte Professor Dr. Kulischer, UK Personalia, K 429; W. Parker Mauldin, "Eugene M. Kulischer, 1881–1956," *American Sociological Review* 21, no. 4 (1956): 504; A. J. Jaffe, "Notes on the Population Theory of Eugene M. Kulischer," *Milbank Memorial Fund Quarterly* 40, no. 2 (1962): 187–206.

39. Alexander Kulischer, *Das Wesen des Sowjetstaates* (Berlin: Verlag für Politik und Wissenschaft, 1921); Mark Tolts, "Alexander Kulischer: On the Demographic Future of Russia," *Demographic Review* 5, no. 2 (2018): 147–168 [Russian]; Schechtman, *The Life and Times of Vladimir Jabotinsky*, 29, 287, 549.

40. Friedrich Ratzel, *Der Lebensraum: Eine biogeographische* Studie (Tübingen: Verlag der Laupp'schen Buchhandlung, 1901); Friedrich Ratzel, *Politische Geographie*, 3. Auflage (Munich: Oldenbourg, 1926), 70; Paul Mombert, *Studien zur Bevölkerungsbewegung in Deutschland* (Karlsruhe: Braunsche Hofbuchdruckerei, 1907); Ernst Georg Ravenstein, *The Laws of Migration* (1885-1889; New York: Arno Press, 1976).
41. Kulischer and Kulischer, *Kriegs- und Wanderzüge*, 3-35, 202; Eugene M. Kulischer, *Europe on the Move: War and Population Changes, 1917-1947* (New York: Columbia University Press, 1948), 8. On the *Lebensraum* concept, see Woodruff D. Smith, *The Ideological Origins of Nazi Imperialism* (New York: Oxford University Press, 1989), 83-111.
42. Kulischer and Kulischer, *Kriegs- und Wanderzüge*, 203-204; Tiander, "Review of *Kriegs-und Wanderzüge*"; Hans Grimm, *Volk ohne Raum* (Munich: A. Langen, 1926), 24-25, 799, 1259; Smith, *The Ideological Origins of Nazi Imperialism*, 224-230; Francis L. Carsten, "'Volk ohne Raum': A Note on Hans Grimm," *Journal of Contemporary History* 2, no. 2 (1967): 221-227.
43. Tolts, "Alexander Kulischer"; Zahra, *Great Departure*, 17, 113, 143; Kulischer and Kulischer, *Kriegs- und Wanderzüge*, 200-204.
44. Kulischer and Kulischer, *Kriegs- und Wanderzüge*, 160-161.
45. Antonio Ferrara, "Eugene Kulischer, Joseph Schechtman and the Historiography of European Forced Migrations," *Journal of Contemporary History* 46, no. 4 (2011): 715-740.
46. *New York Times*, August 19, 1945 (Ferenczi obituary); Walter F. Willcox, ed., *International Migrations*, vol. 1: *Statistics*, compiled by Imre Ferenczi on behalf of the International Labour Office (New York: National Bureau of Economic Research, 1929), 81-89; Imre Ferenczi, *Kontinentale Wanderungen und die Annäherung der Völker: Ein geschichtlicher Überblick* (Jena: Gustav Fischer, 1930), 6-8, 17-18; see also Imre Ferenczi, "Migration, Modern," in *Encyclopedia of the Social Sciences*, ed. Edwin R. A. Seligman (New York: Macmillan, 1933), 10:431-441; Emerich [Imre] Ferenczi, "Das Auswanderungsproblem Nachkriegs-Ungarns: Ein Beitrag zur Lage in Zentral-Europa," *Weltwirtschaftliches Archiv* 18 (1922): 348-376, esp. 370; Kulischer and Kulischer, *Kriegs- und Wanderzüge*, 217n274.
47. Maurice Halbwachs, "Review *Kriegs- und Wanderzüge*," *Annales Sociologiques*, serie E, fasc. 1 (1935): 79-85; see also Alfons Dopsch, "Review *Kriegs- und Wanderzüge*," *Weltwirtschaftliches Archiv* 37 (1933): 259-262; E. Coornaert, "Review *Kriegs- und Wanderzüge*," *Revue d'Histoire Modern* 6 (1933): 62-63; Karl Schlögel, "Verschiebebahnhof Europa: Joseph B. Schechtmans und Eugene M. Kulischers Pionierarbeiten," *Zeithistorische Forschungen* 2, no. 3 (2005): 468-472; Mazower, *No Enchanted Palace*, 115-123.
48. "Nachwort" for new edition of "Juden auf Wanderschaft," in *Joseph Roth, Werke*, 2:895.
49. *New York Times*, March 12, 1933 ("*Forward*'s Reporter Jailed"); Lestschinsky, Petition for Naturalization; Saß, *Berliner Luftmenschen*, 433-435; Estraikh, "Jacob Lestschinsky," 230-234; Jacob Lestschinsky to Abraham Cahan, May 12, 1937; Jacob Lestschinsky to Abraham Cahan, undated (probably September 1938), YIVO,

Abraham Cahan Papers, RG 1139, F91; Dubnov-Ehrlich, *The Life and Work of S. M. Dubnov*, 210–211.

50. Zahra, *Great Departure*, 160; Richard Breitman and Allan J. Lichtman, *FDR and the Jews* (Cambridge, MA: Harvard University Press, 2013), 110; Paul R. Bartrop, *The Evian Conference of 1938 and the Jewish Refugee Crisis* (New York: Palgrave Macmillan, 2018); Jennings, *Escape from Vichy*, 38.
51. Zahra, *Great Departure*, 146–149; *Jewish Telegraphic Agency*, December 27, 1938 ("Jews Suffer in Europe No Man's Lands").
52. Zahra, *Great Departure*, 146–149; Jerzy Tomaszewski, *Auftakt zur Vernichtung: Die Vertreibung polnischer Juden aus Deutschland im Jahre 1938* (Osnabrück: fibre, 2002), 136–144, 178–202.
53. Steven J. Ross and Wolf Gruner, eds., *New Perspectives on Kristallnacht: After 80 Years, the Nazi Pogrom in Global Comparison* (West Lafayette, IN: Purdue University Press, 2019); David Engel, *The Assassination of Symon Petliura and the Trial of Scholem Schwarzbard 1926-1927: A Selection of Documents* (Göttingen: Vandenhoeck & Ruprecht, 2016), 40–42.
54. Suzanne Rutland, *Edge of the Diaspora: Two Centuries of Jewish Settlement in Australia* (New York: Holmes & Meier, 1997), 180–184; Tichenor, *Dividing Lines*, 164.
55. Hilfsverein der Deutschen Juden, *Jüdische Auswanderung: Korrespondenzblatt über Auswanderungs- und Siedlungswesen* (Berlin: Schmoller & Gordon, 1937); Hilfsverein der Deutschen Juden, *Jüdische Auswanderung: Korrespondenzblatt über Auswanderungs- und Siedlungswesen* (Berlin: Schmoller & Gordon, 1938).

Chapter 8

1. *New York Times*, January 9, 1940 (weather reports); Rachel Wischnitzer, *1940 Ship Manifest, New York, NY*, Microfilm Roll 6433, line 14, page number 91, *Passenger and Crew Lists of Vessels Arriving at New York, New York, 1897–1957*, Microfilm Publication T715, 8892 rolls, NAI: 300346, Records of the Immigration and Naturalization Service, National Archives, Washington, D.C. [Rachel Wischnitzer, 1940 Ship Manifest].
2. Mark Wischnitzer, *Die Universität Göttingen und die Entwicklung der liberalen Ideen in Russland im ersten Viertel des 19. Jahrhunderts* (Berlin: Ebering, 1907); Kuzmany, *Brody*, 234–260; *The Jewish Pogroms in Ukraine: Authoritative Statements on the Question of Responsibility for Recent Outbreaks against the Jews in Ukraine by Julian Batchinsky, Dr. Arnold Margolin, Dr. Mark Vishnitzer, Israel Zangwill, Documents, Official Orders, and Other Data Bearing upon the Facts as They Exist Today* (Washington, D.C.: Privately published, 1919), 19.
3. Mark Wischnitzer, *Die jüdische Zunftverfassung in Polen und Litauen im 17. und 18. Jahrhundert* (Stuttgart: W. Kohlhammer, 1927); Mark Wischnitzer, *A History of Jewish Crafts and Guilds* (New York: J. David, 1965).
4. Claire Richter Sherman, "Rachel Wischnitzer: Pioneer Scholar of Jewish Art," *Woman's Art Journal* 1, no. 2 (1980–1981): 42–46; Saß, *Berliner Luftmenschen*, 185;

Marion Neiss, *Presse im Transit: Jiddische Zeitungen und Zeitschriften in Berlin von 1919 bis 1925* (Berlin: Metropol, 2002); Hermann Simon, *Das Berliner Jüdische Museum in der Oranienburger Strasse: Geschichte einer zerstörten Kulturstätte* (Berlin: Hentrich, 2000); Joseph Gutman, "Introduction," *Artibus et Historiae* 9, no. 17 (1988): 11–12.

5. Bericht über eine Informationsreise nach der Südafrikanischen Union, den beiden Rhodesien und Kenya (Britisch-Ostafrika) von Dr. Mark Wischnitzer, LBI—New York, MS 695; *The South African Jewish Board of Deputies—Report of the Executive Council 1935-37* (Johannesburg: Palladium, 1937), 21–25; Edna Bradlow, "South African Policy and Jewish Refugee Immigration in the 1930s," in *False Havens: The British Empire and the Holocaust*, ed. Paul R. Bartrop (Lanham, MD: University Press of America, 1995), 239–252; Richter Sherman, "Rachel Wischnitzer," 42–46; *Festschrift zu Simon Dubnows siebzigstem Geburtstag*; "Hitler Is Conciliatory," *New York Times*, March 12, 1933.

6. *Jewish Telegraphic Agency*, December 27, 1938 ("France Jails Denationalized Polish Jews"), January 28, 1938 ("League to Seek Shelving of Citizenship Decree"); Memorandum to the Committee of Three, World Jewish Congress Executive Committee, January 15, 1939, AJA, WJC Records, MS Coll. 361, Central Files, 1919–1975, Box A1, Folder 1; Gosewinkel, *Einbürgern und Ausschließen*, 369–404; Tomaszewski, *Auftakt zur Vernichtung*; Corry Guttstadt, *Turkey, the Jews, and the Holocaust* (Cambridge: Cambridge University Press, 2013), 104; Deborah Dwork and Robert Jan van Pelt, *Flight from the Reich: Refugee Jews 1933-1946* (New York: Norton, 2009), 62–63.

7. Rachel Wischnitzer, 1940 Ship Manifest.

8. *Statistical Abstract of the United States 1941, Sixty-Third Number* (Washington, D.C.: GPO, 1942), 107–115; *American Jewish Yearbook* 42 (1940–1941): 612–622; Daniels, *Coming to America*, 294–295; Laurel Leff, *Well Worth Saving: American Universities' Life-and-Death Decisions on Refugees from Nazi Europe* (New Haven, CT: Yale University Press, 2019), 3.

9. *American Jewish Yearbook* 42 (1940–1941): 618; *Hilfsverein Jahresbericht für 1928*, 27, 48–52; Wells, *Tropical Zion*, 3–68; Abella and Troper, *None Is Too Many*.

10. *Jewish Telegraphic Agency*, December 27, 1938 ("France Jails Denationalized Polish Jews"); Rosenberg, *Policing Paris*, 101–103.

11. Arieh Tartakower and Kurt Grossmann, *The Jewish Refugee* (New York: Institute for Jewish Affairs/World Jewish Congress, 1944), 142–161; Lisa Moses Leff, *The Archive Thief* (New York: Oxford University Press, 2015), 26–71.

12. Leff, *Well Worth Saving*, 2–3; Eugene Kulischer 1941 Ship Manifest, *New York, NY*, Microfilm Serial T715, 1897-1957, Microfilm Roll 6555, line 1, page number 103, *Passenger Lists of Vessels Arriving at New York, New York, 1820-1897*, Microfilm Publication M237, 675 rolls, NAI: 6256867, Records of the U.S. Customs Service, Record Group 36. National Archives at Washington, D.C. [Eugene Kulischer 1941 Ship Manifest].

13. T. G. Powell, *Mexico and the Spanish Civil War* (Albuquerque: University of New Mexico Press, 1981), 145–159; Alicia Alted, *La Voz de los Vencidos: El Exilio Republicano de 1939* (Madrid: Aguilar, 2005); *New York Times*, April 3, 1941

("Liberals Held in France"); Elizabeth Young-Bruehl, *Hannah Arendt: For Love of the World* (New Haven, CT: Yale University Press, 1982), 145, 153; Daniela Gleizer-Salzman, *Unwelcome Exiles: Mexico and the Jewish Refugees from Nazism, 1933–1945* (Leiden: Brill, 2014).

14. Richter Sherman, "Rachel Wischnitzer," 42–46; *Festschrift zu Simon Dubnows Siebzigstem Geburtstag.*
15. LBI—New York, Rachel Wischnitzer Papers, AR 25657 [Rachel Wischnitzer Papers].
16. Rachel Wischnitzer to Joseph Rosen (Dominican Settlement Association), May 21, 1940; A. M. Warren (chief of Visa Division, State Department) to Rachel Wischnitzer, June 5, 1940, Rachel Wischnitzer Papers; Wells, *Tropical Zion*; Young-Bruehl, *Hannah Arendt*, 150–163.
17. Jose-Alain Fralon, *A Good Man in Evil Times: The Heroic Story of Aristides de Sousa Mendes—The Man Who Saved the Lives of Countless Refugees in World War II* (New York: Basic Books, 2001); Philip S. Bernstein (rabbi, Rochester, NY, for HICEM) to Rachel Wischnitzer, June 12, 1940, Rachel Wischnitzer to Joseph C. Hyman (JDC), June 20, 1940; P. Bernstein to Joseph C. Hyman, June 26, 1940, Rachel Wischnitzer Papers.
18. Rachel Wischnitzer to Eliot B. Coulter (State Department) July 11, 1940; Eliot B. Coulter to Rachel Wischnitzer, July 29, 1940, Rachel Wischnitzer Papers.
19. Patrick von zur Mühlen, *Fluchtweg Spanien-Portugal: Die deutsche Emigration und der Exodus aus Europa 1933–1945* (Bonn: Dietz, 1992); Bernd Rother, *Spanien und der Holocaust* (Tübingen: Niemeyer, 2001), 115–116; Jaqueline Adams, "Why Jewish Refugees Were Imprisoned in a Spanish Detention Camp While Fleeing Europe (1940–1945)," *Journal of Modern European History* 21, no.1 (2022): 110–132.
20. Anna Seghers, *Transit* (Boston: Little, Brown, 1944); Harshav, *Marc Chagall and His Times*, 477–506; Rachel Wischnitzer to Helen Sherry (lawyer, Baltimore), November 1, 1940; Schwarz (Bollack Store, Brownsville, TX) to Rachel Wischnitzer, November 2, 1940, Rachel Wischnitzer Papers. On escape routes through the Caribbean, see Jennings, *Escape from Vichy*; Joanna Newman, *Nearly the New World: The British West Indies and the Flight from Nazism 1933–1945* (New York: Berghahn Books, 2019); Marion Kaplan, *Hitler's Jewish Refugees: Hope and Anxiety in Portugal* (New Haven, CT: Yale University Press, 2020).
21. Wells, *Tropical Zion*, 151–154; Mark Wischnitzer, 1941 Ship Manifest, *New York, NY*, Microfilm Serial T715, 1897–1957, Microfilm Roll 6543, line 12, page number 2, *Passenger Lists of Vessels Arriving at New York, New York, 1820–1897*, Microfilm Publication M237, 675 rolls, NAI: 6256867, Records of the U.S. Customs Service, Record Group 36, National Archives at Washington, D.C. [Mark Wischnitzer 1941 Ship Manifest]; Mark Wischnitzer Naturalization File, November 18, 1941, National Archives at Philadelphia, NAI Title: *Declarations of Intention for Citizenship, 1/19/1842–10/29/1959*, NAI Number 4713410, Record Group *Records of District Courts of the United States, 1685–2009*, Record Group number 21; Richter Sherman, "Rachel Wischnitzer."
22. Patrick Weil, *How to Be French: Nationality in the Making since 1789* (Durham, NC: Duke University Press, 2008), 87–124; Susan Elisabeth Subak, *Rescue and*

Flight: American Relief Workers Who Defied the Nazis (Lincoln: University of Nebraska Press, 2010); Kaplan, *Hitler's Jewish Refugees*; Michael Dobbs, *The Unwanted: America, Auschwitz, and a Village Caught In Between* (New York: Alfred A. Knopf, 2019), 257.

23. Jacques Semelin and Laurent Larcher, *Une énigme française: Pourquoi les trois quarts des Juifs en France n'ont pas été déportés* (Paris: Albin Michel, 2022).

24. Mark Wischnitzer, "Jewish Emigration from Germany 1933-1938," *Jewish Social Studies* 2, no. 1 (1940): 23-44; Wischnitzer, "The Historical Background of the Settlement of Jewish Refugees in Santo Domingo"; Marrus, *The Unwanted*; Amrith, *Crossing the Bay of Bengal*, 228-230.

Chapter 9

1. File Kulischer, Eugene Michael, Emergency Committee in Aid of Displaced Foreign Scholars Records, in New York Public Library, Manuscripts and Archives Division, Mss. Col. 922, Box 84, Folder 29. For background on the Emergency Committee, see Leff, *Well Worth Saving*; Eugene Kulischer, "Three Fifths of Europe's Jews now in USSR, *Rescue* [Bulletin of HIAS], July 1946; Eugene Kulischer, "The IRO and the Jewish Refugees," *Rescue*, April 1947, n.p.

2. Conference on Postwar Population Resettlements, Program, June 27, 1942, Hotel Roosevelt, New York, YIVO, Gottschalk Papers, RG 330; Max Gottschalk, "Report of Research Institute on Peace and Post-War Problems," in 36th Annual Report of the AJC, *American Jewish Yearbook* 45 (1943-1944): 668-677; *New York Times*, October 26, 1941, and June 27, 1942; Max Gottschalk and Abraham G. Duker, *Jews in the Post-War World* (New York: Dryden Press, 1945).

3. Eugene M. Kulischer, *Jewish Migrations: Past Experiences and Post-War Prospects* (New York: American Jewish Committee, 1943), 13, 20, 23, 33; Jean Medawar and David Pyke, *Hitler's Gift: The True Story of the Scientists Expelled by the Nazi Regime* (New York: Arcade, 2012).

4. Kulischer, *Jewish Migrations*, 36, 41; Max Nordau, "II. Kongressrede (Basel, 28. August 1898)," in *Max Nordau's Zionistische Schriften*, ed. Zionistisches Aktionskomitee (Cologne: Jüdischer Verlag, 1909), 72. See also "Rede Dr. Max Nordau's," *Die Welt* (Vienna), January 3, 1902, 4-11; *Stenographisches Protokoll der Verhandlungen des II. Zionisten-Congresses, gehalten zu Basel, vom 28. Bis 31. August 1898* (Vienna: Verlag des Erez Israel, 1898), 24-25.

5. Kulischer, *Jewish Migrations*, 49.

6. Kulischer, *Jewish Migrations*, 49, 42; Abraham Duker and Michael Alper, eds., *Jewish Post-War Problems: A Study Course—Unit VII: Relief, Reconstruction, and Migration* (New York: American Jewish Committee, 1942), 34.

7. Max Gottschalk, "Preface," in Kulischer, *Jewish Migrations*, 7.

8. Eugene Kulischer, *The Displacement of Population in Europe* (Montreal: Inland Press, 1943), 95, 166; *New York Times*, October 1, 1943 (Kulischer's displacement study),

and November 12, 1944 ("Thirty Million in Europe's Darkness"); Hannah Arendt, "The Displacement of Population in Europe by Eugene M. Kulischer (Review)," *Jewish Social Studies* 7, no. 1 (1945): 88; Eugene M. Kulischer, "Displaced Persons in the Modern World," *Annals of the American Academy of Political and Social Science* 262, no. 1 (1949): 166–177, 169.

9. Simpson, *Refugee Problem*, 3–4.
10. Simpson, *Refugee Problem*, 442, 516–545. On Simpson's study, see Matthew Frank, "The Myth of 'Vacant Places': Refugees and Group Resettlement," in Frank and Reinisch, *Refugees in Europe*, 121–146; Naomi W. Cohen, *The Americanization of Zionism, 1897–1948* (Hanover, NH: Brandeis University Press, 2003), 119–128.
11. Sumner Wells to the President, November 28, 1938, in Franklin D. Roosevelt Library Archives, Hyde Park, NY, FDR Papers, President's Secretary's File—Subject File—Refugees, 1938–1944, Box 158; U.S. Department of the Interior, *The Problem of Alaskan Development* (Washington, D.C.: U.S. Department of the Interior, 1940); Henry L. Feingold, *Bearing Witness: How America and Its Jews Responded to the Holocaust* (Syracuse, NY: Syracuse University Press, 1995), 94–140; Zahra, *Great Departure*, 144, 161–164; Steven Seegel, *Map Men: Transnational Lives and Deaths of Geographers in the Making of East Central Europe* (Chicago: University of Chicago Press, 2018), 170.
12. Frank, "The Myth of 'Vacant Places'"; Henry Field, *"M" Project for FDR: Studies on Migration and Settlement* (Ann Arbor: Edwards Brothers, 1962), 328; Henry Field, "How FDR Did His Homework," *Saturday Magazine* (New York), July 8, 1961; Mazower, *No Enchanted Palace*, 109–120.
13. Jennings, *Escape from Vichy*, 38–41; Czeslaw Madajczyk, "Einleitung," in *Vom Generalplan Ost zum Generalsiedlungsplan: Dokumente*, ed. Czeslaw Madajczyk (Munich: K. G. Saur, 1994), v–xxi; "Der Generalplan Ost," *Vierteljahrshefte für Zeitgeschichte* 6, no. 3 (1958): 281–325. For background, see Götz Aly and Susanne Heim, *Architects of Annihilation: Auschwitz and the Logic of Destruction* (London: Orion, 2015); Christian Gerlach, *Kalkulierte Morde: Die deutsche Wirtschafts- und Vernichtungspolitik in Weissrussland 1941 bis 1944* (Hamburg: Hamburger Edition, 1999); Saul Friedländer, *The Years of Extermination: Nazi Germany and the Jews, 1939–1945* (New York: Harper Collins, 2007), 261–328.
14. Tommie Sjöberg, *The Powers and the Persecuted: The Refugee Problem and the Intergovernmental Committee on Refugees (IGCR), 1938–1947* (Lund: Lund University Press, 1991), 75–82; Mazower, *No Enchanted Palace*, 109–120; Matthew Frank, *Making Minorities History: Population Transfer in Twentieth-Century Europe* (Oxford: Oxford University Press, 2017), 242–257; Zahra, *Great Departure*, 162; Field, *"M" Project for FDR*, vii, 1–5, 8, 347–348.
15. Jérôme Elie, "Histories of Refugee and Forced Migration Studies," in *The Oxford Handbook of Refugee and Forced Migration Studies*, eds. Elena Fiddian-Qasmiyeh, Gil Loescher, Katy Long, and Nando Sigona (Oxford: Oxford University Press, 2015), 23–35; Frank, *Making Minorities History*, 179–181; Mazower, *No Enchanted Palace*, 113–125.
16. "Jacob Robinson: In Memoriam," *Israel Law Review* 13, no. 3 (1978): 287–297; *Unity in Dispersion: A History of the World Jewish Congress* (New York: WJC, 1948),

134–154. See also Rotem Giladi, *Jews, Sovereignty, and International Law: Ideology and Ambivalence in Early Israeli Legal Diplomacy* (Oxford: Oxford University Press, 2021).

17. Frank, *Making Minorities History*, 176–178; *New York Times*, May 14, 1923 ("Jewish Congress to Meet"); *Unity in Dispersion*, 135; Stephen S. Wise to Jacob Robinson, May 29, 1941; Max Gottschalk to Jacob Robinson, March 3, 1942, AJA, WJC Records, Institute for Jewish Affairs Records, MS Coll. 361, Box 5, Folder 6.

18. Eugene Kulischer to Jacob Robinson, April 11, 1942, AJA, WJC Records, Institute for Jewish Affairs Records, MS Coll. 361, Box 8, Folder 6; Sarah Cramsey, *Uprooting the Diaspora: Jewish Belonging and the Ethnic Revolution in Poland and Czechoslovakia, 1936–1946* (Bloomington: Indiana University Press, 2023); Gerard Daniel Cohen, *In War's Wake: Europe Displaced Persons in the Postwar Order* (New York: Oxford University Press, 2012), 129–137; Daniel Elazar, "Prof. Arieh Tartakower," *Newsletter (World Union of Jewish Studies)* 22 (1983): 11–13; Jessica Reinisch, "Internationalism in Relief: The Birth (and Death) of UNRRA," *Past and Present* 210, no. 6 suppl. (2011): 258–289; Arieh Tartakower, Report London Trip, Jan.–Mar. 1944, AJA, WJC Records, MS Coll. 361, Central Files, 1919–1975, Box A1, Folder 4.

19. Lothar Mertens, *Unermüdlicher Kämpfer für Frieden und Menschenrechte: Leben und Wirken von Kurt R. Grossmann* (Berlin: Duncker & Humblot, 1997). For an analysis of the economic profile of German Jewish refugees, see Arieh Tartakower, "The Jewish Refugee: A Sociological Survey," *Jewish Social Studies* 4, no. 4 (1942): 311–348; Tartakower and Grossmann, *The Jewish Refugee*; Simpson, *The Refugee Problem*, 186.

20. Tartakower and Grossmann, *The Jewish Refugee*, viii, 2–8; Frank, *Making Minorities History*, 187; Sebastian Musch, "Zwischen Bermuda und Palästina: Arieh Tartakowers und Kurt R. Grossmanns Suche nach Rettung für jüdische Flüchtlinge (1944)," *Zeithistorische Forschungen/Studies in Contemporary History* 13, no. 3 (2018): 576–582; British Embassy, Washington D.C., to Department of State, January 20, 1943, in U.S. Department of State, *Foreign Relations of the United States: Diplomatic Papers, 1943* (Washington, D.C.: GPO, 1963), 134; Feingold, *Bearing Witness*, 144–146.

21. Arieh Tartakower, *Yidishe Vanderungen* (Warsaw: Privately published, 1940) [Yiddish]; Szajkowski, "How the Mass Migration to America Began," 291–310; Zosa Szajkowski, "Materialn vegen der yiddisher emigratzye keyn Ameruje in 1881–1882," *YIVO Bleter* 19 (1942): 275–278 [Yiddish]; Arieh Tartakower, "The Jewish Refugee," *Jewish Social Studies* 4, no. 4 (1942): 311–348; Tartakower and Grossmann, *The Jewish Refugee*, 6–8, 528.

22. Wischnitzer, *To Dwell in Safety*, xi.

23. AJC Research Institute on Peace and Post-War Problems, Report for 1942, December 31, 1942, AJA, WJC Records, Institute for Jewish Affairs Records, MS Coll. 361, Box 5, Folder 6; Mark Wischnitzer, "Die Tätigkeit des Hilfsvereins in der Nachkriegszeit mit besonderer Berücksichtigung der Auswandererfürsorge," in *Festschrift anlässlich der Feier des 25 Jährigen Bestehens des Hilfsvereins*, 47–58; Mark Wischnitzer, *Die Juden in der Welt: Gegenwart und Geschichte des Judentums in allen Ländern* (Berlin: Erich Reiss Verlag, 1935), v–vi, 7, 355; *Philo-Atlas: Handbuch für die jüdische Auswanderung* (Berlin: Philo, 1938). See also Michael Traub, *Die jüdische Auswanderung aus Deutschland: Westeuropa, Übersee, Palästina* (Berlin: Jüdische Rundschau, 1936).

24. *New York Times*, October 18, 1955 (Wischnitzer obituary); Gottschalk, "Report of Research Institute (1943–44)," 674.
25. Wischnitzer, *To Dwell in Safety*, ix, xiii; 3; Wischnitzer's use of the term "Holocaust" is noteworthy; James G. McDonald, *My Mission in Israel: 1948–1951* (London: Victor Gollancz, 1951); Barbara Metzger, "The League of Nations, Refugees, and Individual Rights," in Frank and Reinisch, *Refugees in Europe*, 101–119.
26. Lloyd P. Gartner, "Jewish Migrants en Route from Europe to North America: Traditions and Realities," *Jewish History* 1, no. 2 (1986): 49–66.
27. Eugene M. Kulischer, "Review of *To Dwell in Safety*," *Jewish Social Studies* 12, no. 3 (1950): 281–283.
28. Kulischer, *Europe on the Move*, v–vii, 8; Jennings *Escape from Vichy*; *New York Times*, April 4, 1956 (Kulischer obituary); Mazower, *No Enchanted Palace*, 113; Marcel Fournier, *Marcel Mauss: A Biography* (Princeton, NJ: Princeton University Press, 2006), 333–350; Lewis Coser, "Introduction: Maurice Halbwachs, 1877–1945," in Maurice Halbwachs, *On Collective Memory*, ed. and trans. Lewis Coser (Chicago: University of Chicago Press, 1992), 3–7.
29. Engel, *The Assassination of Symon Petliura*, 40–42; *New York Times*, October 27, 1927 ("Paris Jury Acquits Slayer of Petlura"); Kulischer, *Europe on the Move*, 66n83; Wischnitzer, *To Dwell in Safety*, 143.
30. *The Jewish Pogroms in Ukraine*, 15–16.
31. *The Jewish Pogroms in Ukraine*, 7, 20, 22.
32. "World Revolution Called Stalin's Aim," *New York Times*, February 6, 1946; Dimitry V. Lehovich, *White against Red: The Life of General Anton Denikin* (New York: Norton, 1974); Schechtman, *Pogromy Dobrovolcheskoi Armii na Ukraine*. On Denikin's role during the pogroms, see a translation of a Yiddish study that was first published in 1923 in Berlin: Nokem Shtif, *The Pogroms in Ukraine in 1918–19: Prelude to the Holocaust*, trans. and annotated, with an introduction by Maurice Wolfthal (Cambridge, UK: Open Book, 2019).
33. For recent studies, see Budnitskii, *Russian Jews between the Reds and the Whites*; Lohr, *Nationalizing the Russian Empire*; Gatrell, *A Whole Empire Walking*; Veidlinger, *In the Midst of Civilized Europe*.
34. Kulischer, *Europe on the Move*, 312–318; Mazower, *No Enchanted Palace*, 113; Kulischer, "Displaced Persons in the Modern World," 176; Carl Bon Tempo, *Americans at the Gate: The United States and Refugees during the Cold War* (Princeton, NJ: Princeton University Press, 2008), 24.
35. Joseph B. Schechtman, *European Population Transfers 1939–1945* (New York: Oxford University Press, 1946), 16–22, quote on 467–468.
36. Schechtman, *European Population Transfers 1939–1945*, 16–22, 457 (Palestine), quote on 467–468; Vladimir Jabotinsky, "Proposed Solution by Mass Evacuation," in Duker and Alper, *Jewish Post-War Problems*, 63–65; Mazower, *No Enchanted Palace*, 117–178; Frank, *Making Minorities History*, 179–182; Laurence Weinbaum, *A Marriage of Convenience: The New Zionist Organization and the Polish Government 1936–1939* (Boulder, CO: East European Monographs, 1993), 164–199; Timothy Snyder, *Black Earth: The Holocaust as History and* Warning (New York: Tim Duggan, 2015), 63, 100; Ferrara, "Eugene Kulischer."

37. Kulischer, *Europe on the Move*, 264.
38. Kulischer, *Europe on the Move*, 264, 312–315; Wischnitzer, *To Dwell in Safety*, 248–250. Schechtman later published a controversial book about the Mufti's ties to Nazi Germany: Joseph B. Schechtman, *The Mufti and the Führer: The Rise and Fall of Haj Amin el-Husseini* (New York: Thomas Yoseloff, 1965).
39. Ferrara, "Eugene Kulischer."
40. James Loeffler, "'The Conscience of America': Human Rights, Jewish Politics, and American Foreign Policy at the United Nations San Francisco Conference, 1945," *Journal of American History* 100, no. 2 (2013): 419–420.
41. Mark Wischnitzer, "Review, *Europe on the Move*," *Journal of Economic History* 9, no. 1 (1949): 111–112; Ilya Dijour, "Review, *Europe on the Move*," *Jewish Social Studies* 11, no. 2 (1949): 179–180.
42. Jacob Lestschinsky, "Jewish Migrations, 1840–1946," in *The Jews: Their History, Culture, and Religion*, ed. Louis Finkelstein (Philadelphia: Jewish Publication Society, 1949), 3:1198–1238, quote on 1215; Rachel Wischnitzer, "Judaism and Art," in Finkelstein, *The Jews*, 984–1110; Jacob Lestschinsky, "Remarks on Professor Eugene M. Kulischer's Pamphlet on Jewish Migrations," June 18, 1943, AJA, WJC Records, Institute for Jewish Affairs Records, MS Coll. 361, Box 8, Folder 7; see also Jacob Lestschinsky, "Poland," in *European Jewry Ten Years after the War*, ed. Institute of Jewish Affairs of the World Jewish Congress (New York: Institute of Jewish Affairs, 1956), 13–43.
43. Lestschinsky, "Jewish Migrations, 1840–1946," 1234.
44. "Necrology" (Wischnitzer), *American Jewish Yearbook* 58 (1957): 477; Wischnitzer, *Visas to Freedom*, 12–13; Sherman, "Rachel Wischnitzer."
45. *New York Times*, April 4, 1956 (Kulischer obituary); Kulischer file, WFO 100-17493, August and September 1946, FBI Headquarters File, Subject Silvermaster, File no. 65-56402, Vol. 65, 99, Vol. 67, 122, 130–131, https://archive.org/stream/FBISilvermasterFile; Eugene M. Kulischer, "Migration," *Encyclopedia Britannica*, vol. 15 (1952), 997. Kulischer's research on Soviet forces resulted in one of his last publications: Eli Ginzberg, Edward A. Fitzpatrick, Howard A. Meyerhoff, Eugene M. Kulischer, et al., "Human Resources and National Resources," *Scientific Monthly* 82, no. 3 (1956): 121–135.
46. Schlögel, "Verschiebebahnhof Europa"; Mazower, *No Enchanted Palace*, 113–125. For biographical background and a bibliography of Kulischer's works, see Jaffe, "Notes on the Population Theory of Eugene M. Kulischer"; Ferrara, "Eugene Kulischer."
47. Estraikh, "Jacob Lestschinsky," 230–234; Jacob Lestschinsky, "Jewish Migrations, 1840–1956," in *The Jews: Their History, Culture, and Religion*, 2nd edition, ed. Louis Finkelstein (New York: Harper, 1955), 2:1198–1238; Jacob Lestschinsky, "Jewish Migrations, 1840–1946," in *The Jews: Their History, Culture, and Religion*, 3rd edition, ed. Louis Finkelstein (New York: Harper & Row, 1960), 2:1536–1596; Jacob Lestschinsky, *Jewish Migrations in Recent Generations* (Tel Aviv: Alef, 1965) [Hebrew].
48. Elazar, "Prof. Arieh Tartakower," 13.

Chapter 10

1. *Aufbau* (New York), February 18 and 25, 1949 ("Shanghai Flüchtlinge"—"Gerettet aus Shanghai"); *New York Times*, February 22 and 28, March 12, 1949 ("Israel-Bound DPs"); Anna Pegler-Gordon, *Closing the Golden Door: Asian Migration and the Hidden History of Exclusion at Ellis Island* (Chapel Hill: University of North Carolina Press, 2021), 91–93.
2. Wells, *Tropical Zion*, 139–154; Marion Kaplan, *Dominican Haven: The Jewish Refugee Settlement in Sosua, 1940–1945* (New York: Museum of Jewish Heritage, 2008), 91.
3. Tichenor, *Dividing Lines*, 181–192, quote on 188; Revercombe quoted in Bon Tempo, *Americans at the Gate*, 23; Kulischer, "Displaced Persons in the Modern World," 176.
4. "1,543 from Shanghai," *New York Times*, May 28, 1949; Frank Dikötter, *The Tragedy of Liberation: A History of the Chinese Revolution, 1945–57* (London: Bloomsbury, 2013), 30–32, 94–96; "In letzter Minute. . . ," *Aufbau*, June 2, 1950; "Shanghai Konferenz mit Präsident Truman," *Aufbau*, June 9, 1950; "U.S. Orders 108 Refugees Deported Here Wednesday," *New York Times*, June 19, 1950; "All Hope Vanishes for 106 D.P.'s Here," *New York Times*, June 20, 1950; "Truman Speeding Refugees' Return," *New York Times*, June 21, 1950; "106 Refugees Sail for German Camp," and "Odyssey of the 106," *New York Times*, June 22, 1950.
5. Anna Holian, *Between National Socialism and Soviet Communism: Displaced Persons in Postwar Germany* (Ann Arbor: University of Michigan Press, 2011), 42–43; *Constitution of the International Refugee Organization* (Lake Success, NY: United Nations, 1946), 3, 12–14.
6. "An Act to Authorize for a Limited Period of Time the Admission into the United States of Certain European Displaced Persons for Permanent Residence, and for Other Purposes," June 25, 1948, *U.S. Statutes at Large* (Washington, D.C.: GPO, 1949), vol. 62, part 1, 1009–1010; Daniels, *Coming to America*, 331; Zolberg, *A Nation by Design*, 272, 308.
7. Cohen, *In War's Wake*, 56–57.
8. Ori Yehudai, *Leaving Zion: Jewish Emigration from Palestine and Israel after World War II* (Cambridge: Cambridge University Press, 2020), 66–97; "700 Jewish DPs Return to Germany from Israel," *New York Times*, June 20, 1950.
9. Yfaat Weiss, "The Golem and Its Creator, or How the Jewish Nation-State Became Multiethnic," in *Challenging Ethnic Citizenship: German and Israeli Perspectives on Immigration*, ed. Yfaat Weiss and Daniel Levy (New York: Berghahn Books, 2002), 82–104; Hannah Arendt, *Origins of Totalitarianism* (1951; New York: Meridian, 1958), 279; Arendt, "The Minority Question"; Memorandum, November 12, 1948, AJA, WJC Records, MS Coll. 361, Box 65, Folder 26.
10. Daniel Greene, *The Jewish Origins of Cultural Pluralism: The Menorah Association and American Diversity* (Bloomington: Indiana University Press, 2011); Robert Redfield, Ralph Linton, and Melville J. Herskovits, "Memorandum for the Study of Acculturation," *American Anthropologist*, New Series, 38, no. 1 (1936): 149–152; Mitchell Duneier, *Ghetto: The Invention of a Place, the History of an Idea* (New York: FSG, 2016), 48–49.

Conclusion

1. Chazan, *Refugees or Migrants*, 81, 107, 225.
2. Lederhendler, "The Interrupted Chain," 175.
3. "Refuseniks and other Refugees," *New York Times*, April 12, 1989; Bon Tempo, *Americans at the Gate*, 140–142; Maria Cristina Garcia, *The Refugee Challenge in Post–Cold War America* (New York: Oxford University Press, 2017), 15–34.
4. Yinon Cohen and Irena Kogan, "Russian Jews in Germany: Jewish Immigration from the Former Soviet Union to Germany and Israel in the 1990s," *Leo Baeck Institute Yearbook* 50, no. 1 (2005): 249–265; Christopher A. Molnar, *Memory, Politics, and Yugoslav Migrations to Postwar Germany* (Bloomington: Indiana University Press, 2019), 161–204.
5. For Jews as "migrating people," see Zvi Gitelman, "Native Land, Promised Land: Jewish Emigration from Russia and Ukraine," *Harvard Ukrainian Studies* 22 (1998): 137.
6. John A. Armstrong, "Mobilized and Proletarian Diasporas," *American Political Science Review* 70, no. 2 (1976): 393–408; Leslie Page Moch, *Moving Europeans: Migration in Western Europe since 1650* (Bloomington: Indiana University Press, 1992); Amrith, *Crossing the Bay of Bengal*; Hoerder, *Cultures in Contact*. On the Wandering Jew stereotype, see the essays in *Le Juif Errant un Témoin du Temps*, exhibition catalogue, Musée d'Art et d'Histoire du Judaïsme (Paris: Biro, 2002).
7. Lederhendler, *Jewish Immigrants and American Capitalism*, 69–84.
8. Leo Lucassen and Jan Lucassen, "Migration, Migration History, History: Old Paradigms and New Perspectives," in Lucassen and Lucassen, *Migration, Migration History, History*, 14; Tyler Anbinder and Hope McCaffrey, "Which Irish Men and Women Immigrated to the United States during the Great Famine Migration of 1846–54?," *Irish Historical Studies* 39, no. 156 (2015): 620–642.
9. Zolberg, *A Nation by Design*, 270–272; Weil, *How to Be French*, 87–124; Claire Zalc, *Denaturalized: How Thousands Lost Their Citizenship and Lives in Vichy France* (Cambridge, MA: Harvard University Press, 2020).
10. Hannah Arendt, "The Minority Question," in *Hannah Arendt: The Jewish Writings*, ed. Jerome Kohn and Ron H. Feldman (New York: Schocken, 2007), 130.
11. Simpson, *The Refugee Problem*, 3–4; UNHCR, *Convention and Protocol relating to the Status of Refugees* (Geneva: UNHCR, 2010), 14–15; William Maley, *What Is a Refugee?* (Oxford: Oxford University Press, 2016), 21.
12. James Loeffler, *Rooted Cosmopolitans: Jews and Human Rights in the Twentieth Century* (New Haven, CT: Yale University Press, 2018), 180.
13. Bon Tempo, *Americans at the Gate*, 90–105; Ngai, *Impossible Subjects*; Lia Lynn Yang, *One Mighty and Irresistible Tide: The Epic Struggle over American Immigration, 1924–1965* (New York: Norton, 2020), 62–89; Aristide Zolberg, Astri Suhrke, and Sergei Aguayo, *Escape from Violence: Conflict and the Refugee Crisis in the Developing World* (New York: Oxford University Press, 1989), 3–33.
14. Sharma, *Home Rule*; Alexander Betts, *Survival Migration Failed Governance and the Crisis of Displacement* (Ithaca, NY: Cornell University Press, 2013).

Selected Bibliography

Archives

Austria
Österreichisches Staatsarchiv, Allgemeines Verwaltungsarchiv, Vienna (OeStA/AVA)
 Justiz JM Allgemein Sig 6.

Britain
The National Archives, Kew.
 Foreign Office (FO).

Canada
Library and Archives Canada, Ottawa.
 Canadian Northern Railway (CNR), Deposit No. 56.

Germany
Geheimes Staatsarchiv Berlin (GeSta).
 Preußisches Ministerium für Handel und Gewerbe, Bestimmungen zum Schutze und zur Fürsorge für die Auswanderung und Kolonisation, XIII, 20, No. 1, vols. 1–24.
Universitätsarchiv, Humboldt Universität Berlin.
 Personalakte Professor Dr. Kulischer, UK Personalia: K 429.
Staatsarchiv Hamburg.
 Auswanderungsamt I, 373-7 I.
Staatsarchiv Bremen.
 Auswanderung 3-A.4.

Israel
Central Zionist Archive, Jerusalem (CZA).
 Central Zionist Office Berlin, Z3.
 Isaak Rülf Papers, A1/3.
 Leo Motzkin Papers, A126.
Central Archive for the History of the Jewish People, Jerusalem (CAHJP).
 Berlin Collection, D/Be4.
 DALJEWCIB, Harbin, Far East Collection.
 Danzig Collection, D/Da.
 Königsberg Collection, D/Ko1.
 Insterburg Collection, D/In1.

Switzerland
League of Nations Archive, Geneva (LNA).

Administrative Commissions and Minorities Section, Registry Files, Subseries 4 Danzig, R-140 (Situation of Jews in Danzig).
Dossiers du Bureau International de Travail Service des Refugies, Section C, Reg. 1379-1467.
Russian Refugees, Section 45, Reg. 19-27.

United States
American Jewish Archives, Cincinnati (AJA).
  Jacob Schiff Papers, MS Coll. 456.
  World Jewish Congress Records, MS Coll. 361.
Franklin D. Roosevelt Library Archives, Hyde Park, NY.
  Franklin D. Roosevelt Papers, President's Secretary's File, Subject File, Refugees, 1938-1944.
Leo Baeck Institute, Center for Jewish History, New York (LBI).
  Bericht über eine Informationsreise nach der Südafrikanischen Union, den beiden Rhodesien und Kenya (Britisch-Ostafrika) von Dr. Mark Wischnitzer, MS 695.
  Bernhard Kahn Papers, AR 416.
  Isaak Rülf Collection 1858-1987, AR 3179.
  Rachel Wischnitzer Papers, AR 2565.
The New York Public Library, Manuscripts and Archives Division.
  Emergency Committee in Aid of Displaced Foreign Scholars Records.
YIVO, Center for Jewish History, New York.
  Abraham Cahan Papers, RG 1139.
  Ilya Dijour Papers, RG 589.
  Max Gottschalk Papers, RG 330.

Newspapers and Periodicals

Allgemeine Zeitung des Judenthums, Leipzig
American Hebrew, New York
American Jewish Yearbook, New York
American Railroad Journal, New York
Arbeiter Zeitung, Vienna
Aufbau, New York
Berliner Lokalanzeiger
Berliner Tageblatt
Berliner Zeitung
Bulletin du Comité des Delegations Juives, Paris
Centralblatt der Bauverwaltung, Berlin
Chicago Occident
Danziger Lebn
Danziger Zeitung
Detroit Jewish Chronicle
Hamburger Correspondent
Illinois Staatszeitung, Chicago
Israelitisches Familienblatt, Hamburg
The Jewish Chronicle, London

SELECTED BIBLIOGRAPHY 297

Jewish Telegraphic Agency, New York
Jüdische Presse, Berlin
Jüdische Rundschau, Berlin
Jüdisches Volksblatt, Breslau
Korrespondenzblatt des "Centralbureaus für jüdische Auswanderungsangelegenheiten," Berlin
Memeler Dampfboot, Memel
The Morning Chronicle, Halifax, NS, Canada
Neue Freie Presse, Vienna
Die Neuzeit, Vienna
New York Times
Nieuwe Rotterdamsche Courant, Rotterdam
Ost und West, Berlin
Rotterdamsch Nieuwsblad, Rotterdam
Spandauer Anzeiger für das Havelland, Spandau, Preußen
Spemans Illustrierte Zeitschrift für das Deutsche Haus, Stuttgart
The Times, London
Vorwärts, Berlin
Wiener Morgenzeitung, Vienna
Die Welt, Vienna
Der Zeitgeist, Milwaukee
Zeitung des Vereins Deutscher Eisenbahn-Verwaltungen, Berlin

Published Reports

Annual Report of the Commissioner General of Immigration for the Fiscal Year Ended June 30th 1894. Washington, D.C.: Government Printing Office, 1894.
Bericht über die vorläufigen Ergebnisse des vom k.k. Handelsministerium durchgeführten Untersuchung über die Organisation der Auswanderung in Österreich. Vienna: Hof- und Staatsdruckerei, 1913.
Festschrift anlässlich der Feier des 25jährigen Bestehens des Hilfsvereins der Deutschen Juden, gegr. am 28. Mai 1901. Berlin: Hilfsverein der Deutschen Juden, 1926.
Kaiserliches Statistisches Amt. Zur Eisenbahn- und Bevölkerungs-Statistik der Deutschen Städte: Insbesondere der Deutschen Kleinstädte und Landstädte in der Periode 1867 bis 1875. Berlin: Puttkammer & Mühlbrecht, 1878.
U.S. Senate. Reports of the Emigration Commission, Presented by Mr. Dillingham: Emigration Conditions in Europe. Washington, D.C.: Government Printing Office, 1911.

Memoirs

Antin, Mary. From Plotzk to Boston. Foreword by Israel Zangwill. Boston: W. B. Clarke, 1899.
Bogen, Boris. Born a Jew. New York: Macmillan, 1930.
Cahan, Abraham. Bleter fun mein Lebn. New York: Forverts, 1926–1931.
Cowen, Philip. Memories of an American Jew. New York: International Press, 1932.
Gronemann, Sammy. Erinnerungen. 1947. Berlin: Philo, 2002.
Horwich, Bernard. My First Eighty Years. Chicago: Argus Books, 1939.

La Guardia, Fiorello. *The Making of an Insurgent: An Autobiography, 1882–1919*. Philadelphia: J. B. Lippincott, 1948.
Morgenthau, Henry. *Ambassador Morgenthau's Story*. New York: Doubleday, 1918.
Weizmann, Chaim. *Trial and Error: The Autobiography of Chaim Weizmann*. New York: Harper, 1949.

Novels and Plays

Aleichem, Sholem. *Ale Verk von Sholom Aleichem*. New York: Folks-Fond Oysgabe, 1923.
Cahan, Abraham. *Yekl: A Tale of the New York Ghetto*. New York: D. Appleton, 1896.
Grimm, Hans. *Volk ohne Raum*. Munich: A. Langen, 1926.
Gronemann, Sammy. *Utter Chaos*. Translated by Penny Milbouer. Bloomington: Indiana University Press, 2016.
Nabokov, Vladimir. *Pnin*. Garden City, NY: Doubleday, 1957.
Roth, Joseph. *Das Spinnennetz*. 1923. Cologne: Kiepenheuer & Witsch, 1967.
Seghers, Anna. *Transit*. Boston: Little, Brown, 1944.
Sue, Eugène. *Le Juif Errant*. Paris: Meline, 1844.
Zangwill, Israel. *Children of the Ghetto: Being Pictures of a Peculiar People*. Philadelphia: Jewish Publication Society, 1892.
Zangwill, Israel. *The Melting-Pot*. New York: Macmillan, 1909.

Other Published Works

Abella, Irving, and Harold Martin Troper. *None Is Too Many: Canada and the Jews of Europe, 1933–1948*. New York: Random House, 1982.
Adler, Eliyana. *Survival on the Margins: Polish Jewish Refugees in the Wartime Soviet Union*. Cambridge, MA: Harvard University Press, 2020.
Alroey, Gur. *Bread to Eat and Clothes to Wear: Letters from Jewish Migrants in the Early Twentieth Century*. Detroit, MI: Wayne State Press, 2011.
Alroey, Gur. "Bureaucracy, Agents and Swindlers: Hardships Faced by Russian Jewish Emigrants in the Early Twentieth Century." *Studies in Contemporary Jewry* 19 (2003): 214–231.
Alroey, Gur. "Demographers in the Service of the Nation: Liebmann Hersch, Jacob Lestschinsky, and the Early Study of Jewish Migration." *Jewish History* 20, nos. 3–4 (2006): 265–282.
Alroey, Gur. "Two Historiographies: Israeli Historiography and the Mass Jewish Migration to the United States, 1881–1914." *Jewish Quarterly Review* 105, no. 1 (2015): 99–129.
Alroey, Gur. *An Unpromising Land: Jewish Migration to Palestine in the Early Twentieth Century*. Stanford: Stanford University Press, 2014.
Aly, Götz, and Susanne Heim. *Architects of Annihilation: Auschwitz and the Logic of Destruction*. London: Orion, 2015.
Amrith, Sunil. *Crossing the Bay of Bengal: The Furies of Nature and the Crossings of Migrants*. Cambridge, MA: Harvard University Press, 2013.
Arendt, Hannah. *Origins of Totalitarianism*. New York: Meridian, 1951.
Armstrong, John A. "Mobilized and Proletarian Diasporas." *American Political Science Review* 70, no. 2 (1976): 393–408.

SELECTED BIBLIOGRAPHY 299

Aschheim, Steven. *Brothers and Strangers: The East European Jew in German and German Jewish Consciousness 1800–1923*. Madison: University of Wisconsin Press, 1982.

Avraami, Zwi. *Die jüdische Wirklichkeit und der Zionismus: Eine sozial-ökonomische Studie*. Zurich: Ostheim, 1905.

Avrutin, Eugene M. *Jews and the Imperial State: Identification Politics in Tsarist Russia*. Ithaca, NY: Cornell University Press, 2012.

Baron, Salo. "Ghetto and Emancipation." *Menorah Journal* 14 (1928): 515–526.

Bartrop, Paul R. *The Evian Conference of 1938 and the Jewish Refugee Crisis*. New York: Palgrave Macmillan, 2018.

Bauer, Yehuda. *My Brother's Keeper: A History of the American Jewish Joint Distribution Committee 1929–1939*. Philadelphia: Jewish Publication Society, 1974.

Benton-Cohen, Katherine. *Inventing the Immigration Problem: The Dillingham Commission and Its Legacy*. Cambridge, MA: Harvard University Press, 2018.

Bernheimer, Charles Seligman, ed. *The Russian Jew in the United States*. Philadelphia: John C. Winston, 1905.

Bon Tempo, Carl. *Americans at the Gate: The United States and Refugees during the Cold War*. Princeton, NJ: Princeton University Press, 2008.

Breitman, Richard, and Allan J. Lichtman. *FDR and the Jews*. Cambridge, MA: Harvard University Press, 2013.

Brenner, Michael. *Prophets of the Past: Interpreters of Jewish History*. Princeton, NJ: Princeton University Press, 2010.

Brinkmann, Tobias, ed. *Points of Passage: Jewish Transmigrants from Eastern Europe in Scandinavia, Germany, and Britain 1880–1914*. New York: Berghahn Books, 2013.

Brinkmann, Tobias. "The Road from Damascus: Transnational Jewish Philanthropic Organizations and the Jewish Mass Migration from Eastern Europe 1860–1914." In *Shaping the Transnational Sphere: Experts, Networks, and Issues from the 1840s to the 1930s*, edited by Davide Rodogno, Jakob Vogel, and Bernhard Struck, 152–172. New York: Berghahn Books, 2015.

Brinkmann, Tobias. "Why Paul Nathan Attacked Albert Ballin: The Transatlantic Mass Migration and the Privatization of Prussia's Eastern Border Inspection, 1886–1914." *Central European History* 43, no. 1 (2010): 47–83.

Cabanes, Bruno. *The Great War and the Origins of Humanitarianism 1918–1924*. Cambridge: Cambridge University Press, 2014.

Cecil, Lamar. *Albert Ballin: Business and Politics in Imperial Germany 1888–1918*. Princeton, NJ: Princeton University Press, 1967.

Cecil, Lamar. "Coal for the Fleet That Had to Die." *American Historical Review* 69, no. 4 (1964): 990–1005.

Chazan, Robert. *Refugees or Migrants: Pre-Modern Jewish Population Movement*. New Haven, CT: Yale University Press, 2018.

Choate, Mark. *Emigrant Nation: The Making of Italy Abroad*. Cambridge, MA: Harvard University Press, 2008.

Cohen, Gerard Daniel. *In War's Wake: Europe Displaced Persons in the Postwar Order*. New York: Oxford University Press, 2012.

Cohen, Naomi W. *Jacob Schiff: A Study in American Jewish Leadership*. Hanover, NH: Brandeis University Press, 1999.

Cohen, Naomi W. *Not Free to Desist: The American Jewish Committee, 1906–1966*. Philadelphia: Jewish Publication Society, 1972.

SELECTED BIBLIOGRAPHY

Daniels, Roger. *Coming to America: A History of Immigration and Ethnicity in American Life*. New York: Harper Collins, 1991.

Daniels, Roger. *Guarding the Golden Door: American Immigration Policy and Immigrants since 1882*. New York: Macmillan, 2005.

Davies, Helen M. *Emile and Isaac Pereire: Bankers, Socialists and Sephardic Jews in Nineteenth-Century France*. Manchester: Manchester University Press, 2015.

Dekel-Chen, Jonathan. "East European Jewish Migration: Inside and Outside." *East European Jewish Affairs* 44, nos. 2–3 (2014): 154–170.

Dekel-Chen, Jonathan. *Farming the Red Land: Jewish Agricultural Colonization and Local Soviet Power, 1924–1941*. New Haven, CT: Yale University Press, 2008.

Duker, Abraham, and Michael Alper, eds. *Jewish Post-War Problems: A Study Course. Unit VII: Relief, Reconstruction, and Migration*. New York: American Jewish Committee, 1942.

Dwork, Deborah, and Robert Jan van Pelt. *Flight from the Reich: Refugee Jews 1933–1946*. New York: Norton, 2009.

Endelman, Todd. *Leaving the Jewish Fold: Conversion and Radical Assimilation in Modern Jewish History*. Princeton, NJ: Princeton University Press, 2016.

Estraikh, Gennady. "Jacob Lestschinsky: A Yiddishist Dreamer and Social Scientist." *Science in Context* 20, no. 2 (2007): 215–237.

Estraikh, Gennady. *Transatlantic Russian Jewishness: Ideological Voyages of the Yiddish Daily* Forverts *in the First Half of the Twentieth Century*. Boston: Academic Studies Press, 2020.

Evans, Richard. *Death in Hamburg: Society and Politics in the Cholera Years 1830–1910*. Oxford: Oxford University Press, 1987.

Ewence, Hannah. *The Alien Jew in the British Imagination 1881–1905*. London: Palgrave, 2019.

Fairchild, Amy L. *Science at the Borders: Immigrant Medical Inspection and the Shaping of the Modern Industrial Labor Force*. Baltimore: Johns Hopkins University Press, 2003.

Federman, Sarah. *Last Train to Auschwitz: The French National Railway and the Journey to Accountability*. Madison: University of Wisconsin Press, 2021.

Ferenczi, Imre. *Kontinentale Wanderungen und die Annäherung der Völker: Ein geschichtlicher Überblick*. Jena: Gustav Fischer, 1930.

Ferrara, Antonio. "Eugene Kulischer, Joseph Schechtman and the Historiography of European Forced Migrations." *Journal of Contemporary History* 46, no. 4 (2011): 715–740.

Feys, Torsten. *The Battle for the Migrants: Introduction of Steamshipping on the North Atlantic and Its Impact on the European Exodus*. St. John's: International Maritime Economic Association, 2013.

Field, Henry. *"M" Project for FDR: Studies on Migration and Settlement*. Ann Arbor, MI: Edwards Brothers, 1962.

Fink, Carole. *Defending the Rights of Others: The Great Powers, the Jews, and International Minority Protection, 1878–1938*. Cambridge: Cambridge University Press, 2004.

Frank, Matthew. *Making Minorities History: Population Transfer in Twentieth-Century Europe*. Oxford: Oxford University Press, 2017.

Frank, Matthew, and Jessica Reinisch. "Introduction: Refugees and the Nation-State in Europe, 1919–59." *Journal of Contemporary History* 49, no. 3 (2014): 477–490.

Frank, Matthew, and Jessica Reinisch, eds. *Refugees in Europe, 1919–1959: A Forty Years' Crisis?* London: Bloomsbury Academic, 2017.

Frankel, Jonathan. "The Crisis of 1881–82 as a Turning Point in Modern Jewish History." In *The Legacy of Jewish Migration: 1881 and Its Impact*, edited by David Berger, 9–22. New York: Brooklyn College Press, 1983.

Freitag, Gabriele. *Nächstes Jahr in Moskau! Die Zuwanderung von Juden in die sowjetische Metropole 1917–1932*. Göttingen: Vandenhoek & Ruprecht, 2004.

Friedländer, Saul. *The Years of Extermination: Nazi Germany and the Jews, 1939–1945*. New York: Harper Collins, 2007.

Garland, Libby. *After They Closed the Gates: Jewish Illegal Immigration to the United States, 1921–1965*. Chicago: University of Chicago Press, 2014.

Gartner, Lloyd P. *American and British Jews in the Age of the Great Migration*. London: Valentine Mitchell, 2009.

Gartner, Lloyd P. "Anglo-Jewry and the Jewish International Traffic in Prostitution, 1885–1914." *AJS Review*, nos. 7–8 (1982–1983): 129–178.

Gartner, Lloyd P. *The Jewish Immigrant in England 1870–1914*. London: George Allen & Unwin, 1960.

Gartner, Lloyd P. "Jewish Migrants en Route from Europe to North America: Traditions and Realities." *Jewish History* 1, no. 2 (1986): 49–66.

Gatrell, Peter. *The Making of the Modern Refugee*. Oxford: Oxford University Press, 2013.

Gatrell, Peter. *A Whole Empire Walking: Refugees in Russia during World War I*. Bloomington: Indiana University Press, 2005.

Gatrell, Peter, and Liubov Zhvanko, eds. *Europe on the Move: Refugees in the Era of the Great War*. Manchester: Manchester University Press, 2017.

Giladi, Rotem. *Jews, Sovereignty, and International Law: Ideology and Ambivalence in Early Israeli Legal Diplomacy*. Oxford: Oxford University Press, 2021.

Gitelman, Zvi. "Native Land, Promised Land: Jewish Emigration from Russia and Ukraine." *Harvard Ukrainian Studies* 22 (1998): 137–163.

Glazier, Jack. *Dispersing the Ghetto: The Relocation of Jewish Immigrants across America*. Ithaca, NY: Cornell University Press, 1998.

Gleizer-Salzman, Daniela. *Unwelcome Exiles: Mexico and the Jewish Refugees from Nazism, 1933–1945*. Leiden: Brill, 2014.

Gordon, Milton M. *Assimilation in American Life: The Role of Race, Religion, and National Origins*. New York: Oxford University Press, 1964.

Gottschalk, Max, and Abraham G. Duker. *Jews in the Post-War World*. New York: Dryden Press, 1945.

Granick, Jaclyn. *International Jewish Humanitarianism in the Age of the Great War*. Cambridge: Cambridge University Press, 2021.

Grant, Madison. *The Passing of the Great Race or the Basis of European History*. New York: Charles Scribner's Sons, 1916.

Green, Abigail. "Intervening in the Jewish Question 1840–1878." In *Humanitarian Intervention: A History*, edited by Brendan Simms and D. J. B. Trim, 139–158. Cambridge: Cambridge University Press, 2011.

Greene, Daniel. *The Jewish Origins of Cultural Pluralism: The Menorah Association and American Diversity*. Bloomington: Indiana University Press, 2011.

Grossmann, Atina. *Jews, Germans, and Allies: Close Encounters in Occupied Germany*. Princeton, NJ: Princeton University Press, 2007.

Handlin, Oscar. *Adventure in Freedom: Three Hundred Years of Jewish Life in America*. New York: McGraw-Hill, 1954.

Handlin, Oscar. *Boston's Immigrants 1790–1865: A Study in Acculturation* (1941). Revised and enlarged edition. Cambridge, MA: Harvard University Press, 1991.
Handlin, Oscar. *The Uprooted: The Epic Story of the Great Migrations That Made the American People*. Boston: Little, Brown, 1951.
Herberg, Will. *Protestant, Catholic, Jew: An Essay in American Religious Sociology*. Chicago: University of Chicago Press, 1955.
Herbert, Ulrich. *Geschichte der Ausländerpolitik in Deutschland*. Munich: C. H. Beck, 2001.
Hersch, Liebmann. "International Migration of the Jews." In *International Migrations*, edited by Walter Willcox, 2:471–520. New York: National Bureau of Economic Research, 1931.
Hersch, Liebmann. *Le Juif Errant d'Aujord Hui: Etude sur l'Emigration des Israelites de l'Europe Orientale aux Etats-Unis de L'Amerique du Nord*. Paris: M. Girard & E. Briere, 1913.
Herskovits, Melville J. "When Is a Jew a Jew?" *Modern Quarterly* 4, no. 2 (1927): 109–117.
Herskovits, Melville J. "Who are the Jews?" In *The Jews: Their History, Culture, and Religion*, edited by Louis Finkelstein, 2:1489–1509. New York: Harper & Row, 1960.
Higham, John. *Send These to Me: Immigrants in Urban America*. Revised edition. Baltimore: Johns Hopkins University Press, 1984.
Higham, John. *Strangers in the Land: Patterns of American Nativism 1860–1925*. New Brunswick, NJ: Rutgers University Press, 1955.
Hilberg, Raul, Christopher Browning, and Peter Hayes. *German Railroads, Jewish Souls: The Reichsbahn, Bureaucracy, and the Final Solution*. New York: Berghahn Books, 2019.
Hoerder, Dirk. *Cultures in Contact: World Migrations in the Second Millennium*. Durham, NC: Duke University Press, 2002.
Hoffmann-Holter, Beatrix. *"Abreisemachung": Jüdische Kriegsflüchtlinge in Wien 1914 bis 1923*. Vienna: Böhlau, 1995.
Holian, Anna. *Between National Socialism and Soviet Communism: Displaced Persons in Postwar Germany*. Ann Arbor: University of Michigan Press, 2011.
Howe, Irving. *World of Our Fathers: The Journey of the East European Jews to America and the Life They Found and Made*. New York: Harcourt Brace Jovanovich, 1976.
Huber, Valeska. *Channelling Mobilities: Migration and Globalisation in the Suez Canal Region and Beyond, 1869–1914*. Cambridge: Cambridge University Press, 2013.
Jahr, Christoph. *Paul Nathan: Publizist, Politiker und Philanthrop 1857–1927*. Göttingen: Wallstein, 2018.
Jennings, Eric T. *Escape from Vichy: The Refugee Exodus to the French Caribbean*. Cambridge, MA: Harvard University Press, 2018.
Jockusch, Laura. *Collect and Record! Jewish Holocaust Documentation in Early Postwar Europe*. New York: Oxford University Press, 2012.
Just, Michael. *Ost- und südosteuropäische Amerikawanderung: 1881–1914. Transitprobleme in Deutschland und Aufnahme in den Vereinigten Staaten*. Stuttgart: Franz Steiner, 1988.
Kahn, Bernhard. "Die jüdische Auswanderung." *Ost und West* (Berlin), July and August 1905, 457–480.
Kaplan, Marion. *Hitler's Jewish Refugees: Hope and Anxiety in Portugal*. New Haven, CT: Yale University Press, 2020.
Kaplun-Kogan, Wladimir Wolf. *Die jüdischen Wanderbewegungen der neuesten Zeit*. Bonn: Marcus & Webers, 1919.

Kaplun-Kogan, Wladimir Wolf. *Die Wanderbewegungen der Juden*. Bonn: Marcus & Webers, 1913.
Karlsberg, Bernhard. *History and Importance of the German Control of Emigrants in Transit*. Hamburg: Gebrüder Enoch, 1922.
Keeling, Drew. *The Business of Migration between Europe and the United States, 1900–1914*. Zurich: Chronos, 2012.
Kelley, Ninette, and Michael Trebilcock. *The Making of the Mosaic: A History of Canadian Immigration Policy*. Toronto: University of Toronto Press, 1998.
Klier, John D. *Russians, Jews, and the Pogroms of 1881–1882*. Cambridge: Cambridge University Press, 2011.
Kobrin, Rebecca. *Jewish Bialystok and Its Diaspora*. Bloomington: Indiana University Press, 2010.
Kühl, Stefan. *The Nazi Connection: Eugenics, American Racism, and German National Socialism*. New York: Oxford University Press, 2002.
Kukushkin, Vadim. *From Peasants to Labourers: Ukrainian and Belarusan Immigration from the Russian Empire to Canada*. Montreal: McGill-Queen's University Press, 2007.
Kulischer, Alexander, and Eugen Kulischer. *Kriegs- und Wanderzüge: Weltgeschichte als Völkerbewegung*. Berlin: De Gruyter, 1932.
Kulischer, Eugene. "Displaced Persons in the Modern World." *Annals of the American Academy of Political and Social Science* 262, no. 1 (1949): 166–177.
Kulischer, Eugene. *The Displacement of Population in Europe*. Montreal: Inland Press, 1943.
Kulischer, Eugene. *Europe on the Move: War and Population Changes, 1917–1947*. New York: Columbia University Press, 1948.
Kulischer, Eugene. *Jewish Migrations: Past Experiences and Post-War Prospects*. New York: American Jewish Committee, 1943.
Kuzmany, Börries. *Brody: Eine galizische Grenzstadt im langen 19. Jahrhundert*. Vienna: Böhlau, 2011.
Kuznets, Simon. "Immigration of Russian Jews to the United States: Background and Structure." *Perspectives in American History* 9 (1975): 35–124.
Kuznitz, Cecile Esther. *YIVO and the Making of Modern Jewish Culture: Scholarship for the Yiddish Nation*. New York: Cambridge University Press, 2014.
Lederhendler, Eli. "The Interrupted Chain: Traditional Receiver Countries, Migration Regimes, and the East European Jewish Diaspora 1918–39." *East European Jewish Affairs* 44, nos. 2–3 (2014): 171–186.
Lederhendler, Eli. *Jewish Immigrants and American Capitalism, 1880–1920: From Caste to Class*. Cambridge: Cambridge University Press, 2009.
Lederhendler, Eli. "The New Filiopietism, or Toward a New History of Jewish Immigration to America." *American Jewish History* 93, no. 1 (2007): 1–20.
Leff, Laurel. *Well Worth Saving: American Universities' Life-and-Death Decisions on Refugees from Nazi Europe*. New Haven, CT: Yale University Press, 2019.
Leff, Lisa Moses. *The Archive Thief*. New York: Oxford University Press, 2015.
Leff, Lisa Moses. *Sacred Bonds of Solidarity: The Rise of Jewish Internationalism in Nineteenth Century France*. Stanford: Stanford University Press, 2006.
Leiserowitz, Ruth. *Sabbatleuchter und Kriegerverein: Juden in der ostpreußisch-litauischen Grenzregion 1812–1942*. Osnabrück: fibre, 2010.
Lesser, Jeffrey. "The Immigration and Integration of Polish Jews in Brazil, 1924–1934." *The Americas* 51, no. 2 (1994): 173–191.

Lestschinsky, Jakob. "Die jüdische Wanderung, ihre Ursachen und ihre Regelung Fortsetzung." *Archiv für Wanderungswesen und Auslandskunde* 1, no. 4 (1929): 168–172.
Lestschinsky, Jakob. "Die soziale und wirtschaftliche Entwicklung der Ostjuden nach dem Kriege." *Weltwirtschaftliches Archiv* 24 (1926): 39–62.
Lestschinsky, Jakob. "Jewish Migrations, 1840–1946." In *The Jews: Their History, Culture, and Religion*, edited by Louis Finkelstein, 4:1198–1238. Philadelphia: Jewish Publication Society, 1949.
Lestschinsky, Jakob. *Probleme bei der Bevölkerungsbewegung bei den Juden*. Berlin: Privately published, 1926.
Levene, Mark. *War, Jews and the New Europe: Diplomacy of Lucien Wolf, 1914–19*. Oxford: Oxford University Press, 1992.
Loeffler, James. "'The Conscience of America': Human Rights, Jewish Politics, and American Foreign Policy at the United Nations San Francisco Conference, 1945." *Journal of American History* 100, no. 2 (2013): 401–428.
Loeffler, James. *Rooted Cosmopolitans: Jews and Human Rights in the Twentieth Century*. New Haven, CT: Yale University Press, 2018.
Lohr, Eric. *Nationalizing the Russian Empire: The Campaign against Enemy Aliens during World War I*. Cambridge, MA: Harvard University Press, 2003.
Lohr, Eric. *Russian Citizenship: From Empire to Soviet Union*. Cambridge, MA: Harvard University Press, 2012.
Maley, William. *What Is a Refugee?* Oxford: Oxford University Press, 2016.
Marinari, Maddalena. *The Unwanted: Italian and Jewish Mobilization against Restrictive Immigration Laws 1882–1965*. Chapel Hill: University of North Carolina Press, 2020.
Markel, Howard. *Quarantine! East European Jewish Immigrants and the New York City Epidemics of 1892*. Baltimore: Johns Hopkins University Press, 1997.
Marrus, Michael R. *The Unwanted—European Refugees in the Twentieth Century*. Oxford: Oxford University Press, 1985.
Martin, Susan F. *International Migration: Evolving Trends from the Early Twentieth Century to the Present*. Cambridge: Cambridge University Press, 2014.
Mays, Devi. *Forging Ties, Forging Passports: Migration and the Modern Sephardi Diaspora*. Stanford: Stanford University Press, 2020.
Mazower, Mark. "Minorities and the League of Nations in Interwar Europe." *Daedalus* 126, no. 2 (1997): 47–63.
Mazower, Mark. *No Enchanted Palace: The End of Empire and the Ideological Origins of the United Nations*. Princeton, NJ: Princeton University Press, 2009.
McKeown, Adam M. *Melancholy Order: Asian Migration and the Globalization of Borders*. New York: Columbia University Press, 2008.
Medoff, Rafael. *The Jews Should Keep Quiet: Franklin D. Roosevelt, Rabbi Stephen S. Wise, and the Holocaust*. Lincoln: University of Nebraska Press, 2019.
Miller, Kerby A. *Emigrants and Exiles: Ireland and the Irish Exodus to North America*. New York: Oxford University Press, 1988.
Morris-Reich, Amos. *The Quest for Jewish Assimilation in Modern Social Science*. Abingdon: Routledge, 2008.
Murken, Erich. *Die großen transatlantischen Linienreederei-Verbände, Pools und Interessengemeinschaften bis zum Ausbruch des Weltkrieges: Ihre Entstehung, Organisation und Wirksamkeit*. Jena: G. Fischer, 1922.
Nathans, Benjamin. *Beyond the Pale: The Jewish Encounter with Late Imperial Russia*. Berkeley: University of California Press, 2002.

Ngai, Mae M. *Impossible Subjects: Illegal Aliens and the Making of Modern America.* Princeton, NJ: Princeton University Press, 2003.
Penslar, Derek. *Shylock's Children: Economics and Jewish Identity in Modern Europe.* Berkeley: University of California Press, 2001.
Perlmann, Joel. *America Classifies the Immigrants: From Ellis Island to the 2020 Census.* Cambridge, MA: Harvard University Press, 2018.
Pitkin, Thomas M. *Keepers of the Gate: A History of Ellis Island.* New York: NYU Press, 1975.
Prokopovych, Markian. "Urban History of Overseas Migration in Habsburg Central Europe: Vienna and Budapest in the Late Nineteenth Century." *Journal of Migration History* 2, no. 2 (2016): 330–351.
Rechter, David. *The Jews of Vienna and the First World War.* Oxford: Littman, 2001.
Rischin, Moses. *The Promised City: New York's Jews 1870–1914.* Cambridge, MA: Harvard University Press, 1962.
Ristaino, Marcia Reynders. *Port of Last Resort: The Diaspora Communities of Shanghai.* Stanford: Stanford University Press, 2001.
Rogger, Hans. "Tsarist Policy on Jewish Emigration." *Soviet Jewish Affairs* 3, no. 1 (1973): 26–36.
Rosenberg, Clifford. *Policing Paris: The Origins of Modern Immigration Control between the Wars.* Ithaca, NY: Cornell University Press, 2006.
Roth, Joseph. *Juden auf Wanderschaft.* Berlin: Die Schmiede, 1927.
Roth, Ralf, and Günther Dinhobl, eds. *Across the Borders: Financing the World's Railways in the Nineteenth and Twentieth Centuries.* Aldershot: Ashgate, 2013.
Roth, Ralf, and Henry Jacolin, eds. *Eastern European Railways in Transition: 19th to 21st Centuries.* Aldershot: Ashgate, 2013.
Rülf, Isaak. *Jankel Widutzky, der den Händen der Judenbekehrungsmission entzogene Knabe.* Memel: Ed. Schnee, 1867.
Rülf, Isaak. *Meine Reise nach Kowno um die Uebersiedelung nothleidender Glaubensgenossen aus den Grenzbezirken nach dem Innern Russlands zu ordnen, sowie die in der dortigen Synagoge gehaltene Predigt von Dr. Ruelf.* Memel: Goldschmidt, 1869.
Ruppin, Arthur. *Die Juden der Gegenwart: Eine sozialwissenschaftliche Studie.* Berlin: S. Calvary, 1904.
Ruppin, Arthur. *Soziologie der Juden.* Berlin: Jüdischer Verlag, 1930.
Sachar, Howard M. *Course of Modern Jewish History.* New York: Vintage Books, 1990.
Sanders, Ronald. *Shores of Freedom: A Hundred Years of Jewish Emigration.* New York: Henry Holt, 1988.
Sarna, Jonathan. "The Myth of No Return: Jewish Return Migration from Eastern Europe 1881–1914." *American Jewish History* 71, no. 2 (1981): 256–268.
Saß, Anne-Christin. *Berliner Luftmenschen: Osteuropäischen-jüdische Migranten in der Weimarer Republik.* Göttingen: Wallstein, 2012.
Schechtman, Joseph B. *European Population Transfers 1939–1945.* New York: Oxford University Press, 1946.
Schenk, Frithjof Benjamin. *Russlands Fahrt in die Moderne: Mobilität und sozialer Raum im Eisenbahnzeitalter.* Stuttgart: Steiner, 2014.
Schenk, Frithjof Benjamin. "Travel, Railroads and Identity Formation in the Russian Empire." In *Shatterzone of Empires: Coexistence and Violence in the German, Habsburg, Russian, and Ottoman Borderlands,* edited by Omer Bartov and Eric D. Weitz, 136–151. Bloomington: Indiana University Press, 2013.

Schivelbusch, Wolfgang. *Geschichte der Eisenbahnreise: Zur Industrialisierung von Raum und Zeit im 19. Jahrhundert*. Munich: Carl Hanser Verlag, 1977.

Schlögel, Karl. "Verschiebebahnhof Europa: Joseph B. Schechtmans und Eugene M. Kulischers Pionierarbeiten." *Zeithistorische Forschungen* 2, no. 3 (2005): 468–472.

Schneider, Dorothee. *Crossing Borders: Migration and Citizenship in the Twentieth-Century United States*. Cambridge, MA: Harvard University Press, 2011.

Sharma, Nandita. *Home Rule: National Sovereignty and the Separation of Natives and Migrants*. Durham, NC: Duke University Press, 2020.

Sheffer, Gabriel. *Diaspora Politics: At Home Abroad*. Cambridge: Cambridge University Press, 2003.

Siegelbaum, Lewis H., and Leslie Page Moch. *Broad Is My Native Land: Repertoires and Regimes of Migration in Russia's Twentieth Century*. Ithaca, NY: Cornell University Press, 2015.

Simpson, John Hope. *The Refugee Problem: Report of a Survey*. London: Oxford University Press, 1939.

Sjöberg, Tommie. *The Powers and the Persecuted: The Refugee Problem and the Intergovernmental Committee on Refugees (IGCR), 1938–1947*. Lund: Lund University Press, 1991.

Slezkine, Yuri. *The Jewish Century*. Princeton, NJ: Princeton University Press, 2004.

Sowell, Thomas. *Migrations and Cultures: A World View*. New York: Basic Books, 1996.

Spiro, Jonathan. *Defending the Master Race: Conservation, Eugenics, and the Legacy of Madison Grant*. Lebanon, NH: University of Vermont Press, 2009.

Steidl, Annemarie. *On Many Routes: Internal, European, and Transatlantic Migration in the Late Habsburg Empire*. West Lafayette, IN: Purdue University Press, 2021.

Szajkowski, Zosa. "The Consul and the Immigrant: A Case of Bureaucratic Bias." *Jewish Social Studies* 36, no. 1 (1974): 3–18.

Szajkowski, Zosa. "Emigration to America or Reconstruction in Europe." *Publications of the American Jewish Historical Society* 42, no. 2 (1952): 157–188.

Szajkowski, Zosa. "How the Mass Migration to America Began." *Jewish Social Studies* 4, no. 4 (1942): 291–310.

Szajkowski, Zosa. "Sufferings of Jewish Emigrants to America in Transit through Germany." *Jewish Social Studies* 39, nos. 1–2 (1977): 105–116.

Tanabaum, Susan L. *Jewish Immigrants in London 1880–1939*. London: Routledge, 2015.

Tartakower, Arieh. "The Jewish Refugee: A Sociological Survey." *Jewish Social Studies* 4, no. 4 (1942): 311–348.

Tartakower, Arieh. *Yidishe Vanderungen*. Warsaw: Privately published, 1940.

Tartakower, Arieh, and Kurt Grossmann. *The Jewish Refugee*. New York: Institute for Jewish Affairs/World Jewish Congress, 1944.

Ther, Philipp. *The Outsiders: Refugees in Europe since 1492*. Princeton, NJ: Princeton University Press, 2019.

Tichenor, Daniel J. *Dividing Lines. The Politics of Immigration Control in America*. Princeton, NJ: Princeton University Press, 2002.

Tilly, Charles. "Transplanted Networks." In *Immigration Reconsidered: History, Society and Politics*, edited by Virginia Yans-McLaughlin, 78–95. New York: Oxford University Press, 1990.

Traub, Michael. *Die jüdische Auswanderung aus Deutschland: Westeuropa, Übersee, Palästina*. Berlin: Jüdische Rundschau, 1936.

Traub, Michael. *Jüdische Wanderbewegungen vor und nach dem Weltkriege*. Berlin: Jüdischer Verlag, 1930.
Ury, Scott. "Migration as Redemption: The Myth and Memory of Jewish Migration from Eastern Europe to the New World." *Jewish Culture and History* 20, no. 1 (2018): 3–22.
Veidlinger, Jeffrey. *In the Midst of Civilized Europe: The Pogroms of 1918–1921 and the Onset of the Holocaust*. New York: HarperCollins, 2021.
Vital, David. *A People Apart: The Jews in Europe 1789–1939*. Oxford: Oxford University Press, 1999.
Weil, Patrick. *How to Be French: Nationality in the Making since 1789*. Durham, NC: Duke University Press, 2008.
Weindling, Paul. *Epidemics and Genocide in Eastern Europe 1890–1945*. Oxford: Oxford University Press, 2000.
Wells, Allen. *Tropical Zion: General Trujillo, FDR, and the Jews of Sosúa*. Durham, NC: Duke University Press, 2009.
Wertheimer, Jack. *Unwelcome Strangers: East European Jews in Imperial Germany*. New York: Oxford University Press, 1987.
Whitman, James Q. *Hitler's American Model: The United States and the Making of Nazi Race Law*. Princeton, NJ: Princeton: University Press, 2017.
Wirth, Louis. *The Ghetto*. Chicago: University of Chicago Press, 1928.
Wischnitzer, Mark. *Die Juden in der Welt: Gegenwart und Geschichte des Judentums in allen Ländern*. Berlin: Erich Reiss Verlag, 1935.
Wischnitzer, Mark. *Die jüdische Zunftverfassung in Polen und Litauen im 17. und 18. Jahrhundert*. Stuttgart: W. Kohlhammer, 1927.
Wischnitzer, Mark. *Die Universität Göttingen und die Entwicklung der liberalen Ideen in Russland im ersten Viertel des 19. Jahrhunderts*. Berlin: Ebering, 1907.
Wischnitzer, Mark. "The Historical Background of the Settlement of Jewish Refugees in Santo Domingo." *Jewish Social Studies* 4, no. 1 (1942): 45–58.
Wischnitzer, Mark. "Jewish Emigration from Germany 1933–1938." *Jewish Social Studies* 2, no. 1 (1940): 23–44.
Wischnitzer, Mark. *To Dwell in Safety: The Story of Jewish Migration since 1800*. Philadelphia: JPS, 1948.
Wischnitzer, Mark. *Visas to Freedom: The History of HIAS*. Cleveland, OH: World Publishing, 1955.
Wischnitzer, Mark, Ismar Elbogen, and Josef Meisl, eds. *Festschrift zu Simon Dubnows 70. Geburtstag*. Berlin: Jüdischer Verlag, 1930.
Wyman, David S. *Paper Walls: America and the Refugee Crisis, 1938–1941*. Amherst: University of Massachusetts Press, 1968.
Yang, Lia Lynn. *One Mighty and Irresistible Tide: The Epic Struggle over American Immigration, 1924–1965*. New York: Norton, 2020.
Yarfitz, Mir. *Impure Migration: Jews and Sex Work in Golden Age Argentina*. New Brunswick, NJ: Rutgers University Press, 2019.
Yehudai, Ori. *Leaving Zion: Jewish Emigration from Palestine and Israel after World War II*. Cambridge: Cambridge University Press, 2020.
Zahra, Tara. *The Great Departure: Mass Migration from Eastern Europe and the Making of the Free World*. New York: Norton, 2016.
Zalc, Claire. *Denaturalized: How Thousands Lost Their Citizenship and Lives in Vichy France*. Cambridge, MA: Harvard University Press, 2020.

SELECTED BIBLIOGRAPHY

Zolberg, Aristide R. "The Great Wall against China: Responses to the First Immigration Crisis, 1885–1925." In *Migration, Migration History, History*, edited by Leo Lucassen and Jan Lucassen, 291–315. Berne: Peter Lang, 1997.

Zolberg, Aristide R. *A Nation by Design: Immigration Policy in the Fashioning of America*. Cambridge, MA: Harvard University Press, 2006.

Index

For the benefit of digital users, indexed terms that span two pages (e.g., 52–53) may, on occasion, appear on only one of those pages.

Ahasverus, 1–2
   See also antisemitism
Alaska, 212–13
Aleichem, Sholem, 51–53, 54
Aliyah, 6–7, 167
Alliance Israélite Universelle (AIU), 9, 15, 16, 22–25, 30, 44–48, 59, 63, 108–11, 116, 118–19, 123
American Jews. *See* United States
American Jewish Committee (AJC), 111, 123, 206–7, 209–11, 216–17, 220–22, 223–24
American Jewish Congress, 217, 219
American Jewish Joint Distribution Committee. *See* Joint Distribution Committee
Am Olam, 32, 33, 46–47
Anglo-Jewish Association, 25, 110–11, 116, 149–50
Antin, Mary, 77–83, 92, 95–96, 101–2, 104, 247–48
antisemitism, 1, 61–62, 74, 107, 138–39, 157–58, 171–72, 184–85, 228, 231, 245–46, 249–50
  among academics, 157, 182, 183, 212–13, 228
  Germany, 4–5, 16, 58, 68, 80–82, 108–9, 110, 160, 162, 163, 188, 231
  Jewish migrants from Eastern Europe, 19, 37, 48, 49, 87–88, 90, 95–96, 108–9, 168
  Jewish rebuttal, 4, 46–47, 110, 111, 146
  "Ostjuden," 16–17, 20, 25–26, 30, 81–82, 148, 162, 164, 169–70, 183, 184
  United States, 126, 145, 148–50, 236
  "Wandering Jew," 1–2, 37, 38, 39–40, 164, 173, 175–76, 207–8, 220, 246–47
  See also Holocaust; pogroms

Antwerp, 65, 67, 71, 76–77, 92–93, 113
  See also Red Star Line
Arendt, Hannah, 194, 199, 210–11, 214–15, 229–30, 238–39, 242, 250
Argentina, 8–9, 47, 63, 106, 111–12, 119, 166, 173
Armenians, 135, 246
  genocide, 134–35, 153, 182–83
  refugees 132, 134, 142, 152, 227
Atlantic rate war, 112–18
Auschwitz extermination camp, 81–82, 203
  See also Oświęcim
Australia, 8–9, 119, 132–33, 185–86, 188, 213–14
Austria (after 1918), 11, 118, 137–39, 184, 185–88, 195–96, 197, 199, 203, 206, 225–26, 238–39, 240–41, 248
  Austrian Jews, 7, 170–71, 188, 189, 197–98, 200, 214–15, 235, 249
Austro-Hungarian Empire, 2, 9, 11, 20–21, 62–63, 65, 68
  borders, 65–66, 70–71
  Jewish migrants, 18–19, 38, 109–10, 133, 189, 247, 248
  railroads, 55–56, 62–63
  steamship lines, 69, 70–71, 72, 112
  successor states, 164–65, 188, 249
  See also Austria; Galicia; Hungary
Avraami, Zwi, 40

Ballin, Albert, 9–10, 63–74, 83–84, 114–17
Balta, 32, 33
Bangladesh, 158–59, 252
Baranovich, 51–52, 53, 54–55
Baron, Salo, 177–78, 204–5, 220–21, 244
Basel, 91–92

Belgium, 66, 132–33, 148–49, 151, 195–96, 200, 201, 207
Berlin, 10, 13–15, 18–20, 22–25, 29, 33, 35–36, 53–54, 56, 57–58, 68, 74, 76–77, 83, 89–90, 91–92, 104, 107, 108, 109–10, 115–16, 117, 118–19, 122–23, 150–51, 152–53, 154, 159, 162–69, 173, 178–81, 187, 190–94, 200, 204, 209–10, 218, 231–32, 245–46
Bermuda conference (1943), 219
Bernheimer, Charles S., 96–97
Bernheim petition, 160
Bessarabia, 47, 140–42, 155
Białystok, 47–48, 54–55, 121–22, 164–65
Biharis, 158–59, 252
Bismarck, Otto von, 19–20, 56, 62, 67–68
Bleichröder, Gerson, 68
Boas, Franz, 3–4, 40
Bolivia, 196
Boston, 29, 77, 78–79, 95–96, 101
Bowman, Isaiah, 212–13, 229
Brazil, 130, 163–64, 166, 196
Bremen, 22, 54, 64–65, 66, 69, 70–71, 72, 76–77, 78, 80–82, 88, 92–93, 97–99, 104, 114, 117–18, 119, 130
    See also North German Lloyd (NDL)
Breslau (Wrocław), 23–24, 33, 38–39, 110
Britain, 3–4, 8–9, 10–11, 25, 40, 49–50, 55–56, 59, 63–64, 68, 86–87, 91–92, 96, 108, 109–10, 115–16, 117, 119, 129, 132–33, 149, 151, 157–58, 170–71, 173–74, 178, 179–80, 181, 188
    First World War, 132–33
    immigration restrictions, 37, 95–96, 122–23, 165–66, 219, 229
Brody, 75–76, 88, 91, 138–39, 162, 189–90, 200, 217–18
    1881/82 crisis, 14–15, 32–34, 35, 41–48, 49–50, 108, 110
Brussels, 24, 62–63, 189–90
Budapest, 65–66, 90–91, 93, 112–14, 133–34, 137–38, 180–81
Buenos Aires, 37, 52, 102–3, 111–12, 166, 248
Bundism, Bundists, 37, 38, 135, 149, 175–76

Cahan, Abraham, 33–34, 35, 41, 43–44, 45–47, 55, 88, 94–97, 167–68, 184–85
Canada, 8–9, 71–72, 88–89, 93–94, 111–12, 118, 119, 132–33
    destination after 1945, 240, 241, 242
    immigration restrictions, 165–66, 196
Cape Town, 29, 102–3, 191–92
Cárdenas, Lázaro, 198–99
Caribbean, 4–5, 7, 73, 196, 203
Celler, Emanuel, 236, 238
Chagall, Marc, 53, 191, 200, 202–3
Chicago, 25–26, 27–29, 34–35, 48, 54–55, 96–97, 123–25, 146, 174, 248
China, Chinese, 48, 73, 170–71, 236–38, 246
    Chinese exclusion (see United States immigration policy)
    Chinese migrants, 59–60, 73, 93–94, 104, 126, 247–48
citizenship, 17, 153, 157–58, 171, 178, 250, 251–52
    Austria, 138–39, 190
    Danzig (Free City), 171
    France, 164, 169–70, 189
    Germany, 110, 132–33, 168, 194, 197–98, 214–15
    Israel, 241, 242
    Lithuania, 168
    Poland, 138–39, 187, 189, 242
    Prussia, 13–15, 121
    Romania, 155, 194
    Saxony, 14–15
    Soviet Union, 164
    United States, 99–100, 164, 251–52
    women, 190
    See also statelessness
Colombia, 251–52
colonization, 6–7, 31–32, 46–47, 55, 159–60, 173, 175, 181, 185–86, 200, 208–9, 213–14, 215, 216
    See also Jewish Colonization Association
Comité des Delegations Juives, 150–51, 154–55, 157–58, 217
Constantinople (Istanbul), 62–63, 135, 152, 225–26
control stations. See Prussia
Copenhagen, 150–51, 156

Crémieux, Adolphe, 22–23, 25, 59
Crimean War, 13–14, 60
Cuba, 165–66
Cunard Line. *See* steamship lines
Czechoslovakia, 138–39, 152, 164–65, 185, 186
 See also Slovakia

Danzig, 104–5, 129, 139–40, 152, 170–72
Denikin, Anton, 224–26
Denmark, 21–22, 63–64, 195–96
Deutsch Israelitischer Gemeindebund (DIGB), 20–21, 22
Dijour, Ilya, 169, 185, 200–1, 204, 216, 230
Dillingham Commission, 36, 40–41, 90, 106
disease, 12–13, 30, 66–67, 70–71, 72, 78, 79–81, 82–83, 119, 129, 141–42, 152
 cholera, 18, 70–71, 78, 82–83, 101, 108–9
 typhus, 18, 69–70, 139
Dominican Republic, 48, 185–86, 200, 201, 203, 204–5, 216, 221, 235
DPs (Displaced Persons), 159, 218–20, 227, 235–42
 DP camps, 222, 225–26, 240, 241, 245
 origin of the term, 210–11
Drancy transit camp, 203
Dublin, 29
Dubnow, Simon, 168–69, 176, 177, 178–79, 185, 189–90, 191, 220–21

East Prussia. *See* Prussia
Ecuador, 196
Eichmann, Adolf, 191
Ellis Island, 9, 69–70, 93, 102–3, 234, 252
 deportations, 143–44, 234–35
 detention, 33, 102–3, 135–36, 198, 203, 206, 235
 inspection, 70, 82–83, 103–4, 119, 139–40
 See also United States immigration policy
El Paso, 152–53
Emigdirect, 156, 158, 159–60, 166, 169, 200–1
England. *See* Britain
ethnicity, 5–6

Evian conference, 185–86, 211–13, 230
Eydtkuhnen, 27, 61, 81, 89–90, 92, 101–2, 105, 108

First World War, 3, 8, 120–21, 149–50, 209
 Jewish aid associations, 136, 149
 Jewish displacement, 128, 132–41
 migration restrictions, 130–32, 183
 turning point, 4–5, 132, 151–52, 222–23
Fiume, 54, 82–83, 112–15, 117
Föhrenwald DP camp, 240–41, 242
 See also DP camps
France, 7, 22–23, 41, 48, 55, 59–60, 109–10, 129, 135–36, 142–43, 151, 155, 157–58, 163–64, 165, 167, 169–70, 173–74, 179–80, 185–86, 189, 195–204, 223–24, 240–41, 249–50
Franzos, Karl Emil, 46

Galicia (Austrian Empire), 38, 63, 68, 91, 94, 110–11, 177
 First World War, 133–34, 137
 Jewish migrants, 39–40, 42–43, 75–76, 83, 93, 110, 142–43, 162, 163, 173–74, 177, 207–8, 222–23
 Jewish refugees, 137–39, 183
 poverty, 87, 107, 110, 121–22, 139–40, 247
 See also Austro-Hungarian Empire; Brody; Krakow; Lemberg
Galveston, 123
Generalplan Ost, 214–15
Geneva, 11, 38, 149–50, 154–55, 171, 175, 185
Germany, 4–5, 9, 16, 27, 45–46, 48, 59, 64–65, 66, 67, 72–73, 96–97, 117, 120–21, 132–33, 137, 139, 142–43, 146–48, 149–50, 157–58, 160, 166, 167, 168, 172, 177, 179–82, 184, 186, 189, 190, 191–94, 197, 199, 201–2, 203, 204–5, 206, 209, 212, 213, 214, 218, 227, 235–36, 238–39, 245–46, 249–50
 Alliance Israélite Universelle, 9, 24, 109–10, 118–19
 antisemitic violence, 80–81, 185, 187, 188, 212–13
 destination, 130, 163–64, 165, 167
 DP camps, 222, 225–26

Germany (cont.)
  eastern border, 67, 71–72, 75–76, 88, 108–9
  German Jews, 104–5, 110, 118, 119, 169–70, 172–73, 178, 185–86, 195–96, 197–98, 208, 214–15, 229, 235
  Holocaust, 218–19, 231
  inspections of migrants, 80–83, 105
  Polish Jews, 187, 195–96
  Social Democratic Party, 33–34, 115
  transit, 10–11, 21–22, 75, 76–77, 78–79, 83, 88, 91–92, 109–10, 129, 248
  West Germany, 236–38, 240–41, 242, 245–46
  See also antisemitism; Hilfsverein der Deutschen Juden; Holocaust; Prussia; steamship lines
Goldmann, Nahum, 216, 217
Göring, Hermann, 184–85
Gottschalk, Max, 207, 209–10, 216, 217, 221–22
Grabski, Wladyslaw, 164–65
grain trade, 13, 14, 27, 57–58, 61
Grant, Madison, 145–49
  See also antisemitism; United States immigration policy
Greece, 152, 227, 239
Grimm, Hans, 181–82
Gronemann, Sammy, 75, 76–77, 83, 163
Grynszpan, Herschel, 187
Günther, Hans, 146–48

Haifa, 110–11, 120–21, 234, 240
Halbwachs, Maurice, 206, 223–24
Halifax (NS), 83–84, 93–94
Hamburg, 22, 27, 33, 54, 63–74, 76–77, 78–83, 86–87, 88, 89–90, 92–93, 97–98, 101, 104, 105–6, 107, 108–9, 110, 118, 119
  Auswandererhallen, 79–80, 93
Hamburg-America Line. *See* steamship lines
Hanover, 75, 76–77, 83, 163, 187
Harbin, 159, 170–71
Hebrew Immigrant Aid Society (HIAS), 83–84, 94–95, 102–4, 111, 129, 135–36, 140, 149, 156, 159–60, 165–66, 169, 206–7, 216, 230, 231, 240–41
Hebron. *See* pogroms
Herzl, Theodor, 1–2, 39–40, 46–47, 57, 110

HICEM, 159–60, 169, 216
Hilberg, Raul, 7, 55
Hilfsverein der Deutschen Juden, 36–37, 72, 110–11, 112, 116–21, 122–23, 133, 135, 149–50, 159, 167, 169, 176, 190–92, 199, 204, 216, 221, 250
Himmler, Heinrich, 146–48, 214–15
Hirsch, Baron Maurice de, 40–41, 47, 55, 62–63, 73–74, 107, 111–12
  See also Jewish Colonization Association
Hitler, Adolf, 146–48, 163, 181, 184–85, 191, 209, 214, 226, 231
Holland-America Line. *See* steamship lines
Holocaust, 1, 3, 5, 7–8, 41, 43, 204–5, 220–21, 231, 235, 240–41, 242–43, 245–46
  migration restrictions, 148–49, 209–10, 222
  "resettlement," 215, 227–28
  scholarship, 7, 55, 81–82, 178, 189, 218, 220–21, 228–29, 230, 231–32
Horwich, Bernard, 26–30, 31, 53–55, 68, 101, 248
Howe, Irving, 6, 86
Hungary, 57–58, 113, 138–39, 152, 169–70, 172, 183, 185, 186, 249–50

Ireland, Irish, 3, 21–22, 29, 54, 247
Israel (state), 5, 6–8, 10–11, 43, 158, 178, 191, 205, 221–22, 223, 232–33, 234–35, 236–38, 240–43, 245
Israelitische Allianz, 44, 45
Insterburg, 105, 108
Institute for Jewish Affairs (IJA), 216–18, 230, 232–33
Italy, Italians, 3, 5–6, 55–56, 59–60, 112–13, 173, 203–4, 208, 238–39, 240–41, 246–47, 251–52

Jabotinsky, Vladimir/Ze'ev, 169, 228
Jacobs, Joseph, 1, 2, 3
Japan, 35–36, 49, 114–15, 116, 117–18, 136, 145, 151, 170–71, 217–18
Jersey City, 93, 234–35, 238
Jerusalem, 162, 229, 232–33
Jewish Colonization Association (JCA), 24–25, 40–41, 47, 63, 106, 111–12, 118–19, 140–41, 156, 159–60, 166, 169, 216

Johannesburg, 29, 37, 248
Johnson, Albert, 145, 146–48
Johnson, Lyndon B., 251
Joint Distribution Committee (JDC), 135, 137, 139–40, 149–50, 152–53, 156, 159–60, 164–65, 176, 193–94, 198, 199–200, 207, 216, 240–41
　Agro-Joint, 200

Kaelter, Robert, 139–40
Kahn, Bernhard, 36–37, 72, 118, 120–22, 190–91
Kaplun-Kogan, Wladimir Wolf, 38–40
Kibarty, 27, 89–90, 101–2, 108
Kiev, 31–32, 44, 45, 46, 150–51, 168, 169, 179, 204, 207, 209–10, 224, 225
Kishinev, 2, 35–36, 37, 49–50, 114–15, 121–22, 141
Koellreutter, Otto, 148
Königsberg (Kaliningrad), 12, 13, 14–15, 21–22, 23, 26–28, 29–30, 53–54, 56, 57–58, 61, 68, 91–92
Kovno (Kaunas), 17, 18, 21, 23–24, 26, 27, 28–29, 30, 53–54, 61, 88–90, 129, 133–34, 156
Krakow, 75–76
Kristallnacht pogrom. *See* pogroms
Kulischer, Alexander, 178–84, 203–4, 215–16, 223, 246–47
Kulischer, Eugene, 185, 198, 203–5, 206–7, 218–19, 223, 227, 228, 231–33, 235–36, 239–40, 242–43, 246–47
　background, 179
　Europe on the Move (1948), 223–27, 228–30
　Jewish Migrations (1942), 207–10, 211, 230
　Kriegs- und Wanderzüge (1932), 178–84
　M Project, 215–16
　The Displacement of Population in Europe (1943), 210–11, 217–18

Landsmanshaftn, 25–26, 87, 111
Latvia, Latvians, 88–89, 95–96, 128, 129, 156, 236
Laughlin, Harry H., 146–48
Lazarus, Emma, 123–25
League of Nations, 139, 151–52, 171–72, 183, 227

Jewish representatives, 149–61, 171
　mandates, 151, 171, 172
　refugees, 140–42, 152, 153–54, 175, 211–12, 217–18, 220, 221–22, 234, 249, 251
Lebensraum concept, 180–82, 184
Le Havre, 59–60, 91–92, 189
Leipzig, 14–15, 20–21, 81, 91–93
Lemberg (Lviv), 32, 33, 43–44, 110
Leningrad, 167, 178–79
Lestschinsky, Jacob, 87, 163, 164–65, 173, 182, 185, 204–5, 217–18, 230–31, 232–33
　background, 97–98
　interviews with migrants in 1913/14, 98–100, 248
　interwar Berlin, 168–69, 176, 184–85, 191
Levant, 7–8, 9
Libau, 61, 88–89, 129
Linz, 199
Lisbon, 169, 198, 199, 201, 202–3, 207, 209–10, 216
Lithuania, Lithuanians, 9–10, 12–30, 34–35, 38, 42, 47–48, 53–55, 68, 128, 129, 130, 133–34, 135, 137, 155, 156, 168, 172, 173–74, 216–17, 248
　Jewish migrants, 25–30, 38, 42, 54–55, 68, 130, 173–74, 184–85
　Jewish migration crisis 1868/69, 18–25, 30
　Lithuanian state, 128, 129, 155, 156, 168, 172
Litvaks, 12–13, 14–16, 18, 25, 29, 30, 34–35, 47–48, 107
Liverpool, 27, 33, 65, 91–92
Łódź, 54–55, 57, 217–18
Long, Breckenridge, 235

Mack, Julian, 123–25, 126
Madagascar, 185, 193–94, 212–13, 228
Margolin, Arnold D., 223–24, 225
Mariampol, 25–26
Marseilles, 69–70, 199, 201–4, 209–10, 250
Marshall, Louis, 142–44, 146, 149–50
Martinique, 59–60, 202–3, 223
Mauss, Marcel, 206, 223–24
McCarran, Pat, 236

Memel (Klaipeda), 12–17, 18, 26, 68, 88–89, 172
Mendes, Aristides de Sousa, 200–1
Mexico, 59–60, 82, 152–53, 165–66, 189, 198–99, 202–3
Meyer, Konrad, 214
Miasoedov, Sergei Nicholaevich, 89–90
M Project (Migration Project), 213–16, 223, 227, 229
  See also Roosevelt, Franklin D.
Minsk, 51–52, 189–90, 195
Mogilev, 31–32
Montreal, 93–94, 206–7
Morgenthau Sr., Henry, 134–35, 142
Morocco, 196, 201
Mortara affair, 15
Moscow, 49–50, 53, 57–58, 60, 61, 108, 167, 168, 180–81
Motzkin, Leo, 137, 149–51, 154–59, 160, 169, 171, 216–18, 250
Myslowitz, 75, 76, 92

Nansen, Fridtjof, 153–54
Nansen passport. *See* passports
Naples, 54
Nathan, Paul, 110, 116–17, 118, 119, 120–21, 133
Netherlands, 7, 55, 66, 76–77, 151, 195–96, 200, 201
  First World War, 132–33, 135, 136
New York City, 3–4, 10, 27, 28, 29, 41, 52–53, 54–55, 59–60, 63–64, 69–70, 91–92, 96–97, 114, 139–40, 145–46, 169, 177, 189, 195, 200–1, 203, 207, 209–10, 216, 219, 221–22, 225–26, 232, 235
  immigrant inspection, 93
  Jewish immigrants, 35, 83–84, 87, 96–97, 128
  Jewish migrant assistance, 18–19, 23–24, 102–3, 107, 111, 166
  Jewish newspapers, 33–34, 49, 184–85
  Jewish scholars, 206–31
  Lower East Side, 33, 88, 95, 130
  See also Ellis Island; Jersey City
nonstate actors, 4, 9, 10–11, 71–72, 104, 115–16, 118, 121–22, 151–52, 160–61, 216, 248, 249

Nordau, Max, 174, 208–9
North German Lloyd (NDL). *See* steamships, steamship lines
Norway, Norwegians 3, 65, 153–54, 195–96, 247

Oberländer, Theodor, 240–41
Odessa, 26, 28, 29, 32, 46–47, 69–70, 97, 103
Office for Strategic Services (OSS), 216, 231–32
Orel, 61
"Ostjuden." *See* antisemitism
Oświęcim, 75–76, 81–82, 91, 92–93
  See also Auschwitz extermination camp
Ottoman Empire, 9, 15, 22–23, 27, 40, 47, 62–63, 74, 109–10, 123, 133–36, 151, 246
  See also Armenians; Palestine; Turkey

Pale of Settlement. *See* Russian Empire
Palermo, 54
Palestine, 110–12, 151, 162, 164, 212, 227–28
  assistance for Yishuv, 133, 135, 240
  destination, 4–5, 6–9, 21–22, 31–32, 46–47, 86, 130, 152, 163–64, 165, 166, 167, 172–73, 175, 185, 188, 191–92, 208–10, 218, 219, 220, 221–22, 228–29
  Zionists, 150–51, 153, 154–55, 158, 159, 172–74
  See also Israel; Ottoman Empire
Paris, 9, 10, 14–15, 19–20, 22–23, 24, 31–32, 40–41, 58–61, 62–63, 91–92, 109–11, 118–19, 149–51, 154, 155, 156, 159–60, 169–70, 175, 179, 181–82, 184, 185, 187, 189–90, 193–94, 195, 197, 199–201, 203, 204–5, 209–10, 218, 220–21, 223–24, 225–26, 231–32, 240–41
passports, 89, 111–12, 132, 144, 151–53, 160, 168, 189, 194–96, 197–98, 201
  false passports, 32, 103, 152–53
  Nansen passports, 153–55, 249
  Russian passports, 27, 43–44, 45–46, 65, 67, 94–95, 101, 103
Pereire, Emil and Isaac, 9–10, 56–57, 58–60, 61–63, 73–74, 91–92

Petlura, Symon, 187, 224–25
Philadelphia, 33, 96–97
Philippines, 73
Philippson, Ludwig, 20–24
Piłsudski, Józef, 184–85
Pinsker, Leon, 46–47
Podolia, 32, 47
pogroms, 36, 52, 114–15, 121–22, 123
  Białystok (1906), 121–22
  Budapest (1918), 137–38
  cause for Jewish migration, 1, 2, 3, 32, 34–35, 38–39, 41–42, 49–50, 173–74, 175, 177, 207–8, 244–45, 247
  Galicia (1898), 42
  Hebron (1929), 162, 167
  Kishinev (1903), 2, 35–36, 37, 49–50, 114–15
  Kristallnacht (1938), 7, 142–43, 188, 191, 249
  Russia (1881/82), 32–33, 34, 42, 43–48, 123–25
  Russian Civil War, 132, 133–34, 144, 153, 160, 169, 207, 224–26, 228–29
Poland, Poles, 9–10, 13–14, 39, 41, 49–50, 57, 59, 68, 69, 105, 128, 133–34, 135, 137, 144, 145, 149–50, 151–52, 164–65, 195, 197–98, 209, 214, 215, 217–18, 225, 228–29, 249–50
  Jewish migration after 1918, 166, 167
  Jewish refugees, 138–39, 140, 159, 160–61
  Polish state, 4–5, 139, 151, 154, 155, 171–72, 185–86, 187, 212–13, 231, 242
  population transfer, 216, 226, 227–28
  See also resettlement
Polotsk, 77
Portugal, 200–1
Prague, 92–93, 137–39, 218
Prussia, 12–15, 16–17, 18, 19–20, 64–65, 120–21, 172
  control stations, 70–72, 78, 82, 116–17
  eastern border, 27, 67, 70, 88–89, 97–99, 101–2, 114–15
  East Prussia, 12–15, 16–17, 27, 54–55, 81, 248
  expulsions of foreigners, 35–36, 68–69, 122–23

  as German state, 66, 67
  Jewish emancipation, 17, 20, 21
  Jewish leaders, 20–21, 22–24
  Jewish migrants, 18, 19, 20, 22, 27, 28, 104–5, 108–9
  railroads, 56–58, 61–62, 92
  steamship lines, 35–36, 69, 70–72, 104, 115
  U.S. immigration policy, 67–68
  western border, 107
  See also citizenship; Germany; steamship lines

Quebec City, 93–94

railroads, 7, 9, 55, 64–65, 74, 86, 89–90, 91–92, 94, 159, 247–48
  Brody crisis, 43–44
  construction and impact, 53–54, 55–57, 60–62
  Jewish investors, 47, 55, 57–64, 73–74, 111–12, 248
  Sholem Aleichem, 51–53
  trains stations, 58–59, 91–92, 93, 170–71
  Warsaw-St. Petersburg line, 9–10, 21–62
Red Star Line. *See* steamship lines
Reed, David, 144, 145, 146
refuseniks, 6, 241, 245
resettlement, 215–16, 226, 227, 228–29
  Holocaust, 214, 215
  Jews, 4–5, 8, 17, 23–24, 30, 46–47, 141, 182–83, 185–86, 193–94, 207, 210–11, 212–14, 217–18, 219, 228
  Palestinians, 228
  See also population transfer
Riga, 128, 129, 156, 185
Robinson, Jacob, 216–19, 251
Rohingya, 158–59, 252
Romania, 1–2, 4–5, 8, 24, 36, 39–40, 42, 57–58, 87–88, 107, 110–11, 118–19, 121–22, 123–25, 129, 140–42, 149–50, 151, 152, 154, 155, 160–61, 169–70, 173–74, 177, 185–86, 194, 212–13, 225, 244, 247, 249–50
Roosevelt, Franklin Delano, 7, 185–86, 193–94, 198–99, 215–16, 228
Rosen, Joseph A., 200, 201, 216

Rosenberg, Alfred, 146–48
Roth, Josef, 162–70, 184
Rothschild family, 55
  Rothschild, James de, 22–23, 58–61, 62–63, 73–74
Rotterdam, 54, 65, 71, 75, 76–77, 83–84, 92–93, 107, 113, 139–40
Rowno, 32, 42, 43–44, 53, 189–90, 195
Ruhleben, 76–78, 79–80, 81–82, 92
Rülf, Isaak, 14–15, 18, 20, 21, 22–23, 30, 88, 107
  1881/82 Russian pogroms, 47–48
  1885 Prussian expulsions, 68
  early years in Memel, 12–13, 14–17
  journey to Kovno (1869), 17–18
Ruppin, Arthur, 173–76, 182, 233
Russian Empire, 1–3, 5, 6–7, 9–10, 13, 31, 37, 38–39, 62–63, 96–97, 107, 118–19, 128, 168, 179–80, 189–90, 191–92, 195, 246
  army deserters, 103, 114–15
  First World War, 132–42
  German steamship lines, 64–67, 72, 112, 114
  Jewish internal migration, 51–53, 247
  Jewish migration, 1–2, 6–11, 16–17, 20, 21–22, 45–46, 68, 69–70, 75–76, 78, 107–10, 112–13, 122–23, 142–43, 173–74, 177, 182, 212, 248
  Jewish railroad investors, 57–58
  Pale of Settlement, 2, 17, 23–24, 25, 29–30, 31, 34–36, 39, 44, 45, 47–48, 49–50, 51–55, 57, 65, 77, 87, 98, 128, 133–34, 136, 189–90, 200, 247
  policies toward Jews, 21, 24–25, 35–48, 178, 182–83, 207–8, 249
  poverty, 21–22, 25, 28–29, 30, 34–35, 40–41, 49–50
  refugees, 133–35, 140, 153, 171, 244
  Russian Civil War, 136–37, 140–41, 159, 169, 179, 180, 184, 227
Russo-Japanese War, 115–18
western border, 13–14, 18, 19, 27, 32, 43–44, 76–77, 86–87, 88–92, 98–99, 101–2, 105, 121, 126–27
See also Lithuania; Podolia; pogroms; Poland; railroads; steamship lines; Volhynia

Saint John (NB), 93–94
St. Petersburg (Russia), 3, 9–10, 13, 19–20, 27, 49–50, 53–54, 56–57, 60–62, 65–66, 89–91, 94–95, 108, 179, 189–90
  See also Leningrad
San Francisco, 136, 234–35, 236–38
Schechtman, Joseph, 169, 179, 185, 204, 216, 217–18, 223–24, 225–26, 227–29, 231–32, 242–43
Schiff, Jacob, 55, 116, 117–18, 119, 123, 133
Schwartzbard, Sholom, 187, 224
Seghers, Anna, 202–4
Sephardi Jews, 7–8, 9–10, 23–24, 58, 123
Shanghai, 7, 43, 170–71, 234–35, 236–39, 242
Shavli, 38
Simpson, John Hope, 211–12, 218, 250
Slovakia, Slovaks, 65–66, 113–14, 165–66, 186
smugglers, 9, 10, 13–14, 32, 33, 43–44, 65–66, 75–76, 86–87, 88–91, 94–95, 98, 99, 165–66, 169–70, 202–3, 240–41, 248
Somalis, 158–59, 252
Sosúa, 200, 235
South Africa, 2, 28–29, 38, 49–50, 54–55, 119, 173–74, 185–86, 196
Southampton, 29, 67, 91–92
South Rhodesia (Zimbabwe), 191–92
Soviet Union, 6, 7, 128, 129, 130, 137–42, 144, 152, 153–54, 156, 159, 164, 167–68, 178–79, 195, 200, 208–9, 210–11, 213, 214, 215, 216, 225–26, 227–28, 231–32, 235–36, 238–39, 240, 241, 242–43, 245–46
Spain, Spanish 59–60, 96–97, 238–39, 246
  Jewish expulsion and flight (1492), 6, 23–24, 40, 46, 47–48, 134–35, 220
  Spanish Civil War refugees, 185–86, 189, 197, 198–99, 201–3
  transit of Jewish refugees, 199–203
statelessness, 153, 172, 184, 186, 205, 242–43
  See also citizenship; DPs
steamships, steamship lines, 4, 9, 10, 35–36, 54, 59–60, 63–74, 75–77, 80–81, 82–87, 90–94, 101, 103–5, 107, 108, 112–19, 121, 129, 137, 139–40, 143–44, 197–98, 235, 247–48

Beaver Line, 94
Canadian Pacific Line (CPR), 93–94
Compagnie Générale Transatlantique, 59–60, 91–92
Cunard Line, 71, 112, 113–18, 122–23
Hamburg-America Line (HAPAG), 9–10, 63–74, 76–77, 78–80, 81, 83, 86–87, 92–93, 101, 107, 112–17, 118, 248
Holland-America Line, 71, 92–93, 113
North German Lloyd (NDL), 64–65, 67–68, 69–72, 73, 76–77, 78, 80–81, 92–93, 101, 112–17, 118, 248
pool agreements, 71, 112, 113, 114–15, 117–18
Red Star Line, 71, 92–93, 113
tickets, ticket agents, 10, 26, 27, 29–30, 54–55, 63–64, 65–66, 69, 71, 76–77, 86–87, 88–91, 94, 99, 101, 103–4, 113–15, 116, 117–18, 129, 165, 198
Union Castle Line, 29
Uranium Line, 83–84, 107
White Star Line, 113
See also Ballin, Albert
Stettin (Szczecin), 12, 21–22, 67–68, 69
Stockholm, 38–39
Stoddard, Lothrop, 146–48
Strousberg, Bethel Henry, 57–58, 73–74
Suez Canal, 82, 234
Sweden, 21–22, 28–29, 65, 120–21, 133–34
Swindlers, 27, 86, 88–89, 91–92, 93
Switzerland, 11, 31–32, 91–92, 97, 155
Szajkowski, Zosa, 41, 43, 86, 197–98

Tangier, 201
Tarnow, 177
Tartakower, Arieh, 217–20, 233, 244
Tcherikover, Elias, 41, 168–69, 185, 191
Tel Aviv, 83, 231
Telz, 18
Thomas, Albert, 158
ticket agents. *See* steamship lines
Tilsit (Sovetsk), 12, 13, 27, 29–30, 81
timber trade, 13, 26, 189–90
Tolstoy, Leo, 51–52, 54
transit visa, 70–71, 76–77, 128, 139–40, 154, 156, 168, 198, 200–1, 203, 235
See also passports
Transnistria, 141–42

Treuenfels, Abraham, 21–22
Trieste, 54, 94, 112–13
Trujillo, Rafael, 185–86
Truman, Harry S., 221–22, 235–36, 238, 242
Turkey, 152, 212, 227

Ukraine, Ukrainians, 3, 41–42, 44, 47, 68, 69, 75, 88–89, 93–94, 97, 114–15, 132, 135–36, 137, 140–42, 156, 160, 167, 169, 228–29, 236, 240–41, 249
Ukrainian People's Republic, 187, 190, 215, 224–26
See also Holocaust; pogroms; Russian Empire
United States
destination for European migrants, 3, 6–7, 21–22, 246–47
destination for Jews, 2, 21–22, 23, 25–30, 37, 42, 87, 109–10, 130, 148, 164, 165–66, 167, 188, 208–9, 231
United States immigration policy, 70, 71–72, 82–83, 106, 198, 221–22, 234–40
1882 Immigration Act, 24–25, 48, 66–67
1921/24 Johnson-Reed Acts, 142–49
1948 and 1950 DP Acts, 227, 235–40
1965 Hart-Celler Act, 251
American Jews, 35–37, 49, 95–96, 105–6, 111, 123–27, 142, 143–44, 146, 238
Chinese exclusion, 8–9, 48–49, 66–67, 93–94, 104, 125–26, 145, 170–71, 247–48
restricting Jewish migration, 4–5, 6–7, 142–49, 167, 173–74, 185–86, 191–92, 204, 235–40
See also Dillingham Commission; Ellis Island; Hebrew Immigrant Aid Society; New York
Uruguay, 166, 196

Velizh, 31
Veracruz, 59–60, 152–53
Vienna, 42, 45, 46, 57, 60, 62–63, 65–66, 90–92, 93, 94, 110–11, 112–13, 133–34, 137–39, 164, 177, 184, 185–86, 190, 217–18
Vietnam, Vietnamese, 245–46, 251–52

Vilna, 15, 26, 27, 28–29, 31–32, 53, 56–57, 61–62, 77, 89, 97, 168–69
Vitebsk, 53, 54–55, 57
Vladivostok, 136
Volhynia, 42, 99, 189–90

"Wandering Jew." *See* antisemitism
Warburg family, 73, 119
　Warburg, Felix, 152–53, 164–65
Warsaw, 9–10, 38, 47–48, 53, 54–55, 56–58, 60, 61–62, 97, 99, 129, 139–40, 144, 152, 164–65, 184–85, 187, 189–90, 214, 228
Warsaw Ghetto, 214
Washington, D.C., 103, 125, 134–35, 223, 225, 227, 228, 231–32, 234–35
Weinreich, Max, 168–69
Weizmann, Chaim, 72–73, 150–51, 154–55, 158
Wischnitzer, Mark, 185, 190–91, 225, 230, 232–33
　background, 42, 189–90
　flight from Nazi Germany, 194, 195, 197–98, 199, 200–1, 202–5, 216
　Hilfsverein, 118, 167, 169, 190–92, 193–94
　To Dwell in Safety (1948), 41–42, 43, 220–23, 224–25, 229–30, 231
Wischnitzer, Rachel, 194, 200, 230, 231
　background, 189–90
　flight to New York, 193–94, 195–96, 197–99, 204–5
　interwar Berlin, 191–92
　saving her husband, 200–3
Wise, Stephen S., 177, 217, 219
Wolf, Lucien, 140, 149–51, 154–56, 157–58, 160, 171
Wolf, Simon, 125–26
World Jewish Congress (WJC), 11, 217–18
World War II, 8, 130–32, 196, 197–99, 200, 216, 217–18, 227–28, 238–39, 251
　See also Holocaust

YIVO (Yidisher Visnshaftlekher Institut), 41, 168–69, 176, 178–79, 216, 230
Yizkor books, 7
Yokohama, 136
Yugoslavia, 185, 245–46

Zangwill, Israel, 95–96, 225
Zielonka, Martin, 152–53
Zionism/Zionists, 6–7, 11, 16, 24–25, 26, 28, 33–34, 37, 72–73, 97–98, 110, 111–12, 120–21, 135, 137–38, 149–51, 153, 154–55, 158, 159, 160–61, 162, 163, 167–68, 171–72, 178, 181, 208–9, 217–18, 241
　Jewish migration, 1–2, 39–40, 43, 156, 173–74, 175–76, 208–9, 220, 221, 250
　Revisionists, 169, 179, 228
Zolberg, Aristide, 9, 148–49, 239
Zurich, 97